T0270582

NEVER TURN BACK

NEVER TURN BACK

CHINA AND THE FORBIDDEN HISTORY OF THE 1980s

◇

JULIAN GEWIRTZ

THE BELKNAP PRESS OF HARVARD UNIVERSITY PRESS

Cambridge, Massachusetts | London, England

2022

LIBRARY OF CONGRESS CATALOGING-IN-PUBLICATION DATA

Names: Gewirtz, Julian B., 1989– author.
Title: Never turn back : China and the forbidden history of
the 1980s / Julian Gewirtz.
Description: Cambridge, Massachusetts : The Belknap Press of Harvard
University Press, 2022. | Includes bibliographical references and index.
Identifiers: LCCN 2022001879 | ISBN 9780674241848 (cloth)
Subjects: LCSH: Historiography—China—20th century. | Political
culture—China. | China—Politics and government—1976–2002. |
China—History—1976–2002. | China—History—Tiananmen Square
Incident, 1989. | China—Economic policy—1976–2000.
Classification: LCC DS779.26 .G49 2022 |
DDC 951.05/8—dc23/eng/20220427
LC record available at https://lccn.loc.gov/2022001879

CONTENTS

ILLUSTRATIONS FOLLOW PAGE 176.

Introduction

Forbidden History

On January 18, 2005, tucked away on page four of the official *People's Daily,* just below an article on post-tsunami inspections and above a weather report, a three-line notice reported the death of an eighty-five-year-old man: "Comrade Zhao Ziyang suffered from long-term diseases of the respiratory system and the cardiovascular system and had been hospitalized multiple times, and following the recent deterioration of his condition, he was unable to be rescued and died on January 17 in Beijing at the age of 85."[1]

A casual reader of the newspaper would certainly be forgiven for not noticing the item. The obituary was notable mainly for its brevity and omissions: it did not mention that Zhao had held China's top two leadership posts as premier of the State Council and then as general secretary of the Chinese Communist Party (CCP). Nor did it acknowledge that he had made any contributions to China's "reform and opening," the agenda of economic development and openness to the world China pursued soon after the death of Mao Zedong. "Reform and opening" remained as a centerpiece of official policy, mentioned nearly a dozen times in that day's newspaper, but Zhao's central role in shaping it had already been systematically erased from official accounts of the history of this period. Indeed, well before Zhao's death, the CCP had rewritten the entire history of China's 1980s—a tumultuous, transformational decade—and subjected it to far-reaching distortion, even though it was one of the most consequential periods in the country's history.

In popular accounts around the world—as well as in the official narrative told by China's rulers—the 1980s in China are typically treated as a time of linear change, moving smoothly from Deng Xiaoping's rise to power in 1978 and the leap into "reform and opening" to new heights of wealth and modernization. In this telling, the decade whizzes by; the crackdown on the 1989 Tiananmen protests is at most a harsh interruption before the linear narrative begins again in 1992 with Deng pushing for faster reform on his "Southern Tour."

This story is a myth. It exists in large part because the CCP has suppressed sources and created a powerful and widely repeated official narrative about China in the 1980s that erases key figures, blots out policies and debates, covers up acts of violence, and forbids public discussion of alternative paths. In contrast to that narrative, the 1980s in China were a period of extraordinary open-ended debate, contestation, and imagination. Chinese elites argued fiercely about the future, and official ideology, economic policy, technological transformation, and political reforms all expanded in bold new directions.

These years of tumult, searching, and struggle transformed China, but by the time protesters filled Tiananmen Square in the spring of 1989, the leadership had not reached agreement on how China ought to modernize. Following the crackdown—which included both the massacre of civilians and the purge of top officials—a new consensus emerged, and China's remaining leaders offered a newly consolidated vision of the Chinese system as well as a refashioning of the events of the 1980s designed to serve this post-Tiananmen agenda. Among many other changes, they built up the cult of Deng Xiaoping while erasing Zhao Ziyang and fellow top leader Hu Yaobang, reinterpreted the pursuit of rapid economic growth, and argued for the absolute necessity of fusing the party and the state. They abandoned or left unfinished many of the political reforms pursued during the 1980s. Before even replacing the tank-scarred stones of Tiananmen Square, they had pushed out their new narrative and staked the party's fortunes on it.[2]

What is today called the "China model"—extraordinarily rapid economic growth paired with enduring authoritarian political control—was not the only vision of the future China's leaders pursued in the decades following Mao Zedong's death in 1976. They imagined and experimented with many possible "China models" in the 1980s. Yet China's rulers have worked hard to conceal this fuller story and the pivotal choices that determined China's development. Bringing this forbidden history back into focus is vital. One of the most momentous transformations of the twentieth century has been the subject of immense historical distortion to bolster the legitimacy of the Communist Party's chosen path.

◇

The fundamental question of the 1980s was one that had motivated Chinese officials and intellectuals for a century: how can China become modern? Deng Xiaoping declared in January 1980 that "modernization" was "the essential condition for solving both our domestic and our external problems," and the 1980s would be "a decade of great importance—indeed, a crucial decade—to China's development."[3]

For Chinese officials and intellectuals, the challenge was to find a "Chinese" path to modernization that did not copy or import wholesale a foreign conception of modernity. To be sure, some thinkers embraced the West with few reservations, praising "Americanization" and "Westernization."[4] But those views were unusual. The more important predicament was how to define modernization anew in China—drawing on ideas and innovations from around the world but on Chinese terms.

To Deng Xiaoping, economic development was the essential element of modernization, and to achieve this goal, he was willing to permit markets to multiply and international trade to expand. But becoming richer on its own was not enough. Deng and other senior officials devoted significant attention to other domains that constituted China's modernization, including official ideology, advanced technology for both economic and military purposes, and the political system. They projected confidence, despite daunting challenges. On a hike up Luosanmei hill in Guangdong Province in January 1984, Deng Xiaoping was warned that the path ahead was steep and treacherous—and in a moment made for propaganda, Deng replied sportingly, "Never turn back." The line soon was widely publicized as a mantra for the leadership's resolve to forge ahead with reforms no matter the difficulty, though it belied the fierce contestation raging over China's future.[5]

The Chinese leadership in the 1970s had embraced a set of objectives, proposed by Zhou Enlai, known as the Four Modernizations— developing "modern agriculture, industry, national defense, and science and technology (S&T)." However, the Four Modernizations were only one piece of a much larger agenda.[6] Dissidents called for democratization, which activist Wei Jingsheng called the "fifth modernization," and others sought to modernize Marxism-Leninism for a new era of economic and technological transformation. Theoretician Su Shaozhi said in 1986, "In China, we usually speak of the 'Four Modernizations' but in my opinion, this is not sufficient. . . . In my view modernization should be comprehensive, which means not only economic but also political and ideological."[7]

This book highlights both these debates about modernization and the CCP's repression of this history. After setting the scene at the dawning of the 1980s, it examines four realms of contestation: ideology, the economy, technology, and the political system. It is deliberately selective, revealing how top officials, their policy advisers, and their wider networks grappled with challenges and changes in these domains. Its focus is on domestic policy, though it often references China's intellectual, diplomatic, and economic opening to the world. Then the book shows how the political crises culminating in the Tiananmen crackdown of 1989 led to a systematic rewriting of the history of the 1980s in ways that profoundly shaped China's ongoing transformation.

In many accounts, the 1980s is seen as "the era of Deng Xiaoping," and indeed Deng plays a central role in this story.[8] But one of the objectives of this book is to correct widespread perceptions that Deng Xiaoping was personally responsible for the policies of the 1980s, particularly the economic policies of the "reform and opening." Deng has been the beneficiary of hagiographical treatment. In fact, Deng was not regularly and actively engaged in policymaking throughout the 1980s. He was extremely active in 1978–1980, when he outmaneuvered Mao's designated successor, Hua Guofeng, to take power, and again at certain moments in the subsequent decade, most crucially during the 1989 protest movement and its suppression. However, to understand Chinese policymaking in the 1980s, it is essential to realize that Deng was often disengaged from the details. He would provide broad guidance about objectives, signal his preferences, or give final approval, though he also frequently contradicted himself or offered only vague pronouncements.[9] His age and disposition limited his involvement in the intense work of policy debate and formulation. Deng said in 1982, at the age of seventy-seven, "If you were to ask me to work eight hours a day at my age, I'm sure I couldn't do it." He repeatedly acknowledged that he had great difficulty with his hearing and took meetings at home.[10] In 1979–1980, he appointed key younger individuals to run the country and let them figure out how to solve the massive challenges facing China.

Those younger leaders, CCP General Secretary Hu Yaobang and Premier Zhao Ziyang chief among them, had significant autonomy on a day-to-day basis. Zhao, in particular, had a crucial and understudied role in shaping ideological, economic, technological, and political modernization. At first, he wrote in his memoirs, "My earliest understanding of how to proceed with reform was shallow and vague. . . . I did not have any preconceived model or a systematic idea in mind."[11] But during the 1980s, his views became stronger, as did his expertise and authority. Power ultimately flowed from Deng, but by and large, Zhao and his colleagues were able to develop and implement policies without having to bring Deng directly into the matter. "I am a complete novice regarding the economy," Deng said in 1984, "but Premier Zhao knows the economics well, and he is taking the lead in this regard."[12] In addition to their relationship with Deng, these frontline leaders dealt with the many other revolutionary elders in their seventies and eighties—august veterans like Chen Yun, Li Xiannian, and Hu Qiaomu—who had great prestige and plenty of ideas about how China ought to be run. Party historiography has turned these leaders into stock figures, whether heroes or villains, but this book takes seriously their worldviews and goals.[13]

Beyond the top echelons of the leadership, a range of characters played important roles in the debates of the 1980s. A cast of grizzled state planners, upstart economists, futurist visionaries, and loquacious propagandists showed up to work at the leadership compound at Zhongnanhai. Missile scientists, technology entrepreneurs, and firebrand intellectuals jostled for influence at seaside conferences and in magazine pages. Amid heady growth rates, exceeding 10 percent annual growth for half of the decade, Chinese society became increasingly vibrant and was at times a source of significant pressure on the leadership—from workers who spoke out and sometimes crossed the line, to iconoclastic students who criticized the CCP on the streets and in writing. Many of these figures had profound disagreements about how the country should move forward. Their voices shaped the continuing intensive contestation over China's path forward.

Studying China's 1980s as history opens up new directions for both scholarly and public discussion, building on important studies of the period by political scientists, economists, journalists, and recently some historians.[14] It gives us an important opportunity to situate China at the center of the stories of neoliberal globalization, growing interdependence, and the information revolution, all crucial dimensions of the global 1980s. So often, China seems to sit apart, always an exception to the rule—but in fact, the reemergent Chinese varieties of capitalism and the changes in China's political economy were deeply connected to the international history of the late–Cold War era. Internal debates about how China would modernize were occurring in an explicitly transnational context, with substantial engagement with ideas and trends from both sides of the socialist-capitalist divide. At the decade's end, the collapse of the Soviet Union and the end of communism in Eastern Europe played a particularly powerful role in shaping the worldviews of China's leaders, crystallizing that another pathway—chaos, the loss of power, and the fragmentation of the nation—lurked in wait if their experiments failed.

It is now clear that China's experience is reshaping how scholars and practitioners understand capitalism, development, and modernization in the twentieth and twenty-first centuries. Yet many significant aspects of China's experience, whether the extraordinary fluidity of the 1980s or the role of ideas in shaping China's rise, remain to be reckoned with. There was no clear-cut "state" versus "market" duality but rather a constant intermingling of developmental forces, with trial-and-error policies that arose from the grassroots as well as the "commanding heights."[15] Instead of the factional model of competition over raw political power that has predominated in scholarship on the period, this book foregrounds the informality and variability of political alignments. It argues for the importance of the ideas and beliefs of key actors in the Chinese system and emphasizes how discourse shapes policy outcomes.[16]

In the 1990s, flush with post–Cold War confidence and optimistic about signs of grassroots reform or civil-society vibrancy, many experts predicted that China's rulers would "eventually fail in their bid to achieve order without opposition, affluence without openness, modernity without pluralism."[17] Of course, those predictions may yet prove true. However, it is long past time to face the reality that China's rulers may continue to succeed. The pages ahead show in detail how they settled on and pursued this so-called China model, not through a master plan but incrementally, adjusting to ideas and events as they confronted them—a transformation that has reshaped both China and the rest of the world.

◇

As I researched the 1980s, I understood this history had been the subject of such thoroughgoing manipulation that revisiting it is impossible without also examining what it means in Chinese politics.[18] So this book delves into the dramatic process of rewriting history that followed the violent repression of 1989. Using newly obtained propaganda and censorship directives, I reveal how the CCP rewrote this history: the internal process of erasing Zhao Ziyang, building up the threats of Western infiltration, and recasting the trajectory of China's modernization.

This historical revision went well beyond what I was already aware of, such as the well-known official spin about the decision to use force against the protesters. It went far deeper into how the CCP wanted people—inside China and around the world—to think about China's past, present, and future. China's rulers used the process of rewriting what had happened to dramatically limit the range of possible paths the country could take, seeking to end lingering uncertainties about how it ought to modernize. This was designed to exclude and forbid the representation of forces pushing for alternative paths. Instead, it advanced a triumphant story of wise, resolute decisions propelling China's rise on the single correct path taken, bolstering the CCP's legitimacy.[19] One thinks of the Party's slogan in George Orwell's *1984:* "Who controls the past controls the future. Who controls the present controls the past."[20]

The crucial turning point in these shifts in China was the crackdown of 1989—a pivotal moment after which CCP rulers changed the way they understood and spoke about the country's modernization. In writing on contemporary China, the period immediately after the massacre is often treated as a gap: a time of "freeze," "uncertainty," or "retrogression" between June 1989 and Deng Xiaoping's Southern Tour of early 1992, like a brief parenthesis in a much longer and more important sentence. In this book, I take a different approach. For official views about how China should modernize, the period between the summer of 1989 and early 1992 was in fact of the greatest possible enduring importance. It witnessed the consolidation and "rectification" of ideas about China's political and economic organization, and its modernization, which remain intact today. Deng's Southern Tour marked the acceleration of economic growth but did not fundamentally alter these concepts that undergird the Chinese system.

We have long known that changes like the erasure of Zhao Ziyang took place, of course. What is new is that rather than inferring it from the outside in, we can use documentary sources to see this erasure and distortion happening from the inside out. We can see China's rulers making history just as they made policy.

This process of rewriting history has created pervasive manipulations and limitations in the source base for research on China's recent past. To address these challenges, I have adopted two approaches. First, this book uses internal Chinese documents, many of which are still formally classified but have become available through a variety of channels, from high-profile leaks to quiet appearance in foreign collections. These include reliable and detailed records of leadership discussions, internal briefing documents, unpublished speeches, archives inside and especially outside of China, oral history interviews, and printed materials. I was also fortunate to speak over the years with many former officials, prominent intellectuals, and family members of individuals who were influential during the 1980s. (To protect their identities at a time of intensified repression inside China, I have not used their names.) Of course, in keeping with the theme of rewriting history, memories are sources shaded with personal bias, idiosyncrasies, and the frustrations of episodes of failure and defeat; so, for example, whenever possible, I cite sources like Zhao Ziyang's memoir alongside other materials to corroborate their assertions. Second, to analyze the CCP's constant attention to controlling information and constructing narratives about itself—and to foreground the attenuated and distorted nature of any historical narrative—this book also makes extensive use of hundreds of propaganda and censorship directives, many of which I obtained in Chinese flea markets and online auction platforms over years of collecting. The enormous quantity of paper produced by Chinese bureaucrats meant that some of these directives found their way out. But there are signs that the brief window of opportunity for collectors may be closing. On my most recent trip to China, a crackdown on flea markets in central Beijing apparently also extended into cyberspace. Every time I searched on my favorite auction platform, the only result was "Item Not Found."

Under Xi Jinping, the Communist Party has intensified its attacks on the crime of "historical nihilism"—meaning, accounts of history that undermine the CCP or otherwise fail to comport with the official narrative. Xi's language to describe the role of history is emotive and existential: "Destroying a nation begins with going after its history," he said in 2013.[21] As the CCP celebrated its centenary in 2021, this focus intensified further. Xi rolled out a new resolution on party history that further exalted the party's absolute historical correctness, global significance, and his personal dominance, ahead of his expected third term in power.[22] In tandem, laws have criminalized the "slander" of officially designated CCP heroes and martyrs. Attacks on "historical nihilism" have extended beyond China's borders, targeting foreign scholars and publications, and into cyberspace. Chinese regulators even recently banned a gaming app for "distorting history."[23]

Chinese writers have not stopped trying to record the past, despite these powerful impediments. They use strategic circumlocutions to refer to purged figures, such as calling Zhao Ziyang "a leading comrade in the central government at that time." They push boundaries and test the limits of acceptable discourse. However, it is difficult to be optimistic. "I used to assume history and memory would always triumph over temporary aberrations and return to their rightful place," novelist Yan

Lianke has written. "It now appears the opposite is true. . . . You will be awarded power, fame, and money as long as you are willing to see what is allowed to be seen, and look away from what is not allowed to be looked at; as long as you are willing to sing the praises of what needs to be praised and ignore what needs to be blanked out."[24]

Within China, the safest bet often is simply to pretend that this period does not exist. In 2014, the scriptwriter of a propaganda television series on Deng Xiaoping was asked at a news conference why he had decided to stop the show abruptly in 1984 when Deng had remained powerful for years thereafter. The writer's answer was unexpectedly candid: "After 1984 would be too difficult to write," he said. "It would be too hard to handle."[25]

◇

This book goes to the heart of how the Communist Party understands itself and legitimates its rule. China today has become the world's second-largest economy and a burgeoning superpower. With these successes, the party's argument for legitimacy is also explicitly historical, positioning itself as the natural outcome of China's long history and the one political group that was finally able to "modernize" China after many other failed attempts.[26] And the party remains deeply invested in maintaining its monopoly on how people in China and internationally interpret that rise and talk about its history. It is now speaking much more openly about a "Chinese model" and "Chinese wisdom" for developing countries, all of which are based on its official version of the recent past.[27]

Of course, other governments rewrite history and always have—whether the *damnatio memoriae* of ancient Rome or the Soviet Union's airbrushing of purged officials. National myths, and the brutalities of imperialism, racism, and authoritarianism they elide, are central flashpoints in public life from the United States to South Africa to Eastern Europe.[28] China's rulers themselves have been rewriting history for centuries, with great political effort devoted to crafting the annals of dynasties and suppressing alternative narratives.[29] But as China's power increases, it is more important than ever to understand the political centrality of control over history to this newly restored great power. The narratives China's rulers choose to forbid and occlude are as revealing as what they choose to spotlight.

The erasures and distortions of the 1980s have led to a lack of public awareness about this period inside China, an extension of what journalist Louisa Lim, writing about the Tiananmen crackdown, called a kind of historical "amnesia." The former political reform official Wu Wei has written that "the younger generation is now all but unaware of what happened in the 1980s."[30] It is hard to blame them; stripped of contestation and imagination and turned into a jubilant story of the CCP's stewardship, the official narrative is both dull and vague, making the 1980s sound like a tedious march up the mountain of gross domestic product, beneath the benevolently outstretched hand of Deng Xiaoping.

Yet, in looking beyond the myths the CCP has pushed out into the world, we must also not fall into nostalgia for the 1980s. In the many conversations I had while researching this book, I heard wistful tones in the voices of my interlocutors. One Chinese writer exclaimed as we sipped margaritas, "That was the time to be young!" Of course, living through the period was far from easy. Ideologized initiatives to purge China of new lifestyles and influences were frequent, and crackdowns and violence remained major features of political life. However, we should be able to hold multiple ideas in mind at once, seeing the contestation and violence as well as the optimism and sense of possibility. Saying that China's 1980s were different from what came after is not to say that it should (or could) be sought as the goal for China today or China in the future. But we can acknowledge that this decade's history will remain one of the possible sources of China's future—as material that can serve as a "usable past," in the words of American cultural critic Van Wyck Brooks.[31]

"The ultimate mark of power may be its inevitability; the ultimate challenge, the exposition of its roots," wrote anthropologist Michel-Rolph Trouillot.[32] Unearthing these roots is the task of uncovering the "political architecture" of Chinese development—both how change occurred and how the party-state gave political meaning to those changes.[33] But it is also, ultimately, about investigating the sources, and the limits, of the CCP's power. Power is wedded to how the past is told—in China and around the world.

For China's rulers today, this fuller history of the 1980s is not just "unusable" or useless; it is threatening. But Chinese history has not ended with Xi Jinping's rise to dominance. Prospects for change—whether they come from within the party or outside of it—will one day look to the history of the 1980s to help understand what China might yet become.

CHAPTER 1

Reassessing History, Recasting Modernization

China's 1980s began with both a call for modernization and a reassessment of history. In January 1980, in the same speech in which Deng Xiaoping deemed modernization "the essential condition for solving both our domestic and our external problems," he also turned his attention to another task, one that he believed was intimately connected to the project of modernizing China. The time had come to "tackle historical issues," Deng declared. "We will probably work out a formal resolution on certain historical questions this year."[1]

What Deng had in mind was a reckoning—with the tumult of the Mao era, the crimes and injustices committed, and the uncertainty about what the People's Republic of China (PRC) was without Mao Zedong. Deng had also come to believe that reevaluating the CCP's history was a prerequisite to his ambitious plans for modernization—and not only because it would bolster his own position and power. With historical questions unresolved, restoring the unity of the party and the country after the chaotic conflicts of the Cultural Revolution (1966–1976) would be impossible. And without unity, Deng believed, ideological, economic, technological, and political modernization would be unattainable.

In fact, this shift to reassess the history of the Mao era had started almost immediately after Mao's death on September 9, 1976. Who would succeed Mao and embody his legacy, and how would that legacy be understood? Mao had designated a successor, Hua Guofeng. However, Mao's wife, Jiang Qing—inherently representing a uniquely strong link to Mao—moved rapidly to seize power with three other high officials, Zhang Chunqiao, Wang Hongwen, and Yao Wenyuan. This so-called Gang of Four were viewed as having perpetrated some of the Cultural Revolution's worst excesses, along with Mao's one-time successor Lin Biao (who had died years earlier in a mysterious plane crash).[2] So within weeks of Mao's funeral, Hua Guofeng allied with CCP elders and the military brass—especially Marshal Ye Jianying, a distinguished former military leader with sterling CCP credentials dating back to the Long March of 1934–1935—to arrest the gang and their supporters. The gang was charged with instigating a "counterrevolutionary" plot to take control of the country.[3]

The news was met with public jubilation. Carousing students and teachers emptied store shelves of liquor in Beijing's university district. When photographs of Mao's memorial service were subsequently published, the gang had vanished, airbrushed out of memory and replaced by the Beijing horizon. Shortly thereafter, Hua helped to cement his own legitimacy by revealing a short message Mao had scratched out shortly before his death: "With you in charge, I am at ease."[4] Hua had crushed his biggest threat and, with the Gang of Four safely in prison, seemed to be in a strong position as both CCP chairman (the head of the party) and premier (the head of the government).

Yet Hua still faced the problem of Mao's legacy. Many of Mao's decisions had caused immense human suffering. The Great Leap Forward attempted to revolutionize China's agriculture and industry, but it collapsed into horrific famine, killing an estimated 30 million people. The Cultural Revolution sought to purify Chinese civilization and Chinese communism, but it became a tragedy of mob rule: children denounced their parents and teachers, neighbors turned on each other, and gangs humiliated "counterrevolutionaries." In some provinces, rival factions descended into all-out warfare. An estimated 1.6 million people were killed, and tens of millions more experienced unthinkable anguish.

Mao's call to "bombard the headquarters" meant that nearly the entire leadership had suffered—denounced, sent to conduct forced labor in the countryside, imprisoned.[5] Even so, Mao had been the nation's founder and its paramount leader for many decades as well as the CCP's global symbol. Its legitimacy remained inextricable from Mao, despite his abuses. Hua, like many senior officials, felt that the CCP had no choice but to remain the party of Mao.

After the chaos of September 1976, one of the great questions confronting Hua was what to do with the officials purged by Mao, as well as how to handle the millions of ordinary individuals who had been denounced. One case was particularly difficult: the longtime top official Deng Xiaoping. Deng was attacked during the Cultural Revolution as China's "number-two capitalist roader" (the "number one" title was held by Liu Shaoqi, the president of the PRC who had died in prison in 1969). However, Deng had extraordinary status within the party and in the People's Liberation Army (PLA), having played a prominent role in the revolution and the early decades of the PRC. Around five feet tall, Deng's outsize personality was also unusually popular with the Chinese people.[6]

Deng's case was further complicated because of this intense public concern with his fate. On April 4, 1976, before Mao's death, an estimated 2 million people had gathered spontaneously on Qingming Festival—the traditional day of mourning—to pay homage to longtime premier Zhou Enlai, who had died in January of that year. They laid wreaths with messages to mourn Zhou, praise his deputy Deng Xiaoping, and criticize the CCP leadership's treatment of both men. On April 5, the leadership called in the PLA and other forces in the area to clear Tiananmen Square. This "Tiananmen incident" proceeded without any recorded deaths, though many arrests occurred thereafter, Deng was once again punished, and the spontaneous protests were labeled "counterrevolutionary."[7]

In late 1976, Hua Guofeng began a vociferous nationwide campaign to criticize the Gang of Four, alongside a process of "reversing the verdicts" of people who had opposed the gang. Hua and his colleagues also began to release prisoners who had been punished for their actions during the Tiananmen incident and determined in early 1977 that Deng Xiaoping could return to work in the near future. In all these domains, Frederick Teiwes and Warren Sun have argued, Hua took the lead.[8] Hua also took significant steps to solidify Mao's legacy and even to ensure that he remained an unmovable presence at the heart of Beijing: Despite Mao's request to be cremated, his corpse was embalmed and placed at the center of Tiananmen Square in a mausoleum.[9] Hua took charge of editing volume 5 of Mao's *Selected Works,* which became the subject of significant propaganda efforts.[10] Posters depicted ferocious revolution- aries, fists raised and teeth bared, clutching the new book above the mes- sage, "Angrily denounce the monstrous crime of usurping the power of the party by the 'Gang of Four' anti-party clique!"[11]

In early February 1977, the central leadership under Hua put forward a new slogan to strengthen Mao's legacy: "We firmly defend whatever deci- sions Chairman Mao made, and we will always follow whatever instruc- tions Chairman Mao gave."[12] This was not strictly true, as the reversal of verdicts indicated, but this approach soon became known as the "two whatevers," and later would be used to caricature Hua Guofeng as a toady of Mao blindly following "whatever' the chairman had ordered.[13] Hua continued to authorize the rehabilitation of cadres whom Mao had attacked; by the end of 1977, the leadership had also authorized examina- tions for university entrance to recommence after more than a decade, with approximately 5.7 million Chinese students who had seen their edu- cations disrupted by the Cultural Revolution sitting for the test.[14]

Hua was not making these decisions alone. The CCP elder Chen Yun was particularly active in pushing for Deng Xiaoping's return to work. The resourceful Chen had served on the Politburo since the 1930s, be- coming the party's highest authority on economic matters. Chen helped develop the first five-year plan, working closely with Soviet advisers, and steered the industrial and planning bureaucracies in the early years of the PRC, including leading the economic recovery after the Great Leap Forward.[15] When septuagenarians such as Chen and Deng looked at Hua, they saw a novice in the central leadership who had not shared in their long, tumultuous history together. Although Hua had managed the initial handling of Mao's legacy, many major questions—from the eval- uation of Mao's actions during the Cultural Revolution to the unjust ver- dicts that had been branded onto ordinary people—remained unre- solved. And figures like Chen and Deng would not be happy taking orders from Hua for long.

While these gradual efforts to reckon with historical issues proceeded, Hua Guofeng also moved to aggressively prioritize economic development and modernization. For economic guidance, Hua looked particularly to Li Xiannian, who became a member of the Politburo Standing Committee in 1977 after working as minister of finance and other roles.[16] Hua endorsed a dramatic plan to accelerate economic growth by focusing on boosting enterprises' budgets and importing massive quantities of foreign technology, with Hua even stating at one point that 10 percent growth per year was too low. Hua introduced a ten-year development plan that sought to boost investment in heavy industry, mechanize agriculture, and use imported technology to create new manufacturing plants.[17]

The main reason the leadership focused on the economy was that they assessed it was facing severe challenges and feared its damaged state would derail the post-Mao political transition. In the PRC's first thirty years, some significant gains had been made: between 1952 and 1978, industrial output value had increased by a factor of fifteen, and the output of heavy industry in particular had increased twenty-eight times over. And in the 1970s, after the worst of the Cultural Revolution, communes boosted both agricultural output and rural industrialization, leading to significant increases in standards of living in parts of the country.[18] However, even with the successes of this model, its failures—beyond catastrophes like the Great Leap Forward—were numerous. China remained a poor country, with a per capita gross domestic product of only $175 in 1978. Industrial and agricultural shortfalls were severe; in 1975, for example, actual steel output fell 36 percent short of the planned target, and grain was 9 percent below the planned target.[19] Chinese economists reported scenes of stark indigence: "I remember going to a village where they had only one blanket for the whole family, and only one bowl," a researcher recalled.[20]

Visiting the developed world brought more bad news. After Vice Premier Gu Mu traveled to France, Germany, Switzerland, and other capitalist countries, he estimated that Chinese industry was at least twenty years behind Europe. The senior official Deng Liqun, after a visit to Japan, reported with amazement that more than 95 percent of Japanese households had televisions, refrigerators, and washing machines, whereas almost none in China did. Top leaders warned of grave conse-quences if China did not get on a better track; Hua Guofeng worried that China's economy might be "on the verge of collapse," and Chen Yun even suggested that China risked a rural rebellion if the problem of poverty remained unsolved.[21]

Hua's favored approach—importing technology—was not a new idea, of course. Hundreds of major projects in the 1950s had been set up with Soviet help; beginning in 1973, Zhou Enlai had made plans to import bil-lions of dollars in technology from Japan, West Germany, and the United States. Yet Hua's plan was unprecedented in its speed and scale—ballooning to planned imports of $80 billion by the summer of 1978, earning it the moniker of the "foreign leap forward." Gu's delegation to Europe reported that foreign officials were willing to extend loans to China of tens of billions of dollars.[22] This intensive push to modernize the Chinese economy under Hua Guofeng's leadership also propelled the ongoing negotiations to normalize Sino-American and Sino-Japanese relations. On May 30, 1978, Deng Xiaoping spoke with his adviser Hu Qiaomu, a preeminent theoretician who had served as Mao's secretary before the Cultural Revolution and was leading the newly established Chinese Academy of Social Sciences (CASS). "Western capitalist coun-tries, starting from their own interests, want us to be stronger," Deng said. "They are willing to lend us money. It's very stupid if we don't take it."[23]

◇

Deng Xiaoping, as he was returning to power, consistently supported Hua's agenda. However, Deng soon began working to subtly criticize and marginalize Hua, seeking to take power for himself—and he did so by of-fering an increasingly distinct vision of both history and modernization.

This new initiative was spearheaded by Hu Yaobang. Hu had been one of the youngest participants in the Long March after leaving his family to join the CCP at the age of fourteen, and had worked under Deng in various capacities since the 1940s. Beginning in 1977, Hu led the CCP's Organization Department, and in this capacity, he led the vital work to reverse unjust verdicts on "reactionaries" and "rightists," creating a process for rehabilitation and delivering impassioned speeches on the urgency of this work.[24] Hu also sought to criticize Hua's line by drawing contrasts with the popular, plainspoken Deng—caricaturing Hua as adhering dogmatically to Mao's theories and the "two whatevers." This culminated in a major editorial titled "Practice Is the Sole Criterion for Testing Truth," drafted by philosopher Hu Fuming and published in May 1978. In a dramatic gesture, the essay suggested the CCP's historical errors had been committed because of insufficient attention to "testing truth" through "practice." Some officials feared that the essay's authors sought to abandon Marxism or "cut down the red banner of Mao Zedong Thought," but Deng Xiaoping soon openly endorsed this line.[25]

Yet the contours of Deng's modernization agenda remained unclear. He had promoted much greater attention to science, technology, and education at an influential address to the National Science Conference in March. Deng also encouraged Hu Qiaomu to prepare a speech on observing "objective economic laws," which Hu delivered on July 28, 1978. Hu said that economic laws could not "change according to political needs." From July to September 1978, the State Council convened a series of planning meetings on "principles to guide the Four Modernizations," including dozens of key economic ministers and other officials, as well as Hua Guofeng himself. The pressure from Deng's allies was rising—with Chen Yun complaining to Li Xiannian about the excessively fast importation of equipment and loans that China could not effectively absorb—but Li continued to call for even more rapid adoption of foreign technology and capital.[26]

Foreign observers could tell that significant shifts were under way. When Deng Xiaoping visited Japan in October 1978, signing the Sino-Japanese Peace and Friendship Treaty and touring numerous factories, "he was treated as if he already spoke for China," Ezra Vogel wrote.[27] What remained, however, was for Deng to solidify his power at home.

On November 10, a Central Party Work Conference convened in Beijing. To put it mildly, this monthlong event did not go according to plan. Hua Guofeng's first priority was to garner an endorsement for "shifting the emphasis of the Party's work to socialist modernization." This meant moving from the Maoist emphasis on class struggle toward still-vague goals including greater economic development and scientific and technological advancement. In this, he succeeded. However, as hundreds of elderly comrades gathered, they demanded that the leadership not only focus on future modernization but also reckon with the past by reversing additional verdicts on many individual cadres as well as on the 1976 Tiananmen incident. The leadership was caught off guard, but Ye Jianying, Chen Yun, and other elders encouraged Hua Guofeng to accept these demands.[28] In a speech at the conference on November 25, Hua stated that the Tiananmen incident was "entirely a revolutionary mass movement, and it is necessary to reevaluate it openly and thoroughly." This reevaluation was a significant boon to Deng, and the leadership approved posthumous rehabilitations while reinstating leaders such as Bo Yibo and Yang Shangkun, which gave further impetus to Hu Yaobang's work overseeing the "large-scale reversal of verdicts."[29] Dozens of elderly officials spoke out in emotional tones about their great suffering during the Cultural Revolution—and many also criticized Hua Guofeng and the "two whatevers," demanding a break with the Maoist past. Over and over, Deng Xiaoping was held up as a leader who would be capable of steering the CCP into a new era.[30]

Deng capitalized on this unexpected development to solidify his power. On December 13, he delivered a speech—drafted by Hu Yaobang and his adviser Yu Guangyuan—in which he articulated his goals for China's leadership in powerful, inclusive terms. In a phrase that would become a signature, Deng said that the CCP had to "emancipate the mind" from the strictures of outdated ideology and misguided notions to succeed in "our drive for the Four Modernizations." This "emancipation" would involve learning advanced science, technology, management, and economics as well as updating political norms and the legal system, "so as to make sure that institutions and laws do not change whenever the leadership changes." Deng's call for "emancipating the mind" ended weeks of contentious meetings on a resounding note of inclusive optimism and suggested that a new era was dawning in China.[31] Hua offered a self-criticism for hewing too closely to Mao in ways that "limited everyone's thinking." By the time the work conference concluded on December 15, it was clear to the participants that Deng, not Hua, was ascendant. Deng remained a vice premier and took on no new title (though he would become chairman of the Central Military Commission in 1981), but his unique historical and personal status and his adroit outmaneuvering of Hua ensured that he was now the center of power in the leadership.[32]

These internal decisions were unveiled publicly at the Third Plenum of the 11th Party Congress, which met December 18–22. The meeting, one of the most famous events in China's modern history, announced that a new era was beginning—rising to the "great task of socialist modernization," as its communiqué declared, "to develop our economy with high speed and stability"—with the promise of wealth, power, and participation in the global community.[33]

However, it is important to recognize that no clear end point of the process was established at this famous Third Plenum. The CCP was, in a widely used phrase, "crossing the river by feeling for the stones." The phrase "reform and opening" had not yet been coined—it would only begin to appear in 1984—and Yu Guangyuan recalled that "reform ideas were generally embryonic" at the Third Plenum.[34] Put another way, the leadership had committed itself to modernization, but it had not yet determined what that modernization would entail or what a new Chinese "modernity" would look like.

Resolving the problems of the past hardly seemed easier. Following the work conference and the Third Plenum, the central leadership issued further guidance on the work that Hu Yaobang was leading to correct "unjust, false, and mistaken verdicts," bemoaning that "not even one third of cases have been reviewed." Resolving these historical issues was especially important for "arousing the enthusiasm of the vast numbers of cadres and the masses to take part in the construction of socialist modernization."[35] Without addressing the past, China's modernization would remain out of reach.

◇

As rumors raced through Beijing about the dramatic events taking place at the Central Work Conference, ordinary people started to write comments and essays criticizing the Gang of Four, the Cultural Revolution, and Mao Zedong. They posted these statements on a 200-meter-long brick wall on a tree-lined street off the Xidan intersection in central Beijing. Crowds gathered at this so-called Democracy Wall to read and discuss the posters calling for democracy and freedom. Newly established samizdat journals such as *Explorations* and *Beijing Spring* were sold at the wall for anywhere between five and twenty cents. Petitioners asked for redress of the abuses of the Cultural Revolution.[36] Senior leaders, including Deng Xiaoping, Hu Yaobang, and Ye Jianying, initially praised the activity at the Xidan Democracy Wall. Deng believed that these long-simmering tensions exploding into the open could be useful as he sought to solidify his gains over Hua.[37] However, Deng did not anticipate the extent to which this ferment laid bare disagreements in society over what lessons to draw from this history.

As the work conference proceeded, an electrician named Wei Jingsheng put up a poster calling for a "fifth modernization" to be added to the Four Modernizations: democracy. Invoking the lessons of "the real history and not the history written by the hired scholars of the 'socialist government,'" Wei wrote that the Four Modernizations alone were not enough. His radical manifesto demanded "true democracy" for the Chinese people, including "the power to replace their representatives anytime," which was "the kind of democracy enjoyed by people in European and American countries." Yet this movement's growing ambitions soon would collide with the man whom Mao had once called "a needle inside of a ball of cotton"—Deng Xiaoping.[38]

Deng felt secure in his power by March. When he visited the United States in January and February, he charmed the public by donning a ten-gallon cowboy hat in Texas and stood as an equal with US president Jimmy Carter at the White House. He launched a monthlong, bloody border war with Vietnam, seeking to "teach a lesson" to China's neighbor while shoring up the unity of the CCP and PLA leadership.[39] Deng also decided that the Xidan Democracy Wall movement had served its purpose and become a threat, especially after Wei Jingsheng published another essay on "the new dictatorship" that directly criticized Deng. On March 29, 1979, Wei was arrested.

The next day, Deng delivered a speech to reassert the CCP's authority and set clear limits on public debate. "The basic prerequisite for achieving modernization," Deng declared, was "adhering to the Four

Cardinal Principles." These principles were a collection of the fundamental tenets of China's political system, now presented as an inviolable formula:

1. We must uphold the socialist road.
2. We must uphold the dictatorship of the proletariat.
3. We must uphold the leadership of the Communist Party.
4. We must uphold Marxism-Leninism and Mao Zedong Thought.[40]

There was no ambiguity: whether modernizing the country or reassessing its history, socialism and the CCP could not be negated. Deng's speech had dramatic, immediate effects. Although Hu Yaobang sought to protect the journals that had flourished in 1978 and early 1979, they were closed in line with the Four Cardinal Principles. The leadership made an example of their best-known critic, sentencing Wei to fifteen years in prison in October 1979, and in February 1980, the Central Committee abolished the Cultural Revolution–era policy support for speaking out freely, airing views fully, holding great debates, and writing big-character posters, which were now seen as a source of upheaval.[41] As we shall see, the Four Cardinal Principles would remain central to the story of China's 1980s.

These political shifts impacted the process of historical reckoning. Unofficial attempts to address the Cultural Revolution's traumas became even less politically acceptable, and the process of dealing with history to enable modernization became even more top down. Hu Yaobang and his team continued evaluating and overturning individual cases, but rather than allow pluralistic discussion, the CCP leadership moved to monopolize this process, casting it as a narrow effort to remedy past errors to enable people to look to the future. On the thirtieth anniversary of the PRC's founding on October 1, 1979, Ye Jianying, chairman of the Standing Committee of the National People's Congress, delivered a lengthy speech on the CCP's history. Ye admitted that the party had made mistakes during Mao's rule, caused by the "impatience" of its leadership—an unprecedented, if nonetheless carefully controlled, public acknowledgment of errors made by both the party and Mao himself. Ye also called on the whole country to "achieve better, faster, and more economical results in building a modern, powerful socialist country."

Reckoning with the past was, once again, inextricable from pursuing modernization.[42]

However, Deng and his close advisers knew that a more comprehensive reevaluation and rewriting of the CCP's history was necessary. Working with Hu Yaobang, Hu Qiaomu, and Deng Liqun, Deng Xiaoping's mind turned to a type of document that the CCP had issued only once before: a Resolution on Party History. In 1945, Mao had presided over the drafting of a historical resolution that built up his own status as the leader of the party. Hu Qiaomu had drafted the 1945 resolution. Now, to shore up Deng's position and resolve open questions about the recent past, a new resolution was deemed necessary, and Hu Qiaomu was in the ironic position thirty-five years later of rewriting his own prior version of history.[43] Deng Xiaoping and Hu Yaobang presided over the drafting, canvassing a wide range of opinions, though, as we shall see, those other voices were not always listened to. Deng's comment in January 1980 that the leadership would be able to "work out a formal resolution on certain historical questions this year" reflected his optimism that drafting a new Resolution on Party History could be done relatively quickly.[44]

Early 1980 also saw Deng's allies move into new positions of power at the Fifth Plenum of the 11th Central Committee. Hu Yaobang took up the position of CCP general secretary, which replaced the position of chairman that Hua Guofeng had held. Hua stepped down from this party role, purportedly to focus on his responsibilities as premier. Zhao Ziyang, the top official in Sichuan Province who had become known for the successful "Sichuan model" of industrial development and decollectivized agriculture, was also promoted. He entered the Politburo Standing Committee and was given chief responsibility for economic policy as the head of the Central Finance and Economics Leading Small Group, taking over those responsibilities from Chen Yun, who supported the younger man. In addition to removing officials who had worked closely with Hua, Deng also installed Chen as head of the Central Commission for Discipline Inspection, which carried enormous organizational power, and gave Wan Li, who had spearheaded agricultural reforms in Anhui, nationwide responsibility for agriculture as a vice premier.[45]

All of these officials had demonstrated their loyalty to Deng, but they had differing status with the new paramount leader. Some elders, such as Chen Yun and Li Xiannian, had been senior officials for decades; they respected Deng but never saw him as above needing to consider their views and make compromises with them. Some younger officials ("young" by CCP standards, in their sixties) like Hu Yaobang had worked closely with Deng for many years, whereas Zhao and Wan had risen by making provincial reforms that won them national attention.

Zhao, for example, had become known as a champion of industrial development and decollectivized agriculture in Sichuan province. In industry, this model increased the autonomy of state enterprises and fostered the emergence of small-scale township and village enterprises, with the total output of industrial production between January and May 1978 rising by 47.6 percent compared to the same period in 1977. More importantly, in agriculture, this model pushed forward decollectivization by permitting peasants to conduct sideline production on privately culti-vated plots of land and receive payment according to work, while also giving greater autonomy to production teams by allowing specialized contracts and cash bonuses. This was a significant difference from the so-called Dazhai model, the late-Maoist agricultural policy of intensive, politicized year-round collective labor and local self-sufficiency, centered on strengthening the institution of the people's commune (which in-cluded production brigades and production teams). Recent scholarship has shown that the commune system successfully increased rural produc-tion throughout the 1970s, aided by improved agronomy, but it required significant subsidies from the central government to rural areas. Experi-ments with individual households making decisions about what to grow and sell had cropped up in communes across the country, with particu-larly significant early activity in Anhui province, but ultimately the deci-sion to decollectivize agriculture was imposed from the top down. Hua Guofeng favored the commune as the foundation of China's agriculture, but in a break with Hua, Deng himself eventually supported these re-forms to lessen the burden on the central government and further in-crease nationwide agricultural production, at the urging of Zhao, Wan Li, and others.[46]

Deng's new leadership team had one major task: pursuing "socialist modernization." Several weeks after the plenum, another vice premier and protégé of Chen Yun, Yao Yilin, was placed in charge of the powerful State Planning Commission (SPC).[47] In September 1980, Deng Xiaoping met with Zhao Ziyang and told him that the leadership had also decided to formally appoint the younger man premier of the State Council, taking that role from Hua Guofeng (who remained CCP chairman)—a meteoric rise from a provincial post to the pinnacle of the Chinese government. Zhao protested modestly that he was too inexperienced, but Deng replied, "Practice will toughen you up, and you'll do a good job."[48]

The focus on using the past to promote unity and facilitate the modernization agenda ran throughout the months of work on the Resolution on Party History. Prior accounts of its drafting have focused on how the leadership would evaluate Mao and how this process fit into the power struggle to oust Hua and build up Deng's power and status.[49] It did indeed serve these functions, but this close connection between history and modernization was a third important vector that shaped the resolution and its significance.

Deng had misjudged how difficult the process of drafting the Resolution on Party History would be. Meeting with the drafting committee between March and June, he complained that the resolution was "no good and needs rewriting." Deng was adamant that Mao's prestige must not be significantly undermined and that the document should not be "too depressing" so it could inspire people to "work with one heart and one mind for China's Four Modernizations."[50] Even so, the central leadership also authorized steps to remove many vestiges of Mao's cult of personality. Orders went out to paint over Cultural Revolution slogans, remove and destroy statues of Mao, and suspend distribution of the *Quotations of Chairman Mao,* better known as the Little Red Book.[51] Other efforts continued, such as the posthumous rehabilitation of Liu Shaoqi.[52]

Significant disagreement on how to handle sensitive aspects of the CCP's history persisted among the resolution's drafters.[53] In August, Deng decided to intervene, in a highly public fashion, by giving an interview to Italian journalist Oriana Fallaci. He began the interview by promising to keep Mao's portrait hanging above Tiananmen "forever."

Deng said, "In evaluating his merits and mistakes, we hold that his mistakes were only secondary."[54] He wanted above all to avoid repeating the Soviet Union's repudiation of Joseph Stalin in 1956, which had triggered instability throughout the Soviet bloc.[55] In February 1956, Deng had been deputy head of the CCP's delegation at the party congress in Moscow during which Khrushchev denounced Stalin and was the key intermediary in relaying the news back to Mao—a searing experience that clearly remained in his mind.[56] Deng seemed also to believe that too harsh an assessment of Mao would impede China's modernization. Following the interview, the team rewrote a complete draft of the resolution to present it to a conference of approximately 4,000 senior cadres in October 1980.[57]

The text was being negotiated up to the last minute, with particular tension over new language that had been introduced to criticize the Gang of Four and the years following Mao's death in 1976. Although Ye Jianying, Deng Xiaoping, Chen Yun, Hu Yaobang, and Zhao Ziyang all approved this text, Hua Guofeng remained powerful enough to block the additions, which contained criticisms of decisions he had made.[58]

The "4,000 Cadre Conference" was tense, emotional, and remarkably freewheeling. Many participants invoked their suffering during the Cultural Revolution and clamored for a stronger denunciation of Mao. Some asked that the resolution be delayed so that a fuller historical reckoning, including a more negative evaluation of Mao, would be possible.[59]

As this heated discussion continued, Deng Xiaoping huddled with senior officials. His approach was to reject some feedback from the conference while using other pieces of feedback to advance his aims. He insisted firmly that Mao's status must be upheld. However, with respect to the conference's encouragement that the resolution address the period following the arrest of the Gang of Four—which would criticize Hua Guofeng, build up Deng's role, and highlight the Third Plenum as "a crucial turning point"—Deng said, "It seems that we shall have to write one."[60] Soon after the conference, Hu Qiaomu produced a new draft and called for it to be finalized rapidly or risk "political unrest."[61]

The winter of 1980–1981 also saw the central leadership take public measures to clarify several lingering political issues. In December, to solidify Deng's rise and Hua Guofeng's fall, the Politburo issued a formal criticism of Hua, casting him as a force that had opposed modernization and sought simply to parrot Mao's line, errors and all.[62] Beginning in November 1980, the leadership also launched show trials of the Gang of Four and officials close to Lin Biao. The trials were covered in the official media, with ample spectacle—some of which seemed unplanned. In one extraordinary exchange, Jiang Qing shouted, "Everything I did, Mao told me to do. I was his dog; what he said to bite, I bit. . . . If I am guilty, how about you all?" But the conclusion was foreordained, with the harsh "verdicts of history" announced on January 25, 1981.[63]

Deng was growing impatient. "We have spent more than a year writing this document," he complained on May 19. "People are waiting for it." He dismissed the need to hold further discussions with the 4,000 cadres who had met the prior October, announcing instead to the Politburo that the resolution would be published nationwide on July 1, 1981, the anniversary of the CCP's founding.[64] When Central Committee members proposed significant revisions in a meeting on June 22, Deng snapped, "There is no time—the resolution must be finalized."[65]

On June 27, the resolution was adopted by the Sixth Plenum of the 11th Central Committee. Deng had triumphed, pushing through his preferred version of the CCP's history and positioning himself as the protagonist of China's historical transformation. The resolution told the story of "sixty years of glorious struggle" since the CCP was founded in 1921, emphasizing the paramount importance of Mao Zedong's leadership in the revolutionary fight and the building of socialism. "His merits are primary and his errors secondary," it determined. The resolution devoted particular attention to reckoning with the Cultural Revolution. It was "initiated and led" by Mao, although Lin Biao and the Gang of Four had "committed many crimes." The resolution cast Hua Guofeng as doing too little to set things right after Mao's death, but the Third Plenum of 1978 "marked a crucial turning point of far-reaching significance." The resolution presented the plenum at which Deng had taken control as a shift in all domains, from politics and historical reckoning to agriculture and the economy, rewriting history to present Deng as the key figure who had "made the strategic decision to shift the focus of work to socialist modernization." It concluded by reminding readers that the purpose of rewriting history was to promote unity in pursuit of becoming "a powerful and modern socialist country. . . . Our goal unquestionably can be attained!"[66]

Despite its goal of unity, the resolution was a complicated document that reflected its tortuous drafting process.[67] It required further study, analysis, and explication to truly "unify thinking."[68] Related initiatives got under way immediately, including the ramping up of party history courses in universities and a National Work Conference on Party History Materials in August, which issued a statement that trumpeted, "All participants unanimously believe that the resolution is the best model for doing party history research."[69] Of course, this "best model [of] research" was a selective and negotiated version of facts designed overwhelmingly to create a "usable past" that furthered current objectives.

As Hu Yaobang acknowledged at the time, the process of historical reckoning was in fact ongoing.[70] At the elite level, the resolution left many questions unanswered; the official Xiao Ke stated at the conference on party history that their research should have no "final conclusions that cannot be challenged when they are wrong (including those which were at one time correct but not so later)."[71] Throughout the country, work on reversing verdicts continued for several years, affecting approximately 3 million cases. Even though an official version of events had now been promulgated, contestation over both the past and the future would persist.

At the leadership's retreat in Beidaihe in late July, Deng Liqun delivered an internal analysis of the resolution in a discussion with senior leaders, producing an explanatory text that was subsequently circulated throughout the propaganda apparatus. Deng Liqun devoted significant attention to elaborating on the importance of Deng Xiaoping, adding another layer of narrative on top of the resolution.[72] Classified propaganda directives highlighted this "series of major decisions" made in "the turn from the 1970s to the 1980s," deliberately built up Deng's status as a transformational figure, and laid out a stark conclusion: "Comrade Hua Guofeng obstructed the progress of history."[73] In these accounts, by contrast, Deng Xiaoping was synonymous with "the progress of history"—even with modernization itself.

But what would "modernization" entail? What problems did the Chinese leadership believe they needed to overcome and what was their desired end state? There was no consensus on the answers to these questions or why China was "relatively backward," as the resolution put it. For China's rulers, figuring out how the country ought to modernize was the central story of the 1980s—a decade of tumult that would transform China and the world.

PART I

IDEOLOGY AND PROPAGANDA

◆

IDEOLOGICAL QUESTIONS were at the center of the politics of
the 1980s. China's system of official ideology—the ideas, practices, and language that the Communist Party endorses to ensure
political unity and continuity, mobilize action, and maintain social
control—was a crucial domain of contestation and the terrain on
which every senior leader operated. It remained the foundation of
how they governed and how they spoke both internally and publicly about their actions.[1] Many accounts have described the 1980s
as an era in which there was "no room for ideology" or in which
"ideology was largely spent as a political force."[2] In this telling, it
was an age of "pragmatism," with Deng Xiaoping, hailed as "the
great pragmatist," at its helm.[3] But to understand the 1980s, one
must understand the contours of these debates about official ideology and how they affected policymaking, propaganda, and people's
lives.

Deng Xiaoping had placed immense importance on ideological
and propaganda work in his 1979 speech on the Four Cardinal
Principles; "the basic prerequisite for achieving modernization"
was upholding the socialist road, the dictatorship of the proletariat, the leadership of the CCP, and Marxism–Leninism–Mao

Zedong Thought, the wordy name for China's official theory. Deng called for "unremitting struggle against currents of thought which throw doubt on the Four Cardinal Principles," especially "blind admiration of the capitalist countries." And he tasked the Propaganda Department to rise to the challenges presented by the modernization agenda, which would require "new content and ideas and presented in fresh language."[4] Yet he did not answer exactly how China could be at once modern, open to the world, and ideologically pure. Officials such as Zhao Ziyang, meanwhile, fought to make the economic policy portfolio as distinct as possible from the demands of official ideology, often without success; indeed, it was not easy to separate economic work and ideological work in China's socialist system.

Discarding socialist ideology was never an option. The nature of ideological "struggle" changed in the 1980s, but it certainly did not disappear. Official ideology remained necessary to promoting the "unity" and control of the CCP and of Chinese society. It was often defensive, fending off the "sugar-coated bullets" of bourgeois, capitalistic influences, but it also frequently went on offense.

The chapters in this section go well beyond simply asserting that ideology mattered. Using numerous classified directives and reports, they also reveal the complex and sometimes tortured role of CCP ideologues who were charged with ensuring that China's modernization remained socialist. (The term *ideologues* can sound disparaging to an English-language ear, often evoking an uncompromising or dogmatic attitude, but to these officials, it was far worse to be accused of lacking ideological fervor.)[5] The term *propaganda* is also often used pejoratively, but the propaganda apparatus acted both as the public face of China's rulers, explaining policies and events to the Chinese people and to the world, and as a hidden channel for giving orders, instilling meaning into disparate policy decisions, and unifying the leadership, the party, and the people—building on the Soviet Union's Leninist model of mass mobilization, information control, and discipline.[6] The Chinese system incorporated Mao Zedong's emphasis on "thought work," refined since his rectification movement in Yan'an, on top of these foundations.[7] Too often, the organs of propaganda, cultural oversight, educational affairs, and public morality have been depicted simply as reactionary opponents of reform.[8] Certainly, figures such as Hu Qiaomu, the leading writer of official documents, and Deng Liqun, a powerful veteran of the propaganda apparatus whom Deng Xiaoping once called stubborn "like a Hunan mule," strongly opposed many of the effects of market reforms. However, we should see their work as part of an integral whole with policymaking and party governance.[9] More specifically, what was called "ideological and political work" played a central role in shaping the meaning and content of modernization. Its role was not only to indoctrinate party members and "the masses" but also to influence what policy options were available and how a wide array of individual decisions was understood to "add up."

These chapters center on two major episodes, the efforts to oppose "spiritual pollution" in 1983–1984 and "bourgeois liberalization" in 1986–1987, examining the profound tensions over the meaning of China's "socialist" modernization as signs of capitalism proliferated. In analyzing anew these episodes, access to original internal sources is particularly significant because great importance resides in what Michael Schoenhals calls the "formalized language and formalized speech acts [that] help constitute the structure of power within China's political system."[10] The CCP's belief in the power of text, precise formulations, and even the strict governance of printing is characteristic of this regime and its focus on rendering ideology as a basis for action, especially in the form of policy. Deng Xiaoping communicated in blunt, feisty language, cultivating a plain-speaking persona—and many of those colloquial statements were translated into ideologically correct formulations.[11] Some, such as Deng's famous assertion that "it doesn't matter whether a cat is black or white, as long as it catches mice" (which had once been criticized as anti-socialist) were reworked into principles such as "practice is the sole criterion for testing truth." For other figures, such as the creative theoretician Su Shaozhi, the goal was to remedy a situation in which "Marxism lost its prestige among the masses" after the Cultural Revolution—even if this meant running headlong into the resistance of more orthodox officials.[12]

The content of China's official ideology evolved in the 1980s, as Deng added his distinctive embrace of socialist modernization to "Marxism–Leninism–Mao Zedong Thought." The number of published periodicals and books more than tripled between 1978 and 1985, reflecting an ever-widening range of publicly expressed opinions, which carried with them the threat of error, subversion, and "chaos." For many ideologues, the most fundamental threat to the project of building communism in China was not capitalism but "confusion." If CCP cadres and ordinary people did not know what to believe—if their thinking was not made "clear" and "unified" through ideological work—then the People's Republic of China's revolutionary project could not succeed. These officials made claims on gender, sexuality, and consumerist lifestyles—ranging from lipstick and rock music to pornography and soft drinks.[13] They fostered morality as defined by the CCP and made demands of society as well as individuals' character and spirit.[14] Indeed, the ideological sphere worked closely with China's public security and disciplinary arms, and the need to punish the ideologically "sick" or criminally "polluted" remained a central preoccupation of the regime. Violence targeting these individuals was intended to be both punishment and propaganda, displaying to Chinese society what it meant to go astray and what could happen if one did. Although such violence was magnitudes more widespread in the era of Mao Zedong, it did not vanish in the 1980s.

China's elderly leadership worried particularly about the young generation, which was born years after the communist revolution and thus might not have the same "revolutionary spirit" as their elders. As we shall see, Chinese young people, particularly students, would repeatedly demonstrate that their views of China's future differed significantly from the gerontocrats on the Politburo. With its primary focus on the Chinese elite, this section does not seek to answer the question of whether propaganda "worked" in shaping the minds of the Chinese people (although innovative recent studies in political science and economics suggest the remarkable effectiveness of such propaganda[15]), but it shows the leadership's deep fear that they were failing to put up adequate ideological defenses against the onslaught of global capitalism.

Throughout the 1980s, and indeed into the present, China's rulers remained resistant to the cultural, social, and ideological implications of "reform and opening." They continued to develop their socialist ideological commitments even as they embraced market reforms and dramatically expanded connections with global capitalism, and they constantly grappled with how socialist ideology could constrain, enhance, or give meaning to the modernization agenda. Different voices reached widely differing conclusions, and throughout the 1980s, these tensions were never decisively resolved. But they powerfully shaped this decade's story of ferment, inspiration, and contestation.

CHAPTER 2

Spiritual Pollutions and Sugar-Coated Bullets

Deng Xiaoping began 1980 in a state of high alarm about the changes sweeping through Chinese society. "There are now certain ideological trends in our society, particularly among some young people, which merit serious attention," Deng said darkly in early January. The only solution was a concerted propaganda effort to make sure that, when engaging with the capitalist world, "we must never allow ourselves to worship capitalist countries, to succumb to corrosive capitalist influences, or to lose the national pride and self-confidence of socialist China."[1]

The Propaganda Department leaped into action, starting with using Deng's speech itself as a text for cadres to study. The party committee of each locality and enterprise met to set out its plan. At the Shanghai Daily Hardware Company, for example, the party committee met on February 23, 1980, to prepare to lead the factory's party members to study Deng's speech. They scheduled weekly sessions on Saturdays for the month ahead. The method would be "first, study; second, discuss; third, compare views"—a process of close reading the speech, discussing the major ideas in it, and determining correct interpretations. For workers, they would also carry out larger-scale presentations and lectures.[2] This process was ideological work in action, and it occurred nationwide.

Deng's concerns reacted to a great blooming of artistic production, which was connected to the Xidan Democracy Wall. Underground literature flourished, with the poets Bei Dao and Mang Ke establishing the People's Republic of China's first nonofficial literary magazine in several decades, *Today*, in 1978. Its pages were filled with daringly opaque, surreal poems that broke with the conventions of socialist literature (its detractors called it "misty" poetry). "Scar literature" sought to reckon with the traumas of recent history and the abuses of officialdom. Translations from around the world brought foreign literature into Chinese, and artists—from the Stars Painters Society in Beijing to figures far from the capital—pushed the boundaries of socialist cultural production.[3] This work drew the ire of CCP ideologues; *Today* was soon banned, and on December 25, 1980, Deng Xiaoping again denounced the threats of "ideological confusion" and "corruption by capitalist influences."[4] In early 1981, with Deng's backing, large-scale propaganda attacks targeted individual works, especially the People's Liberation Army writer Bai Hua's screenplay *Bitter Love*, which official media condemned as "reflecting the erroneous ideological trends of anarchism, extreme individualism, bourgeois liberalization, and even negation of the Four Cardinal Principles."[5] Internal propaganda directives provided strict guidance on the urgent need to criticize "counter-revolutionary" and "anti-socialist" remarks, with the paramount objective of "sweeping away confused thoughts and muddled understanding."[6]

These concerns about threats to socialist ideology did not only affect the realm of politics and propaganda. The central leadership became focused in the winter of 1981–1982 on what they called "economic crimes." The initial market reforms and international trade that had begun to ramp up in the 1970s allowed smuggling, corruption, bribery, and other capitalistic crimes to flourish. In 1979, smuggled goods worth 7.3 million yuan were seized, a number that skyrocketed to 100 million yuan in seized goods for the period between January 1980 and June 1981.[7] For CCP leaders, these economic crimes were thoroughly ideological. Some elders, such as Chen Yun (who ran the Central Commission for Discipline Inspection [CCDI]), took the position that the leadership should not be surprised; China's coastal, marketizing southern provinces were "home ground for bad elements" and historical hotbeds of smuggling and bribery.[8] On January 5, 1982, Chen read a report on rampant smuggling in Guangdong and wrote a stern message to his colleagues: "I propose that we severely punish a few, imprison a few, and even kill a few who've committed the worst crimes."[9] Deng responded approvingly, and on January 11, General Secretary Hu Yaobang chaired a Politburo meeting to "strike hard" against economic crimes, issuing an "urgent notice" on curbing these illicit activities and deploying CCDI to Guangdong, Fujian, Zhejiang, and Yunnan Provinces.[10]

A flurry of arrests and official statements followed, with explicitly ideological framing as "an important part of our struggle against capitalist corrosion."[11] At a Politburo meeting on April 10, 1982, Deng called for "a long and frequent struggle" with "two hands": both continuing to pursue economic development and cracking down on economic crimes.[12] Economic crimes were inseparable from conducting market-oriented reforms and opening to global capitalism, and Deng's prescription for "striking hard" required both political discipline and ideological struggle to facilitate socialist modernization.

Circulating the official decision on economic crimes, the Propaganda Department drew a distinction between how this struggle should be characterized internally and publicly. "Internal education" on the struggle against economic crimes should focus on "capitalist corrosion," whereas public reports should focus on people who "successfully resisted" economic criminality.[13] Reflecting these instructions, posters produced to promote the "strike hard" effort showed images of resolute Chinese officials, dressed in white, resisting corruption with a powerful thrust of the palm down toward a proffered bribe. The central leadership's goal was not simply to crack down but also to "foster a correct spirit."[14]

The sense that socialist ideology was under siege intensified in some parts of the central leadership in the summer of 1982. Beyond "corrosive" economic crimes, a seeming onslaught of threats emerged, a torrent of "sugar-coated bullets" spreading bourgeois, capitalist practices and ideas.

These "bullets" could take physical form as money, luxuries, or "promiscuous" women and "spiritual" form as ideas or artworks. In order to diminish their appeal, the Propaganda Department instructed internally, "Reports on the capitalist world should be very grave and wary."[15]

One frightening threat was pornography. Mixing moralistic ideas about gender, sexuality, and capitalism, warnings about pornography focused on the bodies of young people, particularly Chinese men, who were "invaded" by this "very poisonous corrupting influence," which was anathema to "Chinese socialism." The leadership responded with highly publicized arrests and punishment of providers of pornographic books, tapes, and other materials, and schools cracked down on suspicious students. Ideologues even devised the category of "pornographic songs," which were "decadent," "vulgar," and "give people morbid sensory stimulation."[16]

Another new enemy that appeared on the scene was existentialist philosophy. University students were reading widely as a dizzying array of fiction, philosophy, psychology, and poetry was translated into Chinese. On elite university campuses, no foreign thinker was more popular than Jean-Paul Sartre. One popular novel included a youthful, individualistic character, fixated on the French philosopher, who was warned by a friend that he was "a dangerous thing to study."[17] On August 10, 1981, Sartre's play *Dirty Hands,* the story of a disillusioned Communist who realizes that he has been deceived by the party, premiered at a Shanghai theater; it echoed the "scar literature" that appeared as Chinese writers sought to reckon with the violence and suffering of the Maoist period.[18] Existentialist "humanism" and "individualism" seemed at odds with socialism to many CCP ideologues, who soon decided they had seen enough.

On May 4, 1982, a propaganda directive on the topic of "the influence of Western existentialism on some Chinese college students" went out through internal channels nationwide. Sartre had "the greatest influence on the values of university students," it said, denouncing this "Sartre fever" as "an assault on the Marxist worldview," promoting both individualism and estrangement from the CCP.[19] This denunciation quickly shifted the terms in which Chinese intellectuals discussed Sartre and existentialism, including at a national French literature symposium held in June 1982. "Most comrades believe that there is no 'Sartre Fever' in

China," the report from the conference announced, and the "very small number of relatively naïve young students" affected could be saved by stronger ideological and political education.[20]

Attacks on pornography and existentialism cast these texts as the wicked twins of official propaganda: repeated reading of them produced "confusion" and negative transformation, whereas ideological work produced "clarity" and positive transformation. One man who had become fixated on pornography recounted his experience to the *China Youth News*, recalling, "In the process of reading pornographic material over and over again, I became a different person without realizing it." The parallel with propaganda was made even clearer: "When I went to political education class I would stick the hand-copied [pornography] book in my study material or notebook and read it."[21] The ferocity of the attacks on pornography and existentialism underscored how profoundly CCP ideologues believed that language and study could transform individuals and shape China's future—for better and for worse.

Participants in the efforts to repel the "sugar-coated bullets" of capitalism reached to familiar Maoist concepts to make sense of the close connections between the material and ideological realms. The Propaganda Ministry reported in June 1982 that as the "strike hard against criminal activities in the economic field" proceeded nationwide, many comrades have raised the question, "Is this not the same as the 'danger of peaceful evolution' in the past?"[22] The term *peaceful evolution* had been used in Chinese politics since 1959, when Mao Zedong carefully read US secretary of state John Foster Dulles's speeches that discussed his goal of turning the socialist world capitalist and democratic. Mao called Dulles "a man of schemes" who "wants to subvert and change us to follow his ideas."[23] Party propagandists argued that "the nature of imperialism" meant that "peaceful evolution" was still a threat to China.[24]

To build China's defenses, the leadership rolled out a major effort to shore up what they called socialist spiritual civilization—meaning "revolutionary ideals," "advanced culture," and ideological loyalty. Hu Yaobang's report at the 12th Party Congress in September 1982 positioned socialist spiritual civilization as closely linked to China's "material civilization."[25] By pairing these "two civilizations," Hu made several points. First, even if China's level of economic development remained behind the world's most advanced countries for many years to come, its level of "spiritual" development could be world class and demonstrate the superiority of the socialist system. Second, in line with the concerns that had surfaced about "economic crimes," this focus on spiritual civilization could ensure that the reforms remained on virtuous track. Uniting these ideas was a third, even more fundamental assertion: China's modernization remained socialist, even as it opened to capitalism and capitalists. Even if it was difficult to distinguish between a "socialist" product and a "capitalist" product, it should be possible to make that distinction at the level of the people's "spirit," by whether they could effectively resist the threats epitomized by "peaceful evolution."

Yet fundamental disagreements persisted among the senior leadership about whether the "strike hard" campaign had achieved its goals. Deng Liqun complained that much work remained, but Zhao Ziyang declared on November 30, "The social order has improved significantly." In the period from January to September 1982, at least 136,024 cases of economic crimes had been investigated and addressed.[26] For Zhao and Hu Yaobang, the opportunity to push out a positive ideological narrative about "socialist spiritual civilization" was far more appealing than the fearful, violent campaign against economic crime. In early 1983, the leadership also promoted a program with mass organizations such as the All-China Women's Federation and the All-China Federation of Trade Unions to motivate people in loving the motherland, loving socialism, and loving the CCP. These gave a more explicitly ideological cast to this initiative on public morality, underscoring that patriotism and socialism under the banner of the CCP were the foundations of all "spiritual civilization."[27] The demand on individuals was emotional as well as ideational; the leadership called for their "love" as well as their loyalty.

To show the public that these demands produced results, the propaganda apparatus focused in particular on images of rural China. On January 29, 1983, for example, a propaganda report went out that painted a portrait of "a new flower in the construction of rural civilization" in Taixing County, Jiangsu Province. "Unhealthy trends" had melted away thanks to new regulations on spiritual civilization—culminating in a bucolic sketch of increasingly prosperous, virtuous rural life.[28] The task of propaganda, another directive stated, was to foster "socialist spiritual civilization" and encourage the "positive and calm" progress of reform.[29]

Yet significant uncertainty remained about what, positively, "socialist spiritual civilization" meant. CCP ideologues were firm that it should be "scientific," and in early 1983, a propaganda directive circulated with Hu Qiaomu's guidance on "popularizing science and opposing religious superstition."[30] However, Chinese society was full of signs that people were yearning for forms of individual and communal fulfillment beyond the framework of "socialist spiritual civilization." One example was intense interest that spread nationwide in breathing techniques called *qigong*. These techniques promised to allow people to develop "extraordinary powers," such as the ability to read with one's ears. Some figures, such as Yu Guangyuan, denounced qigong as superstition. These denunciations did not significantly stop its rising popularity for both health and spiritual purposes.[31]

For some prominent intellectuals, this uncertainty about "socialist spiritual civilization" underscored an important unresolved issue in Marxism: the value of the individual and the idea of "humanism." Was it correct to emphasize human agency, subjectivity, and values in a Marxist framework? Humanist ideas drew on Karl Marx's early works, particularly the *Economic and Philosophical Manuscripts of 1844*, which gave greater attention to the individual than later work that emphasized the means of production and the laws of historical materialism. International debates on Marxist humanism had been particularly lively in the 1960s, when Erich Fromm published *An International Symposium of Socialist Humanism* (1965) and new journals were founded like *Praxis* in Yugoslavia and the *New Left Review* in Britain. As Chinese thinkers discovered these debates in the late 1970s and early 1980s, they found a development in Marxism that seemed to address the trauma of the Cultural Revolution and the CCP's new focus on modernization.[32]

For Wang Ruoshui, a deputy editor in chief of the party mouthpiece, the *People's Daily,* these debates were perhaps the only way to revive and save Chinese Marxism after the "ultra-left" Cultural Revolution. Wang recalled that he was fixated on the question, "Why do such tragedies happen repeatedly in socialist countries?" Under the new reform policies, he saw a continued "crisis of faith" that only a powerful shift in China's socialist ideology could fix.[33]

Wang Ruoshui's key contribution was the idea of "socialist alienation." In orthodox Marxist theory, alienation occurs in bourgeois society: workers are "alienated" from their humanity by a society based on social classes and from the value of their labor by the bourgeoisie's ownership of the means of production. Wang, however, argued that the concept of alienation could also be used to analyze the problems of socialist societies, as a way of characterizing the forces that "oppress or even control human beings." The Cultural Revolution was his prime example, which had revealed that socialist alienation had manifestations such as "dogmatism" and the "cult of personality." This was a humanist idea because it argued that human nature and class nature were different.[34]

"Humanism" and "alienation" might have remained primarily the realm of academic controversy were it not for the elder CCP theorist Zhou Yang. On March 7, 1983, Zhou Yang delivered a speech at a commemoration of the hundredth anniversary of Marx's death, held by the Propaganda Department, the Central Party School, the Chinese Academy of Social Sciences, and the Ministry of Education, in which he endorsed the idea of socialist "alienation." Wang had helped Zhou write the speech, which Zhou delivered to an audience that included his longtime colleagues, such as Deng Liqun and the powerful elder Wang Zhen. After the speech, Wang Zhen congratulated his old comrade, "Well spoken!" He added a question, "How do you write that word, *yihua* (alienation)?" Wang had no idea what it meant.[35]

But Deng Liqun and Hu Qiaomu were incensed. When Zhou refused to revise the speech and published it in the *People's Daily* (with the help of Wang Ruoshui and the newspaper's editor, Qin Chuan), they went on the attack against this "unauthorized release." Hu Yaobang and Xi Zhongxun sought to moderate the backlash. The situation reached a tense stalemate.[36]

◇

For party ideologues, the cacophonous sense that China was on the verge of a major ideological crisis had reached a crescendo by the summer of

1983. The sight of people drinking Coca-Cola in the streets of Shanghai provoked concerns about the health, both medical and ideological, of the Chinese people.[37] Women's adornment startled the revolutionaries who just a few years before had worn identical, state-provided outfits, as lipstick, perms, and high heels seemed to signal the allure of "bourgeois" glamour.[38] Talk of "alienation" was the latest sign, but the Propaganda Department had been warning for months about the pervasiveness of "spiritual trash" across society.[39] Deng Liqun decided that far more forceful measures were necessary if China's "socialist spiritual civilization" was to stand a chance. On June 4, 1983, he delivered a speech at the Central Party School that criticized the concepts of "alienation" and "humanism," and called on cadres to "eliminate spiritual pollution."[40]

The term *spiritual pollution* was not Deng's invention; it had previously been attached pejoratively to a wide range of hostile forces.[41] However, Deng Liqun's speech vaulted the term to the center of Chinese politics. He warned that some people simply opposed the Four Cardinal Principles outright, but others were more insidious: "They label ['odd' things from the West] as 'new ideas' and let them emit a foul smell among people, polluting and poisoning people's souls, disturbing people's thoughts, and hindering the construction of socialist material civilization and spiritual civilization. . . . All of our comrades engaged in propaganda work have a responsibility to adopt a Marxist-Leninist attitude, carefully analyze all kinds of erroneous trends of thought, and work hard to eliminate spiritual pollution."[42] This was a fierce, sustained attack on the liberalizing trends in intellectual life that had produced "Sartre fever" and the lively debate over humanism and alienation.[43] These denunciations can be seen as part of a long history of movements to rectify ideology in CCP history, connecting back to the Yan'an rectification movement of the 1940s, where Deng Liqun had risen to prominence by helping to purge the writer Wang Shiwei. He reached back to strategies of the era in which he had first made his name, gradually building momentum to confront "spiritual pollution."[44]

Deng Liqun and his allies did not push immediately to widen the attack because they were focused on a banner event for the propaganda apparatus: the publication of the *Selected Works of Deng Xiaoping* in July 1983.[45] This was a crucial undertaking because it provided the textual basis for CCP ideology, propaganda, and political unity in the 1980s. On July 13, Hu Qiaomu delivered an internal speech to celebrate its publication. He acknowledged that there had been significant editing work because if Deng had made impromptu remarks, it was "not possible to say that every sentence is correct."[46] The *Selected Works of Deng Xiaoping* was not a return to Mao's Little Red Book, but it significantly built up the personal status of Deng as the guiding political and ideological force of Chinese socialism. The ideas contained in this official text represented the antithesis of "spiritual pollution."

A new push to crack down on economic crimes soon turned Deng Liqun's rallying cry into action. In the summer of 1983, Deng Xiaoping became fixated on both public order and ideological laxity after visiting the city of Wuxi, where a retired provincial leader told him that the security situation remained precarious. On August 25, 1983, the Central Committee issued a Decision on Severely Cracking Down on Criminal Offences. On September 2, the National People's Congress (NPC) amended the country's laws to increase the severity of permissible punishments for crimes such as "hooliganism," expand the scope of the death penalty, and delegate to provincial courts the ability to quickly approve death sentences, accompanied by decisions that expanded the population of labor camps. Between August and December 1983, the scholar Cui Min estimates that nearly 1.1 million people were arrested, investigated, sent to reeducation through labor, or detained, and tens of thousands were executed.[47] Zhao Ziyang explained this crackdown as necessary for China to avoid "the incurable diseases of capitalist countries, such as rampant criminal activity, very disorderly society, and ever-more-corrupted morality."[48] The ideological nature of this crackdown was front and center to its overseers.

In the same period, Deng Xiaoping worked with Hu Qiaomu and Deng Liqun to craft an address on ideological work.[49] Deng Liqun was once again denouncing "spiritual pollution in all ideological fields."[50] Reflecting Marxist thinking about the relationship of the base and the superstructure, he asserted that improvements in "material civilization" required concomitant developments in "spiritual civilization" in the form of increased emphasis on socialist ideology that gave meaning to economic development and the modernization agenda. However,

Deng Xiaoping's focus in his address on October 12, 1983, was primarily on intellectuals promoting problematic liberal ideas. Deng declared bluntly, "People working in the ideological field must not spread spiritual pollution."[51] Intellectuals, artists, and writers had an obligation to "serve as 'engineers of the soul,'" not raise ideas like humanism and alienation. Most importantly, Deng called for "waging active ideological struggle": "The guiding principles . . . are correct and clear-cut. The problem is that they have not been resolutely put into practice."[52]

On the same day, Chen Yun delivered a speech on party discipline that emphasized the importance of cracking down on criminal activities, and Li Xiannian soon joined the chorus.[53] Deng Xiaoping may have underestimated the extent to which the crackdown on economic crimes, when combined with opposing "spiritual pollution," opened the door to a much wider attack on changes in Chinese society under reform. Whatever his expectations, he had called for a crackdown and he would get one.

In Chinese politics, subtle changes in official formulations can signal life-or-death changes in policy, and the shift to a much harsher attack on spiritual pollution was contained in a single Chinese character: although Deng Xiaoping had ordered that spiritual pollution only be "cleaned up" (清理), Deng Liqun soon pushed for spiritual pollution to be totally "eliminated" (清除). This soon became the dominant motif in propaganda about spiritual pollution.[54] Articles and meetings decried the "sugar-coated bullets" of "bourgeois ideology," from detective novels and pornography to academic research. A bitter joke spread: "'Spiritual pollution' is like a basket. You can fit anything inside it!"[55]

Indeed, the effects were also material. Across the country, reports emerged that local governments had forbidden female staff members from perming their hair or wearing makeup and disciplined individuals who were too xenophilic, and criminals were executed for offenses that were traced back to "spiritual pollution."[56] Central officials were also punished. Zhou Yang apologized publicly for his "erroneous views," and Hu Qiaomu accompanied Deng Liqun to the People's Daily on October 30 to announce the resignation of editor Hu Jiwei and the firing of his deputy Wang Ruoshui.[57] The next day, Xinhua News Service sent out a commentary titled "Struggle against Spiritual Pollution," a further intensification.[58] Internal directives explicitly presented the efforts under way as interconnected: "The negative phenomena in society, evil trends, criminal behavior, and even some people's hostile activities to oppose socialism are inseparable from spiritual pollution."[59]

But in the days after this public commentary, a torrent of negative international media coverage alarmed CCP leaders. Concern mounted that the public perception of a harsh anti-Western campaign would undermine the willingness of foreign investors and businesspeople to engage with China, which was essential to the economic reforms.[60] On November 15, Hu Qili, a Politburo member who served as director of the CCP General Office, told the new editor of the *People's Daily* that opposing spiritual pollution should not negatively affect the economic reforms. The next day, an editorial in the *People's Daily* struck a conciliatory tone, emphasizing the more positive task of "building spiritual civilization." Yet negative press for the initiative continued to mount, worrying Hu Yaobang.[61]

Zhao Ziyang, for his part, saw that what had begun as an effort to rectify the thinking of intellectuals was now threatening the economic agenda. Working with Vice Premier Wan Li, Zhao pushed for the campaign not to apply to economic or agricultural matters. On November 25, Zhao presented his case at a meeting of senior officials to discuss the national economic plan: "Opening to the outside world and invigorating the domestic economy are the unswerving policy of the central government. Now we are talking about spiritual pollution and opposing bourgeois liberalism, but this mainly refers to the ideological front. The central government does not use these formulations on the economic front."[62] Zhao underscored that he saw the "ideological front" and "economic front" as distinct lines of effort. Both were important, but the goals on the "economic front," which centered on economic modernization and development under the umbrella of reform and opening, were "unswerving," whereas the movement against spiritual pollution was temporary. He added, regarding economic debates, "No matter what kind of opinion you have, you can talk about it all."[63] These comments attempted to wall off the "economic sphere" from the sweeping initiative to redress perceived problems in "theoretical work and literature and art."[64]

Deng Liqun was under great pressure and quickly endorsed "policy boundaries regarding eliminating spiritual pollution," acknowledging the importance of assuaging negative reactions to the initiative, including from "foreign journalists." Then, on December 7, he delivered an internal speech that recast the attack on spiritual pollution as a long-term, more ideational effort, focusing less on "men growing beards, or women perming their hair, high-heeled shoes, and lipstick" and more on "a spirit of bitter struggle." In addition, the entire countryside was placed off limits.[65]

Hu Yaobang also worked to stem the tide. At a meeting of provincial and municipal officials on December 13, Hu stated, "Opposing spiritual pollution must not be allowed to arbitrarily expand beyond the scope of Comrade Deng Xiaoping's remarks." According to the recollection of one participant, the room burst into applause.[66] The following day, Hu delivered a similar message in a speech to the leaders of the major propaganda outlets.[67]

For Deng Liqun and Hu Qiaomu, their best opportunity in years to dramatically increase the power of ideological and propaganda work over the entire modernization agenda seemed to be slipping out of reach. Hu Qiaomu, never simply a political operator, remained fixated on the substance. On January 3, 1984, in the same auditorium at the Central Party School where Zhou Yang had delivered his speech nearly ten months before, Hu delivered a speech arguing that alienation occurred only in capitalist societies. It was a carefully crafted rebuttal to these men whom he had already triumphed over politically. Reading Hu's speech, Deng Xiaoping encouraged its publication in the *People's Daily* but also told Hu Qiaomu to "allow debate, and don't hit people with a big stick," meaning to make harsh political attacks.[68] On January 26, Hu Qiaomu wrote a letter to Zhou Yang, enclosing a poem that he had written that promised "the wound will heal, and friendship will remain."[69]

In private, Zhao Ziyang recalled that he continued to argue to Deng Xiaoping that too much focus on "spiritual pollution" would cause serious damage to economic growth and international perceptions of China. This case was helped by economic data presented to the paramount leader throughout the winter—including a 10.2 percent increase in the output value of industry and agriculture—and continued negative reactions from foreign diplomats and media.[70]

Deng Xiaoping was persuaded and met privately with Hu Qiaomu and Deng Liqun at his home on January 18. Speaking at the Central Party

School on January 20, Hu Yaobang urged "vigilance" against people who were "disrupting" economic reform.[71] The official tone quickly softened, and foreign press soon reported that "spiritual pollution" had been placed on the back burner.[72] Zhao and Hu's arguments about keeping the "ideological front" as separate as possible from the "economic front" seemed to have won the day.[73] When Australian prime minister Bob Hawke asked about "spiritual pollution" in a meeting on February 6, Zhao said, "The central government has set a series of policies boundaries, so don't be afraid."[74]

Yet it remained to be seen how CCP leaders would address the initiative to eliminate spiritual pollution's legacy and the profound ideological concerns that it had raised. On February 11, Hu Yaobang criticized the initiative, claiming that it had led to "overreaching."[75] In doing so, Hu risked incurring Deng Xiaoping's ire because, as Zhao Ziyang subsequently observed, "everyone knew that the campaign was waged according to Deng's remarks." Deng's frustrations boiled over in a meeting on March 3 when he told CCP elder Bo Yibo, "Eliminating spiritual pollution was completely necessary." As if warning Hu, Deng said, "This matter is definitely not over."[76]

In May 1984, Zhao made an attempt of his own to address the initiative's legacy in his work report to the second session of the 6th National People's Congress. He underscored that although "inappropriate practices" had cropped up in some locales, clarifying the central government's "policy limits" helped to quickly remedy those errors.[77] By highlighting the importance of "policy limits," he signaled that the goal of setting out a distinct, protected economic policy portfolio would remain a priority. Yet this separation was always partial at best in China's socialist system.

The rapid and ambiguous turn away from attacking "spiritual pollution" had sown confusion and dissatisfaction in the Chinese bureaucracy. Many officials, of course, were relieved that they could get back to promoting economic development. But in September, Xiong Fu, editor of the preeminent ideological journal *Red Flag*, complained in a speech that central leaders had given mixed signals. In the span of a month, they had made a jumble of assertions—that spiritual pollution "has been suppressed," that it was a "long-term struggle," and that terms such as *oppose* and *resist* should be used instead of *eliminating*. Xiong Fu's point was obvious: Did the top leadership want to take "spiritual pollution" seriously or not? Without clear guidance, his hands were tied.[78]

Even Deng Xiaoping acknowledged that the pushback against eliminating spiritual pollution had left him dissatisfied. Once again, this frustration manifested in his displeasure with Hu Yaobang. According to Deng Liqun, when Hu again criticized the term *spiritual pollution* in February 1985, Deng Xiaoping was infuriated: "I will not retract my remarks [about spiritual pollution]," he insisted. "And, in the future, I will still reference this speech."[79] The struggle over the place of official ideology in China's modernization was far from over.

CHAPTER 3

The Scourge of Bourgeois Liberalization

These fitful efforts had failed to resolve debates over how socialist ideology and "socialist morality" should develop in tandem with the Chinese economy. Soon the leadership decided that the time had come to set out its vision more fully. On September 28, 1986, the Central Committee led by Hu Yaobang passed a resolution on "The Construction of Socialist Spiritual Civilization."[1] The resolution was firm on China's commitment to socialist ideology, but it did not use the term *spiritual pollution*. This was no accident. Hu Yaobang resisted including it as he drafted the resolution, compromising only with a single usage of the related concept of "opposing bourgeois liberalization." To a frustrated Deng Liqun, the document remained far too weak. Yet he was hearted by Deng Xiaoping's comments, in discussing the resolution, that opposing bourgeois liberalization "will have to be carried on not only now but for the next ten or 20 years." Wang Zhen, Hu Qiaomu, and Deng Liqun quickly circulated Deng's remarks, ensuring that cadres nationwide understood that opposing bourgeois liberalization remained a high priority.[2]

The decision to issue a resolution on socialist spiritual civilization developed from several years of work that, in the view of some leading officials, had not produced adequate results. In 1984 and 1985, Deng Xiaoping had reportedly complained on multiple occasions about Hu Yaobang's lack of emphasis on the Four Cardinal Principles.[3] However, for Zhao Ziyang and Hu Yaobang, the challenge was to "clearly demarcate unhealthy practices" from reform, as Zhao said to the Politburo on March 23, 1985.[4] Hu Yaobang, speaking at the Central Party School on July 15, made similar arguments, saying that China must keep to "our lofty ideals" and "avoid making big mistakes."[5] In August, Hu also appointed as propaganda minister his ally Zhu Houze, who pledged to liberalize the propaganda apparatus and adopt the "lenient, tolerant, and generous" governance of publishing—comments that were echoed by other senior officials such as Hu Qili, leading to a new wave of bold artistic and intellectual work.[6]

Countervailing trends in both elite politics and society complicated matters further in the fall of 1986. Earlier that year, Deng Xiaoping had also brought renewed attention to political system reform, as will be discussed in Part IV. This push for political reform added a new dynamic to the debates over ideological work, with uncertainty about how to weigh what now appeared to be three priorities—what Zhejiang party secretary Wang Fang described, in an internal speech, as the imperatives to "unswervingly implement economic system reform, unswervingly implement political system reform, and unswervingly strengthen socialist spiritual civilization." Wang observed, "The deepening of economic and political reforms will inevitably lead to profound changes in people's consciousness . . . [which] puts forward new and more demanding requirements for ideological and political work and building spiritual civilization."[7] He left open how to meet these "demanding" requirements.

Outside of the leadership, the atmosphere fostered by Hu Yaobang and his lieutenants led to a new wave of provocative critiques of China's official ideology. On campuses, women's studies groups sprung up, with one group at Peking University committed to consciousness raising and societal support for women's independence. In this period, Chinese women faced contradictory trends, simultaneously finding new opportunities for independent careers and facing severe discrimination. Women had worked in the Mao period, when official policy declared, in Mao's pithy phrase, that "women hold up half the sky." According to the All-China Women's Federation, 76 percent of working women sur-veyed in Beijing, Shanghai, and Tianjin said that they would still want to work even if their family did not require the income. However, as management became even more flexible and decentralized in the mar-ketizing economy, women faced biased treatment in hiring and the workplace.[8] Concerns about unfairness in the marketizing economy were not limited to women, of course. A February 1986 survey revealed that only 29.3 percent of respondents felt that the reforms offered equal opportunity to all.[9]

These views were serious challenges to Chinese socialism, and other thinkers argued that the CCP, despite its focus on modernization, had an incomplete understanding of what modernizing China would ac-tually require. The philosopher Li Zehou, one of China's most promi-nent intellectuals, offered up a shocking phrase: China should adopt "Western learning for fundamental principles and Chinese learning for practical applications." This inverted the Qing official Zhang Zhi-dong's famous formulation to guide the reform of the Qing dynasty (1644–1911) through a system of "Chinese learning for fundamental principles and Western learning for practical application." By contrast, Li argued that modernization was universal and synonymous with "social existence pioneered by large-scale industrial production in the West." China must therefore take "Western learning" as the "essence" of its modernization and could then apply the best aspects of Marxism and Confucianism "in practice." With his interest in Confucian ethics, Li thus also connected to broader debates about "Confucian Marxism" in this period, though his embrace of Western-style devel-opment as the "fundamental principle" of modernization received the most attention.[10]

Other intellectuals delivered even more searing indictments of Chi-na's system. Wang Ruowang denounced the CCP as an "aristocratic overlord" that was "opposed to the working class," while Xu Liangying, Liu Binyan, and Hu Ping called for freedom of expression.[11] Many Chi-nese students, increasingly frustrated with China's system and their prospects, were inspired by these thinkers' iconoclasm and daring. The students' favorite was Fang Lizhi, an astrophysicist and administrator at the University of Science and Technology in Hefei, Anhui, who toured the country delivering speeches that called for democracy and education reform. He declared that the socialist movement worldwide had been a "failure."[12] In this atmosphere, these latent political and social tensions exploded on China's university campuses. In early December, students in Hefei staged short protests, which quickly spread to Beijing, Shanghai, and other cities.[13] The Shanghai protests received particular attention after December 19, when students marched to the municipal government offices.[14]

Initially, several prominent officials, including Hu Yaobang, offered moderate assessments of the student unrest.[15] But others saw a significant threat as well as an important opportunity to combat "bourgeois liberalization." Figures such as Chen Yun (still leading the Central Commission for Discipline Inspection), Deng Liqun, Wang Zhen, and Vice Premier Li Peng (in charge of educational affairs) argued for a strong ideological and political effort to respond to the protests and ensure that they would not recur.[16]

The most significant unresolved question was where the eighty-two-year-old Deng Xiaoping would come down. On December 27, several powerful elders including Bo Yibo, Peng Zhen, Yang Shangkun, Hu Qiaomu, and Deng Liqun reportedly visited Deng Xiaoping at home to warn about the protests and complain about Hu Yaobang's leadership.[17] On December 30, Deng Xiaoping discussed the student unrest with a larger group of senior leaders and blamed it on failure "to take a firm, clear-cut stand against bourgeois liberalization." Deng stated, "We cannot do without dictatorship." He had decided to take severe measures if needed.[18]

These criticisms of bourgeois liberalization made clear that China's elders believed that the student protesters and their leaders in 1986 had seriously erred. The protests gradually subsided as CCP leaders made clear that participating in the protests would damage students' futures. However, Deng was "shocked" by the protesters' statements, Zhao recalled, and had made up his mind to remove Hu Yaobang as general secretary and replace him with Zhao.[19]

On January 2, 1987, Hu offered his resignation, which the Politburo Standing Committee accepted on January 4. The CCP leadership simultaneously targeted certain intellectuals, most prominently Fang, who was fired from his job and expelled from the CCP. Several officials linked to Hu, such as propaganda minister Zhu Houze, were also fired or reassigned.[20]

The leadership subjected Hu's record to sustained criticism in order to build a case against him. On January 10–15, Bo Yibo chaired a series of sessions to criticize Hu, with Hu's longtime opponent Deng Liqun speaking for more than five hours over two days.[21] On January 15, it was Zhao Ziyang's turn to criticize Hu. Zhao spoke cautiously at first but soon raised serious criticisms of Hu's "refusal to be restrained by organizational principles." Speaking to Hu directly, he allegedly added, "You are already like this while the older people are still around. This may become a serious problem when, in the future, the situation changes and your authority grows. . . . We are working together well today, but it is very difficult to say whether we will work together well if such a situation occurs in the future."[22] The next day, on January 16, the Politburo announced Hu's resignation. Xi Zhongxun (the father of China's current leader, Xi Jinping) reportedly protested the decision, but it was final. A summary of the criticism against Hu was published as Document No. 3 of 1987. He was also permitted to retain temporarily a seat on the Politburo and permanently on the Central Committee.[23]

According to some reports, Hu's ouster had long been in the works because Deng believed that his permissiveness with intellectuals had allowed "bourgeois liberal" ideas to fester throughout the 1980s. Hu had made other missteps, including a 1985 interview with the Hong Kong journalist Lu Keng in which he had discussed sensitive topics and allowed himself to be portrayed as an ardent liberal.[24] Other elders, especially Chen Yun and Li Xiannian, resented Hu. As early as the summer of 1986, Deng Xiaoping told the party elders gathered for the annual conclave at the seaside resort of Beidaihe that his greatest "error of the last few years" was to "misjudge that man, Yaobang," recalled Zhao. Many elders had also attacked Hu's "enthusiasm" for the capitalist world.[25]

However, the swiftness with which the CCP elders dismissed this popular, charismatic general secretary after years of dedicated leadership appeared to many Chinese intellectuals, officials, and students to be an injustice. After the meeting to criticize Hu, Li Rui wrote a poem:

Today the pen turns back to the past;
hatreds persist no matter what one does.
With a black-and-white pattern after a loss,
justice endures in people's hearts.[26]

A poignant statement of accepting fate, this poem suggested that even as the CCP laid claim to what was "in the hearts" of both officials and the people, "justice" remained beyond their hold. For years thereafter, ordinary people resented how the popular Hu Yaobang had been treated.[27]

Zhao Ziyang was swiftly named acting general secretary and would serve both in this role and as premier in the coming months. Some of Hu's allies believed that Zhao had stabbed him in the back to seize the general secretaryship—a charge that, unsurprisingly, Zhao vehemently denied.[28] There can be no doubt that tension existed between the two men, that Zhao criticized Hu in January 1987, and that Zhao benefited from Hu's removal. Deng, however, did not make a practice of engaging with Zhao on the highest-level personnel decisions, which remained the purview of the CCP elders. The most plausible interpretation is that Zhao acted opportunistically and pragmatically: he took the far easier path of not standing up to defend Hu and doing what was expected of him in a context where Hu's loss of power was already a fait accompli.

Zhao's power had increased, but many elders did not see him as above attack. Li Xiannian sent a warning to Zhao through Yang Shangkun, cautioning Zhao not to move too quickly with market reform and to avoid foreign and "bourgeois liberal" ideas. "Continuing this is unacceptable," Li said to Yang. "You should tell [Zhao] that."[29]

◇

The CCP's senior ideologues had decried the protests and successfully removed Hu Yaobang from power. They were emboldened to move forward with a broader initiative to attack bourgeois liberalization. Across the country, officials circulated Deng's speeches and worked to put his ideas into practice. In Tianjin, Mayor Li Ruihuan said that ensuring that the student disturbances did not recur was essential to avoid damage to the party and the risk that "foreigners will think less of us, and won't come to invest."[30] These attacks on bourgeois liberalization were explicitly presented as necessary for "reform and opening" to succeed.

On January 28, the central government circulated Document No. 4 of 1987, which focused on bourgeois liberalization and set limits on the scope of the initiative to combat it. It insisted "the struggle is strictly limited to within the party." Zhao was emphatic in his Spring Festival address on January 29 that "we are not engaged in a political campaign."[31]

Reflecting the lessons of "eliminating spiritual pollution," Deng Xiaoping went to great lengths to ensure that the public reform agenda moved forward. He had been willing to fire Hu Yaobang but refused to let this stymie the reforms. On February 6, Deng drew attention to the upcoming 13th Party Congress, planned for the fall. Speaking to leading officials, Deng said that he believed that the leadership had been "much too cautious" in advancing reform. "Why do some people always insist that the market is capitalist and only planning is socialist?" he said. "If they serve socialism they are socialist; if they serve capitalism they are capitalist."[32] Deng's important statement echoed his famous "cat theory" and sought to preserve space for the economic reforms to advance in the run-up to the 13th Party Congress, a major reform milestone, even as the CCP rolled out a "struggle" within the party. The process of reform was external and public, whereas the process of ideological struggle was largely internal. These two lines of effort played out alongside each other.

Indeed, the struggle against bourgeois liberalization continued internally with many new initiatives that sought to interpret and shape the modernization agenda. Vice Premier Li Peng, a favorite of Chen Yun and Li Xiannian, announced that a top priority was "guiding students to fully understand the long-term nature of the struggle to oppose bourgeois liberalization."[33] Around the country, party cadres and enterprise workers were organized to study newly published books that collected and annotated leadership statements. In addition to focusing on the correct views and language in these two texts, a variety of representative "incorrect" statements were also provided to cadres—dissecting language that allegedly revealed blind adoration for capitalism, such as the writings of Fang Lizhi.[34] Of course, not everyone reading Fang's statements found them so reprehensible; some cadres told the journalist Orville Schell that they actually enjoyed their mandatory reading of Fang and only paid lip service to criticizing him.[35] Unintended consequences did not deter the major propaganda push, however, which ramped up with great speed and force.

The CCP ideologues' effort to use bourgeois liberalization to reframe the modernization agenda was on display in a set of classified materials prepared for military units. This slim book contained six lessons on opposing bourgeois liberalization, showing in detail how ideological instruction occurred under "reform and opening."[36]

The book's first lesson was titled "Upholding the Four Cardinal Principles and opposing bourgeois liberalization is a major matter affecting the fate of the party and the nation." The lesson mounted its case against the student protests: some voices had called the Communist Party and Marxism evil; the protests disrupted commerce and people's routines, causing enormous financial losses. The struggle against bourgeois liberalization had "extreme importance" because if it spread unchecked, it could cause the CCP and socialism to collapse. After carefully reading this alarming set of arguments, readers were expected to answer examination questions, including "Why do we say that adhering to the Four Cardinal Principles and opposing bourgeois liberalization is a matter of great importance for the future and fate of the party and the country?" Once readers had mastered the first lesson, in subsequent weeks they moved on to lessons on topics such as the "people's democratic dictatorship," which contained strong criticisms of American democracy that highlighted the role of money in politics and limitations on free speech even in the United States and the United Kingdom, and the importance of the party's leadership. "Our party is good at learning from its own mistakes," one lesson stated. "Our party never hides its faults and mistakes." Most fundamentally, the text demanded "clear-cut adherence to the Four Cardinal Principles and opposing bourgeois liberalization."[37] The central leadership's agenda for ideological "struggle" sought to shape and constrain the modernization agenda by powerfully asserting values and objectives outside of the economic realm that constituted "socialist" modernization.

As the Chinese leadership was presiding over this intensive internal indoctrination effort, observers around the world were attempting to understand the fall of Hu Yaobang and what they could glean about the nationwide focus on bourgeois liberalization. Zhao Ziyang, meeting with longtime East German leader Erich Honecker, said, "Many people considered Comrade Hu Yaobang as the patron for the spread of bourgeois liberalism and placed high hopes on him in this regard."[38] Hu had purportedly not focused enough on ideological work; thus, in Zhao's estimation, he was unfit to serve as general secretary.

Despite these comments, Zhao and his advisers worried about the enhanced power of the propaganda apparatus. So Zhao revived the idea of "policy limits" that had played an important role in delimiting the initiatives against spiritual pollution earlier in the decade. In March, Zhao repeatedly called opposing bourgeois liberalization fundamentally a "political" task, one that "does not connect to the economic reform policies." Ideological work should support, not impede, the modernization agenda, and economic goals should advance separately from ideological work.[39]

As Zhao steered this shift, the propaganda apparatus responded slowly. The editor of *Red Flag,* Xiong Fu, delivered internal talks in late March that acknowledged that although bourgeois liberalization has a "systemic quality," ideological and propaganda workers would "pay attention to policy boundaries and not turn it into a movement."[40] However, the propaganda apparatus remained restive, continuing to convene conferences at which new trends in art and culture, edgy publications, and even specific individuals were harshly criticized.[41]

The press remained full of examples of figures whose woes traced back to bourgeois liberalization. In May, the CCP expelled Ni Xiance, the governor of Jiangxi Province, for adultery and succumbing to "the invasions and attacks of bourgeois liberal thought."[42] That same month, the *Beijing Daily* reported with horror on a college student named Liu Yong who had been accused of a murder-suicide on his campus. He had once been a model Communist Youth League cadre, but, the newspaper recounted, he had been led astray by reading Friedrich Nietzsche and Jean-Paul Sartre and "ruined and destroyed himself."[43]

No matter how different their stories, figures such as Ni and Liu had both come to a bad end because of the enduring threat of bourgeois liberalization. Zhao and other top leaders had shifted their focus elsewhere by the spring of 1987, but the relationship between modernization and socialist ideology remained profoundly unsettled. With signs of capitalist infiltration everywhere, propaganda officials resisted attempts to rein in their work.

Zhao decided to put a stop to this defiance. To do so, Zhao drew on an important formulation that he attributed to Deng Xiaoping: "one central focus and two basic points." This idea characterized the modernization agenda that Deng had developed as having "one central focus" of building socialism with Chinese characteristics and "two basic points" of simultaneously "upholding the Four Cardinal Principles" and "adhering to the policy of reform and opening, and enlivening the economy." Zhao stated in January 1987 that it was unacceptable "to talk about one but not to talk about the other."[44] Combating bourgeois liberalization was frequently framed in terms of "upholding the Four Cardinal Principles," so this strategy was designed to placate ideologues by seeming to reaffirm part of their agenda, while simultaneously seeking to bolster the status of reform as a distinct line of effort.[45]

In the spring of 1987, Zhao turned this seemingly anodyne concept into a political weapon. On April 28, Zhao went directly to Deng Xiaoping to inform him of the "discoveries" that he had made about the resistance to his agenda in the propaganda apparatus and warned Deng that this might prevent the 13th Party Congress from endorsing ambitious reform plans. In response, Deng instructed Zhao to prepare a speech on propaganda work and committed to supporting him.[46] On May 9, with his core arguments developed, Zhao convened a meeting with Bo Yibo, Yang Shangkun, Wan Li, Hu Qili, and Deng Liqun. He delivered a vigorous rebuke: "Some people do not agree with discussing the two basic points and only agree to discuss one of the basic points," but it was wrong to "oppose liberalization and give very, very little attention to reform." This attack made clear that Zhao intended to set a new agenda for ideological and propaganda work that differed significantly from the priorities of its longtime overseers by separating it from the core work of the modernization agenda.[47] Delivering an advance draft to Deng Xiaoping for his approval, Zhao reminded him of their April 28 conversation in a note handwritten around the margins of the speech. Deng responded simply, "Completely agree."[48] Zhao's gambit had worked.

On May 13, Zhao opened his speech with an unambiguous statement. "The tide of bourgeois liberalization has been reversed," he announced. While acknowledging that a certain degree of bourgeois liberalization would persist until the "superiority of socialism" could be proved following a "long-term struggle," the dominant message of Zhao's speech was that "reform and opening" was the topmost priority. Zhao rested his credibility firmly on Deng: "I reported to Comrade Xiaoping, and Comrade Xiaoping said that the storm that occurred last year must not affect reform and opening, and [it] should not only persist but must speed up."[49]

Next, Zhao moved to target his most significant obstacle in the propaganda apparatus, Deng Liqun. Zhao passed along to Deng Xiaoping a letter from the reformist elder Li Rui accusing Deng Liqun of improprieties while the CCP was camped out in Yan'an four decades earlier. These decades-late accusations provided a pretext for action. On July 7, 1987, Deng Xiaoping summoned the top leaders to his home—including Zhao, Yang Shangkun, Wan Li, Bo Yibo, and Hu Qili—and announced his decision to remove Deng Liqun from all his positions except for his seat on the Politburo, because his opposition was undermining reform, and to dissolve the Research Office of the Secretariat that he had led. Deng Liqin's power was dramatically curtailed and his duties were largely transferred to Zhao's ally Hu Qili.[50] Even Deng Liqun's protectors Chen Yun and Li Xiannian, who had once hoped that he might become CCP general secretary, could not push back against Deng Xiaoping's decision.[51] The following month, the decision was also made to close *Red Flag*, the CCP's longtime ideological journal.[52]

Yet the struggle over how ideological matters would affect Chinese politics and the modernization agenda was not resolved for good, even if Zhao had prevailed in mid-1987. The day before Deng's dismissal, the Propaganda Department prepared an internal guidance document, which emphasized opposing bourgeois liberalization and stated firmly, "We must not relax our current work even as we emphasize the long-term nature of the struggle."[53] Deng Liqun vowed to continue fighting, recalling bitterly, "Zhao Ziyang's speech of May 13, 1987, opened the door to the proliferation of bourgeois liberalization"; it was, he believed, a "green light" to the enemies of Chinese socialism.[54]

Ideology and political power were deeply intertwined: Zhao had replaced Hu Yaobang and, after months of conflict, taken control over ideological and propaganda matters. He was poised to use this dominant position to shape an event of extraordinary political significance, the 13th Party Congress. Yet there had been no definitive resolution to the profound question of how to keep China's modernization "socialist" as the sort of capitalistic changes discussed in the next section cascaded across the economy and society. Zhao's repeated attempts to create "policy limits" and a separation between economic and ideological work had found its form in the "one central focus and two basic points." However, many leading officials resisted this separation, fearing that it would undermine the CCP and the cause of Chinese socialism. The connections between "material" and "spiritual" civilization were still deeply ingrained, and their future remained unresolved.

PART II

THE ECONOMY

◆

THE BASIC ECONOMIC story of the 1980s could take just two words to tell: getting richer. Reducing poverty and increasing wealth were the results of what China's rulers called "liberating the productive forces." This "liberation" was a process of loosening the constraints of the planned economy in which state plans set production targets in industry and agriculture, controlled the inputs available to firms, and fixed prices at low levels. Reforming this system meant breaking up collective agriculture to allow Chinese farmers to have greater control over what they grew and encouraging new forms of ownership to make and sell clothes, gadgets, furniture, and much more. It meant welcoming foreign investment and carving out special enclaves for economic liberalization. It was both top down and bottom up. The results were clear: the annual compound growth rate between 1978 and 1989 was 9.5 percent per year; gross domestic product per capita, which had been well under $200 for the entirety of the 1960s and 1970s, doubled over the same period. Exports and imports both increased by more than a factor of ten.[1] In 1978, the number of rural people below the official poverty line was 250 million; by 1988, that number had shrunk to 96 million.

For ordinary people, these changes were tangible. The number of urban households with a washing machine rose from just 6 percent in 1981 to more than three-quarters in 1989; the number that owned a color television rose from essentially zero to more than half in the same period.[2]

Yet there is far more to the economic story. The decisions China's leaders made—what policies they chose, what they avoided, and how they connected their economic agenda to other objectives beyond the economy—powerfully shaped the trajectory of the country's modernization. The system of centralized state planning did not vanish overnight but stayed in place and was retooled for a new era. A new world of economic activity flourished alongside it and in its interstices, like lush, unruly gardens sprouting up around dilapidated buildings. Yet, as we shall see, the building itself was not marked for demolition but for renovation.

The Chinese leadership never intended to give up all their control over the economy. Even the most liberal-minded among them felt that state ownership and allocation of resources had enormous advantages for the broader Chinese system. They wanted to modernize and reform the country's economy and deal with the many obvious problems of state planning, from widespread poverty to severe shortages and serious inefficiencies. State-set prices, for example, did not move without top-down orders, even if production became cheaper or demand fell; from 1965 to 1979, general retail prices increased by an annual rate of only 0.2 percent, and similar rates applied to industrial prices. Firms did not have economic incentives to produce more numerous or higher quality products because they could not gain larger market share or profits, and innovations and improvements brought constant bureaucratic hassles.[3] In Tianjin, for example, new homework

books and even ballpoint pens took up to six months to even receive pricing approval, even though they were needed for students
who were about to start school.[4] Despite these problems, China's
leaders believed that the planned economy had its strengths—
promoting industrialization, ensuring jobs and welfare for China's workers, maintaining fiscal balance, and most of all, ensuring continued control of the economy. They wanted to retain
these benefits where possible, while significantly accelerating
modernization and growth by fostering local experimentation
and initiative, seeking out foreign investment and expertise, and
giving space to firms and markets.

China's leaders had a series of broad, quantifiable objectives as
they set out to modernize the economy. Deng Xiaoping wanted
China to quadruple its industrial and agricultural output by the
year 2000. He also promised that the Chinese people would attain a "moderately prosperous" level of wealth in which well-
being was widely distributed and people could live comfortably.
But he did not know how exactly to achieve these objectives,
and he sometimes changed his mind during this decade. Other
leaders—such as the CCP elders Chen Yun and Li Xiannian and
frontline leaders General Secretary Hu Yaobang and Premier
Zhao Ziyang—competed to develop policies to achieve these
goals.[5] Indeed, the defining characteristic of economic policymaking during the 1980s was contestation, not consensus.

These dynamics of contestation and experimentation meant
that China's embrace of both markets and the international economic system was always limited and always partial, with stark
trade-offs. Building on an important body of existing scholarship, substantially enriched by newly available sources, this section
illuminates the key dynamics and disputes at critical junctures,

underscoring the extent to which the attitudes of China's rulers toward marketization and internationalization of the economy were evolving and conflicting.[6]

This section shows that China in the 1980s was not on a single path toward freer markets. There was no inevitable teleology toward liberalization. To the contrary, the system was being designed piece by piece, often reacting to events, and the model developed was deliberately a mixture of public and private ownership, of centralized control and freewheeling local experimentation, of "socialist" and "capitalist" methods.

The decision making of the Chinese leadership occurred in dialogue with changing economic realities as well as economic ideas. As I argued in my earlier book, *Unlikely Partners,* in shaping debates and decisions, the importance of economists—especially Chinese advisers but also some foreign economists—was enormous. Despite bitter disagreements, what unified these diverse thinkers was a deep hunger to experiment, learn from the world, and contribute to China's modernization. International influences also permeated all sides of this debate over China's economic future. Organizations such as the World Bank and the Ford Foundation consulted on and provided funding for policy measures to "liberate the productive forces" in the rural economy after decollectivization and the fast-developing industrial sectors. International businesses opened shop in special economic zones and started joint ventures with Chinese firms, with activities that included selling consumer goods, building plants, and transferring technology. And leading foreign economists from both sides of the Cold War divide—from Eastern Bloc research institutions and universities in capitalist metropolises—traveled to China, meeting with economic officials to help them interpret the changes under way and determine what China's goals and policies should be.[7] Ideas mattered enormously in China's economic transformation.

As China's rulers grappled with the scope and meaning of the market and faster growth, they worried particularly about the consequences for other values, from CCP control to inequality to price rises. Their economic agenda was sometimes in tension with their ideological, social, and political priorities. As we have seen, economic growth was not the only value they cherished, and senior officials were pulled between the allure of marketization and the resistance to market absolutism. These officials drew on transnational networks of neoclassical economists but also raised fundamental questions about whether the changes under way could be justified ideologically, ranging from reforms to state enterprises that hurt workers' livelihoods to the tolerance of the population for high levels of inflation to the appropriate role of the party.

Focusing on debates about economic growth, this section underscores how the decisions to pursue market reforms, faster growth, and international interdependence were fiercely contested, as was their meaning. It also shows how removed Deng Xiaoping was from these daily debates about the economy and how central Zhao Ziyang was, highlighting the dynamics and tensions that marked the policymaking process. This process stands as one of the most significant stories of national development in the twentieth century.

CHAPTER 4

Liberating the Productive Forces

Before Zhao Ziyang became premier in September 1980, the leadership of Deng Xiaoping, Hu Yaobang, Chen Yun, and others had decided to "liberate the productive forces"—but they remained unsure how and how quickly that "liberation" would occur. Although Deng Xiaoping, Chen Yun, Li Xiannian, and other CCP elders stepped down from their roles as vice premiers at the same September 1980 meeting, these elders continued to hold great power and set the agenda for economic work. After the reforms launched during the 1970s, debates in the early 1980s focused on how much control to give up, how much instability to tolerate, and most of all, how much to pursue economic growth relative to other objectives. In the early 1980s, China's leaders made changes to the price system and state enterprises, continued to decollectivize rural agriculture, and promoted more international trade and the special economic zones (SEZs). But this process was full of tension—not only because of contestation over policy options but also because of acute trade-offs among different values and priorities.

The guiding agenda for economic policy at the start of the decade, following the removal of Hua Guofeng, was what China's leaders called *readjustment.* This readjustment agenda sought to bring heavy industry, light industry, and agriculture into balance and keep growth gradual and largely self-reliant. The dominant view—espoused consistently by Chen Yun and also at this stage by Deng Xiaoping, Zhao Ziyang, and others—was that growth should not occur too fast. Flowing from the long-standing economic ideas of Chen Yun, who had led work to create the first five-year plan in the 1950s and restore economic order after the Great Leap Forward, the goal of readjustment was economic stability; revenues and expenditures should be balanced and inflation avoided. Chen has often been caricatured as a dogmatic opponent of reform, but in fact he was most concerned with avoiding the hastiness and loss of control that had marked the worst economic disasters of the Mao era (and beyond the economic realm, he sought to instill party discipline and stamp out corruption and self-dealing). Even though Chen suffered from poor health, his agenda was as influential in this period as it had been at any prior point.[1] In 1980, Deng Liqun declared in an internal speech to the Central Party School, "Chen Yun is the outstanding leader of China's economic work."[2]

In contrast to Chen, newer leaders like Zhao had not yet developed strong views on the best direction for the nationwide economic reforms. Zhao's approach in Sichuan had emphasized local conditions, fostering the initiative of communities of farmers and workers; now he had responsibility for a country of 1 billion people with immense variation on nearly every metric. Thus, Zhao wrote in his memoirs of this moment that he had only a "shallow and vague" notion of "how to proceed with reform" and no "preconceived model or a systematic idea in mind."[3] His undeveloped understanding concerned not only the substantive "model" of a reformed economic system but also "how to proceed" day to day as a national political leader.

Zhao was expected to execute the policy direction of readjustment, not reinvent it. Zhao had limited status in a central government still dominated by elders such as Deng, Chen, and Li Xiannian. (Hu Yaobang, at least, had served in Beijing for many years.) In 1979, Chen had noted approvingly that many of the officials who had been appointed to run China's economic policy had "done financial and economic work in the comprehensive state organs since liberation. . . . We veterans are still here." The contrast to the newcomer Zhao was clear.[4]

It is important to understand that eighteen months after December 1978's Third Plenum, Deng Xiaoping and his top lieutenants remained focused on the readjustment agenda, and China had not embarked on a massive program of marketization or liberalization. The readjustment responded not only to Maoist economic policy but also to the loosening of central controls under Hua. Investments had skyrocketed as local governments raced ahead with massive new projects that they struggled to pay for, especially when petroleum supplies, which were intended to finance much of this development, fell short of expectations. Overinvestment in some sectors was matched by severe underinvestment in others, a serious energy shortage, and rising unemployment.[5] Yet the top leadership did not agree on the purposes and specific elements of readjustment: for Chen Yun and his protégé Yao Yilin, readjustment was a long-term path forward, whereas Deng Xiaoping and Hu Yaobang understood it as a way to "put the house in order quickly before a renewal of substantial growth." Zhao, for his part, seemed to vacillate between these positions, opportunistically favoring one and then the other as the political winds and economic indicators shifted.[6] These different views about readjustment were not simply factional conflicts. They were substantive disagreements that played out in Politburo meetings and conferences on long-term planning.[7] For many of China's top leaders, the process of experimenting with and debating over policy in the 1980s would itself become a process of clarifying their thinking on these fundamental questions.

Within the framework of readjustment, some reforms—from agriculture to foreign trade—moved forward, often by local initiative in regions far from Beijing. One important example was the controversial practice of "household contracting" in which collectively owned land was leased to individual households that were then required to produce the quota necessitated by state planning authorities but could sell any surplus freely. As noted earlier, although this local experimentation had cropped up in provinces such as Anhui and Sichuan during the 1970s, the decision to pursue nationwide decollectivization was ultimately up to the central government; Deng and Zhao were motivated by a desire to reduce the burden on the state of subsidies to rural areas as well as the goal of increasing agricultural production. The central leadership initially vacillated on whether to endorse household contracting, given the enormous ideological implications of breaking with the Maoist model of agriculture centered on the people's commune. However, after Deng indicated his support for the policy, they promulgated Central Document No. 75 in September 1980, which provided an official, if carefully worded, endorsement of household contracting policies. Zhao, Wan Li, Hu Yaobang, and Du Runsheng began to assertively push forward with household contracting in provinces from Shandong and Qinghai to Guangdong and Fujian. By mid-1982, nearly 72 percent of production teams would adopt household systems, and Document No. 1 of January 1982 formalized the forward march of agricultural decollectivization. That year saw a 9 percent increase in grain output.[8]

Experiments with increasing enterprise autonomy also moved forward, with the State Council granting approximately 6,600 enterprises greater autonomy, including retaining a portion of profits. This policy marked an initial nationwide shift to address enterprises' high dependency on the government, but it had little practical effect because it only created weak incentives for enterprises—a challenge that would persist for much of the decade.[9]

International trade also continued to expand in this period, despite concerns from some quarters that it would cause the party-state to lose control and become dependent on foreigners. On May 28, 1980, in an internal letter to the top leadership, Zhao criticized the analysis of some officials that "the reform of the foreign trade system has brought chaos." The readjustment policy was important, Zhao stated, but it should not cause China to avoid promoting trade, which was essential for China's modernization.[10]

Yet some powerful figures called for faster growth rates and higher levels of investment, contravening the readjustment agenda. Hu Yaobang was the most assertive proponent of these views in internal debates, urging China to hurry to quadruple output by the year 2000.[11] For officials who wanted faster growth, few initiatives were as important as the SEZs that were established in March 1980. With the approval of the senior leadership, Guangdong Party Secretary Xi Zhongxun (Xi Jinping's father) and Vice Premier Gu Mu had taken the lead in early 1979 in organizing the initial SEZs—Shantou, Shenzhen, Xiamen, and Zhuhai—to pursue trade and foreign investment more freely and with less central government involvement.[12] The SEZs soon became a defining element of China's development.

Initially, the SEZs had been conceived of as export processing zones. Gu Mu had traveled to Western Europe in 1978, with orders from Deng Xiaoping "to study the successful experiences of capitalist countries and bring them back to China."[13] The SEZs also took inspiration from Singapore, where officials had created special industrial zones to promote exports.[14] Chinese officials also closely examined the three other "Asian Tigers"—Hong Kong, South Korea, and Taiwan—as well as Japan, which was already also providing foreign investment and expertise to China. These discussions with figures such as Singaporean deputy prime minister Goh Keng Swee and Japanese economist and official Saburō Ōkita broadened the Chinese leadership's ambitions for the zones to "commerce, tourism, and real estate" alongside industry, thereby also positioning the SEZs at the vanguard of introducing new industrial technologies, earning foreign exchange, and promoting deeper integration with the world economy.[15]

As China deepened its interdependence with the international economic system, the leadership decided to rejoin the World Bank, supplanting Taiwan. In mid-April 1980, World Bank president Robert McNamara visited China. In briefing materials, bank officials accentuated the positive. "In terms of economic growth, the performance of the Chinese economy has been quite impressive," McNamara's briefing stated. "Nevertheless, its per capita income in 1978 remained quite low by international standards."[16] When they met, Deng Xiaoping was far blunter: "We are very poor. We have lost touch with the world. We need the World Bank to catch up."[17]

China officially rejoined the World Bank on May 15, 1980, and top leaders including Zhao remained personally engaged in shaping the initial stages of this partnership.[18] Meeting with Shahid Husain, the bank's vice president, on July 16, Zhao said that he hoped China would receive both cash and expertise to support reforms and infrastructure development.[19] Shortly thereafter, the Chinese leadership authorized the

World Bank to conduct a major study of the Chinese economy—a pre-condition for lending—which would be completed in 1983. These inter-actions with envoys from the capitalist world—from Singapore and Western Europe to the World Bank—powerfully shaped the early reform debates and policies. They ranged from technical and financial exchanges to dialogue about the most fundamental characteristics of China's economic system.[20]

Among senior officials, profound concerns about rapid market-driven growth and individuals' self-interested pursuit of wealth persisted, and economic indicators underscored the risks of deviation from the readjustment agenda. An internal directive from the Propaganda Department in August 1980 stated, "It is necessary to come up with specific guidelines, politics, and regulations to define the direction, road, and method of getting rich."[21] New data revealed a spike in state investment, a decline in revenues, an increase in the deficit to upwards of 14 billion RMB (from an original estimate of approximately 10 billion), and a rising inflation rate as high as 8.4 percent in urban areas.[22] The leadership decided to further strengthen the readjustment agenda to control investment and inflation, with Zhao warning of a potential "economic crisis" that might cause "all the economic benefits to farmers and workers since the third plenum to be lost."[23] The readjustment agenda seemed poised to guide China in 1981 and beyond.

◇

Economic modernization was proving no easy task. An initial wave of optimism had given way to relentless anxieties about "chaos" and the perilous forces that might be unleashed by moving beyond the readjustment and embracing markets or pursuing even more rapid growth.

To figure out how to "liberate the productive forces," China's top leaders developed networks of economic advisers, primarily from three distinct generations. First, a set of figures such as the septuagenarians Xue Muqiao and Ma Hong returned to work after the Cultural Revolution—"ready," Xue wrote, "to contribute my last bit of strength to working with my comrades." (Xue had helped author the first five-year plan in the early 1950s and led several economic agencies before being attacked during the Cultural Revolution, while Ma had been a senior planning official in the Mao era and became one of Zhao's key advisers.)[24] Second was a fast-rising generation that had finished its academic studies before the Cultural Revolution, with standouts such as Liu Guoguang and Wu Jinglian. A third, even younger generation had seen its education disrupted by the Cultural Revolution. Forced to go to the countryside, they encountered the bare facts of China's indigence. Economists in these three generations worked for governmental institutions such as the System Reform Commission and the Chinese Academy of Social Sciences (CASS) or held academic perches at major universities and semiofficial organizations. They embarked on an intensive process of developing new economic policy ideas for the senior leadership.[25]

Given the takeoff of agricultural reforms and his background in Sichuan, it is unsurprising that Zhao was initially particularly drawn to experts working on "rural reform." He turned to the senior economist Du Runsheng and what came to be known as the Research Group on Problems in China's Rural Development (Rural Development Group). Formally established on February 12, 1981, this group was led by Chen Yizi, He Weiling, and Wang Xiaoqiang and consisted of economists and scholars who had spent time in the countryside during the Cultural Revolution and conducted research on household contracting soon after the Third Plenum.[26] In March, a classified notice from the Central Committee and State Council called for rural areas to "develop commodity production" and "diversified business" using the "rich natural resources" and "abundant labor" of China's countryside, signaling that the priorities of the Rural Development Group would extend well beyond agriculture.[27]

Other advisers were focused on more theoretical questions about China's economic system, often with reference to other socialist countries that had experimented with market reforms—a natural fit given their shared Soviet planning legacies. At times, they even looked for alternatives within Soviet history—for example, seminars, books, and translations studied Nikolai Bukharin, who had helped Lenin devise the New Economic Policy in the 1920s.[28] Some thinkers looked to Yugoslavia and its system of worker self-management. Many Chinese economists, including Yu Guangyuan and Liu Guoguang, also carefully studied

Hungarian experiences with reform socialism; Deng Liqun said that studying Hungary underscored that China's problems "were not only China's but were common to all socialist countries."[29] They even invited Polish émigré and Oxford professor Włodzimierz Brus—a famed advocate of what was often called market socialism, a system based on the idea that market mechanisms were tools to make planned economies work better and ideologically compatible with socialism—to visit China in 1979–1980. Brus met with Vice Premier Bo Yibo, a powerful CCP elder who subsequently told other officials that Brus "stressed that nowhere in the world was there an absolutely ideal socialist model with no flaws. . . . I am inclined to agree with his view."[30]

Assessing the socialist model, the question of prices was particularly sensitive and complex, inextricably bound up in maintaining economic stability. As part of the readjustment agenda, CCP leaders determined that reform should begin with a reorientation away from investment (most of which came from heavy industry, the traditional focus of central planning) and toward production of consumer goods in light industry, which increased output by 36 percent during 1980 and 1981.[31] However, they knew that these quick successes would have limited long-run effects as long as the price system remained unchanged; without loosening controls through price reform, producers would lack better information and clearer incentives, and supply and demand would remain severely imbalanced. In March 1981, Zhao told the State Council, "We must come up with a long-term plan for price reform as soon as possible."[32]

Later that month, Zhao's call for "a long-term plan for price reform" received assistance when the Czech economist Ota Šik, the author of *Plan and Market under Socialism,* visited China beginning on March 19, 1981. Building on the foundation that Brus's visit had laid, Šik argued in favor of gradual price reform starting quickly, noting that this "incremental" adjustment was essential when demand exceeded supply as it did in China. Ma Hong immediately sent reports on these lectures to Zhao, who responded by proposing that Šik be hired as a consultant to CASS, visit China once a year, and hold an additional seminar with the highest-level economists. When one of Zhao's secretaries, Bai Meiqing, gave an account of this follow-up seminar to Zhao, the premier responded with a decision: the State Council would create a Price Research Center under the leadership of Xue and Ma.[33]

Zhao clearly sensed an opportunity to move expeditiously on price policy, despite the readjustment agenda in place, and thus he provided personnel and institutional support to this initiative. As an initial, transitional step, the Price Research Center began to recalculate prices to more accurately reflect supply and demand, hiring several price-calculation consultants who had been recommended by Šik.[34] Zhao also authorized a pilot program to liberalize the prices of nonstaple food items in Guangzhou in 1981.[35] These changes were not sweeping reforms, but they constituted a first step toward reconciling China's ossified price system with economic realities. And they had brought significant expertise—both from within China and from abroad—into the decision-making process.

A crucial shift took place as Zhao gained experience in managing economic affairs and gradually began to take greater risks. Knowing that Deng harbored hopes that the readjustment agenda could give way to a period of faster growth, Zhao began to suggest that more growth-focused policies might be appropriate. To address this question, at a State Council meeting in April, Zhao issued what would become a signature imperative: "We must conduct research from every angle."[36]

This emphasis on research and debate is essential to understanding Chinese politics in the 1980s. For Zhao and other officials, policy ideas were not simply weapons in political wrangling or factional competition but meaningful, substantive aspects of their work to modernize China, shaping options and clarifying choices. Chen Yun and other longstanding advocates for readjustment had a clearly defined vision and set of priorities for China's economy, but Deng governed mostly by intuition and broad, sometimes vague utterances. Zhao now placed great emphasis on generating ideas and policies for China's economic development that could fill in Deng's gestures.

Zhao began to push internally for reassessing the benefits of faster growth. Speaking with Ma Hong on June 24, 1981, Zhao suggested that Chen Yun was wrong to see parallels to the past and encouraged Ma to research the "large differences between this instance of readjustment and the 1962 readjustment."[37] In July 1981, the State Council introduced regulations to foster the growth of the "individual economy," referring in particular to private, nonagricultural, rural enterprises. Small individual businesses were already widespread in both cities and the countryside, and these regulations gave them further encouragement. Individual businesses were formally restricted from hiring more than seven employees, but in practice, many of these firms had dozens and even hundreds of employees. This entrepreneurial ferment extended to township and village enterprises (TVEs), which developed from "commune and brigade enterprises" and existed in a legal gray zone, combining aspects of public and private ownership that allowed them to grow outside of the planned economy without facing the stringent restrictions on fully private firms. Taken together, the individual businesses and the TVEs would transform the Chinese economy, creating a complex system of capitalistic activity in both urban and rural China.[38] In the same period, Zhao, Du Runsheng, Wan Li, and other officials worked to spread the household contracting system more widely, facilitating faster rural development and the continued growth of agricultural output.[39]

Zhao began to deliver one message in public and another message to his advisers in private, as new sources demonstrate. In mid-October speaking to a group preparing his report for the National People's Congress (NPC) meeting slated to start in late November, Zhao provided guidance on how to publicly characterize the past year: "Achievements from this year that do not connect to readjustment should not be discussed."[40] However, in internal conversations the same month, Zhao raised the possibility of large new capital construction that could potentially "greatly increase revenues and produce benefits" and said that he felt the industrial readjustment was "basically nearly completed."[41]

Important debates emerged outside of the leadership, as bold economists advocated in journals and newspapers for faster market reforms. The economists Liu Guoguang and Xu Dixin published articles that garnered attention for arguing that the market ought to take on a larger role in the Chinese economy.[42] Li Yining, a professor at Peking University, highlighted the need to study "Western bourgeois" economics, citing a tool kit from "the investment multiplier" to "econometric methods."[43] Chinese economists even hosted the American free market evangelist Milton Friedman—who wrote in a letter to a friend that the invitation was "a phenomenon that I find almost literally incredible"—although this 1980 visit collapsed into acrimony when a Chinese researcher critiqued "the internal contradictions of capitalism" over lunch and Friedman responded with an impassioned defense of free markets and attacked Marx.[44] These economists were experimenting with diverse arguments in favor of market reforms and higher growth rates.

One reason for the continuing limits on the official embrace of market reforms was widespread awareness that these changes would have profound negative consequences for other values, from control to equality. An internal propaganda directive acknowledged in the fall of 1981 that the economic reforms would "break the iron rice bowl"—the guarantee of secure employment, income, and welfare benefits at state enterprises and public institutions.[45] Another directive worried about recent adjustments in the prices of goods such as polyester cloth, tobacco, and alcohol, noting that some people did not understand why prices had risen suddenly, creating "turbulence" and "fear."[46] Even at this early stage of cautious change, the leadership knew that the market reforms would profoundly disrupt the lives of many millions of Chinese people. Their hope, of course, was that the positive effects would outweigh the negatives.

By early 1982, these shifts among economic thinkers, alongside opposition to the readjustment from CCP General Secretary Hu Yaobang and other officials, were causing consternation to Chen Yun and the other leaders who had dominated economic policy over the preceding year. Deng Liqun, closely associated with Chen as head of the Policy Research Office of the CCP Secretariat, led the preparation of materials that directly attacked the views of Xue Muqiao, Liu Guoguang, and other economists. Chen also called for a campaign to "strike hard" against economic crimes, as discussed in Part I, and even sought to force the SEZs to "uphold 'the planned economy as primary,'" according to Zhao's recollection of their discussions.[47]

Zhao continued to believe that he needed better, more systematic ideas to respond to Chen's criticisms. In an important step, on March 30, 1982, Zhao and the economic official An Zhiwen inaugurated an organization that would shape the evolution of economic policy: the System Reform Commission. It would "unify theory and practice," Zhao said, pulling together the efforts of the government's many different research units and experts to propel the reforms forward.[48] Zhao himself took on the title of the commissioner, and he named An Zhiwen as his deputy to administer its daily affairs. An Zhiwen made his vision clear: "I have done two things in my life. The first was to sincerely study the planned economy, and the second is to sincerely study how to transform the planned economy."[49] The System Reform Commission drew on a core group of experts and maintained strong networks throughout the central and provincial governments, becoming a locus of activity to promote fast market-driven growth policies.

As these initiatives centered on Zhao moved forward, Hu Yaobang made his own efforts to hasten decentralization and accelerate market reforms that promoted growth. In May 1982, Hu convened a seminar to discuss the sensitive subject of consumerism and consumption. Although saying that China should not "promote 'high consumption,'" Hu made clear that he viewed consumerism as an essential part of economic modernization, praising the greater diversity of brands and competition among different producers of consumer goods to satisfy people's tastes—still a provocative notion.[50] On May 27, the State Planning Commission's (SPC's) Yao Yilin and Song Ping submitted a letter to the senior leadership that criticized Hu's economic ideas as "not in accordance with the central government's strategy." They accused Hu of impatience with the readjustment as well as an excessive interest in delegating authority from the center to ministries, provinces, and workplaces.[51] Tensions only seemed to be growing.

Zhao, meanwhile, emphasized the challenge of reforms to China's state-owned enterprises. "We can't eliminate a lot of enterprises like capitalism does, but it also won't do to eliminate none at all," he said.[52] For Chinese workers, state enterprises provided beneficial outcomes well beyond the narrowly economic: large-scale employment, lifetime tenure, and significant welfare benefits. Reforming these enterprises might make them more efficient or profitable, but market reforms combined with "eliminating" loss-making firms threatened to severely undermine the benefits that they provided to Chinese workers as well as the planning apparatus's control over the economy.[53] In November, working with the Ministry of Finance and the System Reform Commission, Zhao announced a "tax for profit" policy that sought to reform enterprises by changing their fiscal relationship to the state, emphasizing income tax paid on profits (rather than the long-standing profit-sharing system).

This approach was strikingly different from the contracting model that Zhao had advocated for the rural reforms and that Hu Yaobang believed should be the model for industry as well.[54] However, Zhao believed that the economic realities of the urban economy were simply too different for the same decentralizing approach to be used, stressing that over 80 percent of state revenue came from this sector of the economy.[55]

The 12th Party Congress of 1982 reaffirmed the goal of quadrupling China's output by the year 2000. Although the congress's work report was penned in Hu Yaobang's name, it also echoed Chen's statements, asserting the primacy of the planned economy and the "subordinate and secondary" role of market mechanisms.[56] However, in subsequent statements on how to achieve the quadrupling goal, Zhao particularly encouraged foreign trade, stating, "As long as it is not a dependency, a favorable exchange is still self-reliance."[57] Deng, meanwhile, repeatedly raised concerns about why the targets for state plans remained low and promoted more rapid growth. Deng also laid strong emphasis on "building socialism with Chinese characteristics"—an enduring term that offered a spacious, vague, and malleable assertion of the distinctiveness of China's modernization agenda, while subtly suggesting that Chen Yun's ideas were still too closely borrowed from the Soviet planning model.[58] Two visions of economic modernization were taking shape, and their goals seemed irreconcilable.

Facing this growing chasm, Chen delivered the most vivid articulation to date of his views. Comparing the relationship between the market and the plan to a bird and a cage in December 1982, he said, "You mustn't hold the bird in your hands too tightly, or it would be strangled. You have to turn it loose, but only within the confines of the cage; otherwise, it would fly away. The size of the cage should be appropriate." In case his metaphor was not clear, he added, "In short, enlivening the economy and regulation through the market can only operate within the framework of state plans, and must not depart from the guidance of planning."[59]

Within a few months, the balance of debate among the Chinese leadership would shift decisively. The readjustment policies had achieved their desired effects, and the incremental reform policies designed to promote growth were producing results: industrial production had risen by 7.7 percent in 1982, and the budget deficit had fallen to 2.6 percent of revenue (from 11.7 percent in 1981).[60] Thus, Zhao stated on February 13, 1983, "We must speed up the pace of reform."[61]

Despite these ambitious statements, friction between Zhao and Hu over economic policy grew because Hu wanted even faster change. Speaking in Hainan on February 18, 1983, Hu made lightly veiled criticisms of Zhao's economic work as ineffective and insufficiently fast.[62] Zhao recalled in his memoirs, "People became aware of the differences between Yaobang and me on economics." On March 15, Deng Xiaoping called a meeting at his house with the two men and sided with Zhao. The three leaders determined that Zhao would manage economic policy without interference from Hu.[63] Yet Hu's humiliation was not yet complete. On March 17, at a joint meeting of the Standing Committee and the Central Secretariat, Chen Yun surprised Hu and Deng Xiaoping with prepared remarks that harshly attacked Hu. The blindsided Hu conducted a self-criticism on the spot regarding his handling of economic matters.[64] For promoting decentralization and faster growth, Hu Yaobang had been shut out of economic policymaking and received censure from one of the CCP's most powerful elders despite his position atop the party. Privately, Hu was furious and still hoped for greater speed.[65]

With this strengthened authority over the economy, Zhao continued to move away from the readjustment agenda and put into action several new initiatives in early 1983, including measures designed to rationalize and unify the fiscal system and address concerns about wages and bonuses.[66] Deng had made his broad goals clear and empowered Zhao to realize those objectives, relying on him to make the more detailed policies and trade-offs. Their shared agenda for economic work combined limited decentralization, promoting faster growth rates, and targeted reforms to many aspects of the economic system—all of which would be areas of ongoing debate and contestation.

By the summer, Zhao seemed bullish. At the NPC on June 6, 1983, Zhao heralded the renewed focus on reform and emphasized the need to change direction from the readjustment agenda. China should "fulfill or overfulfill" plan targets, he said: "It is imperative to speed up structural reform of the economy."[67]

But the differences between China and the capitalist system remained front and center. Propaganda directives highlighted "economic crises in the capitalist world," including the "trade wars" that had convulsed the United States, Europe, and Japan, in contrast to "the vitality and vigor of China's socialist economy."[68] Officials also developed propaganda to mitigate public discontent over visible inequality that was rising in both urban and rural areas.[69] Internal documents claimed that unlike capitalist countries, China's economic modernization would be driven by both self-interest and "self-sacrifice."[70] Despite these denunciations of capitalism, many Chinese economists quickly began a renewed effort to forge ahead with market reform and intellectual opening to the outside world, including studying what they called "modern Western economics." China's goals differed from capitalist societies, but "Western economics" had become crucial to both to intellectuals and the policy-making apparatus.[71]

◇

Implementation of market reform policies topped the agenda, even as the wave of attacks on "spiritual pollution" discussed in Part I convulsed the ideological sphere. On the rural and agricultural side, on January 1, 1984, the Central Committee released a document that permitted an extension of land contracts in rural areas and further facilitated the marketization of the rural economy, prepared in consultation with the Rural Development Group.[72] On the urban and industrial side, first, Deng Xiaoping reaffirmed his support for economic reform, international opening, and the SEZs by visiting Shenzhen, Zhuhai, and Xiamen in January–February 1984 and opening up more coastal cities.[73] Zhao also made a new push on enterprise reform, calling for speeding up implementation of the "tax-for-profit" system.[74] He urged the expansion of early experiments in "comprehensive urban reform," and the *People's Daily* published a letter from fifty-five factory managers pleading, "Please untie us!"[75] With the goal of increasing the market's pressure on enterprises, the State Council on May 10, 1984, approved a document on expanding enterprise decision-making powers that Zhao and the Central Finance and Economics Leading Small Group had crafted. State-owned enterprises could now freely produce above state quotas, sell such goods at prices within 20 percent of the state-set price, and retain 70 percent of the funds allocated to buy new fixed assets.[76] Soon thereafter, the State Council also approved new urban reforms, and the SPC reformed the planning system to reduce its control over enterprises and pricing.[77] The leadership had made a decisive shift: they were determined to tackle the problems of the urban and industrial economy.

Yet the disagreements over the meaning of market reforms and international opening remained profound, even though the CCP continued to adamantly deny that such contestation was occurring. A classified propaganda directive in July 1984 stated, "Within our party, no forces opposed to reform exist." It explained, "Some comrades are now lagging behind realities in their thinking and are slow in waking up to the need for reform. This is normal. If we do a good job at reform, they will very quickly see things in a new light." For public writing, this meant, "[We should not] in a sweeping fashion label those comrades who are actively pursuing reform as 'reformers,' members of a 'reform faction,' and so forth."[78] But the real question facing China's rulers by 1984 was not one of whether "forces opposed to reform" existed. It was, instead, a question of fundamental and enduring disagreement about what "reform" meant.

CHAPTER 5

The Powers of the Market

As markets expanded across the Chinese economy, both urban and rural communities began to see the results of surging growth. A rise in coal and petroleum production removed many bottlenecks that had stymied growth. Agricultural output increased significantly as decollectivization bore fruit. Foreign exchange reserves rose to $14 billion by the end of 1983; the special economic zones (SEZs) began to grow; and that year, gross domestic product (GDP) rose by 10.8 percent, a high rate that signaled China might reach or exceed Deng's goal of quadrupling industrial and agricultural output by the year 2000.[1] Yet uncertainties lingered about the risks and benefits of this exploding growth, and whether the system should transform to encourage it or constrain it.

The summer of 1984 witnessed intensive debate about these questions. It crystallized around a major, if seemingly quite arcane, decision Zhao and his advisers were considering: whether China ought to be characterized as a "planned commodity economy." The "commodity economy" had been a controversial term in Chinese political and ideological circles for years. It was traditionally contrasted with a "product economy" in Marxian economics. In a product economy, the sale of a product from one state-owned enterprise to another did not involve a change of ownership because both enterprises were owned "by the whole people," but in a commodity economy, ownership changed with a sale.[2] Ma Hong once asked Zhao Ziyang, "What is the difference between a socialist commodity economy and a socialist market economy?" Zhao replied that there was "no difference," explaining, "Using 'commodity economy' is simply a matter of decreasing commotion, since many people find it easier to accept."[3] Zhao recollected that he felt strongly that China should endorse the "planned commodity economy" concept at the Third Plenum of the 12th Central Committee scheduled for October 1984 to strengthen "the national laws of supply and demand and the power of the market."[4]

Yet the push to endorse a "planned commodity economy" faced staunch resistance. It was one thing to debate this term in the corridors of Zhongnanhai or the Chinese Academy of Social Sciences (CASS), but it was another matter entirely to now propose to turn this phrase into the official designation of China's economy. Some officials were concerned about the effect on other aspects of the economy and society (from weakening the state-owned enterprises to increasing inequality), and others had ideological objections to the shift to a "commodity economy."[5] In each draft report for the plenum that the System Reform Commission produced, Zhao's team experimented with using the term *commodity economy*. Every time that the document was returned after being edited by other officials, the term was crossed out.[6]

To break the impasse, Zhao commissioned a report from Ma Hong, who combined stature, expertise, and originality. Working closely with the middle-aged economist Wu Jinglian, who had just returned from studying economics at Yale University, Ma's report emphasized the necessity of high-level ideological support to help legitimate and encourage urban reform. The report argued that guidance planning and indirect administration, rather than mandatory planning and direct administration, were the keys to the next stage of China's economic transformation. Support for this shift, they contended, could only be provided by the formulation "planned commodity economy."[7] In August, Zhao met with the team writing the decision that would be issued at the upcoming plenum and told them, "The key is to clearly state what is the nature of the economic system reform." He also encouraged them to prioritize "enlivening" enterprises, price reform, and executing economic plans through indirect economic incentives and guidance rather than incessant direct commands from the central planning authorities. Overcoming the opposition, the task that remained was finalizing the decision itself.[8]

Of the challenges that Zhao identified, price reform seemed perhaps the most concrete—prices, after all, were a fact of economic life that was familiar to every household and firm—but the leadership's views on the topic were not well formed, even after Ota Šik's visit. Officials knew that because of long-standing state subsidies, the urban consumer price index was artificially low; the government was devoting well over 20 percent of its total expenditures to subsidies, mainly for daily necessities.[9] The situation was similar for industrial products and raw materials.[10] Their sense of urgency was bolstered by a visit in late August 1984 from the deputy prime minister of Hungary, József Marjai, who stressed that Hungary's most important error had been not taking advantage of the period of rapid growth during the early part of the reform process to implement price reform. Zhao subsequently cited Marjai's advice that "right now China is in a golden period for price reform."[11]

To reform the price system, Zhao drew on a different part of his intellectual network: the young generation of economists, born in the 1940s and 1950s, who in general had more advanced training, greater familiarity with both Western economics and rural China, but less policymaking experience than their elders. Some of these younger economists, such as Chen Yizi and Wang Xiaoqiang, joined the Institute for Chinese Economic System Reform, a new research organization created during this period. Chen, who had moved to this new group after several years of working on rural policy, explained they focused on drawing up price reform proposals because of Eastern European experts who had "all mentioned that price reform was key."[12] This new institute served as a way of distilling the ideas of a much wider network of economic thinkers for the senior leaders, especially Zhao.

Indeed, some young economists beyond Zhao's policy apparatus, seeing the power of new ideas in influencing the top leadership, decided to host their own conference at the mountain resort of Moganshan in Zhejiang Province in September 1984.[13] Questions of price reform generated considerable excitement at the conference. Two approaches initially held sway. First, officials at the Price Research Center proposed recalculating state-set prices in one large step. Second, Tsinghua University graduate student Zhou Xiaochuan, CASS graduate student Lou Jiwei, and other young scholars proposed a series of small, swift recalculations of prices. Then, in a dramatic turn, a graduate student named Zhang Weiying intervened, insisting that both approaches were unrealistic and calling for prices determined by supply and demand. A heated debate broke out, after which participants prepared a memorandum for the central leadership that outlined what would become known as the dual-track system. This system required the prices for goods sold within the plan to remain at state-set levels, while permitting goods sold outside the plan to trade at market prices. Coal, for example, was priced under the plan at RMB 22 per metric ton, but the market price was over RMB 100. This built on previous experiments that allowed prices of excess production to float within a small range above or below the state-set price but went much further than any prior decision.[14]

By January 1985, the dual-track system was ratified by the State Council, which permitted parties to negotiate prices for above-plan outputs regardless of the planned price. Zhao also instructed that the Material Supply Bureau, which controlled input allocations, hold constant the size of the central plan, laying the groundwork for the system to produce sustained increases to output outside the plan.[15] The dual-track system would become a defining and controversial feature of China's reforms. That it found favor with Zhao was not entirely surprising because it displayed some of his preferred qualities: it did not overtly impinge on the planned economy but created tremendous new space for market activity and faster growth to take place.

Two crucial policy innovations to advance Zhao's agenda had been produced by the end of the summer of 1984: the concept of the "planned commodity economy" and the development of the dual-track price system. Zhao had built consensus among China's most senior economic officials that the CCP Central Committee should explicitly endorse the "planned commodity economy" as "the basic principles of our economic system reform."[16] In a message addressed to Deng Xiaoping, Hu Yaobang,

Li Xiannian, and Chen Yun, Zhao shared a draft of the plenum decision and stated clearly that China was implementing a "planned commodity economy with public ownership as the basic form." He stressed, "China is implementing a planned economy, not a market economy," but it was a planned economy in which "guidance planning" would predominate, rather than "directive planning." Zhao also explained the price reforms under way, once again citing Marjai's advice that China was in a "golden period" for pushing forward with price reforms.[17] Zhao found a receptive audience. Deng Xiaoping approved the document on September 10, and Li, Hu, and Chen all followed suit.[18]

Zhao had come far since he first became premier and possessed "no systematic idea" about his vision for the path of China's development. By September 1984, drawing on a wide network to generate economic policy ideas, Zhao had garnered the approval of the rest of China's senior leadership for a fundamental refashioning of China's economic modernization. Yet contestation over the benefits and risks of market reform, faster growth, and deeper international integration would continue in the period ahead, even if China would be operating under the banner of the "planned commodity economy."

On October 20, 1984, the CCP Central Committee issued the Decision on the Reform of the Economic Structure, formally endorsing the "planned commodity economy."[19] Deng congratulated Zhao, describing the formulation as a "new theory of political economy," a contribution to official ideology. In a speech two days later, Deng acknowledged the deeper ideological concerns among many CCP cadres that this new system would permit "the sudden appearance of capitalism." But, he promised, "it will have no effect on socialism. No effect."[20]

As Deng's comments indicated, the ambiguous "planned commodity economy" formulation promised further debate about interpretation and implementation. Ma Hong, writing in November, indicated that it remained unclear even to economists who participated in the document's drafting what such a system would entail in practice.[21] Some figures feared that the market reforms and international firms' entry into China would spill over into the ideological and political realms, either by promoting "bourgeois liberalization" or by creating dependencies on foreigners. Inspecting Xiamen, the senior ideologue Hu Qiaomu declared,

"Special economic zones are not special political zones, and wholly-owned [foreign] enterprises are not foreign concessions."[22] The effects on Chinese workers and economic inequality were equally uncertain, despite Deng's promises that the decision would have "no effect on socialism." In the years to come, workers would encounter unexpected layoffs and shifts to fixed-term contract employment.[23] From the perspective of such workers, the marketizing "planned commodity economy" clearly did pose significant dangers, in addition to its economic benefits.

These debates over the newly approved "planned commodity economy" formulation also revealed an important emerging characteristic of China's reform process. Because of the compromises necessary to achieve a consensus on an official formulation, such phrases often contained components in seeming opposition (in this case, "planned" and "commodity"). This, in turn, created a situation in which these formulations were highly generative and required further interpretation even after receiving official endorsement, which generated continued contestation. The debates among Chinese economists often centered on developing a "best" interpretation, a process that often involved the same actors who formulated the phrase in the first place. Even once they had arrived at a "systematic idea," the challenges of interpretation, revision, and implementation remained unresolved.

With this official designation of the Chinese economy approved, another new term began to appear—the phrase *reform and opening* (改革开放). Although it is now well known, this formulation had not previously appeared as a set phrase in *People's Daily,* though of course each component ("reform," primarily meaning measures to develop and modernize the economy, and "opening," primarily meaning measures to increase international interchange) were constantly invoked. But in late 1984 and early 1985, a series of high-profile statements—from a speech by Deng Yingchao, Zhou Enlai's widow who served as chair of the Chinese People's Political Consultative Conference, to articles on agriculture, education, railroads, tourism, and international trade—used this new phrase. By 1986, it would be in uniform use, with figures such as Xi Zhongxun, Hu Qiaomu, and Qiao Shi deploying the term. And soon thereafter, "reform and opening" would become a catch-all used around the world to name the entire era from the late 1970s onward.[24]

In the wake of the consequential endorsement of the "planned commodity economy" concept, China's leading economists debated how to proceed. Their disagreements occurred against the backdrop of the takeoff of several key enterprise reforms, particularly increases in factory manager responsibility and in the ability of enterprises to determine their own output. The use of market prices also became substantially more widespread as enterprises began to conduct transactions outside the plan under the dual-track system. The in-plan price of coal, for example, was raised to RMB 31 per metric ton (from RMB 22, a 41 percent increase), and enterprises were free to sell coal produced beyond the plan quota at market prices. As these changes occurred, in the first quarter of 1985, gross industrial output boomed by approximately 23 percent over the same period in 1984.[25]

Some voices raised concerns that the Chinese economy was "overheating," meaning that excessively rapid growth might be leading to inflation, imbalances, and chaos.[26] However, at a meeting of the National People's Congress (NPC) in March 1985, Zhao stated emphatically that China would "continue reform unflinchingly."[27] Zhao recollected that he worried privately about how to stabilize the economy as "overheating got worse" but felt that he needed to strike a positive note in public and forge ahead with the reforms to enterprises and the price system so as not to lose momentum.[28] This context—a sense of urgency about the need to reform and fears of overheating—shaped the economic debates of 1985.

Several prominent groups of economists with ties to the central leadership developed proposals that would have substantial influence in the latter half of the decade. Wu Jinglian, whom Ma Hong had newly appointed to a senior position at the State Council's Development Research Center, emerged as the leader of one group focusing on "coordinated reform." This group argued for steadily advancing price reform beyond the dual-track system in order to move more fully toward using market mechanisms to guide the economy. In the short run, Wu argued, China should readjust its high-growth orientation and slow down the rate of investment in capital construction and increases in wages and bonuses, to create a favorable environment for those reforms. Acolytes such as Guo Shuqing, a twenty-nine-year-old doctoral student at CASS (and currently the party secretary of the People's Bank of China) joined Wu's calls to formulate a "coordinated" vision of reform.[29]

Other economists refuted Wu's emphasis on moderating growth and prioritizing price reform. Among many younger economists, the pursuit of rapid growth was widely held as the top objective, with no more ardent supporter than the economist Zhu Jiaming, who believed that China must undergo a radically "high-speed growth phase." Citing data from the United States, the Soviet Union, Japan, and Brazil, Zhu contended that during this "high-speed growth phase," inflation was "typical" and not to be feared because high-speed growth provided an "excellent environment" for reform.[30] Inflation, in Zhu's view, was not an insidious force undermining reform; rather, it was a signal that China was booming and catching up with the rest of the world.

A third major group of economists, exemplified by Peking University professor Li Yining, contended that Wu's emphasis on price reform was fundamentally misguided. Some, such as Wang Xiaoqiang, asserted that the dual-track system was necessary to ensure the gradual development of the economy, rather than risking disruption through price liberalization; they caricatured "coordinated reform" as akin to a "big bang." Li argued that, instead, enterprise reform and especially reform of the ownership system should be given priority.[31] Economists associated with Li argued for "restructuring the microeconomic base" and proposed a system in which "returns on assets" would be the primary metric of enterprise success, creating market incentives driven by the pursuit of profit.[32]

These major groups all endorsed the broad goals of market reform, even if they disagreed on priorities or policy measures, and all were developing economic arguments informed by international comparisons. Yet these economists generally continued to describe themselves as "socialist." An influential essay published in late 1985 under the pen name Ma Ding wrote that Chinese economics must go even further, declaring iconoclastically, "No ready answers can be found in *Das Kapital* or any other Marxist classics." It would be necessary to study "contemporary Western economics" and "develop a science of economics in light of China's reality" that could be applied directly to policy challenges. Ma Ding provided an interpretation of the ferment in Chinese economic circles that resonated with many intellectuals, and his article was widely republished and quoted.[33]

Chinese economic debate had shifted significantly by the middle of the decade. The disagreements over policy were bitter, despite an emerging consensus about the necessity of market reform and the use of neoclassical economic logic to support these views. These thinkers had a receptive audience in at least Zhao Ziyang and his close advisers, though the premier continued to oscillate in his support of particular policies.

The debates also prompted economic officials and thinkers to reach out anew to foreign experts. On September 2–7, 1985, a crucial weeklong conference organized at Zhao's direction by the System Reform Commission, CASS, and the World Bank convened on board a cruise ship sailing down the Yangtze River. Advisers to Zhao such as Xue Muqiao, Ma Hong, An Zhiwen, Wu Jinglian, and Gao Shangquan attended what came to be known as the Bashan Conference. Their interlocutors included the American Nobel laureate James Tobin, the Hungarian Harvard professor János Kornai, the Scottish economist Sir Alec Cairncross, Aleksandr Bajt from Yugoslavia, and Włodzimierz Brus, among others. The foreign visitors warned the Chinese economists about the risks of inflation and advocated for an interpretation of the "planned commodity economy" in which enterprises faced greater market pressures and harder budget constraints—which the Chinese officials reported back to Zhao, who studied their recommendations.[34]

Kornai, in particular, proved to be a transformational figure. He became most influential in China for his argument that "shortage" was a "chronic" characteristic of the planned economy. For the firm under socialism, Kornai described a permanent state of "investment hunger," an "almost-insatiable demand" for inputs and factors of production, and a "soft budget constraint" due to primarily political rather than economic incentives.[35] Chinese economists like Wu Jinglian found Kornai's analysis "easy to understand" because it offered a systematic, concrete framework to analyze the problems of the socialist economy.[36]

At the Bashan Conference, Kornai advocated for a model of market coordination with macroeconomic control. In this model, the "budget constraint" on enterprises would be "hard," but the state could in exceptional circumstances come to the rescue of the largest enterprises should they encounter serious difficulties and go bankrupt. In particular, Kornai said the model should be oriented toward creating macroeconomic conditions in which enterprises would shake off their command-economy reliance on political relationships and begin responding to market forces, although indirect administrative controls could act as a transition device. A key measure of success, Kornai noted emphatically, would be the enterprises' "price responsiveness." He argued that the model of market coordination with macroeconomic control was the only sensible choice as the goal for China's reform. Kornai's words resonated deeply; one participant recalled that as the Chinese economists talked among themselves later that day, they believed that for the first time they had reached a consensus about the best possible interpretation of 1984's "planned commodity economy."[37]

It did not take long for Zhao to begin using these ideas. At a meeting of provincial leaders a few weeks later, Zhao described the problem of the expansion of the scale of investment in China by using the term *investment hunger,* explaining that it was "a common disease in socialist countries"—language that came directly from Kornai's work.[38] The public report on the conference, released soon thereafter, used these ideas to describe the goals of the planned commodity economy. Kornai became a popular figure throughout China's economic circles, and the Chinese translation of *Economics of Shortage* quickly sold over 100,000 copies.[39] Kornai, as a neoclassical economist working on the problems of socialist economies, was uniquely positioned to influence Chinese debates at this moment in the mid-1980s. His diagnosis of the problems of socialist enterprises and his model of "market coordination with macroeconomic control" shaped the evolving interpretations of the planned commodity economy and the debate about market reform, while also further connecting China's dilemmas to international debates about socialism and market reform.

Yet the new wave of international advisers who came to China in this period were not only from the West. Just a month after Goh Keng Swee retired from government in December 1984, he was appointed as an official adviser on China's economic work, with a special focus on coastal economic development—with the explicit purpose of bringing to China the lessons of Singapore's experience.[40]

On May 15, 1985, Zhao Ziyang and Goh met in Beijing. According to a newly available transcript of the meeting, Zhao invited Goh's input on China's economic agenda, and Goh focused on two interrelated factors: the need for funds to purchase foreign technology and manufacturing equipment, particularly for energy, mining, and transportation; and the need to obtain sufficient foreign exchange on the path to expanding exports. Zhao and Deng both later cited his advice, and Zhao met with him again in 1986.[41]

Goh worked particularly closely with Gu Mu on matters of export policy, coastal economic development, and the SEZs, in particular on the southern island of Hainan. Goh helped Gu develop a strategy focusing first on tropical cash crops, agriculture, and animal husbandry, then associated products, gradually developing processing industries for export, and also developing tourism. However, as we shall see, the SEZs soon ran into significant difficulties.[42]

◇

The pursuit of faster growth still posed great risks. The continuation of extremely rapid industrial growth—an increase of 23.4 percent in the second quarter of 1985—intensified concern about uncontrolled "overheating."[43] For officials who saw the continued commitment to a balanced, planned socialist economy as essential, this seemed to confirm their worst fears.[44] Even longtime advocates for even faster growth, such as Hu Yaobang, criticized the economic overheating and called for temporarily reasserting "macro-control."[45] Zhao agreed but was cautious about the government's response: "We cannot step on the emergency brakes," Zhao wrote to Hu Yaobang and Hu Qili. "We must gradually reduce the speed."[46]

In the fall of 1985, Deng, Hu, and especially Zhao continued to push ahead and strike an optimistic public tone while seeking to rein in overheated growth, but their disagreements with Chen Yun and his allies over the substance and significance of the economic reforms were widening.[47] Many basic questions remained unanswered. Fundamentally, what level of economic development would be enough, and how would China define success? Of course, the leadership had articulated several goals, including quadrupling industrial and agricultural output by the year 2000 and for the Chinese people to attain a "moderately prosperous" level. Yet those were abstract, amorphous objectives. Even the statistical question of how to describe a "moderately prosperous" level was the subject of debate, with an internal directive on this important term noting the different measurements of "moderate prosperity" that existed, including the "capitalist" measurement of gross national product. "China's current statistics do not use this comprehensive indicator," it declared, asserting instead that China's success would be measured in hybrid indicators to reflect the continuing "socialist" objectives of its economic growth.[48]

Despite these concerns about overheating, the leadership also charged that "too little progress was being made in developing the commodity economy."[49] The reasons for their desire for more pro-growth policies varied, but they often combined a need to improve people's livelihoods by raising their incomes with the ambition to demonstrate a viable alternative to capitalist development. As the prominent economist Yu Guangyuan wrote in 1986, increasing labor productivity to "exceed the level of the capitalist countries" would show the "superiority" of China's socialist system while benefiting Chinese workers.[50]

Several directions appeared particularly promising. First, this period witnessed the continued rise of China's private sector. In 1984, the State Council publicly used the term *township and village enterprise* (TVE) for the first time, providing political support to this distinctive hybrid formation that had developed across China and especially in the countryside. Some of these firms were collectively owned by townships and villages, as the name suggests, but others were "alliance enterprises"—what Yasheng Huang calls a "1980s euphemism" for private firms "with multiple investors and with more than seven employees." By 1985, there were over 12 million TVEs, with collective TVEs employing 41.5 million people and private-run TVEs employing 4.75 million people (and 23.5 million employed in individual household businesses). Eventually, as the private sector became politically permissible later in the decade, the term *private enterprises* would replace *alliance enterprises*. Entrepreneurs and this new "managerial elite" gradually gained in visibility and status in society. These firms contributed significantly to growth, as TVEs spread capitalistic ownership, incentives, and exchange across the country.[51]

Chinese officials and economists also began to openly endorse industrial policy, spanning both public and private sectors, as part of a broader development strategy.[52] This trend was exemplified by a major report on a long-term, state-led development agenda for China titled *China toward the Year 2000*, which was initiated in 1983, completed in May 1985, and gradually rolled out nationwide. Led by Ma Hong and the Development Research Center, it involved more than 400 experts from across the government in work that one described as "large-scale social systems engineering." (They also called it an exercise in "futurology," as we will see later.) The report pursued a development strategy to industrialize the country, boost export-led growth, and reach a "national output value" of $1.2 trillion by 2000, with average annual increase of 7.4 percent. This growth was fast, but they argued that it would not create major problems. Following the submission of the initial draft of the report, the project leaders undertook a separate project on "Industrial Policy and Industrial Restructuring" to map out the future of Chinese industrial policy.[53]

In crafting a development strategy, *China toward the Year 2000* was also significant for the substantial attention that it devoted to a relatively new topic, "environmental protection"—the importance of China "not simply reliv[ing] the 'pollute first, clean up afterward' cycle adopted by the developed countries during their early industrialization." Although it acknowledged that economic development would be a higher priority than environmental protection in the near future, it also made clear that long-term planning should pay attention to "ecological and environmental problems."[54] Of course, this prioritization did not shift significantly before the year 2000, and China's ecological crisis would worsen well into the twenty-first century.

Chinese officials' focus on industrial policy was shaped in particular by the case of Japan, which had grown rapidly as a major source of investment, lending, and expertise. In 1985, the Renmin University economist Yang Zhi published his *Introduction to Industrial Economics,* which presented industrial economics as an example of "modern Western economics used to solve real problems" and centered on the case of Japan. The central aspect of Japanese development that garnered attention was its use of guidance (rather than command) planning, identification of strategic industries, and use of export-focused industrial policies. The State Planning Commission (SPC) and the newly founded Institute of Industrial Economics at CASS were both shaped by Japanese industrial economics. Future policymakers, including Liu He and Ma Kai, were associated with Yang Zhi through the Renmin University economics department during this period and continued later in their careers to develop Chinese industrial policies.[55]

In 1986, industrial policy was formally introduced into the seventh five-year plan, which covered the years 1986–1990. The plan sought to invigorate state-owned enterprises by making them more responsible for production, profits, and losses, expand the scope of markets, and increase the role of guidance planning and indirect macroeconomic levers; it included an entire section under the rubric of "industrial structure and industrial policies" that encompassed agriculture, industry, raw materials, and "commodity circulation."[56] The industrial-policy advocates in China's leadership, including Ma Hong, also explicitly connected their agenda for market reform and fast growth to international debates about "development economics."[57] In a remarkably brief period, the paradigms of "industrial policy" and "development economics" had become part of the Chinese leadership's economic thinking as a way of reconciling modernized state planning and stronger markets.

This vision for fast economic growth gave a prominent role to international trade and the SEZs. Yet they had run into major problems, including disorganized production and significant overinvestment, and their role as export hubs remained undeveloped. The SEZs had made some early progress, with Shenzhen leading the country in implementing price reforms to free up capital goods, liberalizing the system for workers' wages, and becoming the first Chinese city to allow foreign banks, beginning with Hong Kong's Nan Yang Commercial Bank. The SEZs grew quickly in the early part of the decade. Between 1980 and 1984, Shenzhen grew at 58 percent annually, a stunning rate, and Zhuhai grew at 32 percent (followed by Xiamen at 13 percent and Shantou at 9 percent and compared to the national average GDP growth of approximately 10 percent annually). By 1985, they had attracted US$1.17 billion in foreign direct investment, around 20 percent of the national total, and the leadership felt there was significant room for improvement.

The biggest disappointment was that the SEZs were not becoming the export engines that leaders had hoped for. Their growth was coming from investment and domestic production, and as of 1985, Shenzhen, Zhuhai, and Xiamen all exported less than half of their industrial production. The four SEZs had become a drain on limited foreign exchange, reportedly running up a trade deficit of US$900 million by importing nearly four times as much as they exported.[58] Future premier Zhu Rongji, then SPC deputy chairman, acknowledged to a delegation visiting Beijing that Shenzhen's development "obviously isn't running smoothly."[59]

Facing these problems with the SEZs, Gu Mu decided to intervene in 1986. He refocused the SEZs on increasing industrial production and product quality and expanding international trade and exports, while closing failing firms and reining in overinvestment and construction.[60] The SEZs offered less job security and fewer labor protections to workers, and Gu clearly felt that it was time for them to show the promised gains in efficiency and exports. (By 1985, Shenzhen had approximately 400,000 unregistered residents, primarily migrant workers, approximately half of its total population.[61]) Gu Mu's push would pay off. By the end of the decade, exports would soar; Shenzhen's utilized foreign direct investment inflows would grow more than seventyfold from their 1979 levels, and its GDP per capita would rise tenfold in the same period, from US$122 to US$1,279.[62]

This renewed focus in 1986 on promoting China's international trade led to the major step of moving to deepen its integration into the formal international trading system. Zhao Ziyang spearheaded China's application to regain its membership in the global General Agreement on Tariffs and Trade (GATT), of which it had been a founding member in 1947. The predecessor to the World Trade Organization, GATT had market requirements that were far more stringent than the PRC was able to meet only ten years after Mao's death. However, as the Chinese economist Wu Jinglian has written, "this very act signified China's determination to further open itself to the outside world."[63] Zhao also hosted diplomats and business executives from Japan, the United States, West Germany, and the United Kingdom, promising to improve China's policies to promote international investment and trade.[64] These steps to become more fully integrated into the global economic order had enduring importance for China and the world.

◇

As China's leadership prepared to set out its agenda for the 13th Party Congress that was scheduled for the fall of 1987, it faced significant choices for its economic policies. One such choice was the enduring question of whether to prioritize price reform or enterprise reform, and how quickly to implement whichever priority was chosen. After considering numerous proposals, Zhao made clear by late 1986 that he was leaning heavily toward prioritizing enterprise reform.[65] In line with the focus on enterprises, the leadership also introduced a new law to regulate enterprise bankruptcy, a step toward creating a system in which enterprises would be more accountable for their own loss making. This idea had been championed by the economist Cao Siyuan and taken up by Peng Zhen, chairman of the NPC, although implementation proceeded slowly.[66] Yet Zhao continued to vacillate, saying in December 1986, "Prices are key—they are the key to reforming the entire system, and can also be said to be the key to the success or failure of reform. But the reform of prices will bring risks and cause prices to rise." Zhao seemed inclined to prioritize less destabilizing challenges, especially in the run-up to the congress.[67]

Senior officials quickly moved forward with drawing up plans for the 13th Party Congress. In March 1987, An Zhiwen and SPC official Fang Weizhong presented a report to Zhao that included a model of the economy in which "the state plan adjusts and controls the market through a variety of economic means, and, through the market, guides the enterprises," which drew the premier's attention.[68] Also in March, Ma Hong's Development Research Commission submitted a detailed proposal on China's industrial policy that also endorsed an elevated role for the market. Zhao responded enthusiastically, writing, "At this stage for China, it is impossible to solely rely on the market. . . . We must rely on the intervention of the state formulating clear industrial policies as well as policies for the industrial organization structure."[69] He was articulating the contours of a new economic model that built on the "planned commodity economy" but gave greater, if still bounded, status to the market.

Chinese economists continued to partner closely with foreign economic advisers and organizations. The Ford Foundation, which had been a crucial source of funding for research in economics and law, received formal approval from the State Council to open a Beijing office in April 1987. The Ford Foundation had worked with CASS and supported broader training activities, including a series of economics programs that were led by figures such as Princeton professor Gregory Chow, Harvard professor Dwight Perkins, and Stanford professor Lawrence Lau. Its engagement had been premised on mutual benefit to the United States and China: "We see China as seriously trying to move toward incentives, markets, [and a] freer econ[omic] system," said the foundation's executive vice president, David Bell. "We would like to help Chinese—and the rest of us—benefit from it."[70] That approach had paid off: "According to CASS, we are the first foreign private foundation to be authorized to open an office in China," Ford's representative in Beijing, Peter Geithner, wrote proudly.[71] The World Bank also partnered with the System Reform Commission to organize seminars on financial system reform and state-owned enterprise reform.[72]

Many Chinese officials felt that the need for new policies and even an updated economic model was particularly urgent because of the serious distortions that had emerged in the economy. The dual-track price system had succeeded at increasing production and efficiency, but tensions remained high as the production of key industrial commodities climbed steadily even as the in-plan requirements remained basically unchanged; for example, production of steel increased by nearly 10 million metric tons between 1984 and 1987 (an increase of over 25 percent), essentially all of which was produced outside the plan.[73] The dual-track price system also encouraged serious corruption to fester, as discussed further in Part I and Part IV, and the old system remained deeply entrenched. In April, Ma Hong and the Development Research Commission submitted a report to Zhao stating that a consensus had emerged that the fundamental problem confronting China's economy was an overexpansion of demand (assessing problems such as overissuance of currency and rises in commodity prices), although opinion remained divided on which "transitional symptoms" were most dangerous. In July, the SPC submitted a detailed paper on increasing the autonomy of decision making at large and medium-sized enterprises and implementing new measures to control consumer demand.[74] Beyond official channels, in journals and newspapers, numerous economists and intellectuals continued to compete for influence and attention.

As the 13th Party Congress approached, Zhao made decisions among these various priorities. Working with the Central Economic and Finance Leading Small Group, he settled on a policy agenda that would prioritize reforming the enterprise management system while also developing new policies to govern investment, materials management, and foreign trade.[75] State-owned enterprises began to implement a contract responsibility system in which enterprises guaranteed the state a certain portion of enterprises' revenue but otherwise generally allowed them to make independent operational decisions. Enterprise managers and government agencies negotiated the terms of the contracts, an arrangement intended to eliminate "ratchet effects" in which enterprises produced at minimum levels so that planners would set lower production targets. This new model of a contract responsibility system, which Hu Yaobang had advocated in the early 1980s, went beyond any previous management reform, although it did not target the more basic issue of ownership. By July 1987, over 50 percent of state-owned enterprises reportedly had adopted the system.[76]

Thus, by August 1987, Zhao and his economic advisers had developed a vision of China's economy moving toward a system in which "the state plan adjusts and controls the market through a variety of economic means, and, through the market, guides the enterprises." Industrial policy and export-led growth would play a crucial role in this evolving system. The leadership had explicitly set deepening the reforms to enterprises as their priority. As the 13th Party Congress drew near, Zhao called for the bureaucracy governing economic affairs to mobilize and prepare to implement this agenda.[77]

Even as the leadership's comfort with the market increased, concerns persisted about undermining the socialist nature of China's system, as well as the risks of excessively fast growth to society, the environment, and political stability. Yet there was great enthusiasm for China's market reforms around the world, from both capitalist and socialist countries. Even the Bulgarian leader Todor Zhivkov confided in Deng Xiaoping in May 1987 that he felt, "You made a breakthrough in establishing a free market economy," which he hoped to emulate.[78] Yet how far would this "breakthrough" go in China? What other objectives beyond economic growth would it serve? These dilemmas remained unresolved even as China prepared to endorse a central role for the market and embark on a new period of rapid development.

PART III

TECHNOLOGY

◆

THE 1980s WITNESSED rapid technological change around
the world, and China was no exception. On October 9, 1983, Chinese premier Zhao Ziyang discussed this trend in a major speech
at the State Council to officials with responsibility for technology
policy, economic reform, and scientific research. "At the end of
this century and the beginning of the next century," he predicted, a
"global New Technological Revolution" would emerge, with sweeping
implications "for production and for society." On that fall day, Zhao
listed numerous reports and readings that had shaped this vision
of the future, but one stood out: the work of the American futurist
Alvin Toffler. Citing Toffler's book *The Third Wave,* Zhao announced
that Toffler believed that developing countries might be able to
take "an entirely new route" to becoming a technological power-
house. "This view is worthy of our attention," he concluded.[1]

This remarkable endorsement of Toffler from the Chinese premier was neither a passing fancy nor an inconsequential citation.
To the contrary, Toffler had become a central part of Zhao's worldview. And this was only one aspect of a much broader story of
debates over science and technology (S&T), the defense-industrial
base, and futurist thinking in the 1980s. Deng Xiaoping believed

that China had "fallen behind," and his endorsement of what Zhou Enlai had called the "Four Modernizations" placed S&T at the core of the leadership's agenda. Due to the enduring legacies of the Maoist period, S&T and national defense were deeply interconnected, and China's technological drive in the 1980s drew on both military and civilian domains.

These two domains were tied together by the Chinese leadership's interest in futurist ideas and policies. Senior officials and their advisers believed that they urgently needed to respond to major technological changes—what they came to call the New Technological Revolution—that they saw sweeping the world. To meet this challenge, they developed a distinctive set of major policies blending technology, science, defense, and development in ways that powerfully affected China's complex pursuit of modernization in the 1980s.

The imperative to develop the economy shaped nearly every aspect of China's technological agenda in this period, including by reshaping the Mao-era military-industrial apparatus, which spanned the successful program to build a nuclear bomb and the "Third Front" industrialization of China's interior starting in 1964.[2] However, Zhao Ziyang gave "technology" prominence and even preeminence. What he characterized early in the decade in imaginative and futuristic terms—a need to respond to a global New Technological Revolution—soon became a set of major state development projects. This was epitomized by the 863 Program, a multibillion-dollar state technology research and development program established in 1986 that prioritized information technology, biotechnology, energy, and other fields. Chinese leaders' worries were greatly increased by the fact that the cutting edge of global technological development was not static.

The United States, Japan, Europe, and the Soviet Union were all racing ahead in innovating and adopting novel information technologies; China was struggling to catch up to a level that was continuously rising, like Tantalus grasping at bunches of grapes dangling overhead.

Reflecting the "global" scope of this challenge, China's technological drive drew on transfers from abroad, both of expertise and hardware. At this point, the governments of the United States, Japan, and many other countries saw technology transfer to China as in their interests: "One of the most important influences that the United States has [over China] is technology transfer," stated a congressional research report in 1987.[3] And the Chinese leadership was extremely frank about its need for foreign assistance. Vice Premier Wang Renzhong, while on a tour of Europe in 1979, told a Swedish reporter, "To acquire independence we have to get access to technology. Technology is a joint treasure for [the] people of the world."[4] Between 1979 and 1989, according to one estimate, China signed 27,527 contracts for imported technology equipment and collaborative projects, which totaled US$12.38 billion.[5] The eventual goal was "independence"—or "self-reliance," a Maoist phrase that remained frequently used in this period—but to catch up, China would need to use all means to gain access to this "treasure."

The CCP believed that S&T not only served and reflected economic development but also had important political, ideological, and social dimensions.[6] The CCP proclaimed itself to be "scientific," drawing on the idea of "scientific socialism"—that is, socialism based on reason and the prediction of material change and historical trends (contrasted by Friedrich Engels with "utopian" socialism). Paired with the Dengist view that "practice is the sole criterion of truth," the claims of "science" were especially powerful, extending beyond the realm of S&T into many aspects of the CCP's governance. As rehabilitated scientists moved back into positions of authority, and as budgets for institutions like the Chinese Academy of Sciences expanded, the status of S&T was further elevated, and China's capacities grew significantly.[7]

In broadening their understanding of how S&T fit into their agenda for modernization, China's leaders were influenced by futurist ideas and thinkers, exemplified by Toffler. These writers' surprising popularity in China constituted far more than an intellectual fad. They powerfully affected policy measures to ensure that China was not "left behind" in the information age. New expectations about the future, shaped by the transnational movement of ideas, became centrally important to the Chinese leadership as a category of both analysis and action.[8] These visions of the future were a way of fashioning the new goals of China's modernization as well as planning actions to be taken—looking beyond the year 2000 and operating in transnational and even explicitly "global" contexts. And they occurred in dialogue with the need to harness and control information technology and other emerging technologies, as well as new ideas and policies about China's economic system.

The implications of this futurist thinking for how Chinese officials envisioned modernization were more significant than has been previously understood.[9] The widespread reform-era concept of "crossing the river by feeling for the stones" suggested deep ambiguity about what might wait on the far riverbank. Indeed, the "feeling for the stones" metaphor minimized basic elements of the longer-term "planning" ingrained in CCP governance, exemplified by five-year plans. Constructing a new future for China, very much going beyond such "five-year" planning, constituted a central goal for CCP officials so that a modern China could move "to the front ranks of the world." This evolving vision, with a time horizon that stretched well into the new millennium, must be understood not only as a pragmatic or technocratic agenda. The Chinese leadership acted both to prepare for and to shape a radically transformed future as they imagined it—pursuing an idiosyncratic and fluid path that could serve their country's interests. This section demonstrates how China's future was seen through the eyes of Zhao and other senior Chinese officials who developed a large-scale, actionable vision of China's S&T modernization in the 1980s, and assesses its implications.

Ideas about the future matter profoundly to how governments mobilize for and respond to technological change. Top Chinese policymakers embraced what we might term *actionable futurism*— a futurism that required a response from the state and indeed shaped a wide range of important S&T policies. Technological changes affected new ideas about the future, and those ideas in turn affected how governments crafted their agendas for S&T policy.

By the third decade of the twenty-first century, the importance of China's technological rise has become apparent even to a casual observer. But this current public conversation is frequently stripped of historical context, and the technological, futuristic dimensions of the 1980s in China are all too often left out of historical narratives of this period. China's modernization in the 1980s was centrally focused on technological change. The time has come to place these dynamics at the center of the decade's story, where they belong.

Responding to the New Technological Revolution

Deng Xiaoping had many goals for China, but perhaps none was as ambitious as his hope that China could become a superpower of advanced science and technology (S&T). In March 1978, shortly before he succeeded in outmaneuvering Hua Guofeng as paramount leader, Deng delivered a speech to the National Conference on Science. "The entire nation is setting out with tremendous enthusiasm on the march towards the modernization of our S&T," Deng said, calling S&T a core "part of the productive forces," which played "a vital role in economic construction and in building up our national defense."[1]

Deng set out two important goals. The first goal was to "catch up with and surpass" advanced countries. Despite his belief that China was "backward" in S&T, Deng voiced extraordinary ambition that with concerted effort, it could move to the global vanguard. This goal had shaped the Mao era, with limited success, and Deng was now making clear that he intended to adapt it and carry it forward. The second goal was to "learn from those who are more advanced." This reflected the profoundly transnational nature of the scientific enterprise as China had practiced it throughout the entire history of the People's Republic of

China (PRC), despite constant claims of "independence" and "self-reliance." Waves of American- and Soviet-trained scientists formed the core of the PRC's scientific establishment in the Mao era, such as missile scientist Qian Xuesen, who returned to China from the United States in 1995 after having his security clearance revoked in 1950 as McCarthyism and racial discrimination rose. Qian led the development of China's missile system while also helping to establish the University of Science and Technology of China, modeled on his alma mater Caltech. China's first atomic bomb, successfully tested in 1964, drew heavily on prior Soviet help and Western-trained Chinese scientists. These transnational linkages in the scientific establishment only deepened during the 1970s, as US-China relations warmed.[2] Scientific exchanges were also a motivating force behind the US-China rapprochement and the pursuit of normalization in the 1970s, which finally occurred on January 1, 1979.[3]

These exchanges boomed in the 1980s. Chinese officials' strong focus on sending students and scholars abroad was facilitated by agreements on S&T cooperation with France, Germany, Britain, and the United States.[4] The numbers rose quickly, from 6,500 studying in the United States in 1981 to at least 40,000 by 1989—the largest number of any nationality studying in the United States. An estimated 100,000 Chinese students in total ventured abroad as of 1986.[5]

The goal of overseas study was clear: "having more of them return home to serve the socialist motherland," one 1981 guideline stated. Even if students went abroad at their own expense, they should receive "political and ideological education" before departing and be strongly encouraged to return to China.[6] So eager was the Chinese leadership to ensure that Chinese students could study abroad that Zhao Ziyang personally asked Margaret Thatcher to help lower "the level of fees" for Chinese students, noting that they were the centerpiece of Sino-British "technical cooperation."[7] These students were crucial to China's modernization.

From the start, Chinese students were sometimes a source of controversy in their host countries. Many were government funded, and some were even the children of powerful Chinese officials, including Foreign Minister Huang Hua's son, Organization Department head Song Renqiong's children, and even Deng Xiaoping's son Deng Zhifang.[8] The Federal Bureau of Investigation (FBI) monitored these students, looking both for espionage risks and possible defectors. In the *Washington Post,* an FBI official wrote, "It would be arrogant to assume every Chinese student is a spy. It would also be arrogant not to recognize that classified S&T data are up for grabs by many foreign powers."[9]

Another important dimension of Deng's vision was purchasing technology from advanced countries, especially the United States. Although China faced export controls placed on socialist countries and governed by the Coordinating Committee for Multilateral Export Controls (CoCom), the United States and other governments explicitly "develop[ed] a distinction" between China and the Soviet bloc to enable sales of sensitive technology. Deng was particularly frustrated by China's difficulty in obtaining a supercomputer, and he raised it with Vice President Walter Mondale in August 1979. The Carter administration internally supported "liberalizing sensitive exports to China on a case-by-case basis" (including aviation and radar technology), but the slow pace of relaxing export controls—what Foreign Minister Huang Hua called "loud thunder with few raindrops"—was a source of considerable frustration for the Chinese leadership.[10]

Within China, a major effort was under way to reposition S&T as primarily of *economic* value, in addition to its military or strategic value. All S&T work, whether in university laboratories, academy institutes, or the defense industry, was now required to serve China's economic development. The policies of "civilian-military integration" initially meant, in practice, "making military technologies serve civilian uses" and placing civilian interests first.[11]

A series of reforms in 1981–1982 facilitated this work. In 1982 the Chinese leadership created a unified Commission for Science, Technology, and Industry for National Defense (COSTIND), jointly supervised by the State Council and the Central Military Commission. COSTIND had oversight of military research and development, production, and S&T personnel and equipment within the country's military institutions.[12] Although the focus on serving economic development was paramount, Deng also wanted to modernize the People's Liberation Army (PLA) itself. His vision was of an improved economic foundation that would bolster China's defense-industrial base.[13] Following the brief, bloody war with Vietnam in 1979, in which China suffered unexpectedly heavy casualties, the leadership saw the need to modernize the PLA's conventional weapons and logistics and streamline its personnel, in contrast to the Mao-era fixation on promoting nuclear weapons, delivery systems, and satellite technologies above all else.[14]

This project of adapting Mao-era S&T institutions to better promote economic development was not limited to the PLA. The Chinese Academy of Sciences (CAS), the preeminent state research institution, had been founded in 1949 by building on both the Nationalists' Central Research Academy (Academia Sinica) and the Soviet Academy of Sciences. CAS had steered the development of the 1956 twelve-year S&T plan, among other important initiatives, but suffered gravely during the Cultural Revolution. When CAS researchers returned to work, many wanted to resume basic science research and resisted Deng and Zhao's focus on applied S&T. This remained an ongoing source of contestation, especially after reforms in 1981–1982 encouraged CAS researchers to "serve economic construction" and start profitable firms from their state perches. Numerous researchers protested these changes, arguing that basic science should be a goal in and of itself. However, many others took up the opportunity to engage in commercial activities in the marketizing economy, starting some of the most significant technology firms of the period, such as Lenovo Group (founded as Legend), which was established in 1984 and would become the world's largest maker of personal computers.[15] The 1981–1982 reforms of China's S&T sector also strengthened the position of the State Science and Technology Commission (SSTC), which had been restarted in 1978 following its abolition during the Cultural Revolution and was led by Fang Yi. The SSTC assertively pushed for "applied research and technical innovation" that could benefit economic development.[16] It was clear that S&T would occupy a significant, albeit still-evolving, place at the center of the broader modernization agenda.

◇

In addition to seeking technical expertise and reorganizing China's S&T institutions, some Chinese intellectuals and policymakers sought to think imaginatively about emerging technological trends. One such organization was the Chinese Society for Futures Studies (CSFS), founded in January 1979, bringing together prominent engineers, physicists, economists, and officials with the mission "to serve the long-term planning and the modernization construction of the country, and to serve the progress of mankind."[17] As the orthodox Marxist understanding of the future began to be questioned and revised even in official discourse, the study of alternative futures became a matter of great interest to many Chinese intellectuals.[18]

The CCP had cultivated official images of the future that were sometimes quite explicit, such as the popular saying in the early Mao period, "The Soviet Union's today will be our tomorrow." Throughout the era of high socialism, official narratives of the future used a Marxist framework in which Chinese socialism would triumph over capitalism and eventually achieve full communism. However, the Deng era of "reform and opening" raised significant new questions about how to conceptualize the future.[19]

Amid this rising attention to futurology and translations of foreign texts into Chinese, Dong Leshan, a researcher and translator at the CASS Institute of American Studies who had previously translated George Orwell's 1984, traveled to the United States in the spring of 1981. Dong recalled, "Everyone I met and with whom I discussed American intellectual trends [in 1981] talked about *The Third Wave*" by Alvin Toffler.[20]

Indeed, *The Third Wave*, which had been published the previous year, remained on best-seller lists and frequently cropped up in the media. Popular interest in the dramatic changes that the future might bring had risen rapidly in Western countries in the 1970s, thanks to prominent publications such as Toffler's *Future Shock* (1970), the Club of Rome's report *The Limits to Growth* (1972), and Daniel Bell's *The Coming of Post-industrial Society* (1973).[21] These texts were at once descriptive and predictive; they described the economic and social changes wrought by technological change and predicted which structural and personal consequences were likely to be most enduring. In 1980, working closely with his wife, Heidi, Toffler followed on the success of *Future Shock* with *The Third Wave*, which would become his most popular work in China.

In *The Third Wave,* Toffler sketched a unified theory of past, present, and future as three evolving "waves" of change. The "first wave" had arrived as humans settled into agricultural society. (Many developing countries, he noted, remained in this "first wave," including China, which he called "the world's biggest First Wave nation."[22]) The "second wave" of change came with the Industrial Revolution.[23] An equally vast shift was arriving with the "third wave," inaugurating an "emerging civilization . . . based on diversified, renewable energy sources; on methods of production that make most factory assembly lines obsolete; [and] on new, non-nuclear families," among others. In the dramatic, television-ready language that helped make him an international celebrity, he called on advanced "second wave" nations to reconsider the fundamentals of their systems, including "the market" and "democracy."[24] Although some of the attention that Toffler received in the United States dismissed him as an intellectual lightweight, his ideas were treated with great seriousness internationally, including in China.[25]

Considering *The Third Wave* from the perspective of a Chinese reader in the early 1980s, a mixed picture emerges. Some of the book's ideas seem to be readily compatible with the Dengist agenda. Toffler wrote, "Old ways of thinking, old formulas, dogmas, and ideologies, no matter how cherished or useful in the past, no longer fit the facts," which was a statement of the type that was frequently appearing in the official Chinese press around this time. Other statements, however, were clearly problematic, especially Toffler's proud admission that he had been a Marxist as a teenager but had renounced this view as "partial, one-sided, and obsolete."[26] Indeed, his book offered a vision that rejected the orthodox Marxist understanding of historical development—as Chinese conservatives would soon criticize.

Yet these elements of *The Third Wave,* ideologically problematic though they may have been, did not detract from Dong Leshan's enthusiasm for bringing Toffler's ideas to China. Dong quickly published a summary of the book in the leading magazine *Dushu* in late 1981. This introduction to Toffler piqued the interest of *Dushu*'s elite readership. Plans were made to translate the entire book. And in the spring of 1982, several months after Dong's articles appeared, CSFS formally invited Toffler to visit Beijing and Shanghai.[27]

Toffler, who had long harbored a desire to visit China, seized the opportunity. Writing to Dong, Toffler requested "meetings and interviews with your leading political figures and with persons responsible for long-term planning in fields such as the economy, technology, and international relations." Toffler was so eager to visit China that he also informed Dong that he was willing to pay personally for the cost of the trip. He subsequently specifically requested meetings with a list of senior officials including Hu Qiaomu, Yao Yilin, Xue Muqiao, Fang Yi, and the minister of communications, the minister of radio and television, and the chief of the general staff of the PLA—an extremely ambitious list.[28] Toffler clearly hoped to personally make the case for his predictions to many of the high-level officials who would be best positioned to turn those ideas into policies. In a letter to a friend, Toffler outlined his hopes about the potential relevance of his ideas to China. "If my theories prove correct, they will also raise fresh questions about economic organization and development in China and other primarily agricultural societies," he wrote, underscoring, "The implications of THE THIRD WAVE for China are politically significant."[29]

On their first evening in Beijing, the couple was welcomed with a lavish banquet. On January 2, 1983, Toffler delivered a speech at CASS. Interest was high, but Hu Qiaomu reportedly sought to prevent too large a group from attending the lecture because he felt that Toffler was dismissive of socialism.[30]

Although many of the meetings that Toffler requested did not occur, the Tofflers were received by CASS vice president Huan Xiang and vice chairman of the Central Committee of the CCP Zhou Peiyuan, a physicist and diplomat.[31] They visited a genetic-engineering laboratory and a fiber-optics plant and met with Shanghai mayor Wang Daohan and other city officials and researchers. The Tofflers also presented these researchers with a newly released documentary film based on *The Third Wave*.[32]

Toffler recalled that his Chinese interlocutors consistently asked questions with similar preoccupations: "Do we have to go through the traditional industrial revolution in order to feed our people? . . . Or are there other alternatives [for] development, and other alternatives for culture as well?"[33] These questions revealed wide-ranging interest in new perspectives from abroad that might be useful to the intellectuals and officials who were tasked with reimagining China's future. Yet by the time that the Tofflers returned to the United States, it remained uncertain whether their ideas had resonated.

This rising interest in futurism developed in tandem with a growing focus among China's rulers on cybernetics, systems engineering, and forecasting as they sought to help China meet its ambitious development goals for the year 2000, which included quadrupling the gross value of industrial and agricultural output from 1980 levels. "Cybernetics is the science that studies the control laws of complex systems," wrote Tong Tianxiang, a prominent champion of cybernetics, in *People's Daily*. These techniques, he noted, could be applied to automating production, building computers and "artificial intelligence," improving defense technology, and even to "the social system"—that is, to "improving the operation" of society itself.[34]

Soon after the 1978 National Science Conference, Qian Xuesen's book on systems control and cybernetics, *Engineering Cybernetics*—originally written in the early 1950s in English, when Qian was still working in the United States—was republished in Beijing.[35] His expertise in systems engineering as well as physics had led him to become the guiding force in developing China's missile and rocket programs, earning him heroic stature. For Qian, systems engineering sat comfortably alongside his continued commitment to Marxism, and he also partnered with experts in cybernetics from the Soviet Union, where the field enjoyed great popularity. After Mao's death, Qian advocated the establishment of institutes at major universities, the publication of books and journals, and the creation of a Systems Engineering Society.[36]

This focus on cybernetics and systems engineering directly affected policymaking in the early 1980s. In the economic domain, officials at the State Council began to use these techniques to model prices, wages, and financial subsidies and forecast increases in energy usage as China's economy grew, calling cybernetics "a technology that organizes and manages socialist construction." Of course, they also continued to be widely used in the defense sector.[37]

But perhaps the most significant consequence of this scientific field was in policies regarding population control in China. The one-child policy was born out of models and forecasts of the exponential growth of the Chinese population produced by cyberneticists and systems engineers, as anthropologist Susan Greenhalgh shows. Song Jian, a protégé of Qian Xuesen who had worked in China's missile program and would rise to lead the SSTC, played a particularly important role, influenced by the doom-laden population projections of the Club of Rome's *Limits to Growth*. Song and his colleagues argued that with one child per family, China's population would stabilize at 1.2 billion by the year 2000, enabling the leadership to more readily achieve its goals of national wealth and power and averting ecological catastrophe. With the backing of powerful elders schooled in economic planning, such as Chen Yun and Li Xiannian, this new population control policy was approved in September 1980. It would be harshly enforced, with a particularly severe impact on women and girls in China—as Greenhalgh writes, it would "harm women's social status, damage their health, [and] provoke peasants to kill their baby daughters." The task of controlling the "social system" was more challenging in the real world than the cybernetic projections indicated, requiring coercion and violence to achieve its goals.[38]

Even so, the Chinese leadership continued to invest in systems engineering and futurist projections. In 1983, Zhao approved a research outline for a project on "China in the Year 2000," and shortly thereafter, the CSFS held a symposium on this topic. The ideal of managing society as a large mechanical system remained profoundly alluring to the CCP.[39]

Despite these initial efforts in a wide range of scientific and technological fields, by 1983 Zhao had not yet determined how to develop China's S&T capacities or how exactly to integrate emerging technologies with economic development. In March 1983, just two months after the Tofflers' visit, the Chinese-language edition of *The Third Wave* was published in Beijing. Like many translated works during this period, the book was marked for "internal" circulation, with only 3,000 copies printed; the publisher seemed not to be expecting widespread interest.[40] But the book circulated swiftly among China's political and intellectual elites. Soon *The Third Wave* and other futurist ideas found their way into government offices, ministries, and eventually to the State Council, where they came to Zhao's attention.[41]

These futurist ideas provided an unexpected answer to Zhao's need to integrate S&T and economic development, offering an optimistic vision of a technological revolution that could dramatically boost productivity while transforming society. One of Zhao's advisers, Huan Xiang (who had met with Toffler), submitted a report on these trends, which captured the premier's imagination. Huan offered a clear exposition of the three types of industry that could allow China to take advantage of emerging trends and thereby meet long-term goals for the future: labor intensive, capital intensive, and knowledge intensive—a schematic that corresponded, broadly speaking, to Toffler's three waves. China, CCP leaders often remarked, had missed out on the Industrial Revolution. At a moment when the Chinese leadership was rethinking fundamental assumptions about its country's socialist economy, here was a fresh vision of the future in which China could take part.[42] These ideas had rhetorical and practical benefits for Zhao's self-presentation as an internationally minded reformist leader, but they also optimistically suggested that one of China's most lamented weaknesses—its comparatively low level of industrial development—would not prevent China from advancing into the information age. Zhao had found a malleable, actionable framework that appeared to offer a range of benefits.[43]

On October 9, 1983, Zhao opened a major conference on what he called the New Technological Revolution. The conference gathered officials from State Council departments; offices with responsibility for S&T, including the SPC, SSTC, State Economic Commission, and CASS; and coastal regions.[44] Zhao outlined a futurist vision for China's technological development that would "help speed up China's socialist modernization." Zhao explained that he had been reflecting on ideas contained in Toffler's *Third Wave*, John Naisbitt's *Megatrends*, and Japanese technology reporting, and he had come to believe that the global transformation under way centered on innovations such as electronic computers and genetic engineering.[45] He continued,

> Whether we call it the Fourth Industrial Revolution or call it the Third Wave, [these writers] all believe that Western countries in the 1950s and 1960s reached a high degree of industrial-

ization and are now moving to an information society. . . . At the end of this century and the beginning of the next century, or within a few decades, there will be a new kind of situation in which breakthroughs in new technology that are happening now or will happen soon will be used for production and for society. This will bring a new leap in social productivity and thus a corresponding set of new changes in social life. This trend is worthy of our attention and must be carefully studied, based on our actual situation, in order to determine the next ten to twenty years of long-range planning.[46]

Zhao clearly believed that the stakes were high: either China would take advantage of this New Technological Revolution to narrow its technological and economic gap with the rest of the world, or China would be left even farther behind.

Zhao also encouraged the assembled group to look for areas where it might be possible to skip "some of the stage of traditional industrial development" and move directly into "utilizing more advanced scientific and technological achievements." He stated specifically that these views had come from Toffler, who "believes that today's Third World countries may not have fully experienced the 'Second Wave' of development, but that they can take an entirely new route to achieve a 'Third Wave' civilization." The challenge for the gathered officials was thus to determine whether China could "directly adopt the results of the New Technological Revolution." Rather than simply emphasizing imitation and continued technology acquisition, Zhao also highlighted the potential of Chinese "technological innovation."[47] Zhao was developing a broad, ambitious framework for charting the role of technology in China's future.

This interest in skipping the "second wave" and taking "an entirely new route" to achieve advanced technological development recalled prior movements to leapfrog developmental stages—a periodic feature of the PRC's history that appeared most notoriously as the justification for Mao's disastrous Great Leap Forward but also underlay Hua Guofeng's rapid importation of industrial technology after Mao's death, the "foreign leap forward." However, despite rhetorical similarities, one must be cautious not to overstate these parallels. When Zhao invoked a "new leap," he was referring to a global "trend" that China should strive to join through careful, if ambitious, policymaking, rather than a utopian prospect that could be achieved by willpower alone. For Zhao, technology was, like economics, a realm that should be kept distinct from political affairs, whereas Mao had said the opposite: "Politics and technology must be unified."[48] Although Zhao was clearly caught up in his enthusiasm about the potential benefits of the New Technological Revolution, he emphasized the long-term nature of these efforts that would take place over "the next ten to twenty years." Toffler provided Zhao with a sense of urgency and opportunity because Zhao realized that, given China's low level of S&T prowess, taking advantage of "third wave" transformations required decades of work that must begin immediately.

To conduct further research on these ideas, Zhao established two high-level groups. One, based at the State Council, would be led by Ma Hong, president of CASS and senior adviser at the State Council. The second would be based in Shanghai and led by Wang Daohan, who had met with Toffler earlier that year. These groups would seek to provide policy solutions addressing "the global New Technological Revolution and China's modernization."[49] Zhao identified this effort as a priority and tasked trusted officials to develop a response.

Ma Hong set about organizing his research group. On October 21, he delivered a speech at the State Council on "economic strategy and technology policies" in response to Zhao's "important instructions" (as well as citing "the third wave").[50] Shortly thereafter, Ma organized several internal meetings, including a conference with approximately 1,600 cadres, experts, and scientists in attendance, and a seminar for several dozen vice ministers.[51] The announcement that China had developed its first supercomputer, the Galaxy, bolstered the sense that a true technological revolution had arrived in China.[52]

That same month, *Dushu* published a précis of John Naisbitt's *Megatrends*, with a recommendation that it should be read by "the many readers who have requested a deeper understanding of foreign trends" after reading about *The Third Wave*.[53] *Megatrends*, which had been published in the United States in 1982, was best known for its analysis of the shift from an "industrial society" to an "information society." Citing developments including satellite communications, cable television, and companies such as Intel and Apple, Naisbitt described the "information society" as an economy in which "the *strategic* resource is information" (original emphasis) rather than capital.[54] Naisbitt's *Megatrends* contributed to China's strong and growing public attention to what Zhao had labeled the New Technological Revolution.

With this intensive top-level support, terms like *New Technological Revolution, New Industrial Revolution,* and *third wave* spread throughout the country. As Zhao's speech indicated, these terms were frequently used interchangeably. A fusillade of articles followed the premier's endorsement, frequently emphasizing the potential for China to catch up with or even leap ahead of the capitalist world.[55] Hu Yaobang also delivered speeches on the importance of this transformation.[56] On January 28, 1984, Zhao, freshly returned from a state visit to the United States on which he had approved an extension of the US-China Agreement on Cooperation in S&T and a new Accord on Industrial and Technological Cooperation, toured a microelectronics exhibition in Shanghai with Wang Daohan. A news report explained, "Microelectronics are the basis of the 'information society' and an important measure of a country's level of modernization."[57] On February 16, Deng Xiaoping lent his personal support by visiting the same exhibition.[58]

This prominent focus on the New Technological Revolution affected the entire S&T apparatus, from CAS to the PLA. In December 1983, Fang Yi announced policies to ensure "overcoming the separation between scientific research and production" and give S&T personnel more freedom to experiment, debate, and pursue economic activities.[59] With the cooperation of the Ministry of Electronics Industry and other officials, media reports covered the important fields of semiconductors and microelectronics, which were bringing "revolutionary changes in the economy, the military, and social life."[60]

This flurry of activity also resonated with broader cultural and intellectual trends that influenced elite discussions about the future. Chinese intellectuals established a popular series, *Toward the Future*, which published books on topics as diverse as systems theory, cybernetics, and "sociobiology," as well as texts on economics, history, and literature.[61] These works offered inspiration and even provocation, underscoring that interest in Toffler was part of a much broader fascination with new ideas and international trends about technology and the future. Zhao and his advisers remained focused on the New Technological Revolution and the vision of actionable futurism that he had articulated in October 1983, but this interest was also emblematic of broader discourses about reimagining China's future.

Yet this domain was not above the intense contestation that was characteristic of Chinese politics during this period. In late 1983 and early 1984, the broader political environment was not conducive to an open embrace of foreign ideas. As discussed in Chapter 2, Deng Xiaoping had lent his personal backing to a sweeping initiative to "eliminate spiritual pollution" on October 12, 1983, just three days after Zhao's speech on the New Technological Revolution, though there is currently no evidence to suggest that Deng's decision was motivated by Zhao's speech.[62] Thus Ma Hong warned in his October 21 remarks that cadres who would be reading works such as *The Third Wave* and *Megatrends* should be cautious and "avoid capitalist spiritual pollution."[63]

Even more significantly, on February 14, 1984, an internal propaganda directive attacked the ideological implications of "internal discussions as well as open reporting" on Toffler. "The so-called Third Wave is not a scientific concept," the directive stated. "To make use of it when setting forth the party's policies is inappropriate, and likely to create ideological confusion."[64] Despite having "reference value," the propaganda directive explained, "the concept Toffler created is not a purely scientific or technical one, but one used to express laws said to govern the development of society . . . formulated in opposition to the theory of social revolution that describes the victory of socialism over capitalism, and the victory of the proletariat over the bourgeoisie. It is clearly meant to supersede this theory."[65] Most fundamentally, this denunciation showed the remarkable seriousness with which the CCP viewed Toffler's ideas, for good or for ill. Second, significantly, it criticized on ideological grounds a specific concept that had been championed by China's premier, underscoring the pervasiveness of the ideological concerns discussed in Chapters 2 and 3. Although the propagandists attempted to limit their criticism of Zhao by excusing his October 9 speech as using Toffler's ideas only for "reference value," this justification was superficial because the speech was clearly designed to influence policy outcomes. Third, the propaganda attack sought to fundamentally dispute the vision of the future implied in Zhao's response to Toffler's work. At a time of great open-endedness about ideology, the economy, technology, and politics, the introduction of a concept that might "supersede" the Marxist "theory of social revolution" was a serious risk. The battle over *The Third Wave* was thus not only a battle over a foreign text or S&T policies; at bottom, it was also a fight over China's future.

As a result, in early 1984 *The Third Wave* was temporarily banned.[66] Shortly thereafter, Ma Hong spoke to a meeting of provincial officials and walked back his endorsement of what he now called the "currently popular so-called 'Third Wave.'" Toffler's and Naisbitt's works "do not support and even oppose Marxism." Ma said that he had been deeply troubled by an unacceptable comment made by a graduate student at Peking University. "Marxism is out of date," the student had said, adding, "Toffler's *Third Wave* is the most correct way of thinking."[67]

Yet even as Ma criticized *The Third Wave* in public, he continued to work behind the scenes on Zhao's Toffler-influenced policy initiative. On February 23, 1984, the SPC submitted a draft document to the Central Finance and Economics Leading Small Group (CFELSG) on the seventh five-year plan, which included a short section on the New Technological Revolution that highlighted Ma and Zhao's work.[68] Ma's group, the State Council Technological and Economic Research Center (TERC), delivered an initial report on its research to Zhao and the CFELSG on March 13. The report discussed strategies for helping China to "jump" stages—that is, move directly to a third-wave economy without going through a lengthy process of industrialization. That spring, the Central Committee and State Council also held a series of twenty lectures on the subject of the New Technological Revolution and specific technologies, including microelectronics and biotechnology.[69] Soon thereafter, the State Council formally approved implementation of Ma's agenda. This initiated the next stage of work to encourage key new technologies (again, microelectronics and bioengineering were the most prominent examples), align traditional industries and emerging industries, and "jump" developmental stages.

Participants at these meetings, intoxicated by what one called "a great ideological liberation," bandied about fantasies of China's future: A group of young officials imagined having the capacity, by the PRC's centenary in 2049, to clone people and re-create the exact scene that had filled Tiananmen Square when Mao spoke on October 1, 1949. As the political atmosphere warmed, this official attention also led to a surge of popular interest in futurist ideas. The prohibitions of the Chinese edition of *The Third Wave* were relaxed, and the book rocketed to bestseller status. As many as 1 million copies were printed between 1983 and 1988. This extraordinary interest became known as "Toffler fever" or "Third Wave fever."[70] Naturally, Toffler was delighted to learn of this from his Chinese correspondents. On February 21, 1984, Toffler wrote proudly to inform Jan Berris, vice president of the National Committee on US-China Relations who had helped him follow developments in China, "Our efforts have not been wasted."[71]

◇

The Chinese leadership's initiatives to respond to the New Technological Revolution continued apace. In April 1984, a State Council report on the sectors of critical importance to China's development highlighted "information technology, space, aviation, and nuclear technologies" and emphasized the importance of any military technology also being "dual use," meaning that it would also have civilian uses. Premised on the belief that "large-scale war" was unlikely, Deng Xiaoping emphasized in November the need for military technology to serve economic development and "concentrate on civilian products."[72] All technological development, even in the military-industrial base, was being put toward the purpose of "speeding up" modernization, defined as the economic and technological level of the "developed countries."[73]

For Zhao and other senior Chinese officials, the long-term success or failure of China's economic transformation increasingly seemed inextricable from this New Technological Revolution. Discussing the seventh five-year plan on September 12, 1984, Zhao said that in the period ahead, "the rapid transformation of information technology and the increasingly wide range of applications, such as making bioengineering practical, new materials, new energy sources, and marine engineering, will cause great breakthroughs in some areas and open up new applications, allowing the global New Technological Revolution to enter a new stage. Our economic development strategy must develop policies to respond."[74] Several days later, at a meeting of the State Council, Zhao declared, "We can use the experiences and results of the New Technological Revolution to allow our traditional industries to leap over several development stages and attain a new technological level" to propel China's economic development in competition with the rest of the world.[75]

The leadership also promoted a series of organizational changes. The State Council established a leading small group on the electronics industry, explicitly targeted at "meeting the global New Technological Revolution" in the "information industry." This new group, replacing an older group on computing and circuitry, was led by Vice Premier Li Peng, alongside the SSTC's Song Jian, Minister of Electronic Industries Jiang Zemin (a future CCP general secretary), and other officials.[76] Chinese officials hosted foreign technology firms—for example, Vice Premier Wan Li met with IBM executives in 1984.[77] In 1985, a National Patent Law was issued, even though China's intellectual property protections would remain weak. By the end of 1985, under this new law, 13,573 patent applications were filed, approximately 60 percent of which came from domestic filers and 40 percent of which came from foreign sources. Furthermore, more than a quarter of the total output of defense factories went to civilian consumption in 1984, and several popular consumer goods sold in China—from motorcycles to cassette tapes—were primarily made in defense factories.[78]

The initiative that Zhao had developed during the preceding year had become a central part of the official agenda. These ideas were enabling S&T expertise to speak directly to economic concerns and to influence the direction of policy debates. The CCP Central Committee's Decision on the Reform of the Economic Structure, issued on October 20, 1984 (which endorsed the "planned commodity economy" concept, as discussed in Chapter 5), prominently featured "the emerging global New Technological Revolution."[79] At a speech delivered to the National S&T Work Conference on March 6, 1985, Zhao emphasized that the Soviet Union, Eastern Europe, and "some capitalist countries" were all reforming their S&T systems. A week later, on March 13, the Central Committee announced the Decision on Reform of the S&T Management System, which changed organizational and funding structures and shifted more researchers from state institutions to enterprises to propel economic development.[80]

As Zhao's reference to the Soviet Union indicated, the late Cold War context shaped the Chinese leadership's sense of the potential stakes of the New Technological Revolution. The Soviet Union's scientific and technological prowess earlier in the Cold War era—symbolized by the launch of Sputnik 1 in 1957 and including Nobel Prize–winning research in nuclear physics and chemistry—had helped its attainment of superpower status. However, the reality by the mid-1980s was that the intensive progress of the early Cold War period had grown diffuse and sluggish. In computing, for example, excessive quantities of computerized information rendered Soviet cybernetic systems inordinately byzantine, and numerous unsuccessful large-scale projects had undermined the leadership's enthusiasm for further investments. As Zhao feared, the Soviet Union was not moving as swiftly to develop information technologies.[81] After Mikhail Gorbachev became general secretary of the Communist Party of the Soviet Union in 1985, he issued calls that were similar to Zhao's and he even explicitly referenced developments in China and elsewhere in Asia as part of an international "whirlwind of changes—social, scientific, and technological."[82] International comparisons intensified these leaders' sense of urgency in the mid-1980s, just as ideas from abroad had shaped Zhao's initial vision.

Beyond the halls of Zhongnanhai, technological changes inspired entrepreneurs to "jump into the sea" of business, as the saying went. The computing company Stone Corporation is one prominent example. On May 16, 1984—just a few months after Apple launched its first Macintosh personal computer in the United States—a group of technicians spun off a firm in Beijing's university district from CAS, with a start-up loan of RMB 20,000 from a government group. The firm focused on word processing software for Chinese characters, while working with Japanese firm Mitsui to purchase printers that could use the software. In 1985, Stone grew to over 170 employees and it set up a store in Beijing's Zhongguancun area, which was becoming a hub for high-tech firms. Success was extraordinarily quick. By 1988, Stone held approximately 80 percent of the market for word processors in China, generating over RMB 830 million in annual sales.[83]

Popular interest in futurist ideas and advanced technology also continued to widen. Many scientists and engineers became figures of public fascination as their contributions to China's modernization received flattering attention in the official media.[84] Toffler's popularity also continued unabated; for example, in Changsha, over 13,000 copies of *The Third Wave* sold in the first half of 1985.[85]

Within just a few years, the Chinese leadership had raced from Deng's call to raise China's level of scientific expertise and technological development to a far-reaching vision of how technological change, driven by information technology, was sweeping the globe. Despite debate and contestation, Zhao and his advisers believed deeply in the urgency and opportunity of this "revolution." Yet by 1985, they had not yet determined how best to respond in a more coordinated and comprehensive way to this New Technological Revolution and ensure that China was not left even farther behind. They would soon implement a series of sprawling new initiatives to turn these expansive ambitions into reality.

CHAPTER 7

A Matter of the Life and Death of the Nation

The Chinese leadership's intensive fixation on advanced technology in the mid-1980s soon produced a concrete agenda based on the premise that China's technological catch-up was, as one directive put it, "a matter of the life and death of the nation."[1] Chinese elites presented science and technology (S&T) as intimately connected not only to economic development and military modernization but also to the nature of China's system and the fate of socialism. As new voices used the status conferred by their scientific expertise to make bold, often controversial, claims about China's future, China's rulers launched a project to use new technologies to modernize rural China and, most significantly, a massive state program melding the civilian and military research apparatus to fund emerging technologies from automation to biotechnology to satellites.

Reflecting the existential stakes, in 1985 Zhao Ziyang tasked Ma Hong, as one of his senior-most advisers, to oversee the next stage of this work via the State Council Development Research Center (DRC) (which succeeded the Technological and Economic Research Center).[2] Yet some voices began to use the leadership's focus on S&T to raise other matters that they felt affected "the life and death of the nation." Outspoken figures such as historian of science Xu Liangying and physicist Fang Lizhi were leading scholars in prominent institutions at the vanguard of China's response to the New Technological Revolution. In the model of Soviet dissident scientist Andrei Sakharov, these figures deployed their profession's tradition of skepticism and rigorous assessment to critique China's system; the CCP claimed to be "scientific" in its principles and its governance, and these scientists sought to put that proposition to the test.[3]

China's leading scientists rubbed shoulders in elite institutions like the Chinese Academy of Sciences (CAS), the University of Science and Technology in Hefei, and academic seminars around the country. Xu Liangying, for one, had trained as a physicist, worked at CAS for many years, and translated Albert Einstein's writings into Chinese. Mentored by Wang Ganchang, who helped design China's first atomic bomb, as well as the prominent academician Yu Guangyuan, Xu called academic freedom "a necessary condition for human progress." In the tradition of the 1919 May Fourth Movement, he saw science and democracy as symbiotic.[4] His friend Fang Lizhi, who became vice president of the University of Science and Technology in 1984, became an even more outspoken critic of the regime (as described in Chapter 3). Fang toured the country delivering speeches that criticized socialism, Marxism, and the CCP. "Knowledge should be independent of power," he asserted.[5]

Of course, most scientists did not aspire to become critics of the regime. They remained focused on research, development, and the enormous economic opportunities that the drive to modernize had presented. Some, such as quantum field theorist He Zuoxiu, became tenacious advocates of the CCP as representative of scientific development. Dismissing the criticisms of figures such as Xu and Fang, He Zuoxiu argued that Marxism-Leninism should guide research in the natural sciences.[6] For other intellectuals, the emerging "information era" seemed to validate Marx's understanding of technology. Su Shaozhi, liberal-minded director of the Chinese Academy of Social Science's Institute for Marxism–Leninism–Mao Zedong Thought, wrote with his student Ding Xueliang that Marx had understood over a century earlier how new technologies affected the nature of labor and the conditions of workers, which was once again occurring as society shifted toward "informatization," "intellectualization," and the "New Technological Revolution."[7]

As early as 1985, prescient voices in China also began to realize the significant potential of new information technology for governance of society and ideology—a dynamic that built on the leadership's existing interest in applying cybernetics and systems engineering to governing. Indeed, the Decision on Reform of the S&T Management System of March 1985 stated, "With the vigorous development of the global New Technological Revolution, S&T have increasingly penetrated into all areas of society's material life and spiritual life. S&T have become an important source of improving labor productivity and an important cornerstone for the building of a modern socialist spiritual civilization."[8]

As Chinese society became "increasingly penetrated" by new technologies, the CCP would have to stay current in its efforts to "build a modern socialist spiritual civilization"—meaning, China's ideological and political order under CCP rule, as discussed in Part I. For others such as Su Shaozhi, it was important for "Marxist methodology" to absorb "new developments in systems theory, cybernetics, and informatics" to help China understand how new technologies would transform society.[9] Criticizing the excessive "optimism" of Alvin Toffler and his Chinese acolytes, Su said that CCP needed to figure out on its own terms how to respond—politically, economically, technologically, and ideologically—to the changing "social system" in China. If it did so successfully, Su said, "Quite a few Third World countries which tried in vain to follow American or European ways [may] be swayed towards the Chinese model."[10]

As the criticism of Toffler's excessive "optimism" indicated, Toffler's influence was troubling for scientists and intellectuals of many stripes. A survey of college students in 1986 revealed that 78.6 percent of respondents said that they had read *The Third Wave*.[11] Fang Lizhi criticized futurology and Toffler's *Third Wave* as utopian, Christopher Buckley writes, "idealizing science as an easy escape from China's long-standing social and economic problems."[12]

Far more common, however, were critiques of Toffler's ideological orientation. In 1986, a team of theoreticians produced a book titled *Critiquing the Third Wave*, which criticized Toffler's "anti-Marxist" analysis of society and the future.[13] This critique was prominently featured in a report on integrating the New Technological Revolution with Marxism to ensure that people did not feel that global technological advancements meant that Chinese socialism was "out of date."[14] These critiques of Toffler, from opposite ends of the Chinese political spectrum, made clear that the relationship between S&T and the future of China's modernization was contentious and profoundly unresolved.

◇

As Chinese scientists and intellectuals debated these fundamental questions, China's rulers launched a new effort to bring the New Technological Revolution to more parts of China. The Spark Program, which the State Science and Technology Commission (SSTC) rolled out from mid-1985 to early 1986, focused on using new technology to accelerate rural development. As discussed previously, decollectivization of agriculture had transformed China's countryside in the late 1970s and early 1980s—increasing agricultural output and gross domestic product per capita but showing limited improvements in the lives of poor, rural people, some of whom looked back nostalgically to the people's communes. The Spark Program aimed to use new technology to improve the rural economy, in particular by prioritizing technological applications that could quickly be commercialized. With an initial budget of RMB 2.26 billion, the majority of which was provided by local governments, the plan sought to create more technologically sophisticated enterprises in China's vast countryside, train workers, apply new cultivation methods and genetically engineered crops, and produce more advanced equipment.[15] On December 7, 1985, Zhao wrote to Tian Jiyun, "S&T must serve the rural economy, and the rural economy must rely on S&T to further develop and improve."[16]

A 1986 conference in Chengdu to reflect on the Spark Program's first year featured celebratory speeches by Song Jian and Yang Jun of the SSTC, Du Runsheng of the Rural Development Group, and Wu Mingyu, the official who had led development of the program. They highlighted the technological modernization of the Chinese countryside and noted proudly that the World Bank and European countries had expressed interest in helping to fund the program in the future. The conference encouraged S&T personnel to move to small- and medium-sized cities and rural areas to set up firms, with preferential loans from banks and government agencies to cover their initial costs, in order to enrich the countryside. The conference affirmed that the Spark Program was "not a temporary solution but a long-term basic policy," with a fifteen-year plan. Some of these goals were quixotic, but the plan extended more advanced technologies into communities that would not otherwise have gained access to them.[17]

While promoting the deployment of advanced technology in rural China, the leadership also implemented "protectionist" policies to shelter the emerging Chinese electronics industry. Vice Premier Li Peng stated in mid-1986, "China should rely mainly on its own products to push ahead with the modernization drive instead of importing large amounts of foreign equipment."[18] This included decisions to restrict imports of integrated circuits and other favored domestic products. Regarding semiconductors, for example, state planners in 1986 sought to promote an indigenous microelectronics commercial and manufacturing base, though this industry would continue to struggle in the years ahead.[19]

China's emergent class of technology entrepreneurs largely supported these policies designed to protect their industries, but some strongly disagreed. Wan Runnan of Stone Group delivered a searing speech on the "protection of China's information industry" in 1986 at a conference organized by Deng Nan, deputy director of the SSTC's Science and Policy Department (and Deng Xiaoping's daughter). Wan Runnan began his remarks by saying that he had heard many officials and businesspeople talking positively about protectionism because of China's "backwardness," which necessitated giving Chinese firms time to develop and reach international standards. However, Wan believed that protectionism was actually one cause of "the backwardness of China's information technology and industry," using the metaphor of a young child that had long outgrown its pacifier. "We must create a level playing field in China," he said. Calling Stone Group "China's IBM," Wan argued that technological advancement would be stymied without "fierce market competition."[20] Despite this brash call to eliminate protectionism, the leadership moved ahead with these policies and the others that had developed under

Zhao's supervision, which were about to receive an important boost from Deng Xiaoping himself.

◇

The most significant policy to result from the ferment surrounding futurist ideas about the "third wave" and the New Technological Revolution was the 863 Program, a flagship government initiative that provided billions of renminbi in funding to important projects including advanced computing and aerospace technology and has been called "China's premier industrial R&D program."[21] The conventional narrative of the program's origins ascribes the motivating force to Deng and, in line with the CCP's deliberate effort after 1989 to sideline Zhao in the historical record, largely erases Zhao's role. Foreign scholars have followed the conventional narrative about Deng's role because they have unavoidably relied on distorted Chinese source material. New sources now allow scholars to remedy that problem. Additionally, the conventional narratives often overlook the rich debate about S&T and economic development discussed in these chapters.[22]

The 863 Program was proposed to Deng Xiaoping in a March 3, 1986 letter from four prominent Chinese scientists, Wang Daheng, Wang Ganchang, Yang Jiachi, and Chen Fangyun. Their letter described the New Technological Revolution, emphasizing the need to invest in seven key areas: biotechnology, space technology, information technology, laser technology, automation (including intelligent robotics), energy technology, and materials engineering.[23] Deng's handwritten response on March 5 was emphatic: "This proposal is very important. Comrade Ziyang should take charge of this and find some experts and comrades with relevant responsibilities to discuss it and make suggestions, which can be the basis of our decision-making. We should make a decision on this matter right away and must not delay."[24] Deng assigned Zhao the task of making the initiative a reality—a logical assignment given that Zhao had been leading the effort to respond to the New Technological Revolution. The 863 Program was continuous with Zhao's efforts earlier in the 1980s rather than a radical shift in the leadership's orientation. Many of the best scholarly accounts have even quoted what turns out to be a censored version of this note from Deng, which entirely omits Zhao's name and assignment.[25] But the fuller story centers on Zhao as well as Deng.

On March 8, three days after receiving Deng's instruction, Zhao met with the SSTC's Song Jian and informed him of the "great importance" that Deng attached to the proposal. The State Council would lead a process to develop ideas drawing on both military and civilian technologies before reporting to the Standing Committee. Noting the need to compete with the United States, Western Europe, and the Soviet Union, Zhao instructed Song to organize a "capable team" and produce a preliminary plan by August. The overarching priority would be for Chinese scientists to domestically develop cutting-edge technologies, though international cooperation and technology acquisition would continue. Zhao would subsequently suggest that the project be labeled the "863 Program," reflecting the proposal's March 1986 date.[26] The New Technological Revolution, Toffler's ideas, and Zhao's development-focused agenda were the foundation on which the 863 Program was built—with Zhao continuing to coordinate the SSTC, CAS, and the State Planning Commission (SPC), among other government institutions, to develop and implement this strategy.

On March 22, Zhao called a meeting of the senior officials who were newly responsible for the 863 Program. The assembled group included Ma Hong and Song Jian as well as officials from the SPC, the Commission for Science, Technology, and Industry for National Defense (COSTIND), and other agencies. Zhao framed their challenge in long-range terms, differentiating this initiative from the five-year plans by emphasizing that these goals targeted "the end of this century" and even "the next century." The 863 Program would focus initially on several still-embryonic priority areas. First, Zhao discussed efforts already under way on space weapons, explaining that such research would allow them to use the resources and manpower available in this military research "to promote China's high-tech development." Second, Zhao tasked the assembled group to determine which areas should be prioritized, and he suggested a focus on bioengineering. Third, Zhao discussed the process that he wished to see govern the project. He emphasized the need for interdisciplinary work, stressing that the organization and workflow should be "horizontal, not vertical. . . . Otherwise, we'll spend a lot of money and not produce major results." Similarly, he requested that the group develop an efficient appropriations and funding system. Zhao promised to remain personally engaged in the new program.[27]

Zhao envisioned the 863 Program as an arena for actualizing his ideas about the potential benefits of S&T for China's future. Meeting with a large group of scientists regarding the 863 Program on April 7, Zhao reminded the scientists of his personal role in developing this vision of China's response to the New Technological Revolution. Zhao underscored an additional point: "The development of advanced technology is not an end in itself" but rather must always aim at ultimately "serving economic construction" and "China's modernization." Furthermore, he acknowledged that it was not yet possible to know exactly what technologies would best serve this goal, contrasting this situation with the Mao era's strategic weapons program, when "everyone could just focus on the two bombs" program (i.e., nuclear weapons and ballistic missiles). This new program would use vast resources to promote domestic innovation, while also deploying new management systems and studying foreign technologies, under Song Jian of the SSTC as well as Ding Henggao of COSTIND. Drawing on both the civilian and defense establishments, the initiative's guiding philosophy would be, in Zhao's words, "civilian and military integration, placing civilian interests first."[28] It inherited the legacies of decades of past S&T drives but responded to the New Technological Revolution and futurist ideas with a broad initiative designed to last well into the twenty-first century.

In line with these objectives, a new push for "civilian and military integration, placing civilian interests first" got under way, with strong exhortations from Deng Xiaoping and Minister of National Defense Zhang Aiping.[29] A significant shift was in process, with civilian production rising from 8 percent of the total annual output of the defense-industrial base in 1979 to fully 62 percent in 1986.[30] Although these figures are remarkable, the boundary between "civilian" and "military" was porous. Many firms "conducted commercial and defense-related activities simultaneously," as Tai Min Cheung shows: "Production lines were often located next to one another within the same plants, and workers could be assigned to civilian or military projects depending on demand." But the next year, in 1987, a contracting system was extended to the defense sector, with enterprises now required to negotiate contracts, profits, and timetables with People's Liberation Army departments.[31] Well beyond the 863 Program, the prioritization of economic development was continuing to remake China's defense-industrial base. Official propaganda trumpeted that China had formed a "modern defense technology system" thanks to these efforts, although realities on the ground lagged behind this upbeat rhetoric.[32]

By the late summer of 1986, work on the 863 Program had progressed significantly. On September 25, nearly seven months after Deng received the four scientists' proposal, Zhao submitted a letter that informed Deng Xiaoping of fifteen projects developed by a team of 124 experts. By the end of the century, Zhao estimated, no less than RMB 10 billion would be required for the 863 Program.[33] On October 6, Deng responded affirmatively. To garner maximum consensus, Deng instructed Hu Yaobang to review the plan, followed by Chen Yun, after which the entire Politburo would discuss it. The initiative and its projected budget of RMB 10 billion were quickly approved.[34]

Deng seemed very pleased with the 863 Program. Several days later, on October 18, he told Chinese American Nobel laureate Tsung-Dao Lee and Italian physicist Antonino Zichichi, "I am a layman in science, but I am enthusiastic about promoting its development. China cannot advance without science. . . . We have only just begun the modernization drive. We shall probably have made considerable progress by the end of the century and even more notable progress 30 or 50 years after that."[35] With these remarks, Deng underscored the centrality of the 863 Program to China's future. He did not praise Zhao by name, but the lineage of these new policies was clear. The task of responding to rapid global technological change, which futurist writings had crystallized for Zhao, had become a long-term strategic initiative of the Chinese leadership.

Implementation of the 863 Program proceeded rapidly. Its funding reflected Zhao's priorities: nearly a third of the total funding went to biotechnology and approximately a quarter went to information technology.[36] After student protests in the winter of 1986–1987 led to the ouster of Hu Yaobang and Zhao's promotion to acting CCP general secretary, Zhao remained so closely associated with Toffler that a fresh round of attacks on the American futurist served as proxy assaults on Zhao's promotion.[37] Chinese officials and enterprises continued to promote the transfer of technology to China from the United States, Japan, Germany, and other developed capitalist countries. As they had since the late 1970s, China's rulers pursued American and other foreign technology, even while promoting "protectionism" and attempting to build up domestic industry—using any and all means to catch up.

From the US perspective at the time, technology transfer to China was a matter of tremendous mutual benefit, and successive administrations had worked to promote it despite the Coordinating Committee for Multilateral Export Controls (CoCom) and other restrictions. The Office of Technology Assessment (OTA), established by the US Congress, studied the low level of technological development in China and argued that "one of the most important influences that the United States has is technology transfer." OTA offered a strong dose of profit-seeking pragmatism, advising American companies that winning significant orders in China sometimes required "a willingness to transfer the technology of materials and manufacture"—citing General Electric, which received two large locomotive contracts in exchange for giving Chinese enterprises production capacity, and the aerospace firm and defense contractor McDonnell Douglas, which coproduced "25 MD-82 twinjet transports with the Shanghai Aviation Industrial Corp., following a sale of five to China."[38] The Chinese were eager for this technology, and as the decade went on, the United States remained willing to sell as much as CoCom would allow.[39] China's response to the "global New Technological Revolution" depended on help from leading powers around the world.

In the summer of 1987, Zhao's work on S&T policy received a sharp push from Deng Xiaoping, who was repeatedly complaining publicly that China still "lagged behind."[40] Thus, at a meeting on a wide range of economic and development topics on July 7, Zhao ordered, "The question of S&T revolution, and the question of technological progress, must also be combined with reform measures. . . . In the Work Report of the Thirteenth Party Congress, we must include this content." Zhao concluded dramatically, "How to promote future technological progress is a matter of the life and death of the nation."[41] Despite creating the 863 Program and advancing research in this area, Zhao clearly felt that the stakes were higher than ever, and the 13th Party Congress needed to treat S&T as a priority.

Shortly before the congress, directives went out calling for greater propaganda focus on S&T work. The 13th Party Congress, one notice stated, will "make economic construction truly turn to the path of re- lying on S&T progress." Echoing Zhao's language, it declared that S&T affected the entire project of national modernization and is "a matter of the life and death of the nation." The reason for this rhetoric was the same sense of urgency that Chinese leaders had long voiced: "The situ- ation of rapid development of the global New Technological Revolution" meant that "if we do not grasp the opportunity and catch up, our gap with the developed countries in the economic and technological do- mains will grow larger."[42]

The Chinese leadership remained fixated on the risk that the fast- moving technological revolution would allow "developed countries" to race ahead and leave China further behind. Despite a decade of inten- sive work, this prospect remained fearsome. Technology occupied a central place in how China's rulers imagined and pursued modernization in China in the 1980s—both as an engine of development and a way of en- suring the long-term survival of "the nation." For China's rulers, the goal of growing wealthy and powerful would remain unattainable without it.

PART IV

POLITICAL MODERNIZATION

◆

THE CHALLENGE of modernizing China's political system produced profound disagreements throughout the 1980s. As Chinese
leaders and intellectuals looked back on the catastrophes of the
Cultural Revolution and Mao's personality cult, they saw a "backward" and broken political system that needed to be "modernized."[1] But what would political modernization mean?

This section examines the wide variety of proposals that developed in and around the senior leadership during the 1980s. Officials and intellectuals argued about democracy, socialism, and
the nature of power. This remarkably vibrant debate drew on
both domestic lineages and international comparisons. Most fundamentally, it was premised on a central idea: Reforms of the political system were deeply connected to reforms of the economic
system. The CCP has exerted great effort to suppress this idea, as
we shall see, but it was a crucial part of the story of China in the
1980s. The history of political reform chronicled here is among the
most important legacies of this period.

Although the visions of leading officials, intellectuals, and ordinary people often differed—as did their tolerance for change—nearly
all agreed that transformation of the economy necessitated

political changes. Some political changes would enable or support the market reforms by forcibly pulling back centralized control or giving new legal protections to commercial activities. Other changes responded to problems that the economic reforms exacerbated, such as corruption and inequality.

That is not to say the cause of political modernization was purely utilitarian. It also included debates about liberalization and democratization that were idealistic and asserted the superiority or universality of certain freedoms and rights—what Wei Jingsheng had called the "Fifth Modernization" of "true democracy," as discussed in Chapter 1, including "the right of the people to choose their own representatives."[2] Theorist Su Shaozhi quoted British politician Lord Acton, in a line that would frequently be invoked throughout the decade: "Power tends to corrupt, and absolute power corrupts absolutely."[3] Other voices argued that alongside its unprecedented economic transformation, China could also build a novel form of "socialist democracy." At times, Deng Xiaoping himself even supported this goal, pledging "to create a higher form of democracy that is superior to capitalist democracy."[4]

Despite this intellectual ferment, Deng's main priorities for the political system were limited, and his understanding of "socialist democracy" was narrow. He sought to open up greater room for debate and autonomous decision making when it served his ends, but in general, his objectives were to increase the efficiency of administration, decentralize authority to foster local initiative, recruit and promote more talented professional officials, and create legal and institutional structures that would facilitate economic development. Even so, he was willing to consider new ideas and at certain moments, such as 1980 and 1986–1987, showed a real interest in bolder experimentation. He seemed aware, at those moments, that there was a gap between the critiques that he articulated of an inefficient, self-serving, and unresponsive political system and the moderate solutions that he proposed.[5]

Yet other top officials pursued policies that extended far beyond Deng's vision. For Hu Yaobang, Zhao Ziyang, and Wan Li (and even, at times, elders such as Peng Zhen, who led the party's Central Political and Legal Affairs Commission, and younger leaders like Hu Qili), the need to transform China's political system was much greater than Deng understood. These figures sought to advance major structural changes: separating the party and the government, building up more independent institutions of the media, the judiciary, and the legislature, and increasing transparency, accountability, and even freedom of speech and debate. Especially in the latter half of the decade, some senior leaders also sought to significantly increase checks and balances on China's governing institutions.[6]

Political reforms were hotly contested. Forcing cadres to retire and imposing new financial constraints on the bureaucracy directly affected entrenched powerholders. Most fundamentally, China's rulers gravely feared instability after the tumult of the Cultural Revolution. They were determined to avoid losing control again. Those fears of instability were not static but constantly developed in reaction to events at home and abroad—from Poland to the Philippines, from the Soviet Union to Taiwan.

Debates about the political system sought to balance "democracy" and "dictatorship." For many officials, these were not contradictory concepts. The CCP's "democratic traditions" grew out of the Leninist system of democratic centralism, which aspired to lively internal policy discussions combined with total unity in policy implementation after a decision was made. The concept of "democracy" (民主) was not synonymous with American or European notions of liberal democracy, though at times Chinese thinkers (such as Wei Jingsheng) were clear that they had liberal democracy in mind. The term *democracy* had first been translated into Chinese in the late nineteenth century as part of the efforts to reform the Qing dynasty, but the CCP made the term its own. In January 1940, Mao Zedong offered his populist conception of "New Democracy," contrasted with the "Old Democracy" of the West, which represented only the interests of the bourgeoisie. China's new system, led by the CCP, would ensure "a proper expression of the people's will [and] a proper direction for revolutionary struggles," with freedom for "the people" and repression for "enemies of the people." During the Cultural Revolution, as his cult of personality pervaded everyday life, Mao sought to create "great democracy" by assaulting the CCP itself as a privileged bureaucratic class—leading to brutality and chaos. The CCP turned away from this form of "democracy" after Mao's death, but what it would embrace instead remained uncertain. With the rejection of the Fifth Modernization and the crackdown on the 1978–1979 democracy movement, the leadership offered the Four Cardinal Principles: keeping to the socialist road, upholding the dictatorship of the proletariat, upholding the leadership of the Communist Party, and upholding Marxism–Leninism–Mao Zedong Thought. But the CCP continued to describe itself as seeking to expand democracy as well.[7]

Some officials, such as Hu, Zhao, and Zhao's chief aide Bao Tong, experimented with even more sweeping changes, pursuing increased efficiency in the short term and an ambitious longer-term vision of "socialist democratic politics," involving significantly greater public participation, accountability, and debate than had occurred under existing socialist systems. Bao said, "No mechanism can always make correct decisions, but there is a kind of mechanism that can correct its own mistakes. Democracy is that mechanism."[8] This was democracy to them—not necessarily nationwide elections or a competitive multiparty system but a more open, transparent, self-correcting mechanism for governance.[9] Put another way, Chinese officials and intellectuals asked whether they could achieve the benefits of concepts like "checks and balances" or "separation of powers" without directly embracing these ideas, which were anathema "Western" democracy, or sacrificing what they saw as the distinctive advantages of Communist Party leadership. This section brings to fuller light this process of debate, experimentation, and contestation between 1980 and 1987, when plans for the 13th Party Congress gave enormous official support to an ambitious vision for political system reform, preparing for the next stage that was designed to follow the congress and speed up thereafter.

Examining anew the debates over political modernization in the 1980s goes to the heart of why that period matters and how its legacies have evolved. In seeking to understand these debates, we should analyze their aspirations and visions of China's modernization rather than only seeking to assess their effectiveness or implementation. After all, many of the plans drawn up beginning in 1986 were left unfinished after 1989, even though some bottom-up experiments in governance continued in the 1990s and 2000s.[10] Moreover, it is crucial to underscore that these debates should not be understood teleologically: they were not inevitably unfolding toward either the 1989 Tiananmen protests or their brutal repression. Those involved in the debates sought to reimagine the Chinese political system without knowledge of where the decade would end.

These stories remain little known because of the secrecy in which many of the leadership's debates and experiments were conducted, which made their erasure from history after 1989 even easier. Of course, we have long known that intellectuals were writing about political reform in China in the 1980s and that the leadership made some public statements and introduced some policies to reform the political system.[11] What has been less visible until recently is the secretive exploration that occurred within the leadership itself in the latter part of the decade. Wu Guoguang, who worked on these issues in the government, writes that the leadership's debate over political reform "almost totally happened behind closed doors." Zhao Ziyang called this work "very sensitive," and CCP elder Peng Chong told the officials leading it to "please pay attention to keeping it secret."[12]

The questions of political system reform debated in the 1980s and the policy experiments undertaken matter immensely to understanding that period's history as well as its legacies. "China did indeed undergo a political reform" in the 1980s, Bao Tong has reflected, but these reforms suffered two deaths. First, they were killed by the events of 1989. Second, "all traces have been erased from official materials."[13] It is time to return this story to the center of our understanding of China's transformations.

CHAPTER 8

Masters of the Country

On August 18, 1980, Deng Xiaoping gathered the Politburo to discuss one of the most sensitive topics that any Chinese leader could address: reforming the party and state leadership system. "Some of our current systems and institutions in the party and state are plagued by problems," Deng declared. "Unless they are conscientiously reformed, we can hardly expect to meet the urgent needs of modernization."[1]

Deng's call for reforming political "systems and institutions" was more complex than it may initially seem. His goals were intensely practical, motivated by political needs as well as a desire to address the disaster of the Cultural Revolution. But in doing so, he gave voice to criticisms of China's political system—and principles to guide reform—that would reverberate far beyond his initial aims.

In 1980, Deng was looking for ways to further undermine the power of Hua Guofeng. Deng's strategy was to critique what he characterized as "feudal" legacies in the top leadership, such as holding multiple posts at once, ruling in a personalistic, arbitrary style, and lifelong tenure—and even, by implication, naming one's own successor, as Mao had done with Hua.[2] The leadership also believed that addressing the problems in the political system could foster popular support, which had been badly damaged in Mao's later years. Deng Liqun worked to prepare Deng's August 18 speech with several thinkers who were experts on the political structure, such as Liao Gailong, a researcher in the Central Committee's Central Policy Research Office, who prepared the first draft. Liao had grander ambitions for the speech, seeing an opportunity to endorse a more open and responsive political system while also advancing Deng Xiaoping's concrete goals in the realm of elite political maneuvering.[3]

On August 18, Deng began his speech by announcing a series of personnel changes—making clear the highly practical nature of what he would be discussing. Hua Guofeng would cease to serve as premier, retaining his party titles, and would be replaced by Zhao Ziyang. Elders such as Li Xiannian, Chen Yun, and Deng himself would be replaced by "more energetic comrades" as vice premiers, though the elders would hold other positions. Deng explained that these decisions had been taken to avoid an "overconcentration of power," end the practice of senior officials holding multiple posts concurrently, stop unduly giving governmental duties to the party, and help solve the problem of succession by shifting responsibilities to Hu Yaobang and Zhao Ziyang's generation and those even younger.

These statements would have made this speech significant on their own, but Deng was just getting started. With the many upheavals of CCP history in mind, Deng diagnosed five major problems: bureaucratism, the excessive concentration of power, patriarchal methods of leadership, lifelong tenure in leading posts, and the existence of special privileges. China had overemphasized centralism and unified thinking and placed too little emphasis on "any assertion of independence." The system needed to undergo a significant change: "The errors we made in the past were partly attributable to the way of thinking and style of work of some leaders. But they were even more attributable to the problems in our organizational and working systems. If these systems are sound, they can place restraints on the actions of bad people; if they are unsound, they may hamper the efforts of good people or indeed, in certain cases, may push them in the wrong direction."[4] These were sweeping arguments for what he called "planned, systematic, and thorough reforms" of the political system, with the full weight of Deng's prestige and authority behind them.

Despite this serious diagnosis, the remedies that Deng prescribed were relatively limited. Amendments to the People's Republic of China's constitution strengthened state organs, prevented an overconcentration of power, and promoted collective leadership. The power of the State Council, now to be run by Zhao Ziyang, was increased so that the government could take on more responsibility from the party. At lower levels, Deng committed to implementing long-promised policies to enhance worker representation and collective decision making. The most controversial area that Deng touched on was making experiments to increase the responsibility of factory managers relative to party committees, and similar reforms to the role of university presidents, which would limit the party's power, but these were still mostly notional. Deng concluded by emphasizing that his commitment to the leadership of the CCP was unwavering.[5] Deng was willing to articulate a powerful and principled critique of China's political system, but his priorities for action were personnel changes and undercutting the power of Hua Guofeng without weakening the CCP and its control of the country.

Following discussion and editing, Deng's speech was circulated nationwide in early September 1980 as Central Document No. 66. A range of officials and intellectuals took it as a sign: The time had come for ambitious new thinking about China's political system. On September 19, for example, the Theory Bureau of the Propaganda Department met to discuss the speech. A report on the meeting documented a remarkably open discussion of China's political system and the importance of learning from "political management systems and methods" in capitalist societies. Intellectuals founded the Chinese Political Science Society, translated foreign texts, and debated actively.[6]

One scholar-official, Liao Gailong (who, as noted above, had helped to draft Deng's August speech), went further than most. In a report at the Central Party School on October 25, 1980, Liao declared that the party should remove itself from the economy, culture, and the media, and China should permit an independent press and a more independent judiciary. He also called for the National People's Congress (NPC) to be refashioned into a bicameral legislature that would not be a "rubber stamp" but rather could meaningfully represent the interests of society. Liao's ideas extended well beyond the boundaries set out by the Four Cardinal Principles the prior year and came to be shorthanded as the "*gengshen* reform" proposals.[7] Momentum was building fast to move beyond Deng's speech and extend the open-ended spirit of the economic reforms to the immense task of remaking the Chinese political system.

As these proposals bubbled up, a series of alarming bulletins arrived from Poland. Workers had been striking in Gdańsk since mid-August, protesting price increases, economic crisis, and limited civil rights. On August 31, the strikers reached an agreement with the government that would permit the existence of trade unions independent of the Communist Party and promote the freedom of speech and publication. They created an officially recognized union called Solidarność, or Solidarity. On September 6, the first secretary of the Polish United Workers' Party resigned under pressure.[8]

The upheaval in Poland was reported in China's state-run press, and some activists in China seized on the coincidental timing of Deng's speech a few weeks earlier. Liao called for creating independent labor unions in China to prevent worker unrest or "the same things will happen to us."[9] Dissident voices, preserving the waning energies of the 1978–1979 democracy movement, went even further. "None of the so-called socialist countries can any longer ignore the existence of Poland's Solidarity," exulted the Qingdao-based radical socialist magazine *Banner of Theory,* calling for "a revolution against the system of feudal bureaucracy that has ruled China for the last two thousand years and is substantially unreformable."[10] These dissident voices used concepts from Deng's speech—criticism of feudalism and bureaucracy—and the triumph of Solidarity to call for "revolutionary" change in China, a far cry from the moderate measures for political reform that the leadership had endorsed.

These events in Poland initially divided the top leadership. Hu Yaobang and Deng Xiaoping both initially saw a positive example of a socialist country resisting the Soviet Union, but other senior leaders were startled by these events' resonance in China. A few days after Solidarity's establishment, senior CCP ideologue Hu Qiaomu wrote a letter to Hu Yaobang warning, "The combination of a small number of dissidents and dissatisfied workers together can become such a huge force." However, making a comparison to the uprisings of 1956, Hu Qiaomu prom-ised that if the Chinese leadership responded adequately, "the misfor-tunes of others can be turned into a blessing for us."[11] Hu Yaobang permitted this letter to be circulated to the top leadership, and in early October, director of the Propaganda Department Wang Renzhong of-fered forceful support for Hu Qiaomu's view. "We have similar problems to Poland, and their development will have the same consequences," Wang said, ordering an end to propaganda about Deng's speech on re-form of the system of party and state leadership.[12] Chen Yun soon added his voice to the warnings about Poland: "If our economic work and pro-paganda work are not handled well, a Polish incident may occur."[13] These concerns quickly dampened the lively discussion of political ideas that had followed Deng's speech.

As the trial of the Gang of Four began on November 20, China's rulers prepared two significant documents that were, according to Deng Liqun's recollections, specifically designed to avoid the occurrence of a "Polish incident" in China.[14] One was a forceful speech that Deng Xiaoping de-livered in December 1980 on the necessity of ensuring stability, unity, and adherence to the Four Cardinal Principles. Second, in January 1981, the Central Committee issued a secret "Decision on the Current Propa-ganda Guidelines for Newspapers, Periodicals, and News Broadcasts." This decision made explicit reference to Deng's December speech but not to his August speech and required all publications to "maintain uncon-ditional political unanimity with the central government."[15]

The burst of enthusiasm that followed Deng's call for political reform in the summer of 1980 revealed the powerful desire among many people—from the topmost ranks of the party leadership to radicals and dissidents—for significant changes to China's political system. But the potent fear of instability, crystallized by events in Poland, shut down those discussions by early 1981. It would be five years before political system reform returned to the top of the leadership's agenda.

Debates about political modernization continued, but they were more muted and constrained. This was also the result of specific orders from the Propaganda Department to conduct discussion and criticism of ideas about political reform internally rather than in the public eye. On March 25, 1981, a guideline addressed the example of students and workers who "have proposed to establish a 'multi-party system' as well as 'independent labor unions' and 'independent student associations'": "This type of problem should not be publicly criticized in the newspapers, so as not to attract more people to pay attention to these problems . . . [or] make foreigners think that there is a great market for these notions and think that the current political situation in China is unstable."[16] The CCP knew how to use invisibility as a weapon; by controlling the media and not publicizing criticism of problematic political ideas, it would minimize their influence domestically and internationally.

Chinese intellectuals continued to analyze and debate the political system, even if in more restrained tones, exemplified by an essay on "democratic authority" in *People's Daily* by liberal theorist and official Li Honglin, who advised his readers "not to be afraid of democracy."[17] Some of the priorities that Deng had articulated in August 1980 did move ahead. Hu Yaobang took the lead in addressing "feudal" political practices, with particular focus on the cult of personality. In a speech on June 29, 1981, he ordered the propaganda apparatus "not to engage in propaganda worshipping individuals."[18] He raised the importance of a "division of labor" between party and government and focused on improving "party work style" and "political life," terms that broadly referred to intraparty governance. He also terminated the position of CCP chairman, instead bringing back the less exalted role of CCP general secretary, and introduced new guidelines in 1982, stating, "Before the party rules and state law, everyone is equal, and the party will not allow any party members to go beyond the law and party rules." The leadership even initiated some experiments with terminating party committees in factories, enterprises, and research and educational organizations—one of the most controversial proposals in Deng's August 1980 speech.[19]

The area of greatest activity in 1982–1985 was in the domain of administrative reform. At a Politburo meeting on January 13, 1982, Deng demanded massive layoffs and reorganization of the bureaucracy while promoting and hiring younger leaders.[20] Education levels were a source of additional concern; in 1982, among party secretaries at the county level nationwide, only 4 percent were college educated, and the vast majority had not graduated from junior high school.[21] In March 1982, the NPC approved a significant "organizational reform" of the State Council, which clarified responsibilities, implemented promotions and retirements, and downsized the number of ministerial-rank departments. It also eliminated lifetime tenure and imposed age limits on many positions. Over 30,000 cadres retired during the following year.[22] By the 12th Party Congress in September 1982, the CCP also created a body known as the Central Advisory Commission (CAC), which Deng promised would give "elderly comrades who have retired from the forefront of affairs" a position to hold after they left the Central Committee.[23] Despite these institutional reforms, these semiretired "elderly comrades" of the CAC would remain a powerful force.

More broadly, the 12th Party Congress enshrined Hu Yaobang's priorities of promoting a larger role for law in governing China and stricter legal constraints on party members and organizations. In November, a new state constitution was passed by the NPC, which wrote the Four Cardinal Principles into its preamble while also increasing the power of the NPC and announcing term limits of two consecutive five-year terms for top government positions.[24] Following the congress, educational efforts ramped up for party members to "study and abide by the Constitution."[25]

Despite these reforms, the larger questions about the flaws in China's political system that Deng had raised in August 1980 remained extremely sensitive. When the Selected Works of Deng Xiaoping was published in 1983, the Central Secretariat struggled to find a writer who would publicly praise Deng's August 1980 speech in print. Deng's speech was mentioned by name only once in People's Daily in 1984 and zero times in 1985. Deng himself seemed comfortable deprioritizing these statements as the economy grew; he would decide if the time was right to return to them.[26]

However, some voices intensified their calls for greater intellectual freedom and faster political reforms. After many years of preparatory work, Yan Jiaqi established an Institute of Political Science at the Chinese Academy of Social Sciences in 1985 to study politics with "scientific attitudes and methods." In March 1985, gifted writer Liu Binyan—a longtime state journalist who had been denounced during the Maoist period before returning to work in 1979—published an incendiary essay that described two types of "loyalty": one that stresses "obeying orders" and "the approval of superiors" and another that is independent minded and seeks truth and justice at any price. The notion of an alternative source of individual meaning, social purpose, and moral clarity, different and better from "loyalty" to the edicts of officialdom, remained profoundly subversive in the mid-1980s. Soon after the essay's publication, the magazine in which it had appeared, *Pioneer,* was banned.[27]

What did Hu Yaobang and Zhao Ziyang think about all this? Both men had played a role in implementing aspects of Deng's vision in his August 1980 speech—with Hu taking the lead on ending certain "feudal" practices in the party and Zhao overseeing administrative reforms to government bodies. Later in the decade, events would certainly prove that both men harbored more ambitious visions for political system reform. Yet, as late as 1985, neither Hu nor Zhao had pushed significantly beyond the acceptable range of discourse set out in Deng's speech, and their records were significantly more complex than what is indicated in many subsequent accounts, which sometimes seek to portray both men as ardent reformers or even inborn liberal democrats.

Zhao, for one, endorsed "the methods of dictatorship" and "using dictatorship against our foes" on numerous occasions.[28] Throughout his career, Zhao displayed open-mindedness to new ideas about the political system but primarily when those ideas served his cause opportunistically. During the Cultural Revolution, while Zhao was party secretary of Guangdong, three intellectuals—Li Zhengtian, Chen Yiyang, and Wang Xizhe—wrote essays under the pen name Li Yizhe that criticized the Cultural Revolution's radical faction. Zhao fostered these debates initially, seeing political value in giving voice to sentiments that were widely shared but that a sitting official could not openly endorse. The Guangdong leadership's attitude changed only when the writers called for democracy and rule of law, at which point Zhao organized written criticisms and reported the authors to the central leadership.[29] However, Zhao was strongly supportive of Deng's August 1980 speech. On May 26, 1984, Zhao encouraged Deng to take further measures to institutionalize the proposals that he had made in August 1980, citing a window of opportunity while Deng and Chen Yun were "still energetic and in good health" and could "personally inspect and seek compliance," but Deng took no immediate action.[30]

Even Hu Yaobang, who had done so much to encourage intellectuals and reform the party's "work style," emphasized not freedom of the press, but the need to focus on upholding party leadership in news reporting.[31] Hu remained tenaciously focused on reorganizing the party and fostering more "scientific" decision making, but he also felt stymied in his efforts to promote retirements to make room for new leaders. As early as 1984, according to Li Rui's recollections, Hu confided that he was willing to retire at the 13th Party Congress in 1987 in order to also push out other officials who were refusing to step down as they aged, such as Hu Qiaomu and Deng Liqun.[32] Questions of personnel and institutionalization were at the top of Hu Yaobang's agenda for the National CCP Conference in September 1985, which was accompanied by many retirements and new appointments, hailed as the "orderly transfer of power to a new generation of officials."[33]

Hu's focus on improving the party had an insidious enemy that seemed to be growing more pervasive by the day: corruption. A series of scandals battered the leadership as officials were found to be committing fraud, embezzling money, and taking bribes. As a political problem, this went well beyond the ideologized attempts to "strike hard" against economic crimes earlier in the decade (see Chapter 2). Some of the most egregious cases were committed by the children of prominent leaders, such as Hu Qiaomu's son who was arrested for fraud after reportedly embezzling 3 million yuan. Certain regions received particularly intense attention; the southern island of Hainan, for example, was the locus of a major "profiteering scandal" that led to the firing of at least three top officials and investigations reportedly involving eighty-eight of the island's ninety-four administrative departments.[34] At a party mobilization conference on January 6, 1986, Zhao said optimistically, "We are fully capable of eradicating the phenomenon of corruption."[35]

Corruption was not explicitly connected at this stage to official discussion of political system reform. Instead, it was a fixable, localized problem that sat at the nexus of party work style and socialist spiritual civilization. It was discussed publicly, despite the obvious sensitivity, because at this point, it was not seen to be "systemic," and the leadership wanted the Chinese people to know that it was taking action.[36] Ideas about reforming the political system remained low on the leadership's list of immediate priorities.

By January 1986, some officials and intellectuals were looking back longingly at that brief moment of opportunity in 1980 as their frustration with the leadership mounted. It remained possible, at least, to study the problems that Deng had identified. A group of graduate students in the Central Party School's Theory Department in mid-1985 started a research group on political reform, which conducted county-level surveys, with particular attention to the division of labor and responsibility between the party and the government.[37] A few defiant voices saw a regime sinking ever deeper into political inertia, corruption, and hypocrisy. Su Shaozhi, the outspoken director of the Institute of Marxism–Leninism–Mao Zedong Thought, told a foreign journalist in a private conversation in 1985, "We need to make a clean sweep of the leadership."[38]

From the perspective of the Chinese leadership, however, pressures for political change seemed to be growing fast. All around China's periphery, a wave of protest, revolution, and liberalization surged ahead. In late February 1986, the "People Power" revolution in the Philippines toppled longtime dictator Ferdinand Marcos, who fled into exile—a bloodless overthrow that, although reported in Chinese state media and formally accepted by the Ministry of Foreign Affairs, was precisely the kind of insurrection against ossified, unjust rule and widespread corruption that the CCP feared. The Chinese leadership had been monitoring discontent in the Philippines; a classified report from immediately before the uprising described factors including wealth inequality, Marcos's nepotism, and the suppression of dissent that were "increasing people's dissatisfaction with the government."[39] On March 12, another secret report was circulated to the leadership that concluded, "The facts of the collapse of the Marcos regime have revealed that dictatorship and power politics do not win the people's hearts."[40] The implications for the CCP were alarming.

Then, on March 31, Taiwan's politics began a dramatic shift when the Kuomintang's (KMT) Central Committee decided to explore political reforms. An opposition party—the Democratic Progressive Party—was formed on September 28, 1986, with KMT leader Chiang Ching-kuo's permission. On October 5, Chiang said, "The ruling party must push reforms according to new ideas, new methods, and based on constitutional democracy." On October 15, the KMT Central Standing Committee lifted the ban on political parties and announced the end of decades of martial law. As in the case of the Philippines, these events were reported in Chinese state media, and Beijing's reaction was formally positive—and in this case, of course, it was shaped by the CCP's continuing claims to "reunifying" with Taiwan.[41] "Jiang Jingguo [Chiang Ching-kuo] is now also pushing for political reform in Taiwan," Zhao Ziyang's chief of staff Bao Tong said. "We should do our reform better than he."[42]

In this same period, China's largest neighbor, the Soviet Union, was also presenting significant political reforms to the world. On February 25, 1986, at the opening of the 27th Congress of the Communist Party of the Soviet Union, Mikhail Gorbachev hailed the "new political thinking" in the spirit of democratization and transparency. An assessment circulated to the Chinese leadership on March 19 was sternly critical of the Soviet Union, in keeping with the antagonistic relationship between the two powers. Yet its list of causes for the Soviet political ossification— from the "rigidity of management forms and methods" to "the growth of bureaucracy"—were strikingly similar to the problems that Deng Xiaoping had emphasized in August 1980. An attached report elaborated on the intense discussions of "stagnation," "bureaucracy," and "social injustice" at the Soviet congress, making clear that Gorbachev had committed to "enter a new era" and "remove resistant cadres."[43] In the system on which the CCP had modeled itself, significant political reforms were under way, due to deep-seated problems that, in many cases, China's leaders believed that they shared.

This wave of changes on China's periphery was profoundly unsettling to China's rulers. In the Soviet Union and Taiwan, leaders had chosen to launch political reforms to save—and transform—their regimes. In the Philippines, by contrast, Marcos had refused to liberalize and lost "the people's hearts." Unless China could find another way forward, the choice for the CCP seemed stark: reform or perish.

CHAPTER 9

Explore without Fear

Watching this international wave of political liberalization, Chinese intellectuals saw a singular opportunity to test the waters anew for more open discussion of political system reform. "Modernization and democratization are the objectives of our struggle. Reform of the economic and political systems is a way to reach this end," Su Shaozhi wrote in 1986. "What we need now is to explore without fear."[1] Some Chinese leaders agreed. In an internal discussion in late March, Hu Yaobang urged greater freedom to discuss political topics. "If there is no democracy, there is no socialism, nor socialist modernization," Hu said. "If the opinions of the people cannot be heard, we will finally collapse."[2]

Encouraged, a range of scholars organized conferences and convenings in April and May 1986 on questions of political reform.[3] They knew that they were taking significant risks, even more than their counterparts in the economic domain, but that great possibility also existed for influencing debate at the highest levels.

These were gatherings of members of the establishment, not dissidents.[4] One such conference was convened by the Chinese Academy of Social Sciences (CASS) on May 16–17, 1986 with "enthusiastic arguments" by a group of senior researchers, academics, and mid-level government officials. Participants prioritized two goals: first, addressing the "excessive concentration of power" and second, "establishing a highly democratic political system" by fostering popular participation and "checks and balances" through a stronger legislature, judiciary, and mass media. Most fundamentally, the participants agreed that the definition of "modernization" needed to be expanded beyond the economic and technological domains to encompass changes to the political system.[5] All around the country, intellectuals began to speak out with verve, making international comparisons and linking economic and political change by asserting that successful economic development required a more open and responsive political system. What was at stake in these intensifying discussions of China's political system went beyond politics to the future of China's modernization agenda.

Some senior members of the leadership, building on Hu Yaobang's statements in March and these bold proposals in circulation, also began to tread into the sensitive realm of political reform. On May 1, 1986, celebrating International Workers' Day, General Office director and Politburo member Hu Qili delivered a lengthy speech on China's future in which he pointedly added "political reform" to the list of his top priorities, harkening back to Deng Xiaoping's August 1980 speech.[6] A week later, People's Daily ran a front-page commentary titled, "Without Socialist Democracy There Is No Socialist Modernization." This commentary explicitly connected the long-standing discussion of "correcting party work style" to increasing the power of the people relative to party cadres, based on "the right to criticize and monitor" the party—all as a way to "release the enthusiasm and creativity hidden among the people" and propel China's modernization.[7]

For the intellectuals and officials who had been discussing political reform ideas, this call for greater "socialist democracy" was profoundly encouraging. The year 1986 was celebrated as the thirtieth anniversary of the "Hundred Flowers" campaign of 1956. That call for intellectual openness and debate had been followed by a crackdown on critics of the regime; in 1986, Minister of Culture Wang Meng (a prominent writer who had been labeled a "rightist" in the Mao era) called the prior campaign a "dream that did not come true." Now many intellectuals hoped that the CCP had truly begun to embrace the benefits of a reformed political system.[8]

Deng Xiaoping, Zhao Ziyang, and Hu Yaobang had been closely following these emerging discussions but had not given authoritative guidance as the focus on political reform swelled anew. On June 10, at a briefing on economic affairs with Zhao Ziyang, Hu Qili, Yao Yilin, Wan Li, and others in attendance, Deng unexpectedly raised "the problem of political system reform." Perhaps he was prompted by seeing Hu Qili for the first time after the latter's May 1 speech, or perhaps he simply had become frustrated that the bloated bureaucracies were stifling economic growth. Whatever the reason, Deng called for "decentralizing our power"; after years of relative inaction on political system reform, the time had now come to "place it on the agenda," or else the lack of progress would "hinder the reforms."[9] Deng raised these issues again at a meeting of the Politburo Standing Committee on June 28, pointing to "the relations between the party and the government, [and] the country's political system" as a question that should be raised at the 13th Party Congress to be held the following year. Deng called for a year of investigation and planning to commence immediately. He pointed to several principles that should guide their efforts. First was "the separation of party and government," seeking ways to delineate domains of responsibility and policy. Second, Deng forcefully emphasized that future political reforms were inextricable from the economic reforms. They were "interdependent and should be coordinated," he said. "In the final analysis, the success of all our other reforms depends on the success of the political reform."[10]

Importantly, Deng still had a limited set of goals: streamlining the bureaucracy, increasing initiative at lower levels of the party and government apparatuses, and most of all, finding new ways to unleash economic initiatives to promote development and growth. His unexpected return to political reform drew on the discussions among intellectuals that had begun earlier in 1986, but he did not emphasize a more expansive rethinking of the Chinese polity. Former official Wu Wei has reflected that although Deng spoke about political system reform more than a dozen times in 1986, he "did not touch on reforms to promote socialist democracy, open up freedom of speech, guarantee people's fundamental rights, or reform the judicial system."[11]

Yet Deng was not the only figure who would determine the meaning of political system reform. His remarks served to give the topic the unparalleled imprimatur of the paramount leader, and he explicitly called for a year of work on the subject. For a wide range of officials and intellectuals, this launched a fervid summer of political debate and exploration.

Additional voices from the central leadership extended the call for political system reform. Zhao Ziyang publicly signaled the leadership's rationale in early July: "With the economic system reforms in full swing, government functions will change, and government institutions and the cadre system must also be reformed step by step . . . to adapt to the requirements of the economic system reform."[12] The Central Party School convened a symposium on political reform on July 10–12, which featured over 100 attendees, from officials such as director of the Propaganda Department Zhu Houze and economic official Chen Yizi to intellectuals such as Gong Xiangrui and Gao Fang. Zhu urged the attendees to examine areas in which the political system was impeding the "continued development of the economic system reform."[13] These wide-ranging explorations received a further boost a few days later at the graduation ceremony at the Central Party School, when Organization Department head Wang Zhaoguo delivered a speech that placed political system reform on nearly equal footing with economic reform and he encouraged the graduating officials to prioritize it in their work.[14]

The boldest extension of the top leadership's renewed focus on political system reform came from Vice Premier Wan Li. On July 31, at a national conference on "soft science"—meaning the social sciences—Wan delivered a speech that went far beyond Deng's line the prior month. "Leaders should be encouraged to exchange views, swap information, and discuss problems with research workers, experienced people, and men of broad knowledge on a regular, equal, and democratic basis," and even "make close friends with some dissidents," Wan said. The "soft sciences" should be "relatively independent and . . . must not be adjusted to fit the expression of the leaders," he said, calling for legislative protections for policy researchers.[15]

These statements alone were an unusually strong message of support for bold, boundary-pushing research. But Wan was not done. He continued to critique China's lack of "adequate support systems for policy consultation, appraisal, supervision, and feedback" so that "it is often too late when a decision is found to be seriously wrong." The only way to address these persistent shortcomings, he said, was a radical shift:

> I think we should remove the ban on free expression and encourage the free airing of views. We should let people really exercise their constitutional right of free expression. . . . This large socialist country of one billion people won't be brought down by a few unpleasant words or inciting remarks.[16]

Wan Li's speech was published on the front page of *People's Daily* on August 15, 1986, taking up the entirety of the front page above the fold. According to official Chinese sources, upon reading the speech, Deng Xiaoping declared, "Very good, publish it in full!" Chen Yun also praised the speech for "solving an important issue that our party has not been able to solve for many years." Wan Li's message was not that of a radical intellectual or an outsider to the system. It was a message from a vice premier broadcast to the public through the party's mouthpiece.[17]

China's intellectuals were exhilarated. Prominent activist intellectuals such as Hu Ping, Fang Lizhi, and Liu Binyan praised Wan Li for opening up the realm of permissible debate in the true "Hundred Flowers" spirit. Wan Li invited Liu to meet with him at Zhongnanhai; Liu recalled that Wan told him, "A party is doomed if it doesn't tolerate differing views."[18]

Momentum continued to build. On August 30, the front page of *People's Daily* featured an official commentary headlined, in large type: "Political Questions Can Be Discussed." The commentary used a series of metaphors to explain the changes under way:

> At the gate [guarding the discussion] of political questions, it seems that a warning was posted: "Please keep your mouth shut." As a result, many people were intimidated, bowed their heads, and walked away. Comrade Wan Li's speech at the National Symposium on Soft Science Research has torn down this warning. This is undoubtedly very important for the improve-

ment and development of socialist democracy. . . . In the new socialist China, the people have become masters of the country. Is there any reason to forbid them from researching, discussing, and arguing about political questions that relate to their own interests? All power belongs to the people.

Although it emphasized continued adherence to the Four Cardinal Principles and suggested that free debate should be more limited after policy decisions were made, this commentary nonetheless was a startling extension of Wan Li's bold speech. It concluded, "Allowing the broad masses of the people to discuss politics is not simply not contradictory to these [Four Cardinal Principles], but in fact is exactly what is required to adhere to these principles." For intellectuals, officials, writers, or ordinary people who had survived decades of political movements, this was an extraordinary moment of possibility, with fundamental aspects of China's political system seemingly thrown open.[19]

China's magazines, journals, and newspapers were flooded with audacious writing. Although debate was fierce, one point of significant agreement during this period was that economic reform and political reform were strongly connected. Separating party and government functions was the most obvious connection because it meant granting greater autonomy to many government bodies, including state-owned firms. Prominent economist Li Yining, an advocate of reforms to the ownership system for China's enterprises, wrote from the perspective of an economist, "Political system reform and economic system reform are actually integrated."[20]

The connections between political and economic reform were ubiquitous, but Chinese intellectuals, particularly those with ties to the leadership, were sensitive to suggestions that China was exploring political reform only to unseat vested interests that were opposing the economic reforms, as a commentary in Selected Internal Reference noted in late summer 1986.[21] Other voices raised concerns that tying the political and the economic too closely might lead to suboptimal outcomes for political reform. At an academic seminar in October 1986, several participants argued that any political system reform proposal should be developed on its own terms rather than based on what would benefit economic reform.[22]

Commentators across the intellectual spectrum agreed that the overconcentration of power remained a serious problem in China's political system. A brashly independent Shanghai-based newspaper, *World Economic Herald,* ran a front-page essay in July 1986 reproducing and analyzing Deng Xiaoping's 1980 speech on political reform. The paper's commentary on the speech stated that the "overconcentration of power," meaning "inappropriate and indiscriminate concentration of all power in party committees," had reached "intolerable levels."[23] Su Shaozhi said, in even harsher tones, that "the first thing we should solve" is the "dogma" of "the overwhelming and absolute leadership of the party."[24] Critiquing the overconcentration of power had initially seemed like a narrow bureaucratic question that could be solved by streamlining and delegating authority to lower levels. However, these arguments in 1986 made clear that it could also become a critique of the CCP's "overwhelming and absolute" political dominance.

The goal of dividing up overcentralized power ran through many other proposals, including to expand the power of the people's congresses and enhance the role of the "democratic parties" and the Chinese People's Political Consultative Conference, a body composed of these minor political parties that banded together under the CCP's leadership in the "United Front." For others, the only path to permanently changing the system of overcentralized power was to promote attention to law, an independent judiciary, and especially the constitution. Su Shaozhi even suggested a new Constitutional Court, which was an unusual notion because most proposals in this period sought to use existing institutions, such as the people's congresses, the democratic parties, and the legal system, to achieve new goals—namely, separating the party and the government, decentralization, and legal constraints on political power.[25] For the most part, these thinkers were seeking to radically reconfigure China's political system with what already existed.

As these ideas about a stronger legislature and judiciary suggested, some officials and intellectuals were considering ideas that resembled a separation of powers.[26] Wei Haibo, a scholar at the Shanghai Academy of Social Sciences, called for the leadership to study "bourgeois democracy" and "form a system of 'checks and balances' among the legislature, administration, and judiciary" that had "been proven by history to be an important measure in preventing the restoration of feudal dictator-ships," in line with Deng Xiaoping's goals.[27]

To be sure, not all intellectuals saw "bourgeois democracy" as worth learning from. Another Shanghai-based scholar, young law professor Wang Huning, wrote in darker tones about Western political systems. Dismissing the notion of "political pluralism," Wang wrote that Western democracy was a sham, awash with money, and representing only "the interests of the monopoly bourgeoisie."[28] Later in the decade, Wang would become a central figure in developing the ideas of "neo-authoritarianism." (He subsequently entered the government and, as of this writing, is a member of the Politburo's Standing Committee and leads the CCP Sec-retariat.) Even scholars like Wang who did not believe that China could emulate Western political models were committed to envisioning new ways for China to develop a modernized political system.

Deng Xiaoping had gotten far more than what he expected when he called for investigation into political system reform. This diffuse, free-wheeling wave of debate about the political system needed structure and leadership, and he turned to Zhao Ziyang to provide it. First, on Sep-tember 3, Deng said publicly, "Whenever we move a step forward in eco-nomic reform, we are made keenly aware of the need to change the political structure."[29] The Secretariat also held a publicly announced session to study Deng's August 1980 speech. Internally, Deng issued marching orders, once again in the context of a meeting on economic policy. On September 13, 1986, at a meeting of the Central Finance and Economics Leading Small Group, Deng called for drawing up a plan for political system reform to be launched at the 13th Party Congress. His top priority was "separating the party and the government and deciding how the party can exercise leadership most effectively," followed by giving more power to local authorities and streamlining the adminis-trative structure. Reflecting the ferment of the past several months, how-ever, Deng also emphasized what was not permitted: neither "imitating the West" nor "liberalization" would be allowed. Deng assigned the de-velopment of this plan to Zhao.[30]

Zhao immediately sprang into action. On September 18, Zhao met with Hu Qili, Tian Jiyun, and Bo Yibo and decided to establish a cen-tral group on political system reform, composed of the four of them plus

Peng Chong, who was vice chairman of the National People's Congress's (NPC) Standing Committee and led its Legal Committee. This group would thus represent the Secretariat, State Council, Central Advisory Commission, and NPC. It was to be a "discussion group" that did not have decision-making authority; it would "explore ideas and design blueprints for political system reform" for the forthcoming congress in 1987. They also decided to establish a small office under their five-person group, which would manage this work, study a wide array of domestic and foreign materials, hold conferences, and produce internal reports. This office would be led by Zhao's chief of staff, Bao Tong, along with CASS scholar Yan Jiaqi and System Reform Commission official He Guanghui (who was Bo Yibo's former secretary). Zhao set two goals for their work: promoting China's "long-term stability" and accelerating China's modernization. On September 23, Zhao sent this work plan to the rest of the Politburo Standing Committee, which approved creation of this new Central Research Office on Political System Reform (CROPSR).[31] Just as he had done with economic policy and technology policy, Zhao took an instruction from Deng and created an intellectual network with his trusted adviser, Bao Tong, at its center.

Bao Tong recruited experts who were knowledgeable about the Chinese and foreign political systems or who had built up policymaking experience, including Hu Yaobang's aide Zhou Jie, Central Committee researcher Chen Fujin, originator of the gengshen reform proposals Liao Gailong, People's Daily editorial staffer Wu Guoguang, and Bao's soon-to-be secretary Wu Wei. Chen Yizi, who had worked on rural reform and other economic policy issues for Zhao, took up the daily administration.[32] The staff varied in seniority and radicalism, but their overriding belief was that they had been tasked with saving the Communist Party from itself. "The factors that can fundamentally shake our party's position now and in the future can't be born outside the party, but only within the party," Wu Wei has recalled that Bao said soon after CROPSR's founding.[33] There was no time to waste.

Even with such high-level backing, this work was extraordinarily sensitive. Bao sought to create a protected environment of internal intellectual openness combined with total external secrecy. At CROPSR's first meeting in early October, Bao told his staff, "Our research should proceed with no forbidden zones." However, he emphasized that whatever occurred inside their offices at 38 Di'anmen Street must stay confidential.[34] This work would prove so secretive that even the Beijing municipal leadership struggled to find out the ideas that were being discussed under Bao's aegis.[35]

From the start, fundamental issues emerged over the meaning and scope of political system reform. The five-person group of Zhao, Hu, Tian, Bo, and Peng met at Zhongnanhai on November 7–8, 1986, with staff in attendance. "When we discuss political reform," Zhao said, "we're not discussing whether the Communist Party should be in power, but rather we are discussing how the Communist Party should govern." Following Deng, the top priority was "rationalizing" the party-government relationship. But Zhao and his colleagues discussed a wide range of other goals: reforming the leadership system to address the excessive concentration of power; promoting institutionalization, decentralization, and increased efficiency; increasing intraparty democracy and the role of social organizations; and institutional reforms, including to the cadre personnel system.

At one point in the discussion, Bao Tong stated that the notion of a "tripartite separation of powers," as in the US model of executive, legislative, and judicial branches, "could not be simply rejected." Zhao—likely thinking back to Deng's orders that "imitating the West" and "liberalization" were impermissible—responded that such a separation of powers could not work in China. However, he encouraged Bao to "further develop the utility of the people's congresses" and acknowledged, "The beneficial things in Western countries' systems can be absorbed into our system." Although all the senior leaders reiterated to CROPSR members that they had total intellectual freedom to explore new ideas, it was clear that some concepts were unacceptable within the parameters that Deng had set.[36]

Following this meeting, the members of CROPSR prepared a letter that Zhao submitted to the Politburo Standing Committee, which offered an overview of their plans for developing political reform proposals ahead of the 13th Party Congress. "China's socialist system is good, but there are some major shortcomings in its leadership system," they wrote; after starting out as a revolutionary party, the CCP had still not fully become a governing party. Fixing this would require an array of changes, from separating the party and the government to strengthening intra-party democracy, the legal system, and institutionalization of rules and practices. The goals of this work were twofold: to adapt the political system to the tasks of governing in peacetime and to the needs of a "commodity economy."[37] With this letter, a process of investigation, imagination, and contestation began that would push the limits of the Chinese political system.

This work was almost derailed soon after getting under way. The student protests that rocked China in December 1986 also powerfully impacted CROPSR. Initially, as the protests began, the researchers reacted in a scholarly fashion—meeting with groups of workers and students to hear their views on political reform and seeing the protests as evidence of one of their theoretical contentions, namely that socialist society had different interest groups (distinct from their class nature). They watched carefully as senior officials offered internal assessments of the protests and their connections to the political reforms. On December 10, according to Wu Guoguang's recollections, Hu Qili stated, "Their zeal is praiseworthy, but their thinking is not clear." If the CCP accepted the students' demands, "the result will be chaos, not democracy." Senior ideologues such as Hu Qiaomu and Deng Liqun fully agreed.[38]

Even so, Deng Xiaoping's strident speech on December 30, 1986 (discussed in Chapter 3) shocked many CROPSR members, especially his harsh statements about the student protests as "bourgeois liberalization." When the group met to discuss Deng's speech and its implications, Bao Tong urged that their work proceed as planned. "Is there any big mistake in our work? Or is there any big change in the situation? No. . . . I will still go all out, trying to reform, working without any doubts."[39] After Hu Yaobang's removal, however, Hu Qiaomu and Deng Liqun targeted several CROPSR members during the initiative against bourgeois liberalization, including Liao Gailong and Yan Jiaqi, and the purges of figures such as Fang Lizhi and Su Shaozhi chilled the intellectual environment. In response, Bao Tong doubled down on the secrecy of CROPSR activities. This, in turn, meant that the content of their work would remain even less known outside of the central leadership.[40]

The full group chaired by Zhao met six more times to prepare for the congress, and CROPSR remained a hotbed of activity. Beginning in January, Zhao even invited Deng Liqun and Hu Qiaomu to attend some of these meetings.[41] Leading this work, Zhao was both a visionary and an opportunist.[42] Zhao initially had accepted Deng Xiaoping's narrow view but soon embraced a much farther-reaching set of reforms to the political system. His changing views were motivated primarily by his concern that the political system was impeding the success of the economic reforms by fostering corruption and abuse of power as well as by his desire to be seen publicly as an enlightened reformer. Zhao did not have multiparty democracy in mind, but his emerging priorities were numerous: to increase transparency, strengthen other political parties and social groups from labor unions to women's organizations, raise the number of appointments made through elections, protect citizens' rights, and entrench the separation of party and state, making the party "not be so controlling or so severe."[43]

This ambitious initiative to reimagine China's political system consistently sought to ensure that such work started from "the realities of China"—its historical experience, low level of economic development, and extraordinary size and scale. Those "realities" also included resistant cadres, a myriad of different interests, from enterprise managers to critical intellectuals, and of course, the limited tolerance of many in the leadership. As one CROPSR member put it, "Deng Xiaoping is China's biggest 'reality.'"[44]

Zhao and his advisers also knew that not every objective or experiment could be made explicit at the 13th Party Congress or even included in its public report. Much of their agenda would turn on what they could accomplish after the congress was held. They would consistently stress that their work was in line with Deng's vision, even when that claim stretched the truth. To this end, CROPSR employed a researcher who had been an editor of the *Selected Works of Deng Xiaoping* and could readily provide choice quotations from Deng's long career to pepper their proposals. Despite ostensibly deriving from Deng's August 1980 speech, the political reform agenda that developed ahead of the 13th Party Congress would go well beyond Deng's goals.[45]

CROPSR spent the first six months of 1987 developing its proposals. Facing these stringent constraints and "realities," its work constituted one of the most remarkable efforts to reimagine the Chinese political system in a long twentieth century shaped by repeated efforts at reform, revolution, and rejuvenation.[46]

The first task was a priority that even Deng had endorsed: separating the functions and responsibilities of the party and the government and reversing the excessive centralization of power in the central leadership. CROPSR members concluded that this would entail not only addressing the party's relationship to government bodies but also its relationship to enterprises and organizations in society: forbidding party officials from managing government work or holding government positions concurrently and abolishing party departments that had the same responsibilities as government administration (for example, in industry, trade, and urban planning). They also positioned enterprise reforms (discussed in Chapters 4 and 5) as an important test case for these priorities; the factory manager responsibility system both lessened the power of party committees in running enterprises and decentralized authority from central bodies such as the State Planning Commission to the firm level. They drew up plans for similar reforms at universities, schools, and research institutions, thus increasing the power of principals and university presidents. They even proposed marginalizing or fully eliminating party cells at many institutions.[47] Their goal was to increase the independence of more decision makers in the government, enterprises, and across society, diffusing power throughout the system and across the country.[48]

In line with the goal of separating the party and the government, CROPSR also developed a significant proposal for a new civil service system. Separate from the party organization, it would be based on rigorous testing, legal protections, and merit-based promotion. Although China had long traditions of civil service examinations and imperial promotion systems, Zhao and his advisers were more interested in international examples, including civil service systems in Japan and France as well as Taiwan. However, in assessing any comparative cases, Zhao emphasized that China's system would have to incorporate "political criteria" in addition to professional standards.[49] These changes sought to reorder China's massive bureaucracy, the actual apparatus of the party-state.

Well beyond these major reforms to existing systems, Zhao and his advisers also developed proposals for what Zhao called "opening up all kinds of permissible democratic consultation and lively social dialogue" as well as village elections, which was an area of significant activity in 1987, with elder Peng Zhen successfully steering through the NPC a proposal for the election of village committees. Even as the anti-bourgeois liberalization initiative raged, Zhao encouraged CROPSR to develop proposals for "grassroots elections" at both the county level and in schools.[50] Rather than "elections without choices," Zhao proposed differential elections—meaning a preselected slate of candidates more numerous than the number of positions—including for leaders of the provincial people's congresses and provincial governors and vice governors—to be voted on by all the delegates. "It is necessary to really have some democracy," Zhao urged. "I don't see any danger."[51]

For Zhao and his advisers, this difficult balancing act required strengthening the role of law and institutionalizing rules for party and government work. That included increasing the independence of the judiciary as well as the legal protections for the population, civil rights, and freedoms to publish and speak. CROPSR also continued to prepare proposals on boosting the legislative power of the NPC, enhancing the role of the "democratic parties," and even strengthening the trade unions that represented China's workers. "Criticizing trade unionism in the past has caused us to lose an effective link to the masses," Zhao said at a CROPSR meeting, with Bo Yibo agreeing. Despite the political risks of strengthening the legislature, other political parties, or trade unions, Zhao seemed confident that the CCP could maintain its leading role even with a more pluralistic political order. His goal, he recalled, was "a kind of distribution of power, so the CCP would not monopolize it all," even if the CCP was still in charge. "If there is no small chaos, there will be big chaos," Zhao said. "Society needs 'safety valves.'" These ideas seemed to be particularly influenced by Mikhail Gorbachev's reforms in the Soviet Union, which Zhao had asked CROPSR to study.[52]

The pieces seemed to be coming together for the 13th Party Congress. On April 7, state media announced that the congress would put forward a program for political system reform.[53] Three weeks later, when meeting with Zhao, Yang Shangkun, and Bo Yibo, Deng agreed to authorize the republication of his August 1980 speech to emphasize his personal investment and insulate the proposals from criticism when they were unveiled.[54]

Yet, as late as May 1987, the content of the political system reform proposals was still being hammered out, especially as CROPSR's more ambitious ideas were receiving significant internal pushback. On May 27, 1987, Deng summoned Zhao to his home after receiving a draft of the 13th Party Congress's work report. "We cannot imitate the tripartite separation of powers," Deng said sternly. "You all didn't write out that you want [that], but haven't you moved a bit in that direction?" Deng shifted away from this accusatorial tone: "The main issue is to enable administrative agencies to work more effectively and not to interfere too much with their work. When we decide something, we can just do it. This is our advantage, and this advantage cannot be lost. We cannot abandon dictatorship; we must not accommodate the mood of demanding democratization."[55] Deng's remarks were a blow to the work of Zhao and his advisers, who had expected their proposals to satisfy Deng's priorities and constraints while also fulfilling their own ambitious vision of a reformed political system. At Zhao's orders, Bao Tong and his staff sought to scrub their proposals of any "trace" of a three-branch system and separation of powers. Yet Zhao said that he still supported the reforms that they had prepared to strengthen the NPC, promote democracy, transparency, and rule of law, develop grassroots democracy and "social consultation dialogues" with the "democratic parties," trade unions, and other groups, and limit "the party's leadership to political leadership." Zhao emphasized, "We are not copying the system of checks and balances, but the issue of democracy cannot be avoided. . . . The report must talk about supervision by the people, about the guarantee of the people's rights, and about elections"[56] Zhao responded to Deng's feedback but did not entirely shift direction.

Even so, CROPSR moved to water down the language in the "General Program for Political Reform" for the 13th Party Congress's work report, making it vaguer and adding more material on the Four Cardinal Principles. If these statements seemed to contradict other explicitly stated priorities in the document, Zhao told the staff not to worry. One recalled that Zhao "felt that any contradictions on paper would be resolved by society." Yet Zhao also predicted serious challenges, particularly related to forced retirements and financial constraints, once they moved to implementing the reforms.[57] Zhao's difficult interaction with Deng Xiaoping had clearly reminded him of how immensely challenging it would be to move these proposals from the protected domain of CROPSR into the messy, resistant system that Zhao was trying to change.

As this process unfolded internally, CROPSR and its nationwide network of researchers churned out books and articles on political reform for public consumption. They anthologized officials' speeches on political reform, collected wide-ranging reports on comparative political systems, and convened a series of high-level conferences to discuss political system reform. The *New York Times* reported that summer, "The political ferment in China is as palpable as the economic progress."[58]

◇

On July 1, 1987—the sixty-sixth anniversary of the CCP's founding—*People's Daily* republished Deng Xiaoping's August 1980 speech on "the system of party and state leadership." It ran as a banner headline on the front page, accompanied by a photograph of Deng speaking in 1980; the complete text of the speech took up all of the newspaper's second page. It was accompanied by an editorial titled "Put Political System Reform on the Agenda," which Wu Guoguang had helped draft in consultation with Bao Tong and other CROPSR members. This editorial emphasized the interconnection of economic and political reform and provided a high-level overview of reforms involving the separation of party and government, decentralization, and the personnel system, while making only vague references to "fully mobilizing the enthusiasm of the grassroots and the people" that alluded to highly sensitive proposals such as expanded grassroots elections. Most of all, this major propaganda push to support political reform emphasized the urgency and opportunity of the upcoming 13th Party Congress: "Now it is time to put forward and solve this problem systematically."[59]

Yet it was clear that a fissure had opened up between Zhao's long-term ambitions for reforming the political system and Deng's enduringly narrow vision. On August 29, Deng met with leaders of the Italian Communist Party to brief them on the upcoming 13th Party Congress. "We have to proceed one step at a time, in a well-directed and orderly way," Deng said. "We cannot allow anarchy."[60]

A yearlong process at the highest levels of the Chinese leadership to develop proposals for remaking China's political system—building on nearly a decade of ferment, exploration, and new thinking—was on the verge of being approved by the 13th Party Congress. A transformation was in the offing. However, its fate would turn on whether Zhao's growing ambition could coexist with Deng's fear of "anarchy."

◆ Chinese leaders vote "yes" to the economic report submitted by Premier Zhao Ziyang (first row, lower left) at the National People's Congress in Beijing, 1981. In the second row (left to right) are Hu Yaobang, Deng Xiaoping, Li Xiannian, Chen Yun, and Hua Guofeng. AP Photo/LHS.

◆ Deng Xiaoping, Chen Yun, Chen Haosu, and Hu Yaobang in the lounge of the 11th National Congress of the Communist Youth League of China in December 1982. Apollo News Network.

◆ Hu Yaobang (left) and Zhao Ziyang (right) in Beijing. AFP.

◆ Ma Hong (front, third from left), Xue Muqiao (front, center), and other senior economists at Zhongnanhai, 1980. Courtesy of Xue Xiaohe.

一九八七年十一月七日合影 于中南海紫光阁

♦ Zhao Ziyang (center, seated) meets with the members of the Central Research Office for Political System Reform in Zhongnanhai in Beijing, 1987. BBC Chinese.

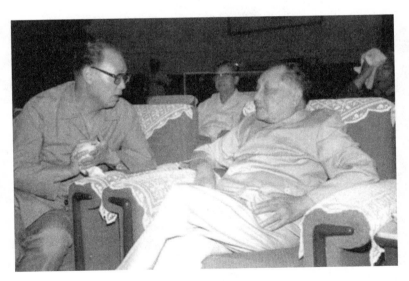

♦ Deng Xiaoping (right) speaks with Zhao Ziyang, 1987. EFE.

◆ **Xue Muqiao, Ma Hong, Li Kemu, and Wu Jinglian, 1985.** Courtesy of Xue Xiaohe.

◆ **Zhao Ziyang (right) speaks with Deng Xiaoping (left), 1987.** AFP.

◆ Zhao Ziyang with the Chinese and international press at the 13th Party Congress, 1987. FlorCruz Library.

◆ Yang Shangkun speaks at the memorial service of Hu Yaobang, with Zhao Ziyang, Deng Xiaoping, and Li Peng, 1989. Kyodo via Nikkei Asian Review.

◆ **Zhao Ziyang addresses protesters in Beijing on May 19, 1989.** AFP.

◆ **"Mourning turning into protesting," Tiananmen Square, 1989.** Photo by Edgard Huang. Indiana University Library Digital Collections.

改革开放的总设计师邓小平

◆ Poster of Deng Xiaoping billed as the "Chief Architect of Reform and Opening Up." Created by Chongqing Chubanshe, designer unknown, 1991. Stefan R. Landsberger Collection, International Institute of Social History, Amsterdam.

◆ **Zhao Ziyang poses for a photo in the garden of his Beijing home, April 17, 1990.**
Reuters/New Century Media and Consulting Co., Ltd.

◆ **The National Museum in Beijing celebrates the fortieth anniversary of "reform and opening" in 2018.** © Julian Gewirtz.

PART V

BEFORE TIANANMEN

◆

CHAPTER 10

Two Rounds of Applause

Applause washed over Zhao Ziyang as the 13th Party Congress came to an exuberant close on November 1, 1987. It had been a tumultuous year from the first days of January, which began with student protests and the firing of Hu Yaobang. But the party congress, held once every five years, had been a triumph for Zhao. He now officially took up the mantle of CCP general secretary, having outmaneuvered some of his bitterest rivals and pushed forward his favored policies. One participant recalled, "A new era seemed to be at hand."

In a break with convention, the sixty-eight-year-old Zhao held an unscripted dialogue with the press corps just after the congress's conclusion. One reporter recalled that he was "preternaturally tranquil" and "beamed with a relaxed confidence." A Japanese journalist asked about Zhao's double-breasted pinstripe suit, a notable variation from the Mao jackets that elders like Deng Xiaoping and Chen Yun wore. "Made in China," Zhao replied, with evident pleasure. "I hope that you can file a special report that Mr. Zhao Ziyang's clothes are all made in China and they are all very beautiful. This may promote the export of Chinese garments to your country." Zhao pointed out that members of his leadership team, including the new acting premier, Li Peng, were similarly attired. "They look smart, too."

Zhao held a cup of tea in hand as he took questions from the reporters, who pressed up in a scrum, holding out their tape recorders. Zhao spent an hour in the room, talking with the journalists and cracking jokes. He was making a point: a theme of the congress had been the importance of political system reforms and promoting transparency, and he was putting those principles into action while the ink was still wet on the announcements.

Another reporter asked him if there were factions in the leadership. "Why is there so much ado when there are differences in our views?" Zhao replied. "Different points of view will encourage democratization and ensure that we don't make mistakes."[1]

These were noble sentiments. The future of Zhao's "new era" would depend on whether they proved to be true.

◇

The 13th Party Congress of 1987 captured the state of play at the elite level of the myriad debates about modernization that had shaped the 1980s. And it marked the solidification of the evolving agenda that the central leadership had pursued throughout the decade: renovations to the ideological foundations of CCP rule, fast, market-oriented economic growth, the central role of emerging technology in China's development, and an ambitious set of ideas about political reform. For those in search of a single moment that can best represent China's elite politics in the 1980s, the 13th Party Congress is a prime candidate. After the thematic organization of the prior sections, this chapter takes the congress as an occasion to sum up and look ahead.

Deng Xiaoping gave Zhao significant leeway and strong backing to develop his priorities for the 13th Party Congress. Deng also designated Bo Yibo to run the personnel process, reflecting the continuing dominance of the CCP elders over promotion of cadres. Zhao drew on his intellectual network to develop an expansive agenda with a new ideological grounding. The congress was intended to mark the culmination of the advances made throughout the 1980s and set goals for the next stage of "reform and opening." It was presented explicitly as an epochal event, the apotheosis of "nine years [of] profound changes" since the Third Plenum of 1978 and the result of "a new era of development."

The congress's work report articulated an important and comprehensive vision for China's modernization. It had taken over a year of drafting, beginning under Hu Yaobang's auspices in October 1986. Zhao had been preparing a "development report" to accompany what would have been Hu's "political report," but after Hu's removal, Zhao was appointed to deliver the sole work report. The first full draft was prepared by May 1987. Following a discussion at the leadership's seaside enclave at Beidaihe in July, 5,000 copies were distributed to officials and experts. Their thousands of comments informed the final major revision, which Zhao presented to the Politburo on September 30 for discussion and approval.[2]

This highly consultative process tempered some of the most radical proposals that Zhao and his network had considered, but it ensured that the contents of the report carried real weight despite the political tumult during its drafting. In some areas, such as ideology and economic policy, the report was at the cutting edge of what the top leadership was considering. In other areas, especially political reform, it marked a significant endorsement but avoided directly taking on the most sensitive questions that were being debated internally—and indeed, there were gaps between what was said publicly and internally.

The 13th Party Congress was the high-water mark of Zhao's authority and public approbation, symbolized by the applause that greeted the congress's conclusion. This chapter describes the areas of its greatest consequence: personnel, ideology, economic policy, technology policy, and political reform.[3] But a second, far more secretive round of applause for Zhao would come to matter nearly as much. That applause ratified a secret agreement of the greatest importance—and, as we shall see, greatly complicates the story of the congress as a triumph of transparency. Between these two rounds of applause rest the great paradoxes of Chinese politics—the gaps between public pronouncements and internal decision making, between political change and the CCP's entrenched hierarchies, and between innovation and continuity.

On October 25, CCP elite from across the country assembled in orderly rows in the Great Hall of the People as the 13th Party Congress began. One of the congress's areas of greatest significance was a generational shift in who sat in those chairs. Of the new Central Committee, including both full and alternate members, 46 percent were now fifty-five years old or younger and only 20 percent were over age sixty. All of the CCP's "Eight Immortals" were now officially retired from the Politburo Standing Committee, though Deng Xiaoping retained his post as chairman of the Central Military Commission (CMC). Zhao became the first-ranked vice chairman of the CMC, further bolstering his position by giving him additional authority over the armed forces. The eighty-two-year-old Chen Yun, meanwhile, was appointed to chair the Central Advisory Commission (CAC), with Bo Yibo as his deputy, which gave them a continuing power base. Li Peng, a favorite of Chen Yun and Li Xiannian with experience in education and industry, was set to take over Zhao's duties as premier and joined the Standing Committee alongside Hu Qili, Qiao Shi, Yao Yilin, and Li Ruihuan.[4] The balance of views in this group ensured that the direction of the reform policies would remain contested in the period ahead. Yet the generational shift at all levels of the top CCP leadership was clear.

With the goal of institutionalization in mind, the leadership tested out political reforms for the congress itself, including a new voting method for election of the members of the Central Committee: a "preliminary election" with approximately ten more candidates than spots. This election was unexpectedly powerful, at least for Deng Liqun, who placed in the bottom ten—a stunning outcome for a prominent figure whose patrons had planned for him to join the Politburo. Because of this dismal showing, he was not selected to the Central Committee and was ineligible to join the Politburo. Facing this humiliation, Deng Liqun joined the CAC, where Chen Yun ensured that he retained access to the luxurious life of a senior official.[5] It was a particular irony that the idea for this balloting method had originally been advocated by Hu Yaobang, whom Deng Liqun had pushed hard to remove from power. From his place on the leadership rostrum, far from the general secretary's seat that he had once occupied, Hu Yaobang must have felt bittersweet emotions at his rival's surprising downfall.

These personnel changes were important, but the true breakthrough of the 1987 congress was conceptual, oriented toward mapping out a direction and making a powerful case for the necessity of new market reforms. The freshly issued criticisms of "bourgeois liberalization" were still circulating—and indeed, China's fundamental commitment to socialism not only could not be called into question but also seemed particularly sensitive at this charged moment. Zhao's solution was to embrace an inherited ideological formulation that could be reworked to encompass a range of new policies. His choice was seemingly innocuous: the "initial stage of socialism." This was a concept intended to explain China's unusual circumstances as a socialist country born not out of capitalism but rather out of a largely agricultural economy and underdeveloped industrial base that needed to develop the "productive forces" before it could progress further down the path to socialism and eventually full communism.

The concept derived from Mao's remark in November 1958 that Chinese socialism was at an early stage of a "long-term transition" that would require development of the productive forces.[6] However, Mao had not elaborated on this "long-term transition." Some thinkers, including Su Shaozhi, Xue Muqiao, and Yu Guangyuan, had returned to this and similar ideas like "underdeveloped socialism" in the late 1970s, sensing its potential usefulness to explain why China had chosen to focus intensively on economic development and to place these changes in a much longer-term framework.[7] Ideologues such as Deng Liqun had criticized these initial forays, but the phrase had appeared in passing and without explanation in the 1981 Resolution on Party History and other official party documents.[8]

Zhao and his chief of staff, Bao Tong, returned to "the initial stage of socialism" in late 1986. Initially, Zhao and Bao demonstrated interest in the term in the context of their plans for political reform.[9] On November 18, 1986, following a briefing from Bao and the Central Research Office on Political System Reform (CROPSR), Zhao sent a letter to Deng Xiaoping, Hu Yaobang, Li Xiannian, and Chen Yun that reintroduced the concept into the leadership's discourse. "We are currently in the initial stage of socialism," Zhao stated, and thus China's political structure was not yet fully institutionalized, requiring "gradual" reform alongside development of both "material civilization" and "spiritual civilization."[10] This was his first known usage of the term, and it is apparent that he and his advisers believed that it had the potential to explain major incongruities in China's system and to justify reforms that some officials might deem contrary to a traditional socialist system or Leninist party. Yet in November 1986, Zhao did not further elaborate on the concept.

Zhao and Bao soon realized that the "initial stage of socialism" formulation had even larger potential for interpreting China's modernization. This phrase would not visibly undercut China's commitment to socialism but would shift the emphasis: If China were in the "initial stage of socialism," development became the indisputable and critical task so that China could move to a more "advanced" stage of socialism in the future. This concept opened up a long-range vista to the future and justified further market reforms without "sparking major theoretical debates," Zhao recalled.[11] In early January 1987, even as the attacks on bourgeois liberalization continued, Bao Tong tested out this broad application of the concept in *People's Daily*. Shortly thereafter, Zhao also used the "initial stage of socialism" in this wider context, urging progress on both reform and economic construction.[12]

By March 1987, Zhao had decided that it would be the bedrock concept on which he would build the agenda of the 13th Party Congress. On March 21, Zhao sent a letter to Deng Xiaoping on the drafting of the work report for the 13th Party Congress. Zhao stated clearly, "The entire document is based on the initial stage of socialism." Zhao explained the advantages of this formulation "articulating clearly the nature and basis of China's reform" and reminded Deng that it had previously appeared in official documents "but has never been fully brought into play." On March 25, Deng responded to Zhao's letter with a brief message: "This plan is good."[13]

From this interaction and the larger process of endorsing the "initial stage of socialism" concept, it is possible to discern important characteristics of Zhao's role in governing both policy and ideology in China in the latter part of the 1980s. Zhao acted with a large degree of autonomy, despite the extraordinary importance and potential sensitivity of the "initial stage of socialism" concept. Zhao did not elevate the concept to Deng Xiaoping's attention until nearly half a year of internal usage and three months of public usage. This concept had wide-ranging implications for the entire future of the reform agenda, but Zhao evidently did not even discuss it with Deng in person. Instead, Zhao oversaw a wide-ranging process to develop the concept and garner high-level support for it. This included an important shift from using the concept as the basis of a proposal for political reform to elevating the concept as part of the long-term ideological basis of the reforms going forward. Zhao also deployed aides and proxies such as Bao Tong to test possible applications of the concept. Deng's characteristically succinct agreement was the final stage of a lengthy process of planning and developing this concept for the congress.

These shifts in ideology and personnel would dominate discussion and analysis of the congress, but the event's significance extended to many other areas as well. Regarding the economy, it revealed how far Zhao's views about the proper relationship between the state and the market had come since codification of the "planned commodity economy" in 1984. In a sweeping gesture, he redefined the goal of the economic reforms in line with the proposals that had been developed earlier in the year: "The system must be one in which 'the state manages the market, and the market guides the enterprises.'" By endorsing this formulation, which was first raised to Zhao by the System Reform Commission and the State Planning Commission in March (discussed in Chapter 5), Zhao established an expansive and pro-market interpretation of the "planned commodity economy." The significance was enormous: after years of debate, Zhao and his network of economists had made a landmark change that solidified the explicit, central, and comprehensive role of the market.[14]

Alongside this support for the market, Zhao endorsed the "one central focus and two basic points": pursuing the overall objective of building socialism with Chinese characteristics while simultaneously "upholding the Four Cardinal Principles" and promoting economic growth through "reform and opening." He noted the ideological threats of "bourgeois liberalization" that had received such significant focus during 1987 but cautioned against overusing this label.[15]

Building on these conceptual innovations that bolstered the role of the market, the work report addressed economic policy in greater detail, emphasizing the importance of market forces in guiding enterprises of all ownership types and using indirect macroeconomic controls. Zhao also encouraged the growing role of private enterprises, then only about 2 percent of industrial output value but 16 percent of total retail commodity sales. This gave formal status to private enterprises, rather than only "individual businesses" and township and village enterprises. In addition, he said, the role of economic planning should become "formulating industrial policies and hastening their implementation." Zhao also gave attention to economic policies that sought to promote social welfare, ranging from mitigating demographic challenges such as an aging population to environmental protection.[16] Yet it is also important to note that many of the specific policies to achieve these goals were not fully articulated, which was one important reason why Zhao would soon embrace a new "coastal development strategy" with such enthusiasm immediately following the congress.

In discussing China's "development strategy," Zhao also ensured a prominent place for his priority initiatives related to science and technology (S&T). Invoking the need to "catch up with the global New Technological Revolution," Zhao emphasized the "dual task" of applying advanced technologies to traditional industries while also ensuring the emergence of high-technology industries. Although he touched only passingly on foreign affairs and national defense, Zhao noted the importance of "defense technologies" and defense modernization; once again, however, he placed them firmly within the broader category of "economic construction" and development, particularly regarding technology.[17] Zhao ensured that the S&T agenda that he had pursued as premier and that Deng Xiaoping had encouraged would remain central to the leadership's agenda.

The most unusual and complex aspect of the 13th Party Congress's work report was the significant emphasis that it gave to political system reforms. This section of the work report grew out of the proposals developed by Bao Tong and CROPSR, as discussed Chapters 8 and 9. The logic of the political reforms endorsed in the work report was simple: a significant number of major reforms were openly ratified, which was intended to pave the way for other, more controversial policies that CROPSR had been discussing.

In meetings with the group drafting the work report, Zhao warned that political system reform was the most "difficult" and sensitive part of the document. CROPSR prepared a freestanding "General Plan for Political System Reform" that was synthesized into the work report. In briefing his colleagues on the document, Zhao relentlessly emphasized the "benefits" of separating the party and the government at the central, provincial, and local levels, as well as in state enterprises. However, many provincial party secretaries voiced opposition to the reforms, and some even called the separation of party and government "anti-party."[18]

The work report presented the logic for pursuing reforms to the political structure as squarely focused on supporting China's economic development. Priority reforms encompassed separating party and government functions and powers, delegating authority to lower levels, promoting the creation of a civil service system, and enhancing the role of representative assemblies. This also included the downgrading or removal of party cells in many government bodies, enterprises, and universities—a major step. Zhao called separation of party and government "the primary key to the reform of the political system." He and his advisers saw this as a universal necessity in socialist countries that were experimenting with political reforms.[19]

These changes sought to strengthen the functioning of the CCP and the government to allow both entities to more effectively lead the economic reforms; they were predicated on a continuing commitment to stability and gradualism in the political reforms, although they were given greater prominence and detail than many analysts expected at the time.[20] They affirmed that greater accountability and transparency—including new systems for the people to communicate their "grievances" and "demands" to the leadership and laws to "guarantee the citizens' rights and freedoms as stipulated by the Constitution"—were essential to the CCP's overall ability to lead China's reform and opening.[21] The congress prepared and solidified the leaders' consensus around political system reform so that they could push further in the months and years ahead.

The 13th Party Congress concluded on November 1 with formal ratification of Zhao's work report. The Propaganda Department had been preparing a nationwide initiative to study the congress and propagandize its conclusions, focusing on the "initial stage of socialism" concept and the agenda of "one central focus and two basic points." Propaganda director Wang Renzhi also discussed the need to promote political system reform, and he even described reforms that he would be overseeing in the propaganda apparatus, including changes to separate the functions of party and government.[22] Immediately after the congress closed, propaganda work was launched to explain the "initial stage of socialism" to cadres across the country. Detailed instructional materials were produced in typical pedagogical styles: study materials, summaries and explanations, and major themes addressed in question-and-answer format.[23]

Despite this major propaganda initiative, not everyone was pleased with the results of the congress. Some members of the elder generation, reportedly including Chen Yun, were dismayed with the work report's open embrace of the market. Chen's hopes for a more planning-focused approach rested in his protégés Li Peng and Yao Yilin, and in the fact that in Zhao's new job as general secretary, Zhao had less direct daily control over economic policy than he had as premier. Other criticisms of the congress came from liberal intellectuals who wanted faster change, but these were relatively muted for the time being: the overriding mood was one of optimism and opportunity for the modernization agenda under an empowered Zhao.

Yet this was not the whole story. One additional decision was made on November 2, at the First Plenum of the 13th CCP Central Committee that immediately followed the congress. That decision was a secret protocol to keep significant power in Deng Xiaoping's hands—an internal agreement made by Zhao and the new Politburo Standing Committee, despite the public fanfare surrounding Deng's retirement from official positions.

At this meeting, Zhao promised that the new leadership would continue to "seek the advice and help" of the elders, and "Comrade Xiaoping in particular." But this was not simply a polite show of deference. Even when Deng did not serve on the Standing Committee of the Politburo, Zhao continued, "The status and value of Comrade Xiaoping as a decision-maker on the major problems for our party and nation did not change." Zhao concluded, "We still need Comrade Xiaoping to continue on at the helm at this critical juncture. The Politburo Standing Committee believes that from today on, when we encounter major problems, we still have the need to consult Comrade Xiaoping, and Comrade Xiaoping will still be able to convene our meetings. We earnestly make this request of the plenary meeting and of Comrade Xiaoping, because it is necessary for the cause of our party, and we trust that the plenary meeting will agree with our request."[24] Zhao's "request" was met with "warm applause." Despite its informality, this served as sufficient ratification.[25] The internal agreement gave Deng continuing paramount authority. This fact would not stay secret for long.

When Zhao made his "request" of the Central Committee, he was not speaking off the cuff. In fact, although it was not based on any official party rule, this agreement had been carefully planned. At a meeting at Deng Xiaoping's house on July 7, 1987, Bo Yibo suggested, according to Zhao's recollection, that Zhao say a few words immediately after taking up the position of general secretary about his intention to continue to consult Deng. Deng reportedly replied that it would be good if this state of affairs were also known internationally, given the degree of international speculation about Deng's role and China's stability. To Zhao, this prospect did not seem very constraining, given how hands-off Deng had behaved toward much of the policymaking throughout the decade.[26] No public announcement was made about Deng's continued status, though when a reporter asked Zhao if he would continue to consult with Deng, Zhao replied that he intended to "seek his advice in making major decisions."[27] Deng's status was ambiguous in public—was he a mere "advice" giver or still a political decision maker?—but it was far clearer in private. Deng retained tremendous authority, including the right to convene meetings of the Politburo Standing Committee. A hearty round of applause had left a shadow leadership in place even as Zhao asserted the bold agenda of the 13th Party Congress, reflecting the persistence of informal and nonpublic political arrangements based on the entrenched hierarchies of the CCP. So much of what occurred at this seemingly public event—one that was celebrated for its unprecedented level of transparency—was in fact unknown to outsiders, hidden from view.

In retrospect, one might reasonably ask whether the 13th Party Congress was actually a representative moment or whether, with its reformist exuberance and patina of consensus, it was instead an aberration. Certainly, its vision of China's future was only partially realized. Yet it is important to note that even after the crackdown that ended the decade, and the purges to come, the Chinese leadership never repudiated the congress or its work report.[28] Its signature concepts remain in circulation. When Xi Jinping presented his namesake ideology, Xi Jinping Thought on Socialism with Chinese Characteristics for a New Era, in 2017, he used a familiar phrase. "China," he declared, "is still at the initial stage of socialism."[29] In this sense, too, the congress is representative—its status ambiguous, downplayed but enduring, like the history of the 1980s itself.

CHAPTER 11

A Great Flood

On the evening of November 9, 1987, members of the Central Research Office on Political System Reform (CROPSR) gathered to celebrate in the immediate afterglow of the 13th Party Congress. They were joined by Wen Jiabao, director of the CCP's powerful General Office, whom Zhao had sent as his representative. Wen raised a toast, saying that CROPSR "had done a good job and completed the historic task assigned to it." He thanked them "on behalf of the central government, and on behalf of Comrade Ziyang."

The next day, the group met with Zhao, who asked them to help him implement the vision of political system reform they had laid out at the congress. Zhao reorganized the office as a permanent body rather than the ad hoc structure that he had used in the lead-up to the congress. Zhao committed to push ahead with the separation of party and government and specific mechanisms that would need to change as a result, including the personnel system, the factory manager responsibility system, and the trade unions. He also requested new proposals for the CCP Central Committee on increasing "societal consultation," for the State Council on institutional reform, and plans for reforms in the provinces and cities to come the following year.[1]

The specific next steps that could realize the ambitions of the 13th Party Congress remained challenging and uncertain. In all domains—from economic and technological policy to the evolving official ideology and political system—further effort was needed to turn the promises of the congress into reality.

The next stage of the political system reform agenda centered on a highly publicized rollout in late November and early December, which underscored that economic and political modernization were deeply connected. Yet already there were signs of difficulties. As early as the prior year, CROPSR had received reports from the governor of Liaoning Province that when local party officials were told about the plans, which they saw as undermining their authority, they "felt a big shock, and most of them could not accept them."[2]

The central leadership, however, appeared unified on the matter. On December 1, the State Council convened to hand over the reins to Li Peng. He delivered an extended speech giving his support to the political reform plan. Dismissing the "turbulent emotions in some departments" as "completely unnecessary," Li praised Zhao's work and committed to personally carry out the institutional reforms that had been discussed.[3]

While these political reforms got under way, Zhao also moved to implement the next stage of his economic agenda and canvass widely for new ideas. For example, he invited eight prominent economists, including Liu Guoguang, Li Yining, and Wu Jinglian, to design the "1988–1995 Medium-Term Reform Proposals," which would provide a buffet of concrete options to help him flesh out the policy direction.[4] Most significantly, in the period immediately following the 13th Party Congress, Zhao endorsed a new strategy for China's economic development, which came to be known as the coastal development strategy.

Beginning in June 1987, a researcher at the State Planning Commission (SPC) named Wang Jian had published articles that argued China should take advantage of what he termed the "great international cycle." This cycle involved Chinese industry first using international markets to purchase inputs, primarily raw materials for production. Then firms would conduct manufacturing within China using low-cost labor primarily in four areas: textiles and garments, food and beverages, sundry light industrial goods, and electrical consumer products such as household appliances. Finally, China would sell these finished products on the world market. As industrial coastal regions rapidly accumulated foreign exchange and attracted foreign capital and technology, this would in turn produce funds the government could spend on fostering rural development. Wang predicted that it would take two or three decades to achieve these goals.[5]

Drawing on the debates about industrial policy that had flourished in China throughout the 1980s, this conception of a "great international cycle" reflected many of the realities of the special economic zones (SEZs) and the coastal regions' position as the vanguard of China's economic transformation. The initial SEZs—Shenzhen, Zhuhai, Shantou, and Xiamen—were all coastal cities, and due to additional port cities being designated SEZs, by 1987 the zones stretched along the coast through the Pearl River delta, the Yangtze River delta, and the Shandong and Liaoning Peninsulas. The government frequently cited the opportunities of coastal economic construction for the whole country's development, and regions such as Fujian and Guangdong had been some of the fastest growing in China. In Guangdong, for example, between 1978 and 1989, industrial output increased by a factor of four and gross domestic product increased by more than a factor of three.[6] Wang Jian also drew on Chinese economists' and officials' studies of Japan, Singapore, Hong Kong, and the other "Asian Tigers."[7] What was new about Wang's ideas was that they systematized these experiences into a long-term framework for export-led growth and China's integration into the international economy. Although the coastal regions played a pivotal role, the aims of the policy were truly national.

In the fall, Zhao encountered Wang's arguments in an essay in Xinhua News Service's internal journal, *Trends and Proofs*. On November 1, the day that the 13th Party Congress concluded, Zhao ordered that Wang's essay be circulated to the State Council and the Central Finance and Economics Leading Small Group (CFELSG). Then, at a several-day planning meeting that ran November 3–5, 1987, Zhao cited Wang Jian's ideas, praising the "great international cycle" as "very reasonable." China's primary economic advantage, Zhao stated, was "labor resources"—adding that he meant "not only people, but also, most importantly, low wages." If China could raise the quality of its labor force, including through increasing its technological and managerial capacities, China would become globally competitive. Zhao encouraged the leadership to implement a crucial capitalistic idea that Deng and others had advocated: deploying China's cheap, plentiful labor as a source of competitive advantage on the global market.[8]

In the subsequent months of 1987, Zhao personally pushed forward this idea by conducting inspection tours of coastal areas. Speaking on November 26 with officials in the city of Suzhou, Zhao outlined the mechanism of the great international cycle, driven by imports of raw materials and exports of finished products. "This is very much possible," he emphasized, as long as China created a situation of cheap labor, improved business mechanisms, and resolved the institutional question of how to reform the trade system for imports and exports. Following from these objectives, on December 30, meeting with officials from the Xiamen SEZ, Zhao urged them to learn from Taiwan about management methods and especially the creation of successful joint ventures. An export-led growth strategy had enabled Taiwan to engage in a technological transformation after the 1970s, Zhao stated, reflecting his long-standing preoccupation with the central role of technology in advancing economic development. "We must further open the entire coastal region and further promote the export-oriented economic development of the coastal region," he declared. Zhao had concluded that the "coastal development strategy" could propel China to extraordinary economic growth, facilitate technological development, and become a signature agenda of his tenure as general secretary.[9]

Thus, in January 1988, Zhao moved decisively to turn this coastal development strategy into policy. First, his allies sought to bolster the standing of these ideas with front-page coverage of Wang Jian's ideas in *Guangming Daily* and *Economic Daily*. Second and most importantly, Zhao submitted a report for approval by Deng Xiaoping and the central leadership. Citing his investigations since November of the previous year, Zhao explained, "Labor-intensive industries are always transferred to places where labor costs are low," and because of currency appreciation in Japan, Taiwan, and elsewhere, the moment was right for China to open up further. Voicing a sense of urgency that recalled his remarks on the New Technological Revolution, Zhao declared, "Throughout history, China has missed several development opportunities. We must not miss the opportunity this time."[10]

In addition to seeking to attract foreign investment and managerial expertise, Zhao proposed an approach that he called the "two ends extending abroad." This denoted a dual integration of China's production processes into the international system, as Wang Jian had described: coastal areas would import raw materials from abroad, so as not to be limited by the availability of domestic raw materials, and then export finished products to international markets. While reforming the foreign trade system, China would obtain more foreign exchange and capital. Zhao also included in this report a strong reminder of his strategic commitment to respond to the New Technological Revolution, encouraging Chinese scientists to create products with commercial applications and participate in international exchanges and competition. Zhao concluded by stating that this coastal development strategy would propel the entire country, both coastal and inland regions, to a more advanced stage of development and "resolve all kinds of contradictions."[11] On January 23, 1988, Deng Xiaoping approved the strategy with a characteristically brief message: "Completely agree. Be especially bold, speed up the pace, and do not miss the opportunity."[12]

Zhao was eager to introduce this new initiative to foreign investors. On February 2, Zhao delivered a video message by satellite to the World Economic Forum in Davos, Switzerland. "China's labor costs are relatively low; production efficiency is increasing; and various laws and regulations are being perfected," he told the Davos audience, while also announcing the decision to open Hainan Island as a new SEZ. "China, and especially China's coastal region, is a very attractive place to invest capital and technology."[13] Several days later, on February 6, a Politburo meeting chaired by Zhao formally adopted the coastal development strategy as an official strategy for a "faster and healthier pace of growth."[14]

The coastal development strategy involved the entire nation, from the coastal regions that would lead the way in interfacing with the global economy to the rural areas that would provide the low-cost labor and inputs. By opening itself to the "great international cycle," China would become deeply enmeshed in the global economic system. It embraced cheap labor as a distinctive international competitive advantage for China, and it further enshrined the pursuit of rapid growth as the over-riding priority of the CCP's economic governance. China's growth would become ineluctably bound up with its role as both an importer and ex-porter, which would mean pursuing large sums of foreign exchange and exposing China to the risky fluctuations of the global economy. The rewards, Zhao promised, would surpass even what China had already witnessed during the 1980s.

The propaganda apparatus promoted the coastal development strategy both domestically and overseas.[15] A directive instructed that external propaganda should highlight China's "abundant labor resources," "low production costs, increasing S&T strength, good industrial and agricul-tural foundations," and "much improved" infrastructure in order to entice "foreign investors." However, it also counseled caution, especially with regard to countries that China would now be competing with for market share. (On even more politically sensitive issues, such as "the in-troduction of capital and technology from Taiwan," the guidance was "to do it without talking much about it.") The goal was to present a posi-tive message to the world that China was more open for business than ever before.[16]

The coastal development strategy sought to enmesh China in the in-ternational system by deepening economic interdependence. China's embrace of foreign trade and investment had remained limited throughout the 1980s; the SEZs were economically liberal enclaves in an otherwise tightly controlled environment for foreign trade. The coastal development strategy was a commitment to change those realities and to transform China's economy into an environment in which export-led growth, taking advantage of low-cost labor, could occur rapidly. Beyond what Zhao acknowledged directly, its ideological implications were sig-nificant. The global capitalist market would now play an even larger role in China's economy. As China became more open to foreign trade and capital, the future of what its commitment to socialism would mean in practice—in the "initial stage" and beyond—was even more uncertain.

Reforms to the political system continued apace with the permanent establishment of CROPSR.[17] In early February, an essay in *People's Daily* endorsed freedom of speech: "The general trend of the world is irreversible: No matter what the social system is, thought and speech will be increasingly open and free."[18] Bao Tong also oversaw the introduction of provincial and municipal competitive elections, including for several deputy governors and party congress leaders. Competitive elections were also held for the Standing Committee of the National People's Congress (NPC) that convened in March 1988, with the number of votes received by the elected chairman and the vice chairmen made public—making it what Yiu-chung Wong calls "the most open and democratic congress the PRC had ever had."[19]

Chinese intellectuals wrote of an extraordinary change under way, describing these processes of political and economic change as inextricable. Fudan University law professor Wang Huning (currently a member of the Politburo Standing Committee) declared that due to the reform process, "China's political culture is undergoing a profound transformation; the traditional, conservative, closed, concentrated, subjective, and arbitrary elements of political culture are transforming into new, open, decentralized, objective, and democratic elements." Wang offered survey data that showed "74.4 percent of people surveyed believed that if there was no political democracy, even with economic growth, it could not be considered true modernization, and 81 percent said that the time was ripe for China's political system reform."[20] He voiced great optimism about the progress already made and the opportunities that remained.

Bao Tong also decided to take on the challenge of corruption in the spring of 1988. Zhao Ziyang had ordered several public opinion surveys, and CROPSR's investigations revealed widespread public discontent with the enduring problems of corrupt officials. Following research tours of Jiangsu and Zhejiang, Bao Tong concluded that addressing corruption through increasing the openness, transparency, and legal accountability of grassroots government work—including tax offices, public security, traffic supervision, food management, and the power supply—would benefit both economic and political reform and generate even greater popular support for the leadership. These proposals were piloted in Beijing and in Shanghai, where party secretary Jiang Zemin also banned party and government organs from engaging in business activities.

According to CROPSR's surveys, these measures significantly improved public satisfaction with the handling of corruption in both cities.[21]

◇

The period from the 13th Party Congress in 1987 to the rollout of the coastal development strategy in 1988 had marked the zenith of Zhao Ziyang's power. Yet almost immediately thereafter, Zhao's authority began to fracture. He made a crucial decision in the formulation of the coastal development strategy that soon returned to haunt him—a deliberate judgment (or misjudgment) that was based on his economic ideas about growth and inflation.

Initially, the reaction to the coastal development strategy was positive, and the criticisms came from familiar sources: the officials who had consistently resisted market-oriented change and fast growth. For example, Chen Yun voiced displeasure with the perception that it might cause the SEZs to become a model that the rest of China would follow. Zhao seemed prepared to address these concerns directly and met with Chen on January 29, 1988; on February 15, Chen told colleagues that he supported the coastal development strategy and the "two ends extending abroad," although he still warned his colleagues not to underestimate the difficulty of the development path that they were undertaking. (Chen also noted that he had never been to an SEZ, but he had followed their progress closely.)[22] Perhaps with this in mind, shortly thereafter, Chen's ally Deng Liqun traveled to inspect the Shenzhen SEZ. They could do little when the constitution was amended to fully legalize the private sector, meaning that these firms would no longer exist in a legal gray zone or need to avoid appearing to employ too many people.[23]

However, some senior officials returned to a different problem: the risk of economic overheating, meaning excessively rapid, imbalanced, inflationary growth. Two important high-level officials, Premier Li Peng and Vice Premier Yao Yilin, became increasingly assertive critics of the new economic policies on these grounds, citing government reports that prices were rising well beyond the targeted increases of approximately 6 percent.[24]

However, Tian Yuan, an official at the State Council's Development Research Center, disputed these negative assessments and argued that the conditions in the Chinese economy were "very good." Rather than caution, he encouraged rapid implementation of sweeping reforms, especially to the price system.[25] At this moment, Zhao made a crucial choice: he revealed that he believed inflation and overheating were less risky than Li and Yao had warned or, at a minimum, that he was willing to tolerate this risk to pursue his objectives. It seemed as if, now that he had become general secretary, succeeded at the 13th Party Congress, and presented the coastal development strategy, Zhao believed—or wished to believe—that the Chinese economy could handle higher inflation. In tense meetings, Li and Yao repeatedly argued that the coastal development strategy might make "malignant inflation unavoidable," to which Zhao responded that it was a "needless" concern.[26] On April 2, meeting with senior economists, Zhao said assertively that he believed that if commodity prices and wages were to rise significantly as the economy developed, "I think that doesn't seem so terrible."[27]

By the spring of 1988, Zhao made clear that he believed rapid growth was essential to the success of the reform policies because it "minimized contradictions" in a mixed system; that the economic conditions in 1988 were not dangerous, even if they were inflationary; and most basically, that a rapidly developing economy could tolerate high levels of inflation. This was a remarkable development from the CCP's top leader, signaling a brash willingness to tolerate higher social costs to pursue faster economic growth.

To strengthen the case for the high-growth coastal development strategy in an inflationary environment, economic officials Zhu Jiaming and Chen Yizi traveled to Brazil and Chile in late April 1988. This may seem surprising, given that pernicious hyperinflation had (and would again) severely affected Latin American countries, but Zhu and Chen found reason for optimism. In Chile, they reported observing widespread satisfaction with the economic governance of Augusto Pinochet's authoritarian regime. Next, in Brazil, they visited Rio de Janeiro, Brasília, and São Paulo, seeing how foreign investment had helped power Brazil's economic growth. From the Chinese consulate in São Paulo, they sent a telegram back to Beijing.[28] Upon returning to China, Chen briefed Zhao on the trip, focusing on foreign investment and inflation. "Infla-tion will exist in any country that undergoes rapid economic develop-ment, and this includes socialist countries," Chen recalled that he told Zhao. "Of course, we are not encouraging inflation, but rather we are recognizing its reality and its extent."[29] Zhu put it in plainer terms: "It seems impossible to have both low inflation and high economic growth."[30] However, other economists with close ties to Zhao disagreed strongly. Guo Shuqing (currently party secretary of China's central bank) argued that "one-sided pursuit of a high-speed growth policy is detrimental—even devastating—to the economic system."[31] Zhao's network of eco-nomic advisers had become bitterly divided over this fundamental question.

To understand these acute disagreements, it is important to recall that they were shaped by the deep belief of many in the CCP leadership that inflation had helped facilitate the collapse of the Kuomintang (Nation-alist Party) and the success of the communist revolution, a lesson in the serious risks that inflation posed to political stability.[32] In addition, after decades with state-set prices, most Chinese economists had little recent experience with inflation. Partly for this reason, they disagreed about what caused inflation and whether inflation was beneficial or harmful for economic growth. Zhu Jiaming was clearly in the minority; most Chinese economists believed that inflation created shortages and social problems and had long-term "corrosive" effects on the economy.[33] Yet all sides had little recent evidence from China on which to draw, a situ-ation that likely contributed to their difficulty in reaching a shared un-derstanding in 1988.

Zhao seemed to feel that he had too much at stake in the coastal de-velopment strategy—and that the opportunity was too significant—for compromise. Yet Zhao found himself unexpectedly weakened. In a bold maneuver, Li Peng downgraded the role of the System Reform Commis-sion; because the State Council was now under Li's purview, this was his prerogative (just as its creation had been Zhao's).[34] That same month, economic indicators dealt a blow to Zhao's agenda: consumer prices in Beijing rose by at least 30 percent, suggesting that economic overheating was indeed a reality.[35]

Zhao attempted to continue with business as usual, but pressure grew. On May 12, in the coastal province of Zhejiang, Chen Yun harshly criticized the excessive focus on "fast results." Chen continued further, offering a veiled ad hominem attack on the general secretary himself by opining that China's senior leaders needed to do a better job of studying Marxist philosophy.[36] Zhao also encountered an intensifying resistance from some of his advisers. At a meeting of the SPC, senior economic official Xue Muqiao broke sharply with Zhao's views: "In provinces and cities at all levels, there is the phenomenon of overheating. Not only does no one dare to comment on this, but in fact it has received praise," Xue stated bluntly. "We really must get inflation under control."[37] Yet, at a Politburo meeting in May, Zhao called for liberalizing the price system in "approximately five years" because he insisted that overall conditions were favorable.[38] Zhao was obstinate that the conditions in the economy were advantageous and that inflationary growth posed a low risk. However, prospects of a serious crisis were mounting.

As these policy debates raged, many Chinese intellectuals began to clamor for even more sweeping changes that would reflect their assessments of both history and modernization. The most indelible statement of this argument came in the early summer of 1988, when Chinese Central Television broadcast a six-part television documentary called *River Elegy*. This documentary offered a shatteringly iconoclastic perspective on Chinese civilization, engaging in unprecedented speculation about the underlying causes of China's continued "backwardness." *River Elegy* scoured China's history, usually the recipient of reverential treatment, and found it wanting, comparing it to the slow-flowing, loess-filled Yellow River. The narrator intoned, "We must create a brand-new civilization. . . . [Our civilization] needs a good scrubbing by a great flood."[39]

Yet "Chinese civilization" was not the only culprit. The documentary announced that Karl Marx's predictions of the death of capitalism were wrong and said, "Only healthy markets can link opportunity, equality, and competition." Trumpeting economic and ideological change, the documentary also lauded new technologies and underscored the importance of political system reform to the overall modernization agenda.[40] With more than 200 million viewers, *River Elegy* exposed a vast audience to ideas previously confined to relatively rarified circles in the policy debates of the period. Historian Rana Mitter has written that "it may be the single most-watched documentary in the history of television."[41]

River Elegy was an unabashedly intellectual project designed for wide viewership. Its critical tone reflected the widespread frustration with the trade-offs and unresolved questions that the reforms had raised: What "Chinese" qualities, exactly, did "socialism with Chinese characteristics" contain? Could socialism, markets, and a reformed political system co-exist?[42] The documentary also directly addressed the personalities and dynamics at the top of the leadership. River Elegy treated Zhao Ziyang as the harbinger of China's transformation into this "brand-new civili-zation." In its fourth episode, titled "The New Era," Zhao was presented as a hero.[43] Black-and-white images of Mao Zedong, Zhou Enlai, Deng Xiaoping, and others appeared, followed by a color close-up of Zhao that quoted language from his work report at the 13th Party Congress. After this image of Zhao, the phrase *The New Era* appeared on the screen, making clear that the filmmakers viewed Zhao as the vanguard of this "new era." The film then endorsed the coastal development strategy as a "once-in-a-millennium chance."[44] In the sixth and final episode, "Blue-ness," Zhao's image again appeared, this time alongside the words, "The marks of a democratic government should be transparency, responsive-ness to popular will, and a scientific approach. We are right now moving from opacity to transparency."[45] The documentary was an extraordinary endorsement of Zhao's economic and political reform agenda, which it argued were intimately interconnected. Yet it was also based on a caustic rejection of "Chinese civilization" and acceptance of precisely the kind of ideas that had been branded "bourgeois liberalization" just over a year earlier.

The film produced dramatically divergent responses from the senior leadership. Zhao viewed the documentary and recommended it to for-eign leaders, evidently including Singapore's Lee Kuan Yew. However, many other officials, such as Deng Liqun and Wang Zhen, were incensed. They saw it as an ideological attack, even as "nihilistic," in Deng Liqun's words. To them, the film's popular success seemed to be fearsome evi-dence of the enduring problems of bourgeois liberalization, and Zhao was not doing nearly enough to halt its spread.[46]

Of course, these officials were not entirely wrong that Zhao had a different conception of ideological and political work. On April 24, 1988, Zhao spoke with Bao Tong and said that ideological work should continue in a new form, focusing more on promoting "ideals and morality" than the CCP's traditional methods of top-down indoctrination. If the relationship of the party to the government (as well as factory managers, university leaders, and other administrative authorities) was changing, then its mode of promoting "socialist spiritual civilization" would need to evolve as well.[47] The central leadership implemented reforms to "modernize" the propaganda apparatus and the work of party building, both of which were designed to bolster the political reforms—seeking to "deepen the roots of democratic politics" and "carry out the spirit of openness."[48] Even so, the old methods did not disappear. A directive from June 1988 instructed cadres to spend several hundred hours studying documents explaining the concept of the "initial stage of socialism."[49]

The central leadership also implemented new measures to promote technological development. These reforms continued the decade-long emphasis on using science and technology (S&T) to promote economic development and the futurist focus of the 863 Program and other efforts to respond to the global New Technological Revolution. On May 3, the State Council announced the use of "competitive mechanisms" in scientific research institutions, including implementation of a contract responsibility system and public bidding for research contracts. It also explicitly encouraged the growth of S&T institutions of "different ownership forms," including private enterprises, and continued the emphasis on using new technology to develop the countryside, exemplified by the Spark Program.[50] Other measures expanded the use of agricultural technologies, including an investment of RMB 60 million to fund upgrades ranging from high-yield hybrid crops to ground coverings made from synthetic materials. Song Jian of the State Science and Technology Commission also announced launch of the Torch Program, which fostered high-tech industrial development zones (such as creating the Caohejing Microelectronics Park in Shanghai and giving official recognition to the Zhongguancun High Technology Zone in Beijing) and promoted the growth of thousands of new advanced technology firms with a combination of state funding, bank loans, and borrowing from foreign governments and institutions.[51]

Political reforms proceeded, further fusing economic and political changes. "In China, establishing a socialist commodity economy order has two aspects: one is economic system reform, and the other is political system reform," Bao Tong said. In mid-May, more steps were taken to separate party and government: for example, the Central Politics and Law Leading Group, a party body, would not be permitted to interfere in specific legal cases and would be required to allow the Ministry of Public Security, the procuratorate, and the judicial system to operate independently.[52] In a significant development, a new civil service system was established at the 7th NPC in 1988, with Shenzhen taking the lead in implementing this system on an experimental basis. In the central leadership, staff were transferred from the CCP Organization Department to the State Council, though the Organization Department fought to retain control over officials at the level of vice minister and higher.[53] At the grassroots level, new measures were implemented to hold differential elections, remove the party from daily management of administrative organs, and forbid government agencies from running for-profit businesses. Other policies mandated increases in government transparency and began to reform the people's congresses, the media, and the legal system.[54]

Despite this wave of activity, some limits to the political system reform were clear. In early June 1988, small-scale protests broke out at Peking University, which the top leadership watched closely, thinking back to the unrest of the winter of 1986–1987. A group of students even marched to the Ministry of Public Security, voicing criticisms of the leadership and the CCP. The students were punished, and Zhao gathered with officials including Hu Qili, Beijing mayor Chen Xitong, and State Education Commission head He Dongchang to discuss how to update ideological and political work at universities. Zhao decided to focus the upcoming Third Plenum on modernizing ideological and political work in both enterprises and universities—underscoring that he and his advisers knew that the political system reforms could only move forward if they maintained social stability. "Western-style civil liberty" was not what China "needed most at this stage," Zhao said.[55]

As Bao Tong and CROPSR assessed these imperatives, they became increasingly worried about what would happen to Chinese workers after the enterprise reforms were fully implemented and a commodity economy developed. Reforming enterprises would inevitably affect the employment and income of workers, Bao said in late June. "What other troubles will arise when many workers are out of work?" There was a paradoxical element even to these concerns, which produced increasing caution in implementing the political reforms, because other members of society complained that these reforms were not proceeding more quickly.[56] Whether too fast or too slow, too deep or too shallow, these reforms seemed to generate strong emotions and concerns no matter what the leadership tried. Yet Zhao, increasingly out of step with his economic and political advisers, still felt considerable optimism about the prospects for the political reforms.[57]

However, in the late summer of 1988, the top leadership made a series of significant misjudgments that would permanently change the trajectory of the 1980s. Chief among these errors was a failed attempt at rapid price liberalization. This failure—a decision made by Deng but facilitated by Zhao—greatly undermined the leadership; Zhao bore the brunt of the blame and saw his authority over policymaking disintegrate, and the broader agenda of economic and political reform was newly thrown into question. Despite the ideological, cultural, and political debates epitomized by *River Elegy*, it would be economic policy that would cause the greatest tumult in 1988.

The push for price reform in mid-1988 came directly from Deng Xiaoping, who made a rare direct intervention in economic policymaking. He seemed intent on moving away from the dual-track system toward letting prices fluctuate more freely in response to market conditions, and he was pushing for even faster growth. Following a May 5, 1988, conversation between Deng and Li Peng, Li reported to the Politburo that Deng wanted to speed up reforms to solve the price system's problems.[58] However, Zhao did not treat this comment as suggesting an immediate push on price reform but rather as a goal for "the next few years." In a conversation with Ma Hong and An Zhiwen, Zhao emphasized, "We cannot allow the living standard of workers to fall." Looking ahead to the Beidaihe meetings that would begin in July, Zhao encouraged

Ma to "organize some seminars" so that Zhao could comment on price reform there. At a Politburo Standing Committee meeting on May 16, Zhao acknowledged urban price rises of 15–18 percent and warned against "dragging it out again and not making a systemic decision." Yet Zhao stated that this meant deciding on "a long-term plan" for price reforms that could replace the dual-track system "step by step" and also prioritizing enterprise reforms, rather than a sweeping liberalization of prices: "If price reform is carried out without any plan, all the localities will engage in pursuing spontaneous efforts and do as they please, which will bring much greater costs and create much larger contradictions." A few days later, Zhao announced that the State Council had appointed the conservative planner Yao Yilin to develop this five-year plan for price and wage reform.[59]

Deng was displeased with this measured approach. If, as Zhao had stated so often, inflation was not to be feared, then why should price reform be approached with such trepidation? On May 19, Deng complained, in a manner that he had seldom done over the preceding decade, "The problem of prices has remained unsolved for many years. . . . We have no choice but to carry out price reform, and we must do so despite all risks and difficulties."[60]

Zhao's tone changed in response to Deng's comments. Speaking to the Politburo on May 30, Zhao now gave a different assessment of the economy: "Production is booming, people's incomes are continually increasing, and this affords us a certain degree of [leeway] for the reforms." Citing the lessons of the Eastern European experience—which he believed pointed toward moving ahead with price reforms when conditions were favorable rather than waiting for a potential future situation in which growth slowed—Zhao also referenced what his advisers' study of Latin America had argued: "[Our prices] go up 15 percent, and our debates become horribly mixed up. In Brazil, they go up 15 percent in one month, and they get through it." Zhao still spoke of "next year" as the time frame for the price reforms, but he called for an intensive effort to begin preparing for them.[61] On July 5, meeting with the president of Brazil, José Sarney, Deng stated, "Price and wage reforms have many risks. Deepening the reforms will bring about inflation . . . but the reforms must be carried out resolutely."[62]

As Deng's impatience became sharper, it was clear that Zhao and other officials were uneasy. In July, Zhao warned against excessive optimism that price reform was a panacea or that "a market system would appear after a price reform without reform of the public sector," which was impossible.[63] With prominent exceptions, such as Zhu Jiaming and Tian Jiyun, leading Chinese economists voiced major reservations about rapid price reforms. Zhao heard proposals from the eight teams of economists that he had assigned to prepare competing "1988–1995 Medium-Term Reform Proposals," none of which supported sweeping price reform, recalled one former official.[64] Yet Deng's insistence trumped all.

Deng's sense of the potential opportunity for rapid price reform seemed, in part, to be an unintended consequence of Zhao's arguments that the Chinese economy's conditions were not highly inflationary and that a higher rate of growth was not problematic. Zhao made these arguments to justify his coastal development strategy, but they clearly influenced Deng's thinking about price reform in a way that he did not explicitly intend. Deng had long favored the pursuit of faster growth rates, and the notion that overheating was less of a risk than the CCP had assumed aligned well with the paramount leader's priorities.

As the summer conclave at Beidaihe drew near, tensions ran high. One former State Council official recalled that the planning-oriented staff of Yao Yilin's group that had been assigned to develop a price reform plan largely excluded the market-oriented economists who were associated with Zhao. Zhao would also later claim that Yao was making decisions behind his back and trying to marginalize him. Chen Yun, who had stayed on the sidelines throughout these debates, also allegedly had the SPC secretly prepare an austerity plan that would be ready if the price reform did not succeed.[65]

As meetings began at Beidaihe in July, Deng continued to make his case for rapid price reform. Zhao again displayed concern about the potential consequences. On July 30, Zhao said, "Price reform is not isolated. Whether or not price reform is successful depends not only on the price reform itself" but also on whether it is part of "an appropriate program."[66] Amid fears about continued inflation and large increases in the urban retail price index, on August 5–9, Li Peng chaired a State Council meeting, with Politburo members attending, that struck a decidedly cautious note about the near-term prospects for the Chinese economy, explicitly endorsing a "safe and feasible" pace for implementing price reforms.[67] On August 15–17, Yao Yilin presented his plan for price and wage reforms. Yao talked about a multiyear time frame for price reform, projecting that 1989 would be a "new start" and discussing a strategy that included freeing steel prices and raising consumer prices.[68] Intense debates continued, but Zhao once again adjusted his position. Despite worrying aloud about inflation and the "significant" consequences if the reform failed, Zhao unexpectedly voiced optimism that the reform could succeed. He had clearly realized that Deng's mind was made up.[69] Deng prevailed, and on August 19, the Politburo approved a plan for broad price decontrols.[70]

The leadership was aware that how it announced and discussed this decision would be of the utmost importance. At Beidaihe, Xi Zhongxun had underlined the need for "prudent" news reporting. However, Xinhua News Agency announced the decision in bold language, stating that the meeting had determined "price and wage reforms are the key to the reform of the entire system." In language that echoed Zhao's comments on May 30, the report continued, "The meeting emphasized that at present China's economy is full of vitality and developing rapidly, and thus the timing is favorable to implement price and wage reform." The announcement concluded by noting, "General Secretary Comrade Zhao Ziyang chaired the meeting."[71]

A crisis immediately followed. Consumers faced with the prospect of soaring prices drove an extraordinary spate of panic buying. Bank runs across the country led to savings withdrawals of an estimated RMB 38.94 billion.[72] In Wuhan, crowds practically laid siege to a store that sold gold. Through a tightly sealed metal gate, consumers waved thick wads of renminbi bills, urgently withdrawn from banks, as men fought violently to the front of the mob, climbing on top of other bodies, stepping on people's heads with their shoes, and gripping the doorframe for support. The frantic saleswoman inside grabbed their cash as fast as she could, doling out as much gold as the shop possessed. The price of gold had risen, almost overnight, to RMB 140 per gram and was expected to rise even higher as people tried to convert their cash into precious metal.[73] One woman in Shanghai, interviewed in front of a crowd lining up at a department store, said, "I took my money out of the bank and bought a bed. . . . I already have a bed at home, I really didn't need to buy a bed [but] everyone is buying them, and I'm also afraid that prices will rise."[74] Other reports cited frantic consumers buying "enough matches to last them twenty years," as well as cotton shirts and soap and a "toilet paper crisis" in Beijing, where some people had bought as many as fifty rolls at once.[75] Rather than evincing confidence, Chinese consumers responded to the news of price reform with a show of extreme anxiety about the prospects for the economy.

This panic buying led to a further inflationary spike. A survey of thirty-two large and medium-sized cities revealed a 24.7 percent price increase during the month of August.[76] An atmosphere of crisis descended on CCP leaders. On August 24, Zhao convened a meeting of the CFELSG on the "lack of public confidence in the price reforms," and in the subsequent days, he spoke repeatedly with Yao Yilin and Li Peng about the panic buying. On August 30, Li Peng held an emergency meeting of the State Council, which made the decision to shift direction dramatically away from the rapid reforms announced only eleven days earlier. The State Council instead focused on restoring stability and confidence by "curbing price hikes and panic buying." It was a rare admission of substantial error. Price reform, meanwhile, was characterized as a goal that would take five or more years to achieve. Following this meeting, the State Council released an "emergency notice" on stabilizing the economy.[77]

The most radical reform attempt to date had ended in failure and a complete policy reversal. It was, according to Ezra Vogel, "perhaps the most costly error of [Deng's] career."[78] Yet this was Zhao's blunder, too; he had facilitated it, been its public face, and overlooked the repeated warnings from many of his advisers and other officials. Zhao had made at least two errors: he underestimated the Chinese public's economic anxiety about inflation and overheating, and he had not expected Deng to become so personally involved in pushing forward a price reform plan. At a Politburo meeting on September 2, Zhao acknowledged the many problems in the economy that had resulted from the announcement of rapid price reform—necessitating strong economic "rectification" measures to control soaring prices and "raise people's confidence in the reforms."[79] Zhao recalled in his memoirs that he realized that Yao Yilin and Li Peng would then more openly push to exclude him from economic policymaking. Li also revealed that he had spoken with Deng Xiaoping on the sidelines of a National Women's Conference the prior day, with Deng telling Li that he supported the new price-control measures, suggesting that Li now had Deng's support on economic matters.[80]

At this meeting, Li Peng also noted that foreign media had reported on the State Council's decision to begin a period of "stabilizing the economy" as a split between the party and the government. This comment suggested a serious problem that had resulted from the voluminous comments on separating the party and the government. Li's comments thus also implicitly raised questions about the political reform agenda. Bo Yibo even asked Li in a private conversation whether he felt that Zhao was blaming Deng Xiaoping for the failure of the price reforms.[81] Bao Tong told his colleagues at CROPSR that they would likely need to "adjust their work" on political system reform to reflect this dramatic turnabout, but no one could foresee how profound those adjustments would be.[82]

On September 12, Deng called a meeting at his home with the top leadership. He acknowledged the need for retrenchment to improve the economic environment, but he insisted that these reversals should not affect the overall policies of reform and opening. He even held out hope that the leadership could still eventually return to implement price reform, whereas Li emphasized the negative consequences of the rise in prices and Zhao stressed his view that price reform could only occur successfully in the context of a "comprehensive" reform plan. It was clear that numerous divergent views still existed among the senior leadership, but Deng did not decisively move to resolve these disagreements. However, Deng had no intention of accepting public responsibility for the failed price reform attempt. Zhao, as general secretary and the public face of the reforms, bore the blame.[83] Thus, meeting with a Japanese official a few days later, Deng publicly addressed the failure of the price reform as having been caused by "poor management" and "a lack of experience," casting Zhao's governance in a negative light.[84]

Presiding over the Third Plenary Session of the 13th Central Committee in late September 1988, Zhao admitted that inflation had not been properly controlled. The leadership's focus for the coming two years would be "managing the economic environment and rectifying economic order."[85] This meeting also discussed ideological and political issues. CCP elders ramped up their criticism of Zhao's policies in this domain, with PRC vice president and CCP elder Wang Zhen specifically accusing Zhao of promoting *River Elegy* and protecting it from criticism as "intense bourgeois liberalization"—a stunningly direct attack on the sitting general secretary.[86] This resurgent emphasis on stability and control also directly affected the political reforms. At this plenary meeting, Zhao reasserted his commitment to the Four Cardinal Principles and promised anew that the political reforms would not disrupt stability.[87]

Zhao recalled in his memoirs that he even began to fear that his position might be imperiled as Li Peng, Yao Yilin, and their allies promoted a narrative that the reckless pursuit of fast market-driven growth had permitted inflation to get out of control, which had caused the failure of the price reform and endangered the Chinese economy.[88] Zhao's advisers were crestfallen at the impact on the reform plans that they had been developing.[89] International observers began to speculate that, as a British diplomat reported to Margaret Thatcher, "Zhao Ziyang's position might be under some kind of threat."[90] The year had begun with Zhao at the apex of his power, but by late summer, his entire agenda seemed newly at risk.

In this vulnerable position, Zhao held several meetings with prominent foreign thinkers who returned to China after visits earlier in the decade: Alvin Toffler and Milton Friedman. Zhao sought to bolster his damaged standing through well-publicized interactions with distinguished foreign visitors, while also perhaps identifying new policy ideas that could be of use. On September 13, Zhao met at Zhongnanhai with Alvin and Heidi Toffler, the American futurists who had inspired his S&T agenda since 1983 and were visiting China as guests of *People's Daily*. Zhao stressed China's commitment to responding to the "New Technological Revolution," telling the Tofflers that the CCP was "studying the advanced technologies of developed countries." However, reflecting the lessons of the failed price reform, Zhao stated firmly, "Stability is necessary to make democratic advances."[91]

Several days later, on September 19, Zhao met with American economist Milton Friedman. Unlikely as it might have seemed, Zhao's advisers hoped that Friedman's monetarism might offer new ideas about how China could control inflation.[92] In their discussion, Zhao asked, "Why did inflation occur in China?" Friedman asserted that the dual-track price system was one reason, making goods "more expensive, not less," because although prices were still held down, the costs of queuing, shortage, and other negative effects were high. Friedman argued that inflation would persist as long as the dual-track system remained in place. They did not reach a substantive agreement on this topic, and the meeting ended inconclusively.[93] Yet Zhao followed the meeting with an unusual gesture of friendship, walking Friedman to his car and opening the door for the American economist. The next day, *People's Daily* buoyantly summarized their meeting, concluding with a comment Friedman had made to Zhao: "You may be a general secretary, but you have the temperament of a professor."[94] Friedman's visit was presented in the state-run media as a public relations boost for Zhao, emphasizing the image that he had cultivated—reflected in his portrayal in *River Elegy*—as uniquely able to lead China's modernization. But it also served a more specific goal: displaying Zhao's seriousness about addressing inflation at a moment when economic overheating had imperiled his entire agenda.

◇

The pursuit of market reform and fast growth faced a significant challenge from the newly implemented retrenchment policies. Prominent economists like Li Yining criticized the policies, warning that retrenchment would produce "stagflation," and enterprise managers voiced fears that the "achievements of the reform will be destroyed in a day."[95] However, Deng Xiaoping and Chen Yun were in agreement that these policies were necessary. "In a socialist country like ours, it seems extremely difficult to emulate the methods of Western market economies," Chen told Zhao on October 8. "Some problems are inevitable. You can continue to explore and sum up experience."[96] Zhao would be permitted to continue as general secretary, but the priorities for economic work would need to be significantly adjusted. On December 1, Zhao met with Xue Muqiao, Liu Guoguang, and Wu Jinglian and invited their criticisms of his work. According to Xue's recollections, Zhao stated that he had recently made serious errors with regard to inflation during the preceding year, but Xue responded that in fact the errors had occurred at least for the preceding three years with negative effects on the reforms. Zhao's standing was gravely damaged, and criticisms came from all sides.[97]

On December 5, Li Peng delivered an address to the National Planning Conference in which he cautioned cadres that they should not underestimate how difficult it would be to salvage the economy. Stating that CCP leaders would cut down on excess demand by curbing investment and instituting other administrative measures, Li reimposed broad price controls. Zhao, in his speech at the conference, echoed these decisions.[98] The shift in economic policy to state-led retrenchment to slow growth and regain control was complete.

After a surge of activity that followed the 13th Party Congress, the summer of 1988 had witnessed a debacle that raised questions about the entire modernization agenda that Zhao and his advisers had developed, from the coastal development strategy and its vision of export-led, market-driven growth, to the close connections between economic and political reform. And it had revealed, in the whirlwind of panic buying and bank runs, the profound anxieties of the Chinese populace about the condition of the economy and the direction of the reforms. The retrenchment imposed in the fall sought to reassert central control over the economy and calm those widespread anxieties.

Zhao was weakened but had not lost power, and many of his favored initiatives still seemed poised to move forward, perhaps with a delay to accommodate the retrenchment.[99] As of the fall of 1988, it remained unclear whether these challenges would lead to a broader and longer-lasting reckoning over the policies pursued during the 1980s and China's future direction.

CHAPTER 12

We Came Too Late

Concern about social unrest ran high among China's rulers in late 1988. A "social outlook study" conducted by the Central Research Office on Political System Reform (CROPSR) indicated there was widespread public anger about corruption, especially among intellectuals and students. It seemed that the panic buying in the summer of 1988, which had revealed deep economic anxieties, might only have been a prelude; the study predicted "a degree of social turmoil" in the year ahead.[1]

Economic pressures remained significant, with inflation continuing to rise despite the retrenchment. By the end of October, year-on-year price rises topped 26 percent, leading the government to offer monthly subsidies of 10 yuan per month to urban residents to compensate for increased living costs, though some complained they were "inadequate."[2] Official profiteering and other forms of graft—what had previously been denounced as "economic crimes"—were obvious to ordinary people in their daily lives, engendering complaints about the unfairness and inequity of China's system.[3] Media articles described cases in sensational detail. One bank vice president in Shenzhen, for example, had misappropriated 7.26 million yuan of public funds and was depicted as "captured by rotten bourgeois ideology, becoming a depraved criminal."[4]

As this language indicates, the official interpretation of corruption in this period remained highly ideologized. Rather than suggesting that corruption was a structural problem in the dual-track price system or the CCP, it was cast as yet another manifestation of "bourgeois liberalization." Propaganda work was designed to show the public that the leadership was addressing the problem. The People's Liberation Army (PLA), too, received instructions on the "planned commodity economy" and the need to avoid corruption and profiteering.[5]

Yet it was clear that even some figures with unimpeachable CCP credentials had succumbed to temptation. Deng Xiaoping's son, Deng Pufang, who had been violently attacked during the Cultural Revolution and remained a paraplegic, was one such suspected case. The CCP cracked down on Kang Hua Development Corporation, a large conglomerate established by the China Welfare Fund for the Disabled, which Deng Pufang led. Zhao Ziyang's sons were also rumored to have benefited from corruption and nepotism in their business dealings in southern China.[6] Nepotism at the highest levels revealed that the marketizing system was easily exploited and grossly unfair. In these negative ways, corruption also underscored the interconnections among the economic and political systems.

Zhao's advisers tracked these issues closely, and reflecting its new political strictures, CROPSR began to devote attention to the less sensitive goal of "establishing a clean government." Building on the trial initiatives that it had launched in Beijing and Shanghai in the spring, it focused in particular on measures to increase transparency and regulate cadres' behavior. The hope was that "democratic supervision" could rein in corruption while also providing new momentum for political system reform; in other words, instead of campaigns against corruption, the hope was to develop institutions, laws, and norms that would reduce corruption at the root.[7]

Yet anger was mounting outside of the leadership. In October, an editorial in *World Economic Herald* decried China's "crisis in moral values." The "old morality" based on Confucian ethics had been destroyed as the commodity economy developed—a necessary development, in the authors' view—and "the Communist morality and the socialist morality" were "mere slogans without substance." No new common morality had replaced those old orders, and the authors saw no easy answer.[8]

Louder cries for pushing ahead with political reforms accompanied the laments by intellectuals about China's "crisis in values." Several bold thinkers called for a more robust system of checks and balances centered on elevating the role of the National People's Congress (NPC), while experiments with creating a more empowered and representative local people's congress were tested in Shenzhen, far from the capital.[9] Intellectual Cao Siyuan, who had previously led the development of bankruptcy reform proposals, wrote in *World Economic Herald* in November 1988 that the NPC should "shed the elegant name of a 'rubber stamp' and really exercise the power of installing or removing a government according to the socialist parliamentary democratic system." Cao also led the newly established Stone Corporation Social Development Institute, a private research institute founded by Wan Runnan's computer firm Stone Corporation to focus on promoting political reforms.[10] The political reforms had not progressed nearly as far or fast enough for these figures, and patience was wearing thin.

Groups across China increased their calls for democratic change and legal rights that they had made over the preceding years. Sometimes this took bizarre and unsettling forms; in December 1988, for example, students in Nanjing became angry that visiting students, including those from African countries, appeared to enjoy greater privileges and legal protections than did Chinese students. Following an altercation at Nanjing University that led to rumors of a murder, Chinese students began to riot, shouting slogans that mixed blatant racism and chauvinist nationalism with other aspirations: "Beat the black devils," "Punish the criminals," and "Human rights and democracy!" As the immediate conflict subsided, demonstrators shifted their focus to the provincial government, calling for "protecting human rights" and legal system reform.[11] Religious and ethnic minorities also pushed back and encountered brutal repression. In March 1989, Tibetans protested in Lhasa to commemorate the 1959 Tibetan uprising, and armed police opened fire, killing over 400 people, according to one estimate.[12] Across China, the degree of agitation and discontent remained high.

Officials in the propaganda apparatus were alarmed by this degree of popular discontent. Directives called on publications to issue more optimistic and upbeat assessments of the economic situation and the past decade's work, signaling fears that the economic retrenchment and the critical, crisis-laden propaganda surrounding it were pushing public attitudes in a more negative direction. One directive declared, "Pessimism is unfounded."[13]

Of course, not everyone was preoccupied with the political system and social instability. While the economic retrenchment predominated, some new initiatives to promote economic and technological development moved forward, such as elements of the coastal development strategy and the Torch Program. On October 24, 1988, in a show of the senior leadership's unity, Deng Xiaoping, Zhao Ziyang, Li Peng, Yao Yilin, and other senior officials inspected an electron-positron collider, and Deng renewed his calls for China to "take its place in the field of high technology."[14] A wide range of scientific and technical exchanges were under way, ranging from a prominent dialogue on international nuclear arms control that began in 1988 to continued engagement with leading foreign futurists on emerging technologies and trends.[15] These multiple vectors—economic retrenchment, debate over political reforms, popular discontent and unrest, and technological development—were all unfolding at once.

◇

The year 1989 was laden with historical import from the start: it would mark the fortieth anniversary of the People's Republic of China's (PRC's) founding in 1949, the seventieth anniversary of the May Fourth Movement in 1919, and even the 200th anniversary of the French Revolution. These seemingly unrelated anniversaries "have a common theme," Su Shaozhi wrote in January, "namely, denouncing feudal despotism and carrying forward the spirit of democracy and science." Su marveled at the fact that China, the Soviet Union, and many countries in Eastern Europe had all launched reforms of both the economic and political systems. "Modernization is by no means merely economic modernization, or 'Four Modernizations,'" he wrote. "It should be political modernization and the modernization of people."[16]

At the start of the fateful last year of the 1980s, Su gave voice to the central question of China's 1980s: What constituted modernization? His answer was a holistic transformation, from the systemic to the personal, encompassing not only the material realm of economic and technological development but also politics, "democracy," and the individual spirit. Su held out hope that this vision of modernization could be realized within China's "socialist system," so long as it was profoundly reformed.

Activist and physicist Fang Lizhi had a more extreme judgment. "Forty years of socialism have left people despondent," he asserted. Fang saw a system that could not even correctly implement the "formula" of "political dictatorship plus free economy" because "its ideology is fundamentally antithetical to the kind of private property rights that a free economy requires." However, he perceived a rising tide of democratization in society, largely driven by anger with corruption: "There can be no denying that the trend toward democracy is set."[17] Fang submitted a letter to the leadership in January calling for the release of Wei Jingsheng and other political prisoners, which was followed by several open letters from groups of scholars—one calling for "genuine implementation of political structural reform" written by Xu Liangying, and another calling for general amnesty for all political prisoners.[18]

Discussion groups on political reform, known as democracy salons, bloomed in bookstores and on university campuses across the country. Su Shaozhi, Fang Lizhi, and several other intellectuals organized a New Enlightenment Salon at Dule Bookstore in Beijing, while a charismatic student named Wang Dan organized salons at Peking University, describing his mission as pursuing "full freedom of speech and academic freedom." Wang said that Peking University "should serve as a special zone for promoting the democratization of politics," a parallel to the special economic zones' focus on political reform.[19] Cultural activity also continued unabated. In February 1989, a sprawling exhibition of several hundred artworks, titled "China / Avant-Garde," opened at the National Art Museum in Beijing to celebrate the experimental art that had been created in the PRC in the 1980s. Posters advertising the exhibition showed a U-turn arrow crossed out, as if to say, "There is no turning back." The exhibition was closed down a mere two hours after opening, when artist Xiao Lu fired a gun into her installation *Dialogue*.[20]

Amid this ferment, Zhao Ziyang continued to push for political system reform. Deng indicated that he was willing to consider increasing the participation and supervision roles of the other political parties, so Zhao instructed Bao Tong to work on "not changing the basic structure, but making them more substantial in content and form," including permitting them to have their own newspapers and even their own funding.[21] CROPSR also discussed reforming and strengthening trade unions—the goal of which was to ensure, Chen Xiaolu said in January 1989, "that if the government makes a mistake in decision-making (which is possible), causing dissatisfaction among the workers, the trade union can come forward to speak, coordinate, and maintain social stability."[22]

In addition, the leadership authorized important legal reforms that limited the power of the government, most importantly the 1989 Administrative Litigation Law, which gave citizens the right to sue government officials (but not CCP officials) for legal violations. This legislation, which Peng Zhen promoted, embodied at least one fundamental element of a true "rule of law": that law constrains the government itself, not simply private parties. These reforms provided new rights to Chinese citizens and increased the accountability of officials, but they were evolutionary and gradualist in nature.[23] CROPSR and Zhao also held high-level discussions of new press freedom laws, and the State Press and Publishing Administration specifically identified its interest in studying "press freedom" in the United States.[24]

Zhao also continued to envision economic policies that could follow the retrenchment. On March 14, in a meeting with State Planning Commission official Fang Weizhong, Zhao sketched his vision of a "long-term plan" for the Chinese economy. He focused on marketization and "interdependence" with the world in line with the coastal development strategy, emphasizing especially "international economic ties," the benefits of which China "had not fully utilized." However, these efforts were limited by new policies that Li Peng and Yao Yilin developed to strengthen the state's role in managing enterprises as a means of extending the power of the rectification policies. Zhao continued to support this official line even as he considered alternative policy directions that might soon become possible again.[25]

Facing the stalling of his agenda, in early 1989, Zhao and his advisers considered more extreme measures. They became enamored of a concept known as "neo-authoritarianism." This complex concept was influenced by the fast-growing authoritarian Asian Tigers, Deng's style of rule in China, and even foreign scholars such as Samuel Huntington who had examined the role of political order in facilitating economic development. Prominent advocates of neo-authoritarian ideas included Shanghai-based academics Wang Huning and Xiao Gongqin and Beijing-based scholars and officials, such as Chen Yizi and other members of the System Reform Commission and the Development Research Center. They supported a system of "hard government and soft economy," meaning an authoritarian system with freer markets. These neo-authoritarian advocates believed in the necessity of reassessing the political structure to strengthen the central leadership if economic and political reforms were to make next-stage breakthroughs.[26]

On January 16, 1989, official and scholar Wu Jiaxiang published an essay on neo-authoritarianism, which defined the concept as "using authority to remove obstacles on the way to developing individual freedom." Economic freedom should come before political freedom, Wu argued (explicitly citing "various East Asian countries" and Samuel Huntington, whose *Political Order in Changing Societies* had recently been translated). A powerful, charismatic leader would promote modernization, "allow the development of individual freedoms," and eventually oversee a transition to a more pluralistic order. Wu Jiaxiang and other thinkers who advocated these ideas positioned Zhao as the natural candidate for this leadership role. The essay generated tremendous debate, with hundreds of articles published in the following weeks and numerous seminars addressing neo-authoritarianism.[27]

To Zhao, this concept seemed to provide a way to reassert his authority at a moment when it had been imperiled by the difficulties of 1988. This concept could lay the groundwork for Zhao to return to ascendancy and push forward market reform, international opening, and political system reform.

Paradoxical as it may seem, Zhao believed that neo-authoritarianism could actually promote his vision of political reform. Neo-authoritarianism was a style of rule that its supporters articulated as a mechanism for achieving reform. Chinese proponents of the idea saw it as similar to Mikhail Gorbachev's forceful use of his authority to push forward glasnost and perestroika but with markets preceding and serving as the basis for democracy.[28] They cast this as a hard-nosed, "anti-romantic" concept in place of more "idealistic" democratic visions. The newspaper *Guangming Daily*, popular among intellectuals, declared, "Neo-authoritarianism is a 'special express train' to democratic politics via marketization," albeit an express train that would take a few stops before its "democratic" destination.[29]

On March 4, Zhao described neo-authoritarianism to Deng. "The main point of this theory is that the modernization of backward countries inevitably passes through a phase in which it has to turn to a politics that cannot follow Western-style democracy, but instead is centered on strong, authoritarian leaders who serve as the motivating force for change," Zhao said. Deng responded, "That is exactly what I stand for. But it is not necessary to use that formulation."[30] Deng lent his support to the idea in substance but warned Zhao to stay away from using "authoritarian" language that might raise serious concerns both domestically and internationally. Thus, when Zhao spoke with US president George H. W. Bush on February 26 in Beijing, Zhao presented these ideas but followed Deng's instructions and did not use the phrase.[31] Even so, in internal discussions, Zhao called for additional research on how to advance political reforms and economic reforms through the methods of neo-authoritarianism: "The process of democratization cannot be stopped."[32]

Some figures raised concerns about whether the Chinese leadership should draw on the experiences of societies like Singapore, Taiwan, and South Korea. In remarks delivered on March 7, Chen Yun said, "We cannot compare ourselves to the 'four little dragons.' . . . We have over 800 million peasants; this is always our starting point in considering a problem."[33] To Chen, as always, China's enormous size and rural population meant that the leadership of the CCP was crucial and that growth should be relatively slow and balanced. Neo-authoritarianism, with its focus on rapid market-oriented growth and strongman rule that would give way to pluralistic politics, seemed to threaten aspects of both priorities.

Many intellectuals attacked neo-authoritarianism as antidemocratic. These critics fundamentally disputed its claims of a "democratic" orientation—suggesting, in the words of Qin Xiaoyang, that it would fall into the "vicious circle" of elitist, corrupt, repressive rule that he felt had recurred throughout Chinese history. Qin dismissed the notion of "using the milk of the beast of autocracy and despotism to feed and nurture the baby of democracy." Other critics suggested that authoritarian leaders were ill-equipped to create the free markets that neo-authoritarian thinkers craved.[34]

Huntington himself, interviewed by his graduate student Pei Minxin, voiced reservations about the application of his ideas in China.

Pei: To a certain extent, the basis of legitimacy for what some people in China have advocated under the aegis of "new authoritarianism" is economic growth and economic results. Would such a foundation of legitimacy be feasible?

Huntington: In comparison with the foundation of legitimacy, economic results are even more directly related to the effectiveness of government. . . . This could allow that government to postpone, over the short run, the development of an even deeper foundation of legitimacy [such as democracy]. However, if a government's legitimacy were entirely and merely dependent on economic results, when it begins to lose its effectiveness economically, it would be faced with many problems.[35]

Fundamentally, the debate over neo-authoritarianism reflected the unresolved dilemmas of China's modernization in the 1980s. It was an argument among intellectuals and officials who wanted to see China "modernize" but who disagreed on what that meant: whether market-oriented economic development or political liberalization should be given priority; whether the economic and political realms were separate or interconnected; and whether China's objective ought to be ever-faster growth, consistent stability, greater freedom, various combinations of these things, or something else entirely. They drew on international influences and domestic assessments of China's situation. Most of all, this debate suggested how open-ended China's path to modernization remained in 1989—with a wide range of political, economic, and social futures all still plausible.

As these debates raged among intellectuals, the leadership began to plan for the Fourth Plenum Congress of the 13th Party later in the year to discuss the political structure. They were carefully monitoring protests in Eastern Europe and particularly the ongoing tensions in Poland. Just as talks between the leadership and opposition groups began in Warsaw in February, a Chinese government report stated, "The Polish authorities are eager to convene the roundtable talks to alleviate the tense domestic situation and stabilize the people's emotions," driven by the worsening economic situation, which included high inflation, the declining prestige of the Polish United Workers' Party, and the need to obtain new loans from the West.[36] In March, watching this situation play out, Deng Xiaoping insisted, "We must counter any forces that threaten stability, not yielding to them or even making any concessions. . . . Tightening our control in this area will not deter foreign businessmen from investing in China; on the contrary, it will reassure them."[37] Stability, always a strong goal, gained heightened importance in the face of domestic challenges and was sharpened by the situation in Eastern Europe. However, there was still room for debate and experimentation about political reforms; after all, the proponents of such reforms argued that they would provide the best foundation for long-term stability.

At a meeting in early April to prepare for the plenum, Bao Tong said, "We must give two signals: one is not to introduce the Western system in full, and the other is that the process of democratization cannot be stopped, and must be steadily and securely promoted." They planned to discuss "stability, reform, and democracy," analyze "the dissatisfaction of intellectuals, workers, and migrant workers," increase the use of legal processes to resolve problems, and "explain democracy to party and government leaders."[38] Hu Qili, meeting with Herbert Naumann of *Neues Deutschland* on April 9, stated, "The problems we currently have are problems resulting from the success of reform. . . . Very complicated tasks are awaiting us. And we have no other models we can learn from."[39] As of the spring of 1989, the potential pathways for China's modernization were numerous, open, and hotly contested.

◇

On the morning of April 8 at Zhongnanhai, the Politburo gathered for a routine discussion of educational affairs. In the midst of the meeting, Hu Yaobang stood up suddenly before collapsing back into his chair. His startled colleagues suspected that the former general secretary was having a heart attack. They rushed him to receive medical attention, but it was not enough. Hu died a week later on April 15, 1989, just over two years after his removal from power. His friends, family, and former colleagues were shocked at his sudden death.[40]

The loss of the sympathetic Hu triggered outpourings of grief around the country. On the evening of April 17, 3,000 students marched from Peking University to Tiananmen Square, the center of Beijing, where they camped overnight.[41] The next day, a group of liberal officials and thinkers, including Yu Guangyuan, Li Rui, Hu's son Hu Deping, and other prominent intellectuals such as Yan Jiaqi, Su Shaozhi, and Dai Qing, gathered for a memorial service. Their eulogies lamented the challenges that China's liberalization had encountered. "But it can be said that his death has given the CCP a historical opportunity," historian Zhang Lifan said. "This may be the last chance to strengthen its cohesion and revitalize its spirit." After the meeting, the participants joined the mourners at Tiananmen Square to present their wreath, which bore a message: "Comrade Yaobang lives on in our hearts forever."[42]

By Hu's funeral on April 22, the number of mourners in the square had swelled to 100,000. No longer were they only mourning Hu, but they were also calling for faster reform and greater freedom.[43] Three students knelt in front of the Great Hall of the People and lifted a seven-point petition over their heads:

First, reevaluate and praise Hu Yaobang's contributions.

Second, negate the previous movements against "spiritual pollution" and "bourgeois liberalization."

Third, allow the unofficial press and freedom of speech.

Fourth, publish government leaders' income and holdings.

Fifth, abolish the "Beijing ten points" [that restricted public assembly and demonstrations].

Sixth, increase education funding and the salaries of intellectuals.

Seventh, report faithfully on this movement.[44]

Inside the Great Hall, Deng Xiaoping, his hair freshly dyed black, stood stonily before the body of his onetime protégé. Zhao Ziyang delivered the official eulogy, taking a conciliatory and understanding tone: "The entire party and the people of the whole country profoundly mourn Comrade Hu Yaobang, and this is because of his great revolutionary spirit and noble ideological and moral qualities. . . . Comrade Hu Yaobang is immortal!"[45] However, the government did not respond to the seven-point petition's demands, and the crisis continued to escalate, with the students calling for comprehensive democratic political reform.

The protest movement had clear antecedents, including the student protests of the winter of 1986–1987 that had hastened Hu's removal and the earlier 1978–1979 Xidan Democracy Wall movement. However, this time, the protesters were more numerous, building on the mass success of critiques such as *River Elegy,* and their sense of frustration, impatience, and opportunity were far greater, also strengthened by economic grievances. Workers began to join the protests, motivated by inflation eating into their wages, enterprise reforms producing layoffs, and injustices that limited upward mobility even as the well-connected grew richer. They criticized those who lived grandly, from wealthy businessmen driving fancy foreign cars to Zhao Ziyang's penchant for playing golf, while so many laborers toiled fruitlessly.[46] According to a survey conducted in 1989, corruption was seen by approximately 70 percent of respondents as the most likely cause of the social unrest in China, and the protesters' anti-corruption slogans received even more enthusiastic support among respondents than their calls for democracy and justice.[47] Once again, the economic and political systems were seen as inextricable—not only by the leadership but also by these protesters.

With crowds filling Beijing's central square, Deng Xiaoping's mind turned to Poland, which he continued to follow with great concern. On April 4, 1989, Poland's Round Table Agreement effectively dissolved the position of the Communist Party general secretary and set the stage for a large-scale electoral victory for the Solidarity coalition in the upcoming national elections. Deng was determined to prevent the CCP from meeting the same fate as its Polish counterpart.[48] One senior Chinese official told Egon Krenz, the second-ranking official in East Germany, that the Chinese leaders believed that "legalizing the opposition would be the beginning of the end of socialism in China" because of the Polish experience with Solidarity, and they were prepared to take extreme measures to stop it.[49]

However, many leaders, most importantly Zhao Ziyang, felt that the leadership's goal should be to "reduce tensions" and to engage in dialogue with the protesters. The thousands of students camping out in the square should be encouraged to return to their classes, and only people who engaged in "beating, smashing, looting, burning, or trespassing" should be punished. Finally, "bloodshed must be avoided, no matter what." Zhao met with Deng Xiaoping on April 19 to discuss the developing unrest and outlined these views.[50] On April 23, believing that Deng supported this approach and the situation was under control, Zhao departed at Deng's orders for a long-planned state visit to North Korea. His actions clearly demonstrated that he believed matters in Beijing were not likely to escalate. He appeared to believe that the student movement should be treated as an opportunity to apply the principles of greater openness and responsiveness in the CCP's style of rule that undergirded the political reform agenda.[51]

Yet this was a profoundly consequential misjudgment. With Zhao away, Li Peng, Beijing mayor Chen Xitong, and Deng Xiaoping himself branded the protests a rebellious political "turmoil," posing a severe threat to CCP rule and requiring a forceful response. An agitated Deng met with Li Peng and Yang Shangkun on April 25, exclaiming, "We have several million PLA soldiers, what do we have to fear?"[52] The next day, the front page of *People's Daily* carried a headline that shocked the students: "Take a Clear-Cut Stand against the Disturbances." The protests were described as opposing the CCP under the manipulation of a small group of malicious leaders. "Their purpose is to sow dissension among the people, plunge the whole country into chaos, and sabotage the political situation of stability and unity," it stated. "This is a serious political struggle confronting the whole party and the people of all nationalities throughout the country."[53]

This editorial's tone was intended to intimidate the protesters, but it caused a dramatic escalation. The leaders of the protests reacted by hardening their stance and intensifying their criticisms of Li and Deng, with a new wave of protests involving an estimated 150,000 people occurring in Beijing the following day.[54] According to a report by the Beijing Armed Police Corps, following publication of the editorial, protesters targeted *People's Daily* headquarters to show their anger. (What went unmentioned in this report, however, was that many members of the newspaper's staff had joined the protests.[55]) A group of protesters at Beijing Normal University declared, "All we want is an honest government, a wiping out of corruption, and a speeding up of reform. . . . We strongly demand that the government have a peaceful dialogue with us and stop accusing the students of creating 'turmoil.'"[56]

In line with the April 26 editorial's demand for a "clear-cut stand," officials put immense pressure on thinkers, writers, and publications to support the official line. In Shanghai, the bold *World Economic Herald* was the focus of this pressure. As tensions rose in Beijing, Jiang Zemin, party secretary of Shanghai, decided to make an example of the newspaper. Following an inspection by his lieutenants, Zeng Qinghong and Chen Zhili, Jiang suspended the chief editor, Qin Benli, and shuttered the paper.[57]

Zhao returned from North Korea on April 29. In his and his allies' telling, he immediately sought a way to reduce tensions. He decided to deliver a set of public remarks on the seventieth anniversary of the May Fourth Movement, the 1919 student movement that the CCP celebrated because it had criticized imperialism, highlighted the value of science and democracy in rejuvenating the Chinese nation, and helped lead to the birth of the CCP in 1921. Zhao sought to walk a fine line, taking a more conciliatory tone than the April 26 editorial without directly contravening it—in other words, seeking to apply pressure on his colleagues and signal to the students that channels for dialogue remained open.[58] First, on May 3, Zhao delivered a speech that hewed to the official line, stressing the paramount importance of "maintaining social stability" and adhering to the Four Cardinal Principles, though he refused to add language about "opposing bourgeois liberalization."[59] The next day, May 4, Zhao spoke in a markedly warmer tone in public comments at a meeting of the Asian Development Bank (ADB). Zhao declared that the majority of the students were "not opposed to our basic system." Promising "no major turmoil," Zhao called for dialogue and consultation between the leadership and the protesters. Many would later believe that Zhao was making a bid to appeal directly to the protesters; some would see this message as an attempt to diffuse tensions, and others would describe it as terribly naive.[60]

Zhao came under strong criticism from Li Peng, Chen Yun, and others for going off message and for using an international venue to pressure his colleagues.[61] The protesters responded more warmly to his tone, but some leaders of the movement also used the anniversary to formalize a new declaration, the "May Fourth Manifesto," which was read out in Tiananmen Square by Örkesh Dölet (Wu'er Kaixi), chairman of the Beijing Students' Autonomous Federation.[62] Groups of students, workers, and other protesters began to form distinct identities, such as the newly established Beijing Workers' Autonomous Federation, the PRC's first independent trade union, and to branch out nationwide, with sympathetic protests and organizations cropping up from Guangdong to Hohhot.[63] Zhao's gambit, premised on his view that dialogue would produce a better outcome than opposition or repression, had produced at best an ambiguous result. Two rifts—between the party leadership and the protesters, and within the party leadership itself—were obvious and widening.

Following Zhao's speech of May 4, events quickly began to spiral. On the same day, according to Li Peng's diary, Yao Yilin stated that he believed Zhao to be encouraging the turmoil and seeking to "attack Deng, topple Li, and keep Zhao."[64] Zhao continued to emphasize the need for a peaceful resolution, arguing that the student movement should be seen as largely patriotic; that the leadership should respond to the students' demands, especially their anti-corruption stipulations; and that all matters related to the protests should be handled according to "democratic and legal procedures."[65] He also instructed Hu Qili and Rui Xingwen, who oversaw the propaganda apparatus, to remain committed to transparency and openness by reporting fairly on the demonstrations.[66] With these actions, Zhao displayed a characteristic combination of visionary and opportunistic behavior—tenaciously pushing for a more transparent, responsive political system, while also seeking to bolster his own position as other senior leaders criticized him.

Zhao had also been attempting to secure a meeting with Deng, but the paramount leader remained worryingly unavailable. On the morning of May 11, Li Peng recollected, Deng's secretary, Wang Ruilin, called Li and urged him to adhere to the April 26 editorial—a remarkable gesture from the paramount leader that clearly indicated his displeasure with Zhao's ADB speech.[67] Zhao "always believed that Deng supported his reforms, and didn't consider what would happen if Deng withdrew his support," Wu Wei recalled.[68] The crisis was worsening.

On May 13, a group of students including Wang Dan, Chai Ling, Örkesh Dölet, and Li Lu commenced a hunger strike, demanding that the leadership engage in a meaningful dialogue with the protesters. Writer Liu Xiaobo called for democratization with real "checks and balances" and no "absolute power."[69] On the same day, after more than a week of trying, Zhao, accompanied by Yang Shangkun, finally met with Deng. According to Zhao's recollection, Deng again stated that he supported Zhao's approach to the protests. They also discussed the importance of taking action against corruption. Yet Deng evidently complained, "I am so fatigued right now, my brain isn't up to the task, and my tinnitus is intense. I can't hear clearly what you are saying." Even so, Zhao left the May 13 meeting feeling buoyed by Deng's approach.[70]

The next day, Zhao told Bao Tong that he wished to make public the decision of the Central Committee to ask Deng to remain "at the helm" on major issues following his retirement at the 13th Party Congress, as a way of "defending the image of Comrade Xiaoping." This may have been thoroughly self-serving, but Li Peng had acknowledged the reality of Deng's paramount status in his February meeting with George H. W. Bush—Deng "remains China's paramount leader," Li had said, "but he leaves the details to us"—but those statements were not made public. Zhao sought to use a similar format: he was slated to meet with Gorbachev on May 16, a major state visit that marked the warming of Sino-Soviet relations, and he told Bao Tong to include this information in his notes for this meeting.[71] However, tensions within the leadership continued to grow, and on May 15, Zhao and Li had a heated argument about the April 26 editorial, which Zhao still felt was a serious problem—a conversation that Li recalled Zhao ended in great frustration and anger.[72]

On May 16, as the students continued the hunger strike, Zhao and Deng held separate meetings with Gorbachev.[73] Although Zhao dismissed the students as "look[ing] at many things naively, simplistically," the most significant statement that he made in the meeting came at the beginning, as television cameras rolled. Zhao stated, "All our party comrades know that they cannot do without [Deng's] leadership, wisdom, and experience. At the First Plenum, elected by the Thirteenth Congress, a fairly important decision was made—that in all big questions we should turn to Deng as to a leader. This decision was not published, but I am informing you about it today."[74] Zhao's statement "surprised" Gorbachev. "I got the impression that with his statement he sort of wanted to face Deng with the situation," Gorbachev recalled. "I thought that there was some deep meaning behind this."[75]

The effect of Zhao's public comment was what Zhao, in his memoirs, calls "a great misunderstanding." Deng and his family immediately declared that Zhao had betrayed the paramount leader by forcing him out from behind the curtain at the moment of maximal risk. On the morning of May 17, Deng's daughter, Deng Nan, vented her rage in a call with Zhao.[76] Zhao may well have intended to use this revelation to pressure the rest of the leadership or avoid personal blame for the escalating crisis, but even if he did not intend it, that was the effect. Protesters including intellectuals Yan Jiaqi and Bao Zunxin issued a declaration stating, "Yesterday afternoon, party General Secretary Zhao Ziyang announced that every important policy decision in China must be approved by this senile autocrat. . . . Down with autocracy!"[77] Some of the protest leaders worried that they were becoming pawns in an elite power struggle, but large crowds filled the streets calling for Deng and Li Peng to step down.[78]

On May 17, Deng convened the senior leadership of Zhao, Li Peng, Yao Yilin, Hu Qili, Qiao Shi, and Yang Shangkun at his home. The topic was whether to implement martial law in the capital. A fierce debate ensued, during which Zhao opposed martial law and designation of the protests as "anti-party" and "anti-socialist." Li and Yao accused Zhao of causing "two voices [to have] emerged at the party center" due to his ADB speech. By the meeting's conclusion, Deng made the decision to impose martial law, demand the cessation of all hunger strikes and demonstrations, and deploy the PLA to restore order in Beijing. Deng's worries about his own public image were powerful; Zhao recalled that Deng stated, "Don't reveal that it was I who made the decision to impose martial law!"[79]

Zhao's approach had lost out. On the early morning of May 18, he and Li Peng visited the hunger-striking students at the hospital, after which Li held an acrimonious and disorderly dialogue with student leaders at the Great Hall of the People.[80] Li Peng also visited Capital Iron and Steel to listen to and calm workers' complaints, but the participation of workers in the protests became even more prominent in the following days. The workers were sometimes critical of the students as elitist and held a negative view of the market reforms and of Zhao Ziyang, whom they saw as too eager to allow price increases that hurt ordinary people. Their vision of democracy focused on increasing workers' voice and decision-making power in enterprises and workplaces. They formed a powerful (if too often overlooked) force in the movement, with leaders such as railway worker Han Dongfang delivering impassioned speeches demanding the right of Chinese workers to organize their own unions and praising the "national patriotic movement that directly affects the interests of the working class."[81]

As the leadership began to implement the decision to impose martial law to quell the protests, Zhao went on sick leave and decided to make a public statement. In the early morning of May 19, Zhao walked to the square to speak directly to the protesters. This gesture was not unprecedented; he and Li had visited students and workers before, as noted above, and Zhao likely saw the gesture of a leader reaching out to the people as continuous with the CCP's populist style of rule, epitomized by Mao's dialogues with the Red Guards. However, his message was remarkable. Urging them to call off the hunger strike, Zhao—his voice filled with emotion as he held a small megaphone—told the students,

> Students, we came too late. Sorry, students. Whatever you say and criticize about us is deserved. My purpose here now is not to ask for your forgiveness. . . . Now what is most important is to end this hunger strike. I know that you are doing this in the

hope that the party and the government will give a most satisfactory answer for what you are asking for. I feel our channel for dialogue is open and some problems need to be resolved through a process. . . . You are not like us, we are already old, and do not matter. . . . Students, can you think rationally for a moment? Now the situation is very dire as you all know, the party and nation are very anxious, the whole society is worried. Besides Beijing is the capital, and each day the situation is worsening; this cannot go on. You mean well, and have the interests of our country at heart, but if this goes on, it will go out of control and will have various adverse effects.[82]

Zhao concluded his speech to the students by thanking them and bowing his head several times. What began for Zhao as a response to the movement that was both visionary and opportunistic had grown into a moral stand, with Zhao seeking to warn the students that they risked endangering their lives to a greater extent than they realized. The famous phrase "we came too late" held several meanings: that Zhao felt the leadership should have had a meaningful dialogue with the students earlier, that the decision to impose martial law had already been made, and that the situation in the central leadership had gone too far already for anyone to protect the students.

Reflecting Zhao's instructions to the propaganda apparatus to report on the movement, this speech and a photograph of Zhao delivering his remarks, with his aide Wen Jiabao staring anxiously by his side, appeared on the front page of People's Daily.[83] Twelve members of the NPC's Standing Committee made an "emergency appeal" to convene the group to discuss how to respond to the movement, but their request went unanswered.[84] Among Zhao's advisers, the situation had grown chaotic and tense. Chen Yizi was organizing intellectuals and officials to support the protesters, drafting a statement that demanded that the leadership reveal its decision making on the crisis and convene special sessions of both the NPC and the CCP congress, which several State Council research organizations and the Beijing Association of Young Economists signed. Chen believed that many senior cadres were supportive of the movement and that numerous PLA leaders, both current and retired, did not want to use force against the protesters.[85] Evidence suggests that Chen was correct, with several prominent generals circulating letters expressing their concerns, and the commander of the 38th Army, Xu Qinxian, refusing to lead his troops into Beijing before swiftly being arrested.[86]

The next day, on May 20 at 10:00 a.m., the imposition of martial law began. Li Peng read out the decree announcing that China had entered a state of emergency. Li did not mention Zhao's name, though he decried individuals whose "goal is precisely to organizationally subvert the CCP leadership." Li promised "resolute and decisive measures to put an end to the turmoil." Yang Shangkun spoke next, promising that martial law would be orderly and that the troops would not hurt the protesters.[87]

On the same day, Deng held another meeting at his home at which the leadership (including Chen Yun, Li Xiannian, Peng Zhen, Yang Shangkun, Li Peng, and Yao Yilin but not Zhao) reaffirmed support of the April 26 editorial. This meeting concluded that "the root of the crisis" originated "within the party." Deng had decided to remove Zhao from power and appoint Jiang Zemin as the new CCP general secretary. The decision was not yet formal since a Politburo meeting would be required to dismiss Zhao, but it was conclusive. Zhao had lost Deng's support, and his downfall had occurred with extraordinary speed.[88] Zhao subsequently wrote letters contesting the decision and pressing for the use of peaceful, legal means to resolve the standoff, but Deng ignored him.[89]

As news of the martial law declaration circulated among the protesters, some felt optimistic, while others were panicked. "The soldiers are not our real enemies," a group of students from Peking University wrote on May 20. "They have been tricked into coming here, and they do not really understand the situation. . . . So we must tell them the truth and make them understand the people's intentions."

The next day, the independent student association of Beijing Normal University issued a plea to the troops: "Soldiers, we love you. The people love you. Your hands must not be stained with the people's blood!"[90]

PART VI

TIANANMEN AND AFTER

CHAPTER 13

Political Crackdown and Narrative Crisis

In the weeks that followed the declaration of martial law on May 20, 1989, the CCP leadership made a series of decisions that would forever alter its rule—including, above all, the violent suppression of the protest movement centered on Tiananmen Square. The world's attention understandably has focused on this brutal crackdown of June 3–4. But to comprehend the meaning of the crisis of May–June 1989 and its effects for the CCP, we must see the crackdown in a longer time frame, stretching from May 20 to June 30 and beyond. For the CCP, this was not only a political crisis, a social crisis, and a military crisis. It was also a narrative crisis or even an epistemic crisis—a rupture in ways of understanding the world among elements of the leadership, the party, and Chinese society.[1]

To respond to this epistemic crisis, the CCP leadership went beyond the well-known political crackdown following the bloodshed of early June. It initiated a thoroughgoing political process called a "rectification"—reeducating party members and overcoming ideological deviation as it had done before at key junctures, epitomized by Mao's rectification movement at Yan'an in the 1940s.[2] China's rulers also introduced internally many concepts and formulations that provided the official way of interpreting the crisis (following from the discussion of propaganda and ideology in Chapters 2 and 3). Deng Xiaoping's views, set out in a series of remarks during this six-week period, were the most definitive statements, but other senior officials offered variations, additions, and different points of emphasis. They found a variety of avenues for debating the meaning of the "turmoil" of 1989 and reinterpreting the history of the decade that had led to the crisis. This gradual process of rectification in fact began weeks before the violent suppression of the protest movement and intensified thereafter. The top-down processes of crackdown and rectification were interrelated, and taken together, they had long-term effects on the leadership's priorities.

The basic timeline of the six weeks chronicled in this chapter is well known. After declaring martial law, the CCP leadership promoted Jiang Zemin to replace Zhao Ziyang as general secretary, unsuccessfully tried to move troops into Beijing, and gathered repeatedly to debate what to do. On the night of June 3–4, with the approval of Deng, the troops were authorized to clear Tiananmen Square and restore order in Beijing by any means necessary. Hundreds and likely thousands of civilians died. This violence horrified observers around the world, but the Chinese leadership maintained the fiction that the process had been peaceful, marred only by counterrevolutionary "rioters" who had instigated violence against the troops. In the subsequent weeks, the leadership regained its unity, punished participants in the protests, purged Zhao, and in late June held a series of meetings passing judgments and describing how it had "controlled the turmoil and quelled the counterrevolutionary rebellion."[3]

Yet this narrative tells only part of the story. The six-week period between May 20 and June 30 also witnessed, as one propaganda document phrased it, "an important historical period—reflecting on many problems and experiencing rapid changes in our understanding to an unimaginable degree."[4] Several changes were most significant. While holding firm to the mantra of "reform and opening," CCP leaders argued that the 1980s had tolerated excessive "bourgeois liberalization" with insufficient attention to Deng Xiaoping's authoritarian "Four Cardinal Principles." They endorsed the centrality of a single "core" leader, built a renewed cult of Deng Xiaoping, and forbade public disagreements among the leadership. And they revived the Maoist idea of "peaceful evolution" as a pervasive and central threat.

This process was the beginning of an important and largely overlooked consolidation of a new vision for China's modernization, reinterpreting the preceding decade and articulating principles to guide China's future. After a decade that had seen the development of many openly contested paths for China's future, the weeks immediately following the declaration of martial law on May 20 witnessed a radical recasting of the 1980s as a period of history and a reorienting of China's future based on constricting that open-endedness. The CCP leadership's response to this crisis produced a process of rewriting history—an effort that new evidence now allows scholars to understand in unprecedented depth.[5] The violence of the military repression was accompanied by a severe indictment of errors made during the 1980s and a decisive shift toward a more limited and authoritarian vision of how China could change in the future.

◇

After the declaration of martial law, internal deliberations continued in an atmosphere of great tension. It became clear that the removal of Zhao and the decision to use overwhelming force against the protestors would enable the deeply divided leadership to reunite against a common enemy—namely, the forces that allegedly sought to overthrow the party from within and without.

As the troops attempted to enter the city, Beijing residents blocked them from advancing for at least fifty hours. The participation of workers in the movement became even more prominent, with the Beijing Workers' Autonomous Federation (BWAF) swelling in size to 10,000 members, calling for a general strike, and forming brigades to stop the troops' movements. On the morning of May 22, the troops received orders to withdraw. The next evening, the students unveiled a statue called the Goddess of Democracy. Although the number of protesters was evidently declining as time passed, a large group remained committed to staying in the square.[6]

The leadership moved swiftly to impose "unity of thinking" on the CCP and the People's Liberation Army (PLA). On May 24, an alarmed Yang Shangkun—the CCP elder who served as secretary general of the Central Military Commission (CMC) and had replaced Li Xiannian as president of the People's Republic of China—spoke at an enlarged CMC meeting, demanding discipline in the ranks and criticizing Zhao for having created "two different voices in the Standing Committee."[7] On May 27, Li Xiannian delivered a speech in which he stated that responsibility for the turmoil rested specifically with "an individual person within the CCP leadership"—a formulation that a former aide to Li recalled was proposed directly by Deng.[8] Documents criticizing Zhao circulated among the leadership, and on May 28, Bao Tong was imprisoned. Meanwhile, Zhao was "detained and isolated," as he described it, at his home.[9]

Even before the military crackdown to clear Tiananmen Square, the senior leadership had decided to implement a major new initiative to strengthen Deng Xiaoping's position in response to the protesters' fierce criticisms. They created a powerful new moniker for Deng: "the chief architect of reform and opening." The history of this term, which is still in widespread use today, turns out to be inextricable from the Tiananmen crackdown and the purge of Zhao.

The notion of Deng as the "chief architect" was endorsed at a late-night meeting in Zhongnanhai on May 22, with Li Peng, Qiao Shi, Yao Yilin, Yang Shangkun, and several other elders. "Who is the core of our party, who represents reform and development—is it Comrade Zhao Ziyang or Comrade Deng Xiaoping?" Li asked rhetorically. "Comrade Xiaoping is the chief architect of the reform and opening policies. Of course, Comrade Zhao Ziyang also did a little work, but it was the implementation of Comrade Xiaoping['s designs]. . . . We must make a clear stand to safeguard Comrade Xiaoping."[10] On May 26, the formulation received its major propaganda debut on the front page of *People's Daily*. "The chief architect of China's reform and opening is Comrade Deng Xiaoping and not any other person," Li Peng was quoted as saying.[11] The vague phrase "not any other person" pointed to the purged Zhao.

This important new concept of Deng Xiaoping as the "chief architect of reform and opening" not only codified a prevailing view and shored up Deng's prestige. It also offered a prominent boost to the concept of "reform and opening" while imposing martial law—affirming that this agenda had not been in error, even if as-yet-undefined mistakes had led to the upheaval. This lent a more positive face to the decision to "resolutely stop the turmoil" and underscored that reinterpreting the official narrative of the preceding decade would remain a central area of focus.

In addition to rolling out these propaganda messages, the Chinese leadership continued to closely follow the popular movements in Eastern Europe and the Soviet Union. Watching "turmoil" at home and abroad, prominent members of the senior leadership reflected on the deeper causes of the crisis of 1989. If long-term responsibility for the "turmoil" rested with Zhao Ziyang, then where exactly had he gone wrong? Li Peng's answer was primarily the corrosive effects of Western influence and "the West's so-called democracy, freedom, and human rights"; for Chen Yun, the primary cause was neglect of "Marxist ideological education." By the end of May, the consensus term for both pernicious foreign influences and domestic ideological laxity had been found by reviving the concept used in 1987 to criticize the prior student protests: "bourgeois liberalization."[12]

Deng Xiaoping remained focused on installing the new leadership of Jiang Zemin and building up another concept, that of the leadership "core." In a conversation with Li Peng and Yao Yilin on May 31, Deng offered his perspective on recovering the leadership's unity. He reaffirmed his, Li Xiannian's, and Chen Yun's support for "reform and opening" as well as the 13th Party Congress's work report, stating, "Not a single word can be changed." Jiang Zemin, who was the only figure able to garner consensus support of the elders, would be the "core" of the new third generation of leadership. Deng warned that all of the new leaders, including Li and Yao, should follow Jiang. "Do not be dissatisfied with each other, do not deplete your own power," Deng concluded. "The key is the leadership core."[13]

This focus on absolute loyalty to the leadership core was particularly important in late May as troops mobilized to retake Tiananmen Square. Over the coming days, hundreds of thousands of troops moved from the outskirts of Beijing into the center of the city in small, secret groups, moving gradually so that the crowds could not again block them. They readied weaponry, including tanks and armored vehicles. The leadership remained concerned about insubordination; not only had Xu Qinxian refused to lead his troops into Beijing but seven prominent retired generals including Zhang Aiping had written a letter demanding that there must be no "bloody incident." As political scientist Joseph Torigian has shown, the head of the PLA's General Political Department, Yang Baibing (the half brother of Yang Shangkun), acknowledged on May 31 that "some comrades" had "doubts" and were even "scared," due to their "lack of deep understanding."[14] Directives that circulated on June 2 from the PLA General Political Department emphasized the necessity of firm unity with "our party's leadership core" of Deng Xiaoping and his generation of revolutionary elders.[15] The intensified focus on both Deng and the concept of a leadership core were invoked as strategies to respond to the immediate crisis of May 1989, but they would endure for decades to come.

On the night of June 3, the troops received orders to assemble in Beijing and march toward the square. At 3:00 a.m. on June 4, the Romanian ambassador telegrammed to Bucharest, "On the major boulevards and in Tiananmen Square over 1 million people gathered. Appeals were read over loudspeakers [asking] the population not to be intimidated and to show its solidarity against the government and against those in the leadership which declared and are applying martial law. During the [army's] attempts to reach Tiananmen overnight, some [demonstrators] were killed when transports [ran] over people. . . . An extremely confrontational situation evolved."[16] Sitting in the courtyard of his home in central Beijing, Zhao Ziyang could hear gunfire. The troops fired on groups of protesters, and young people ran through the streets carrying the dead and the wounded.[17]

According to PLA accounts from 1989, government personnel and buildings came under attack. So-called violent mobs attacked the Ministry of Radio, Film, and Television, which had been broadcasting government propaganda. At approximately 2:55 a.m. on June 4, according to the ministry's account, "bricks, stones, bottles, and Molotov cocktails were used to injure the guards"; the attackers were "thugs and people who did not understand the truth."[18] A Beijing detachment of the People's Armed Police reported in similar language that it had come under attack from "a small number of bad guys" and "people who did not understand the truth."[19]

In the leadership's self-justification of the crackdown, this emphasis on "people who did not understand the truth" was highly significant. For the CCP, broader participation in the riot, beyond simply "thugs" and "bad guys," reflected an epistemic crisis among people who lacked a clear understanding of "the truth." Thus, this crisis required more than a violent crackdown to restore order; it also required a major effort to restore "understanding of the truth."

By the morning of June 4, Tiananmen Square had been emptied. An unknown number of civilians had been killed, and many more had been wounded. The clearing of the square took less than twelve hours, though violence on the streets continued for several days thereafter.[20] Security forces killed protesters in Chengdu, the capital of Sichuan Province, and other crackdowns and arrests occurred in Guangdong, Hangzhou, Heilongjiang, Shandong, Shanghai, Shenyang, Xi'an, Urumqi, and other places.[21] Former senior official Li Rui, in his diary, called it a "black weekend." He observed acts of spontaneous mourning around Beijing, spotting "wreaths dedicated to dead martyrs," "children's shoes, women's shoes, watches, and other remnants," alongside scattered white flowers.[22]

The brutality of the crackdown stunned observers around the world. "Chinese troops of the PLA opened fire with automatic weapons early today on huge crowds of civilians in Beijing," Jim Mann and David Holley wrote in the Los Angeles Times. "For China, it was a fundamental turning point."[23]

Even so, the US government immediately emphasized that its relationship with the Chinese government would endure. On June 5, President George H. W. Bush reaffirmed, "I don't want to see a total break in this relationship."[24] Socialist countries, meanwhile, doubled down in support of the CCP. East German state security issued orders to "effectively suppress" any activities and public statements critical of the CCP.[25]

On June 6, the Chinese leadership held a press conference with State Council spokesman Yuan Mu, who declared that "a shocking counter-revolutionary rebellion, unprecedented in the history of the Republic, has occurred in the capital." Despite ample evidence to the contrary, he insisted that only approximately 300 people had died, and the handling of the movement was "peaceful." With chilling attempts at humor that would earn him a worldwide reputation as "Li Peng's 'hatchet man,'" Yuan continued, laughing sarcastically, "For a period, class struggle was not stressed at all and even political struggle was not stressed. It was said that they were all gone . . . and that the world was full of love."[26] The Chinese leadership had no desire to pretend that it believed the world was "full of love." Instead, a major period of "political struggle" was in the making.

In the heat of this ongoing crisis, rumors swirled. Had Li Peng been shot during a failed assassination attempt? Had Deng Xiaoping died? Were PLA soldiers fighting each other? Yet, internally, the leadership remained focused on the ideas that had been set out in the weeks prior to the violent crackdown, which remained remarkably unchanged by the violence itself. On June 8, Chen Yun commented on a draft of a report on Zhao Ziyang's errors. "For a long time, Comrade Zhao Ziyang has repeatedly shown himself to be someone with severe bourgeois liberal thinking," Chen wrote, praising Deng as "the core of the party center" who had "initiated reform and opening." Chen also voiced concerns about "mistakes in economic work" over the preceding decade—an important, if vague, comment that was in tension with Deng's continued embrace of "the achievements of ten years of reform."[27]

The economic situation remained highly uncertain after the crackdown, especially in the face of international sanctions. The United States quickly suspended government-to-government sales and weapons exports and eventually prohibited the US Export-Import Bank from providing financial assistance to China, while calling on international institutions such as the World Bank to freeze new loans; Japan, Italy, Belgium, and Canada also froze lending and imposed sanctions.[28] Commerce Minister Hu Ping said that "relatively large volatility" in the domestic market was possible and he called for new measures to "stabilize the market."[29] Even so, given the CCP's view of the "turmoil" as an epistemic crisis, greater public clarity was needed to foster a stable, unified "understanding" about what had occurred. Although the violence of June 3–4 marked the bloody end of the 1989 protest movement in Beijing, it was in fact only one part of a larger process of the CCP reasserting nationwide social, political, ideological, and narrative control.

With this need in mind, members of the senior leadership began to reappear publicly. On June 9, Deng Xiaoping delivered a speech to military officials whose continued fealty the CCP needed. In one of the most significant speeches of his career, Deng offered "tribute to the martyrs" from the PLA who had died in clashes with the protesters, but he also did much more: Deng's speech mapped out the official line, producing definitive language to facilitate the leadership's recovery from the crisis of 1989. It merits close reading.

Some aspects of this speech were lifted directly from Deng's comments on May 31. He once again stressed that the "reform and opening" would continue and he praised the correctness of both the 1978 Third Plenum and the 1987 13th Party Congress. He added, "We must stick with a combination of planned economy and market economy."[30]

However, the most significant aspect of Deng's remarks was his analysis of the "turmoil." First, Deng asserted that it was "inevitable": Because of international and domestic factors, he said, it was "bound to happen and is independent of man's will. It was just a matter of time and scale." This claim was not simply rhetorical. Deng's use of "inevitable" invoked the Marxist theory of historical forces, positioning the "turmoil" and subsequent ongoing crackdown as part of a historical teleology toward triumph of the CCP and socialism. Second, the threat was existential: a "rebellious clique" sought to work with hostile foreign forces "to establish a totally Western-dependent bourgeois republic," taking advantage of "ordinary people who are unable to distinguish between right and wrong." This escalated the stakes of the epistemic crisis. Third, Deng offered his fundamental interpretation of the crisis as "the confrontation between the Four Cardinal Principles and bourgeois liberalization." He said, "It is not that we have not talked about such things. . . . What we have not had is continuity in these talks, and there has been no action—or there has been hardly even any talk." Deng made clear that he was talking about not simply the preceding months but "the past ten years."[31]

Deng's analysis of the crisis of 1989 was thus also a reinterpretation of the decade of the 1980s. Fast economic growth and market-oriented reform were the right goals for the economy, Deng stated, but the open consideration of other forms of liberalization during the 1980s had been a serious error. The 1980s were recast as a decade in which too much "bourgeois liberalization" had been tolerated, and the leadership had placed insufficient focus on the Four Cardinal Principles. This was a fundamental indictment of many visions of China's modernization that had been considered but were no longer permissible. Instead of debate and experimentation, Deng now asserted a simple schematic—"the confrontation between the Four Cardinal Principles and bourgeois liberalization"—as the core challenge confronting China, which would require continuous education and action to remedy. These would be the central tasks for the CCP in the period ahead.

◇

Efforts to build up the cult of Deng Xiaoping accelerated after his speech on June 9. Official media called Deng's speech "completely correct," and it was circulated to cadres nationwide for mandatory study. The propaganda apparatus asserted extraordinary control over the publication and printing of Deng's major speeches during the crisis, especially the June 9 speech. The concern was that any deviation—whether a mistyped word, misplaced comma, or more deliberate editing of his comments—might interfere with the process of ideological and political education that these documents were supposed to produce. On June 16, an urgent notice prohibited "the self-publication or printing of Deng Xiaoping's important speeches and other documents." In an unusual step, the State Council declared that these documents were only to be printed by People's Publishing House under direct supervision of the central government.[32] Deng's speech was a "powerful weapon for unifying the party, the army, and the people," said a PLA propaganda document on June 21.[33] The dominant concern was that the narrative of the crisis must be standardized in a top-down process guided by the central leadership to impose nationwide unity.

However, Deng felt that more needed to be done than simply circulating and studying his speeches. On June 16, he summoned the Politburo Standing Committee for a meeting focused on improving the party's public image. Deng called on the assembled leaders to affirm their support for reform and opening and to confront corruption so as to gain greater domestic public support and mitigate international concern. Yet it was equally important to "clear up what aspects of our past [work] were mistaken." He even addressed the political system, the reform of which had been such a priority under Zhao, but Deng now focused on stability and the Four Cardinal Principles. However, referring to American "abuse and rumors," Deng advised, "We can talk less about dictatorship, or just not talk about it at all." (Somewhat ironically, given the initiative under way to build up Deng's image, he also stated that it was "very unhealthy" for "the destiny of a country to be built on the prestige of one or two people.") He concluded by calling for further "party building" efforts, which would focus on attacking bourgeois liberalization and strengthening the Four Cardinal Principles.[34]

Deng was also acutely aware of the multiple audiences for the leadership's words and actions: the CCP itself, the broader Chinese populace, and international observers. As a result, public pronouncements would be relatively few and would primarily seek to put forward the CCP's official narrative for public consumption. The deeper process of rectifying this epistemic crisis would take place primarily in secret, with key decisions left unannounced to the public and important directives transmitted through internal channels. This secret process would produce a dramatic continuation of the crackdown as well as powerful new ideas about China's future.

By mid-month, June 1989 had already contained a world of change for China and the CCP, but the fast-moving process of rectification was far from over. The next task was to formally criticize Zhao Ziyang, whose status had remained suspended since May 19. On June 19–21, an enlarged Politburo meeting gathered to make decisions that would be announced at the Fourth Plenum of the 13th Central Committee, which was slated to begin on June 23. Unusually, important documents that became available in the summer of 2019 reveal what happened at this meeting in great detail.[35]

This three-day meeting began formally, with Beijing party secretary Li Ximing delivering a report that established the official chronology of events, while attacking Zhao's negative effect on propaganda, education, and the Four Cardinal Principles. Evaluating the "achievements" and "mistakes" of the preceding decade, Li called for rectifying and purging the party to maintain its "ideological and organizational purity" and "restore the party's image with the people."[36]

The meeting then shifted to focus on denouncing Zhao more specifically, with Li Peng presenting a report on Zhao's wrongdoings. This was about indicting Zhao; his erasure from history was yet to come. Li's report, prepared with Qiao Shi, Hu Qili, and Yao Yilin, endorsed stripping Zhao of his positions. The report stated, "At a critical juncture in the life and death of the party and the country, Comrade Zhao Ziyang made the mistake of supporting the unrest and splitting the party." It also asserted that Zhao had made significant mistakes in economic policy during the 1980s—pursuing results with "too much impatience" and allowing inflation to get out of control in 1988—and in ideological and political work. The source of the CCP's crisis was not only Zhao's actions in April–May 1989 but also the decisions made during his decade in power.[37]

On June 20, Zhao was allowed to leave his home to appear in front of his former colleagues and speak in his own defense. He acknowledged "shortcomings, errors, and mistakes" in his work and accepted his dismissal from his leadership posts, but he defended his economic record. Most importantly, he refused to accept the accusations that he had "supported the unrest" and "split the party." He stated, "There may sometimes be differences in the emphasis of public statements made by leading personages, or their approach may not be quite the same, or people may come up with differing comments. Such things have occurred time and again and cannot be called 'splitting the party.'"[38] Clearly and boldly, Zhao insisted that political reform must remain a priority: "Reform includes reform of the economic system and reform of the political system. These two aspects affect one another. . . . If [political system reform] lags too far behind, continuing with the reform of the economic system will be very difficult and various social and political contradictions will ensue."[39]

Although he spoke forcefully, there was no changing the verdict. After Zhao spoke, Beijing mayor Chen Xitong responded quickly, "I feel that Comrade Ziyang is making excuses."[40] Yao Yilin demanded that "all comrades" must "spend some hours seriously studying [Deng's June 9] speech in order to attain a unanimous ideological understanding." Yao urged his colleagues to remember how high the stakes were: "The imperialists . . . came to cooperate with us and express friendship not only for the purpose of making money but also for the purpose of changing the nature of our country and remodeling our country to be a capitalist society." Only the CCP could ensure that China remained "a genuinely independent state."[41]

The next day, other officials spoke to denounce Zhao and demonstrate their "unanimous ideological understanding." The typical form of these comments was to begin by expressing agreement with Deng's speeches and Li Peng's report and invoking the perils of bourgeois liberalization and the importance of the Four Cardinal Principles. Then, speakers added additional information or commentary.

Several attacks were particularly significant. Many speakers expanded the critique of the 1980s to encompass other domains. Although many of these comments were framed as attacks on Zhao Ziyang, they extended beyond specific issues for which he might be punished and instead sought to criticize aspects of the overall direction pursued during the preceding decade. First, party elders saw a wide range of political errors; Zhao had "violated collective leadership," complained Yang Shangkun, and after becoming general secretary, "the Standing Committee never formed a core."[42] Second, some of the decade's economic policies came under harsh attack, with Li Xiannian blaming Zhao for "deficits, inflation, rising prices, and unfair distribution" and accusing him of favoritism for private enterprises, which produced "long-term overheating and serious imbalances between aggregate supply and aggregate demand."[43] Third, some of the strongest attacks were reserved for the perceived ideological laxity and political openness of the 1980s, which had permitted public opinion and propaganda work to be overrun by bourgeois liberalization and led to a loss of "unified thinking." Song Ping denounced "people who do not understand China's national conditions" and "want to apply the shallow claims put forward by Western theory"; instead, leadership should be "put in the hands of true Marxists."[44]

In line with these powerful concerns, nearly all the speakers focused on the existential threat of what they called "peaceful evolution," a term that denoted the desire of the United States and other foreign powers to gradually change the socialist countries into capitalist democracies.

Criticism of peaceful evolution in the 1950s and 1960s, launched by Mao, initially waned during the 1970s and 1980s, but in the midst of the domestic and international crises of 1989, it returned to the center of official discourse. This revival featured a large cast of villains: American, French, and British officials, and even Hungarian financier George Soros. Minister of Public Security Wang Fang focused on the allegedly close connections between Soros and members of Zhao's "brain trust," pointing to purported agreements with Zhao's adviser Chen Yizi as well as funding of over US$1 million that Soros had provided.[45] More broadly, the usage of "peaceful evolution" indicated that the CCP leadership was seeking to reappropriate elements from its own history to interpret the crisis of 1989 and justify its decisions.

In addition to this focus on "peaceful evolution," some leaders accused the US government of deep-seated hypocrisy. Jiang Zemin invoked then-governor Ronald Reagan's use of troops to crack down on California student protests in 1969 to complain that the United States was using double standards.[46] Other aspects of this alleged foreign hypocrisy were seen as more beneficial to China. Wang Zhen responded to concerns that foreign investment in China would decline because of the massacre by predicting that "foreign capitalists" will "definitely not give up the big world market of China. If they see your country is stable and can make money, they'll come." The United States was thus portrayed as a meddling superpower intent on subverting the CCP and socialism but at the same time riven by hypocrisy.[47]

Beyond removing Zhao, other officials who were closely associated with him and perceived to have followed his line were also criticized. Hu Qili, Rui Xingwen, and Yan Mingfu delivered strong self-criticisms. The three men would be removed from their positions without further punishment, but participants in the protests would not be so lucky. To regain stability, Wang Zhen encouraged severe punishments: although stating that cases should be handled lawfully, "those who should be killed should be killed, those who should be sentenced should be sentenced, and we can use reeducation through labor for a large number."[48]

At this secret June 21 conclave, the most fundamental means of recasting the history of the 1980s was a purported distinction between

Deng Xiaoping's "intentions" and Zhao's erroneous mode of implementation. Wang Zhen provided a pungent statement of this idea:

> The reform and opening that Comrade Xiaoping talked about is different in its essence from the reform and opening that Comrade Zhao Ziyang talked about. Comrade Xiaoping's reform and opening aimed to uphold national sovereignty and ethnic group respect, uphold the socialist road, uphold a combination of a planned economy and market adjustment, continue to protect the creative spirit of bitter struggle, and to direct investment toward basic industry and agriculture. Comrade Zhao Ziyang's reform and opening was taking the capitalist road, increasing consumption, and generating waste and corruption. Comrade Zhao Ziyang was definitely not the implementer of Comrade Xiaoping's reform and opening policy but was its distorter and destroyer.[49]

This extraordinary statement asserted that Deng and Zhao had two fundamentally different conceptions of "reform and opening." Deng's conception, in this telling, was an essentially conservative vision, premised on the Four Cardinal Principles and economic policies that sounded more like Chen Yun than Deng. Zhao, meanwhile, was purportedly "taking the capitalist road" and pursuing wasteful, consumption-oriented economic policies and permitting corruption to flourish. Wang's comments recalled the long history of "line struggle" in CCP history, especially Mao's purge of his longtime deputy Liu Shaoqi (and Deng Xiaoping as Liu's chief lieutenant), whom Mao branded a "capitalist roader" during the Cultural Revolution—events that Wang and the other assembled leaders experienced firsthand.[50] Like Mao and Liu in a prior era, Wang positioned Deng's and Zhao's visions as antithetical, even antagonistic, despite the fact that all assembled knew that Deng and Zhao had worked closely together throughout the 1980s.

Wang's claims that Zhao was the "distorter" and "destroyer" of "Comrade Xiaoping's reform and opening policy" drew a sharp division between the 1980s and China's future. Instead of Zhao's liberalizing, capitalistic vision for China's modernization, Wang called not only for ruling out political system reform but also for promoting economic policies that would strengthen the socialist, planned aspects of the Chinese system.[51] Attacking Zhao offered an opportunity for this searing indictment of the history of the 1980s and a call for a profoundly different path going forward.

◇

What explains the dramatic and complete downfall of Zhao on display in these June meetings? Several views have emerged from the recollections of participants. One view comes from Zhao himself, who believed that a series of misunderstandings about his intentions had caused the rapid breakdown of Deng's trust in him; Deng felt "he saw through me during the June 4 events and said I myself 'revealed my true colors.'"[52] A second view emphasizes that a large-scale, destabilizing protest movement necessarily led to a forceful crackdown because from the perspective of CCP ideologues such as Deng Liqun, impermissible bourgeois liberalization needed to be repressed.[53] A third and related view accentuates the tensions between Deng's economic aims and political aims, the latter of which he now pushed aside. As Bao Tong phrased it, Deng had been "both a sincere supporter of the reforms and a determined defender of the things we had to reform."[54] A fourth view emphasizes Zhao's own errors in judgment about the political dynamics around him. Singaporean prime minister Lee Kuan Yew, a frequent interlocutor with the CCP leadership, said in a confidential conversation with British officials in July 1989 that Zhao had "miscalculated" because "he was clearly no 'street fighter.'"[55]

Each of these views explains elements of the rapid loss of support that Zhao suffered. It is clear that even though different views were often aired on matters of policy during the 1980s, the disagreements did not reach the level of dissonance displayed in May 1989 between Zhao and the rest of the leadership. The basic tensions inherent in the system the CCP had developed—with frontline leaders managing affairs and elders wielding influence backstage—further primed the CCP to overreact when faced with unprecedented domestic instability. In addition, the cumulative effect of Zhao's misjudgments on economic policy and political maneuvering during the 1980s had severely weakened his position well before the spring of 1989. As a result, when he stepped far out of line, removing him became both feasible and, to Deng and the other elders, desirable. An additional error was that Zhao seemed not to understand how politically weakened he had become. When he failed to sway his colleagues to try to lower tensions through conciliation and dialogue, he grew isolated in both his public and internal statements, culminating in his warning to the students. Although there is no evidence that Zhao sought to "overthrow socialism," he did break with the official line of the party center, the April 26 editorial, and the decision to impose martial law—a fact made apparent to all by his public statements from May 4 to his remarks in Tiananmen Square on May 19. This was an unsustainable position for the CCP's general secretary.

At the Fourth Plenum of the 13th Central Committee, which convened on June 23–24, the party leadership formally approved the purge of Zhao. It labeled the student movement "a planned, organized, and premeditated political turmoil" that "further developed into a counter-revolutionary rebellion in Beijing." Crucially, these decisions were made together; the determinations about Zhao and about the student movement were now permanently interconnected. The Fourth Plenum communiqué stated, "Although [Zhao] did some things that were beneficial to the reform, the opening of China to the outside world, and economic work when he held principal leading posts in the party and the state, he obviously erred. . . . He took a passive approach to adhering to the Four Cardinal Principals and opposing bourgeois liberalization and he gravely neglected party building, the building of spiritual civilization, and ideological and political work, causing serious losses to the cause of the party."[56] When Jiang Zemin spoke to accept the position of general secretary on June 24, he praised the leadership for "correctly handling the issue of Comrade Zhao Ziyang." Economic development under the mantle of "reform and opening" could proceed but in a more conservative form, and only if it did not require or produce political or ideological liberalization that might undermine the Four Cardinal Principles. Zhao became emblematic of the "split" between these two guiding ideologies; Jiang made clear that the party would never again countenance such a "split."[57]

As the senior leadership was presenting these decisions to the public at the Fourth Plenum, a major wave of propaganda directives circulated internally. These documents emphasized that with order "restored," the focus of work was now to acknowledge the deeper roots—a long-term plot to "replace the Four Cardinal Principles with bourgeois liberalization"— and the equally long-term effort to solve those problems.[58]

Importantly, these materials described an epochal shift in "under-standing" that had occurred over the preceding months. One propaganda document acknowledged, "This struggle only lasted two months from its beginning to the present moment, but regarding our thinking, it seems that we have experienced an important historical period—reflecting on many problems and experiencing rapid changes in our understanding to an unimaginable degree."[59] Another instruction document elaborated that the crisis was "the product of an entire historical era," particularly the failure of ideological and political work during the 1980s.[60] The severity of this situation was the subject of a report on "spiritual civilization" by state investigators, which depicted Chinese society as wracked with "insecu-rity," superstition, violent crime, gambling, indiscipline, and a "loss of faith" in the party and socialism. It called for ideological and political work to be treated with the same seriousness as economic development, demanding that "spiritual civilization guidelines and targets" be imple-mented as thoroughly as "economic guidelines and targets."[61]

These statements provided the ideological basis for a major disci-plinary drive that accelerated in late June. The Central Commission for Discipline Inspection conducted a careful review of all party members in Beijing. Investigations also targeted individuals and organizations that were believed to have aided or participated in the movement. For example, Beijing municipal officials, working in tandem with PLA of-ficers, occupied the headquarters of the Stone Group, which they accused of providing equipment and funding to the "illegal" student organ-izations. Stone's leader, Wan Runnan, fled the country, while Cao Si-yuan and other researchers at its in-house think tank were arrested.[62] Leaders of the movement were punished severely. Han Dongfang, the railway worker who had helped lead the BWAF, was imprisoned without trial; several dozen workers were announced to have been executed, with actual numbers estimated to be well above 100. Student leaders such as

Wang Dan, Zhou Fengsuo, and Liu Gang were jailed, while others, such as Örkesh Dölet, Li Lu, and Chai Ling—along with officials and intellectuals such as Yan Jiaqi, Chen Yizi, and Su Shaozhi—escaped from China.[63]

Unsurprisingly, given the central role of students in the protests, universities came under special scrutiny. On June 22, the Organization Department issued regulations that students who were already provisional party members but had participated in the protests would be suspended from the party, subject to intensive review, and all new applicants to the party would be judged on their "performance in the struggle."[64] For students who had been involved in the protests, graduation and work assignments were suspended until they participated in "ideological-political education" in order to ensure that they could "distinguish between right and wrong and raise awareness." However, the central government also requested that special efforts be made to ensure that students could find jobs; clearly, the leadership remained concerned that unemployment would make it more difficult to keep graduating students in line.[65] As we shall see, rectifying the party, the economy, and society would intensify significantly in the coming months.

The central leadership also began to "rectify" media and publishing. Periodicals that had supported the movement were punished or terminated. The works of people "who participated in the counterrevolutionary rebellion" or "advocate for Western capitalism or bourgeois liberalization and refute the Four Cardinal Principles" came under severe new prohibitions.[66] Subsequent notices listed the names of individuals whose works were particularly important to ban, including Fang Lizhi, Liu Binyan, Yan Jiaqi, Chen Yizi, and Su Shaozhi, as well as protester leaders such as Wang Dan and Liu Xiaobo. These bans were to be conducted in secret: "This notice should not be made public and should not appear in newspapers."[67] The goal of this wave of censorship in the immediate aftermath of the crisis was not only to remove now-illegal content from bookshelves; it was also to begin laying the foundations for removing these figures, and their ideas about alternative paths for China's modernization, from history.

◇

During the twenty-six days after the violent clearing of Tiananmen Square, the leadership had initiated a sweeping program of control amid crisis and recovery: a series of nascent political and ideological initiatives that gave unprecedented emphasis to the Four Cardinal Principles and combating bourgeois liberalization, built up the leadership "core" and the cult of Deng Xiaoping while purging Zhao Ziyang and other undesirable elements, and consolidated an official interpretation of the crisis and its deeper causes during the 1980s. It had indeed been "an important historical period" of "rapid changes in our understanding."

On June 30, the leadership formally issued Central Document No. 3, laying out nationwide plans for the rectification that had already begun, and Beijing mayor Chen Xitong delivered a report on the "quelling of the counterrevolutionary rebellion." This report was given to Chen to be read out; it thus should be seen as a document produced by the leadership rather than as his personal report.[68] It chronicled how the student movement developed into a "counterrevolutionary rebellion" that was stopped by "resolute measures" and it cataloged Zhao Ziyang's "serious mistakes." It also indicted what it called Zhao's "brain trust," meaning his network of advisers and intellectuals. Yet its dominant criticism returned to the "split" that Deng had articulated "between bourgeois liberalization and the Four Cardinal Principles." This remained the "fundamental lesson" about the errors of the 1980s, which had now been recast through the frame of the events of April–June 1989.

Chen concluded his speech with a call for a major new drive not simply to impose stability on society but also to assert more powerfully a new official narrative. The task that lay ahead was to refocus the attention of the party, the Chinese people, and the world on where China was headed in the future under CCP leadership. However, this goal was bound up with recasting history. Chen's parting words made this clear: "The rumors will be cleared away and the truth and facts will come out."[69]

CHAPTER 14

Recasting Reform and Opening

With the new critique of the preceding decade now clear, the months between July and November 1989 witnessed significant and enduring changes in how the CCP intended to guide China's modernization in the future. The crackdown and rectification quickly became a vast campaign to promulgate a new official narrative while implementing retrenchment policies in the economy, strengthening "ideological and political work" across society, and eliminating the now more broadly defined category of bourgeois liberalization. Some thought that policymaking was in a deep freeze, but in fact the leadership was in a period of frenzied activity. This post-Tiananmen campaign constituted a comprehensive attempt to more strictly impose limits on all forms of liberalization, including China's openness to global capitalism. This campaign focused with particular intensity on the CCP itself. After all, if the "root of the crisis" of 1989 "originated within the party," preventing "turmoil" in the future would require focusing on the party that was supposed to be the vanguard of society in China's Leninist system. In contrast to the leadership's previous endorsement of separating the party and the government, this period witnessed the consolidation of party leadership at all levels.

The goal was to strictly bifurcate economic development and political liberalization so that the latter would wither.

The task often required using historical revision to develop and legitimize the party's vision for China's future. As party members were investigated for their loyalty, intensive domestic and international propaganda efforts got under way to recast the history of the 1980s to emphasize a battle between "bourgeois liberalization" and Deng Xiaoping's authoritarian Four Cardinal Principles, as discussed in the prior chapter. The official narrative systematically erased Zhao Ziyang from the historical record and attributed even higher historical status to Deng Xiaoping. Unlike the analogous activity after Mao's death, which prepared for the open-ended pursuit of modernization, this process in 1989 dramatically limited the range of possible paths forward for China. Although debate continued over the direction of the economy, the CCP ruled out political system reforms, elaborated on the need for strengthening party leadership, villainized the protest movement, and intensified the rhetoric of "peaceful evolution" and antagonism between China and the capitalist world. This new official narrative was engineered to achieve significant political goals: to present a triumphant story of resolute decisions propelling China's rise on the single correct path taken, to erase and exclude the representation of forces that were pushing for alternative paths, and to end lingering uncertainties about how China ought to modernize in the future.

On July 1, less than one month after the violent clearing of Tiananmen Square, the Central Organization Department held its annual celebration of the founding of the CCP. Chen Yun's speech at this event warned that "some people had lost confidence in the party," requiring the party to earn anew the people's faith. Hu Qiaomu elaborated on the need for deepened rectification: "Lingering unclear questions must be solved now."[1] Although these speeches consistently repeated the official line, some CCP elders found space for more creative verbal expression. Party elder Chen Pixian used a striking pun: he said that the protesters had "loving capitalism disease," playing on the Chinese term for AIDS, *ai zi bing* (艾滋病). This pun replaced *ai* and *zi* with the characters *ai* (爱), meaning "love," and *zi* (资), meaning "capitalism," creating the homonym "loving capitalism disease" (爱资病). A small number of AIDS cases had appeared in China beginning in the mid-1980s, and the disease had been ideologized as a foreign, "capitalist" affliction that was "invading" China. Chen urged cadres to "set straight . . . why socialism is good and capitalism is bad," adding, "Right now some people have 'loving capitalism disease' and want to do something like reevaluate capitalism." This phenomenon of "loving capitalism disease" endangered socialism in China, and Chen called on the entire CCP to work to eliminate it.[2]

The case of the "loving capitalism disease" pun is illustrative of the rapid proliferation of official language and formulations in the immediate aftermath of the 1989 crisis. Following Chen's speech, it became one of a wide range of metaphors for bourgeois liberalization that commentators in the post-Tiananmen period deployed in their writings. Zhou Zhiliang, party secretary at Beijing Normal University, argued, "It is precisely because their minds had 'loving capitalism disease' that they confounded right and wrong, and confused the enemy and ourselves."[3] Aurally identical to the Chinese term for AIDS, "loving capitalism disease" was characterized as one of several "wrong tendencies in the ideological field" that had allegedly caused the turmoil of 1989.[4] CCP leaders believed deeply that the specific language used for "ideological and political work" was, as former vice premier Kang Shi'en stated, capable of "shaping the soul of man and the worldview of man."[5] This was the goal of the rectification agenda.

Of course, this rectification was far more than simply rhetorical.[6] The leadership remained fixated on pernicious foreign forces allegedly pushing for "peaceful evolution." On July 2, Deng Xiaoping met secretly with two personal emissaries of President George H. W. Bush, National Security Advisor Brent Scowcroft and Deputy Secretary of State Lawrence Eagleburger. Bush had sent the officials on a clandestine mission to assure Deng that the United States remained committed to a strong relationship with China and to encourage the leadership to limit the scope of the rectification, especially executions. However, Deng, accompanied by Li Peng, voiced anger at the alleged US role in fomenting the "turmoil" while emphatically denying "the so-called bloodbath." In response to Deng's accusations, a stunned Scowcroft asked Deng to be "sensitive" that "what you do and the way you do it will have a major impact on opinion in the United States and throughout the Western world."[7] As we shall see, China's "sensitivity" about foreign opinion primarily manifested itself in maintaining the secrecy with which the rectification campaign would be conducted.

The purported US involvement motivated the Ministry of Public Security to ferret out Zhao's alleged collusion with "foreign forces." In July, following from Wang Feng's accusations at the enlarged Politburo meeting, the ministry arrested and interrogated the representatives of George Soros's China office. Soros reportedly sent a letter directly to Deng Xiaoping, offering him "the opportunity to examine in detail the fund's operations" in China, but the damage had been done.[8] The leadership continued to attack Soros. In a speech on August 18, the head of the Central Organization Department, Song Ping, denounced Soros's foundation for providing funding to "train people who have advocated peaceful evolution and total Westernization."[9] The CCP saw an ongoing global plot to destroy it.

Despite these tensions, in July and August of 1989, the leadership congratulated itself on emerging from the immediate crisis and implementing the beginning stage of the rectification campaign. On July 14, Jiang Zemin told a senior East German official that "many people in China are today more clearheaded than before," but much work remained. The core task, Jiang added, was "socialist and patriotic education." Complaining about Western news reporting, Jiang uttered a phrase that could itself describe the CCP's own approach to propaganda: "A lie becomes a truth when you repeat it a thousand times."[10] Watching Chinese politics closely, Mikhail Gorbachev told Rajiv Gandhi, "I am confident that now the Chinese leaders have extinguished just the external manifestations of conflict but the conflict itself is not over. . . . And one will need measures of anything but military character to settle it." The task facing the Chinese leadership, Gorbachev mused, was "to orient themselves" now that they had rejected Zhao Ziyang as "unduly keen about liberalization" and mounted a "defense of socialist principles."[11]

Gorbachev was partly correct. The top CCP leaders had determined the direction of the system going forward; they now saw their task not as orienting themselves but as orienting the rest of the party and society through the epistemic dimensions of the rectification that was under way. A major new narrative push took place from July through the early fall of 1989, which not only sounded the core themes that had emerged in the preceding months but also presented a significant new official narrative. This encompassed both the backward-looking indictment of China's 1980s, discussed in the previous chapter, and a new forward-looking teleology for China's continued rise.

The propaganda apparatus was a key site of this work. For example, a notice to publishing houses on July 11 emphasized the need for publishing to reflect "the core values of socialism," "loyalty to the one-party spirit," and "firm opposition to capitalism."[12] Patriotism, national unity, and the pedagogical role of history remained central to propaganda, with new attention to the important concept of China's distinctive "national conditions." Understanding "national conditions" would inspire an appreciation of the necessity of socialism and CCP rule as well as "profound sentiments toward the motherland akin to what they feel toward their own mother."[13] However, it is important to note that patriotism and nationalism were not, as some scholars have suggested, kept distinct from "ideology" or offered up by the CCP to "replace Marxism-Leninism and Maoist ideology."[14] The Chinese leadership sought to infuse patriotism and nationalism even more fully into the official ideology, and this campaign also included a strong focus on the idea of class struggle.

The propaganda apparatus had a more important role to play going forward than at any other point since Mao's death. At a propaganda conference on July 20, Li Ruihuan discussed how to recover from the "crisis" in propaganda work that Zhao Ziyang had caused. With Zhao gone, Li said, "Now you can do many things that you wanted to do in the past but were unable to do."[15]

With this strong encouragement, the propaganda apparatus followed Zhao's purge and criticism with another decision of enduring importance: it erased Zhao from the record. This was not just downplaying his role or criticizing some of his policies; it was a totalizing effort to ensure that the history of China's 1980s could be told without reference to the man who had led the country for the entirety of the decade. A propaganda directive sent to publishers across the country on August 7, 1989, provided detailed instructions on how to erase Zhao. For one, it announced that no further books on Zhao could be published. It also elaborated on the specific rules for handling Zhao's name, quotations, and image—in essence, a targeted guide to censorship. In compilations and other contexts in which quoting Zhao's writings or reports was necessary, these materials must be "treated with earnest skill," excising his quotations when possible, and if not possible, "the quoted material may be retained but should not include his personal name." No biographies of Zhao would be permitted and any that already existed "shall be destroyed." In addition, books and magazines "would no longer publish photographs of Comrade Zhao Ziyang . . . and reprinted or republished books will remove photographs of him." Propaganda texts, if they mentioned him at all, would focus on Zhao's misdeeds during April–June 1989 and briefly reproduce the official interpretation of his tenure as marked by permitting "bourgeois liberalization" to run rampant and neglecting the Four Cardinal Principles.[16] Zhao was to become a historical nonperson, invisible in official accounts of the era that he had shaped and cast as irrelevant to China's future—as he watched, silenced and under house arrest.

What would fill the void left by Zhao's erasure? To a remarkable degree, the answer was Deng Xiaoping. A wide range of policies, ideas, and legacies that Zhao had developed were now directly attributed to Deng. These came under the banner of Deng as the "chief architect of reform and opening," which became directly linked to the need to assert a new narrative for China's 1980s and China's future. Deng, as the leadership core, was now firmly depicted as the protagonist, originator, and designer of "reform and opening," the preeminent figure entitled to decide how China should modernize. The positive decisions of the 1980s were the product of his heroic vision and even purportedly the results of his direct, detailed management of economic policymaking. On July 10, a notice titled "Deng Xiaoping Is the Chief Architect of Reform and Opening" declared that Deng "personally planned the blueprints" and "took charge of implementing reform and opening." Bemoaning the "vicious" attacks on Deng, the directive said that understanding Deng's role "is not a personal question for Comrade Deng Xiaoping, but rather a major question related to whether reform and opening can continue and proceed in the correct direction."[17] This "correct direction" was pursuing economic development with a firm and even violent rejection of anything that might resemble "bourgeois liberalization."

In other words, the decision to erase Zhao and build up Deng was not only an act of censorship or rewriting history; it was a way of crafting an argument about China's modernization going forward. A directive circulated to all People's Liberation Army (PLA) units on July 20, 1989, hammered home this point. Assessing "the past ten years of reform," it stated flatly, "all of [the major policies] were put forward by Deng Xiaoping, and all drew on the hard work and political wisdom of the elder generation. Comrade Deng Xiaoping is the standard-bearer and chief architect of reform and opening." The directive acknowledged internally that Zhao Ziyang "did a bit of useful work in the implementation," but underscored, "he was not a reformer but rather an agent of bourgeois liberalization within the party."[18] China's future depended on rejecting Zhao's legacy and instead following Deng's edicts.

Rejecting Zhao involved casting political reform as pursued in the 1980s as totally impermissible. Whereas a wide range of ideas about political modernization had been considered by the senior leadership throughout the 1980s, and especially in 1986–1989, the new official narrative left no room for such open-endedness. A secret directive circulated on September 13 laid out clearly the new line: "Political system reform must be conducive to strengthening and improving the party's leadership. It by no means may downplay or weaken the party's leadership, let alone abolish the party's leadership."[19] Political reforms to marginalize party cells and increase the power of university, school, and research institution heads were rolled back in August. Enterprises faced a similar fate after Li Xiannian demanded that state factories that had implemented the contracting system must focus on "how to strengthen the party's leadership instead of weakening the party's leadership."[20] Books on political system reform that had been planned for publication were canceled or rewritten, and the central offices that had been managing the political system reform were suspended indefinitely.[21]

However, this newly constructed distinction between Deng and Zhao raised a fundamental question: Did rejecting Zhao also mean rejecting his economic policy agenda or only his ideas about political reform and "bourgeois liberalization"? After all, Deng had reaffirmed "reform and opening" and even the 13th Party Congress's work report, but many other voices were eager to push back against the agenda of market reforms and rapid growth. For example, on July 26, Wu Shuqing, vice president of Renmin University, delivered a stern speech on widespread public dissatisfaction with corruption and economic unfairness, arguing that "reforms only talk about the role of entrepreneurs," making workers and farmers "feel as if they are not respected and their political status has declined." Wu blamed officials who "believed that Western economic theory can save China" and "confused the distinction between the economic system and the social system, and even promoted the convergence of capitalism and socialism"—all veiled references to Zhao Ziyang. For thinkers like Wu, doubling down on China's "national characteristics" was the best answer to regain the trust of workers, farmers, and intellectuals.[22] Reflecting the high-level support for these views, Wu was promoted to president of Peking University shortly thereafter in August, replacing Ding Shisun, who was viewed as having been insufficiently tough on the student protesters.[23]

Senior officials also seized this opportunity. Breaking with Deng's affirmation of the 13th Party Congress, Chen Yun explicitly attacked "Zhao Ziyang's slogan of 'the state manages the market, and the market guides the economy'" (the main economic slogan of that congress), which he believed had led to excessive decentralization and the loss of control over the economy.[24] While voicing his fealty to "reform and opening," Chen thus pushed back against what had been Zhao's—and Deng's—favored interpretation of that agenda after 1987.

In line with Chen Yun's criticisms, Li Peng and Yao Yilin ensured the deepening of the economic retrenchment policies of 1988, but now this retrenchment was openly presented as the result of Zhao's alleged mismanagement of the economy. In July and August, the State Council met repeatedly to discuss the economic situation, with Yao taking the lead on policies to control inflation, and a three-year retrenchment plan got under way. The leadership mainly blamed the economic overheating on the policies of decentralization, especially the loosening of controls in the planning and fiscal systems, which had permitted local governments to make reckless investments that led to shortages and bottlenecks. To Chen, Yao, and Li, a firm clampdown by the central government was the only solution.[25]

On August 28, the State Council approved the State Planning Commission's plan for the remainder of the year. This plan focused on controlling prices, boosting agricultural production, promoting thriftiness in production to relieve shortages of energy and raw materials, reducing expenditures in governments and enterprises, reducing the scale of investment, and tightening the money supply. All of these measures were designed to further cool down the economy while laying the foundations for the three-year retrenchment, which was approved by the Central Committee in early November. These measures for "stable and coordinated" development were extremely effective at reining in growth, with the annual growth rate of gross national product falling from 11.2 percent in 1988 to 3.9 in 1989. As of the fall of 1989, Deng did not push back significantly against these retrenchment policies, contenting himself with the fact that "reform and opening," at least as a slogan, remained in place.[26]

◇

For Deng, another crucial priority was strengthening the leadership "core" of General Secretary Jiang Zemin. Although his own prestige had been damaged by the upheavals of 1989, and despite being in his mid-eighties, Deng remained the CCP's preeminent living leader. To confer the mantle of leadership, Deng told the Central Committee on September 4 that he had at last decided to retire fully and pass his title of chairman of the Central Military Commission to Jiang.[27] On October 10, a commentary in *People's Daily* referred publicly to Jiang as the "core of the third generation of leadership" for the first time.[28]

To understand the significance of Jiang's public designation as the leadership "core," it is important to place this moment in dialogue with the process of removing and criticizing Zhao Ziyang, Jiang's predecessor. On September 3, Zhao was informed that he was under investigation for manipulating the student turmoil, leaking information to the outside world, taking a line that contradicted Deng and the party center, tolerating bourgeois liberalization, and advancing his personal ambition via the concept of "neo-authoritarianism" and public portrayals such as *River Elegy*. Bao Tong was charged with leaking state secrets and other crimes, but Zhao was not charged with a crime or expelled from the CCP. Zhao and Deng, who had worked together to construct the policies of "reform and opening" for the entirety of the 1980s, would never speak again.[29]

Jiang's elevation and Zhao's removal together became a way of mapping out a vision for a new conception of the leadership "core" as a central institution in Chinese politics. Although both Hu Yaobang and Zhao had been positioned as successors to Deng, neither man was designated as the "core." In their era, airing dissenting views was part of the process of policy competition in which Deng, Chen Yun, Zhao, Hu, and others disagreed openly as well as in private. Provided that these disagreements did not undermine the foundations of the CCP's authority, this debate over policy, even if contentious, was a part of advancing "reform and opening." Yet Zhao's downfall on charges of having "split the party" required a renewed emphasis on intellectual and political unanimity under a single supreme arbiter—a pattern set by Mao and carried forward inconsistently by Deng. For decades to come, the legacy of 1989 meant that this institution of the "core" would remain in constant tension with the system of collective leadership. Zhao would be treated as an enemy of the regime and erased from the record, but in this way, his ghostly outline would continue to shape the form and practice of politics in China under the CCP.

In the summer and early fall of 1989, the propaganda apparatus also aggressively villainized the protest movement while building up the heroism of the PLA "martyrs." It demonized prominent figures in the protest movement, such as Fang Lizhi—then still ensconced with his wife, Li Shuxian, in the US embassy in Beijing, where they had fled during the crackdown—by circulating materials offering evidence of their alleged crimes.[30] As the sanctions placed on China began to cause significant economic pain, this period also saw the strengthening of a narrative placing China in opposition to the capitalist world.[31] By July, despite the stringent measures taken to promote stability at home, threatening assessments of the international environment only became more numerous. One instructional document admitted that since the 1960s, capitalism had gained "vitality" and "prosperity," while the socialist countries struggled. This gave great power to "the American warlords' tricks and schemes of the Cold War and ideological struggle." However, even more importantly, this meant that economic engagement with the capitalist world posed severe risks to China. Mocking the idea of "free trade," the author noted that the United States and Western Europe had "expanded their economic ties with China," but "they do not favor Chinese socialism or the CCP. . . . The Americans give the Chinese some economic benefits to keep the Chinese oriented toward the West."[32] Going forward, the leadership made clear that in addition to opposing bourgeois liberalization, it would more assertively seek to limit the pressures that came from economic ties with the capitalist world.

Yet China's rulers clearly wanted the sanctions to be removed and to see China's image improve. A report on international public opinion anticipated hopefully, "when most countries know the truth, they will support the measures taken by the Chinese government and will restore and strengthen their economic and technological exchanges with China."[33] To this end, on August 1, the central government held a forum for overseas propaganda units on remedying "serious damage to our country's international image," which made clear that certain aspects of the process under way would not be suitable for international audiences: "We should say little or not discuss at all issues concerning ideology and different value concepts. It is not suitable to report abroad the actions that are difficult for foreigners to understand." As for punishing the protesters, the document advised, "talk little about tracking people down, arrests, trials, and executions."[34] International audiences were to have evidence of as few changes as possible. Instead, they were to be presented with an image of China that was growing economically and stable politically—with the rectification and "ideology and different value concepts" kept hidden.

On the same day as this forum on international propaganda, the Chinese leadership received a boost when former US national security advisor and secretary of state Henry Kissinger published an op-ed in the *Washington Post* titled, "Caricature of Deng as Tyrant Is Unfair." To Kissinger, Deng was not a "tyrant" but rather, a tragic hero: "His tragedy," Kissinger wrote, was that "he has been too committed to communism to be prepared to face the fact that free-market economies cannot be instituted by a totalitarian Communist Party; but he was also too committed to progress to abandon a course bound to undermine one-party rule."[35] What Kissinger did not state was that Deng and other senior members of the CCP leadership did not see this state of affairs as a "tragedy" at all. Whereas during the 1980s, they had considered many forms of economic and political reform, now they had recommitted themselves to a narrower and more authoritarian agenda for modernization.

When Kissinger next visited China in November, Deng received him warmly in the Great Hall of the People. Kissinger was quoted in a short, prominent item in *People's Daily,* praising Deng by using the exact phrase that official propaganda now deployed: "In the future you will still play a huge role in China's development, just as you have in the past. You are the chief architect of China's reform and opening."[36]

Well beyond presenting this major new official narrative of the past and the future, CCP leaders were engaged in a secretive and far-reaching organizational rectification. This combined the targeting of individuals for "political offenses" with a broader anti-corruption campaign. In total, according to official statistics, 13,254 cadres were subject to disciplinary measures for "political offenses," and 1,179 were punished for direct participation in "mass demonstrations and related disturbances" (although Richard Baum notes that these numbers seem quite small, given that approximately 800,000 party members had supported the student movement). However, by October 1992, the anti-corruption drive had led to the disciplining of 733,543 party members, of whom 154,289 were expelled from the party, although they were almost all low-ranking cadres.[37] The evidence cited above that the propaganda apparatus was explicitly instructed to carry out punishments "without open reportage" underscores that the real number of individuals arrested, punished, or executed during the rectification is certainly higher than the public, official numbers.

Yet the rectification campaign involved more than punishment. It also required "education" and "unifying thinking"—instilling the core ideas of the new narrative in party members and society. Publishing houses remained under scrutiny, and universities held repeated investigations. The Organization Department also reported that a large number of students and postdoctoral scholars who had gone abroad for research had not returned on time—suggesting that they perhaps planned to stay abroad indefinitely—and called for a stricter political review of scholars who wished to go abroad in the future.[38] The rectification campaign may have been most consequential within party organizations. With a focus on party building and anti-corruption, the summer and fall saw a wave of decisions to guide the "education" of party members who had participated in the protests but were not beyond saving. As long as these cadres reflected appropriately on their "mistakes," their cases could be "settled."[39]

Less forgivable, as new regulations announced on September 8, were crimes of bribery, graft, and corruption, including the much-discussed crime of "official profiteering," meaning officials who exploited the dual-track system to resell goods at market prices that had been obtained at low in-plan prices. This facet of the rectification campaign was designed to appeal to the wider public. It included stricter rules governing state-owned companies, regulating the use of automobiles by officials, and banning lavish official banquets—and intensive propaganda to build up the party's image. The campaign benefited from the centralization of party-building work within a central leading small group, while a new periodical, *Party Building*, publicized the latest ideas about how to strengthen the CCP.[40] In this campaign, public propaganda seemed of equal importance to actual implementation; put another way, the rectification remained a matter of both political reality and control over narrative and understanding.

The rectification in the military remained particularly sensitive. After all, the PLA's valor had been the focus of significant attention in the aftermath of June 4, even though the leadership knew that resistance within the military to the use of violence had presented a serious problem. Yang Baibing announced the punishment of 110 officers who "breached discipline in a serious way" and 1,400 soldiers who "shed their weapons and ran away." PLA rectification targeted corruption and military enterprises that were abusing their privileges, while stressing the party's "absolute leadership" over the military.[41]

Would this major rectification campaign have any effect? Many reports from 1989 and 1990 noted passive resistance to the rectification efforts. Yet this ideological and political work was backed up with the threat of punishment, and it was forcefully tied to Chinese nationalism and patriotism through its focus on China's "national conditions" and resisting "peaceful evolution." As we have seen, studies in political science and economics suggest the remarkable effectiveness of such propaganda, and the leadership's continued recourse to propaganda methods suggests that many in the CCP, at least, believed it to be effective.[42] What is clearest, for our purposes, is that these ideas about China's recent history and modernization remained politically powerful both within China and around the world.

For the CCP leadership, the urgency of succeeding in the rectification campaign grew in the fall, as it followed developments in Poland, elsewhere in Eastern Europe, and the Soviet republics that were jostling for independence.[43] Deng met with Jiang Zemin, Li Peng, and other senior leaders on September 4 and stated, "The current problem is not whether the Soviet flag will fall. The Soviet Union will definitely become chaotic. The question is whether China's flag will fall." The priorities for China should be to maintain stability and persevere in reform and opening, Deng added, ensuring that economic growth continued: "We must be calm, calm, and calm again, and work hard, do a few things well, and mind our own business."[44]

The next day, however, Li Xiannian wrote to Jiang Zemin and Li Peng in a much harsher tone. "History has proven that imperialism and the Western powers' designs on us will not die," Li wrote. The only remedy was to intensify the rectification campaign and increase the coercive power of the "security organs" to implement it. Jiang Zemin immediately approved the letter, and Li Peng committed to taking the lead in "strengthening the security front" and especially the Ministries of State Security and Public Security.[45]

◇

A somber, tense mood prevailed on National Day, October 1, 1989. With martial law still in effect, heavy security patrolled the anniversary gala in Beijing. The military parade was canceled to avoid the sight of tanks once again rolling past Tiananmen.[46] Jiang Zemin delivered an address to celebrate the fortieth anniversary of the People's Republic of China's founding, but his language suggested that a long-term battle for survival still lay ahead. Jiang affirmed the CCP's continued support for the decisions of the 13th Party Congress (even though important substantive elements of that congress's agenda, including the political reforms, were no longer permissible), while also stressing the connection between patriotism and socialist ideology, which he called "fundamentally unified."[47] This focus on patriotism would develop, most notably, into the Patriotic Education Campaign of the early 1990s.[48] Soon thereafter, Jiang also gave his personal imprimatur to attacks on "historical nihilism," using the term to criticize those who clung to incorrect interpretations of the party's history and otherwise suffered from "confused thinking."[49]

In late 1989, many more orthodox Marxist assessments emerged, asserting that market reform was a root cause of the crisis and should be limited going forward. On October 13, Deng Liqun convened an internal symposium on the "lessons of the turmoil." According to historian Xiao Donglian, criticisms flew freely, asserting that "the root cause of the political storm was errors in the economic reform."[50] "We cannot rely on the economic support of any big country and take shortcuts to developing the economy like South Korea," a propaganda guidance circulated on October 15 stated, or else "the international monopoly capitalist economy will soon penetrate the Chinese market, and China's national economy will swiftly be destroyed."[51] Figures who supported these arguments maintained their nominal commitment to "reform and opening," but they critiqued both elements of this policy as it was pursued in the 1980s. Market reform was cast as leading to loss of control, corruption, and unfairness, and international trade and investment risked creating dangerous dependence on the capitalist world—both of which threatened to "destroy" the Chinese economy.

The epistemic dimensions of the rectification remained a priority, and some materials on bourgeois liberalization became even more creative. Propaganda official Yu Xinyan offered eight lines of algebra that got from "$x = y$" to "$1 = 2$": "The result of this calculation is obviously ridiculous," Yu wrote, but it might fool a novice who did not know algebra. Similarly, inexperienced young people in China had been led astray by bourgeois liberalization, leading to the turmoil of the spring and summer, and they had been as wrong as someone who claimed "$1 = 2$."[52] Even missile scientist Qian Xuesen wrote an essay that fall arguing that "basic scientific research should be guided by Marxist philosophy."[53]

Reflecting the centrality of the propaganda apparatus to all aspects of Chinese politics in the second half of 1989, Jiang Zemin laid out a fuller vision of how he understood the role of the media in late November. His speech to other officials made clear that the experiments with greater press freedom in the late 1980s were unwelcome. Notions such as "freedom of the press" and "transparency" primarily "confused people's thinking and caused a mess in our country." Jiang continued, in an epistemological vein, "Some matters should be limited to only a portion of people to know and master.... What can be transparent and what can't be transparent [all] depends on whether it is conducive to social stability, political stability, economic stability, and stability in the people's hearts."[54] Jiang's statements were targeted at journalists in November 1989, but they applied equally well to the overall rectification that had occurred during the preceding months. The new official narrative reflected the teleology that the CCP had settled on for China's modernization, pairing economic development with strict political control, and "some matters," such as the "complicated" story of the 1980s, the killings of June 4, or the role of Zhao Ziyang, were now "limited to only a portion of people." In the months after the crisis of May–June, the CCP's relationship to truth itself had shifted more fully in the direction of ensuring "stability and unity" over all other values.

If these ideas seemed rather abstract, Jiang had good reason to feel philosophical. In the weeks before his National Day speech, the Berlin Wall—long a symbol of the Cold War, dividing the German capital into west and east—fell when the East German government announced that its citizens could freely cross the border. The socialist world seemed on the verge of collapse.

CHAPTER 15

The Socialist Survivor in a Capitalist World

Even before the Berlin Wall fell, the Chinese leadership was anxiously watching the tumult sweeping across the Eastern Bloc. On September 4, Li Peng wrote in his diary, "In my view, chaos in Eastern Europe and the Soviet Union is unavoidable." On October 19, he noted laconically, "Socialism has ended in Hungary." Increasingly, it seemed that "socialism's success" would depend on the CCP's survival.[1]

As one regime after another faced explosive upheaval, the Chinese leadership began to see itself in a new way, as the great socialist survivor in a capitalist world, uniquely able to exploit the benefits of openness to global capitalism while resisting the perceived dangers. (Of course, other socialist countries, such as North Korea, Vietnam, Laos, and Cuba, would also survive the 1989–1992 period, but they did not have the size or influence of China.) This chapter charts the intensive debates within the leadership and in elite circles about how China could achieve this goal during the period from November 1989 to Deng Xiaoping's Southern Tour in early 1992. This period witnessed an effort, spearheaded by Deng himself, to reconcile the pursuit of fast market-driven growth with the new narrative about China's modernization. Deng's economic priorities were not fundamentally at odds with the new official narrative, so long as there were no political system reforms or "bourgeois liberalization" of the sort that had allegedly flourished in the 1980s.

The aftermath of the Tiananmen crisis and the collapse of the Soviet Union were profoundly interrelated for the CCP. The international upheavals of the 1989–1992 period assured that the ideas about China's modernization that had gained currency in the summer of 1989 became permanently entrenched. The collapse of other socialist regimes validated the CCP and encouraged it to further promote the idea that this configuration was the only viable path for China, while it held firm to the rewritten history that suppressed the fact that it had considered and experimented with significant alternatives.

◇

The fall of the Berlin Wall in November 1989 caught China's rulers, and the rest of the world, by surprise. In October, *People's Daily* had proudly declared, "The East German people are now strengthening their unity under the leadership of the party." Erich Honecker's government stood with the CCP after the Tiananmen crackdown, and Yao Yilin visited East Germany in October to celebrate its fortieth anniversary and reaffirm their shared commitment to socialism.[2]

When the border between East and West Germany opened, the CCP leadership took a cautious attitude. On November 16, Li Peng, who was asked while visiting Pakistan about the fall of the Berlin Wall, stated that events in Germany should not be linked to events in China, and China did not interfere in the internal affairs of other countries or communist parties.[3]

However, soon thereafter, Li took a more assertive stance internally, delivering a speech on the events in Eastern Europe to a military conference on November 26 in Xinjiang—a location that could hardly have been a coincidence at a time of ethnic movements in the Soviet Union just across the border. Li stated that "China is a socialist country, so naturally we are very concerned about the destiny and future of socialist countries." Li blamed two factors for the Eastern Europe situation: the "peaceful evolution strategy of Western countries" and "some mistakes in the process of building socialism" that these countries had made. Li said, "The fortress has always been easiest to break from within, and the greatest danger is splits among the leadership." Li affirmed the bifurcation of economic and political change in China, also pointing to the pernicious consequences of the Soviet Union's "political reforms." China, by stopping the "turmoil" in June 1989, had successfully "defended the People's Republic of China (PRC) and defended the socialist banner in the world."[4]

"So long as socialism does not collapse in China, it will always hold its ground in the world," Deng said to former Tanzanian president Julius Kambarage Nyerere on November 23.[5] With the CCP firmly in charge, he vowed that China would be a socialist survivor no matter what happened in the Soviet Union and Eastern Europe.

With the Velvet Revolution in Czechoslovakia and the Romanian Revolution that led to the execution of Nicolae Ceaușescu, the CCP leadership doubled down on these ideas. On December 5, in a meeting with senior officials, Li Peng predicted that "[Mikhail Gorbachev's] regime may be overthrown. Now only China has the conditions and the ability to hold firmly to the banner of socialism."[6] On December 27, Jiang Zemin chaired a meeting of the Politburo Standing Committee on the situation in Romania; although Ceaușescu had been a favorite Eastern European leader, the PRC promptly recognized the new Romanian government.[7]

In response to the crisis in Eastern Europe and instability in the Soviet Union, the Chinese leadership prioritized political and ideological work and the economic retrenchment policies. China's rulers felt that to avoid "chaos," they needed to ensure strong economic results; however, their approach at this moment was not to pursue rapid growth rates but rather to strengthen the central government's control, bring down inflation, and empower state-owned enterprises. As references to "class struggle" continued to appear in official media, Li Xiannian, consulting with Chen Yun, wrote to Jiang Zemin and Li Peng in October to call for making the economy more "centralized and unified" and recalibrating "the proportion of the public and private economy."[8] Li Peng repeatedly echoed these priorities that winter, and a series of Central Committee decisions endorsed the formulation "the planned economy combined with market regulation," a return to placing the plan well above the market. The Fifth Plenum of the 13th Party Congress on November 6–7 praised Chen Yun's economic guidance and, with Deng's permission, implemented a thirty-nine-point economic retrenchment program. Soon thereafter, Li Peng established a State Council Production Commission to better coordinate implementation of state plans.[9]

This economic retrenchment embraced the goals of stability and control and rejected rapid growth and marketization. It did not reject the framework of "reform and opening," but it broke explicitly with elements of Zhao Ziyang's market-focused agenda because Chen, Li, and Yao felt that their earlier disagreements with Zhao had been confirmed by the inflation and overheating of 1988–1989. If China was to survive an era of domestic and international "turmoil," they believed not only that the retrenchment policies should stay in place but also that CCP control and centralized authority must be clearly articulated as a priority *above* economic growth—for the long term. Full-scale marketization and privatization were simply cover for "peaceful evolution," scholar Wei Xinghua wrote in *Guangming Daily.* "Theories about a 'socialist market economy' should not be bandied about."[10]

Amid the intensified politicizing of the economic realm, the concerns about deficient ideological and political work in enterprises were just one example of how the rollback of political reforms and the sanctification of the Four Cardinal Principles directly affected economic policy. The central government investigated "the economic situation and political attitude" of private enterprises, finding them to be beneficial on the whole but, in Li Xiannian's words, also revealing "corrupt practices and problems."[11] Even longtime supporters of market reform such as Xue Muqiao wrote in support of the retrenchment, invoking China's "national conditions" and criticizing "one-sided pursuit of too high a speed of development."[12] On November 10, Song Ping strongly criticized what he described as the "obviously dangerous guiding ideology" of the 1980s: Zhao Ziyang "believed that as long as the economy is doing well, everything will be fine, and ideological and political work is of little use." Song suggested that the factory manager responsibility system should remain intact, but it should "strengthen party building and strengthen ideolog-

ical and political work," meaning "the factory manager and party secretary must be of one mind and work together."[13] As was so often the
case, these proposed changes were achieved by keeping the superficial
form of policies intact but meaningfully shifting their content and execution. Because the fundamental goal of this system originally had been
to delegate authority to the enterprise level and separate party and government functions, Song's comments fully reversed the prior intention
of the policy, but this was clearly in line with the new official narrative
about China's future modernization.

On January 8, 1990, Li Peng delivered closing remarks at an Economic
Work Conference, calling for reform to be put on a "healthier" track combining "the planned economy and market regulation." Some of this rhetoric was no doubt self-serving, as the retrenchment policies and international sanctions caused growth to slow. However, it was also connected to
newly predominant ideas about the Chinese system. An article in *People's
Daily* narrated the history of "ten years of reform and opening" by emphasizing improvements to the system of state planning and the importance
of state-owned enterprises. Too much decentralization, excessive speed,
and significant imbalances had thrown the modernization agenda off
track, it said, which the retrenchment would remedy; the policies of the
1980s "lacked a comprehensive and profound understanding of national
conditions and national power."[14] This emphasis on "national conditions"
would become even more prominent in the coming years.

Two days later, on January 10, 1990, Li Peng issued orders to begin
lifting martial law in Beijing, which had been in place since May 20, 1989.
Extraordinary changes had taken place in China and around the world
since that fateful declaration. In a photograph on the front page of
People's Daily, Li wore a Western suit and striped tie as he painted China
as an island of stability: "No matter what kind of storms occur in the
world, we will unswervingly follow the socialist road."[15]

Martial law had been lifted, but the new narrative of China's modernization remained firmly in place. Reports described the success of the
epistemic dimensions of the rectification, trumpeting that the party
members and the populace had "deepened their understanding of the
nature and meaning of this struggle" as well as their loyalty to the
People's Liberation Army (PLA) and the CCP center.[16]

This victory lap was short lived. In early 1990, the Soviet Union was rocked by Lithuania's demands for independence and Gorbachev's promises to create a process for the Soviet republics to secede.[17] The Chinese leadership watched these events with concern. In Moscow, protests called for an end to the party's monopoly on political power, with as many as 100,000 people in the streets as the Central Committee convened in early February. At the opening day of an extraordinary session of the party's policymaking Central Committee, Gorbachev announced that the Communist Party of the Soviet Union (CPSU) would "give up any legal and political advantages" and would compete "strictly within the framework of the democratic process." This new system of "political pluralism" terminated the CPSU's privileged status.[18]

In response, the Chinese leadership even more sharply asserted the absolute imperative of CCP leadership over all. The propaganda organs did not immediately announce the Soviet decision. First, on February 8, *People's Daily* printed a front-page spread on the importance of the CCP's "leadership position" over the "democratic parties" and Chinese society.[19] The next day, the paper carried the news from Moscow about the CPSU giving up its monopoly on power—a sequence that made clear that the CCP saw itself on a profoundly different path from its former Soviet "elder brother."[20] In a slew of commentaries that soon followed, the term *political system reform* was deployed with a new meaning: explicitly strengthening the leadership of the CCP over government functions and society and rejecting the concept of "separating party and government."[21] In March, Jiang Zemin hammered this point home: "The party has absolute leadership over the state organs. . . . All the state organs, including the People's Congress, the government, the Supreme People's Court, and the Supreme People's Procuratorate, should be under the leadership of the party."[22] China's new leaders would countenance no form of political change that undermined or adjusted the "absolute leadership" of the CCP.

Propaganda work remained the crucial conduit for presenting China's new official narrative to domestic and foreign audiences. In *People's Daily* on February 22, Wang Renzhi stated that the struggle of the past few years was in fact "to a large extent a struggle between capitalist reform and socialist reform."[23] All historical writing was required to serve these aims: Hu Qiaomu declared at a national meeting on party history in March 1990 that party history "is not orientated to the past; it is to confront the present and face the future" and "support the leadership of the party."[24]

These initiatives aligned with efforts to conduct "patriotic education," which further melded anti-foreign nationalism with anti-capitalist "struggle" and highlighted the paramount importance of China's "national conditions." The propaganda apparatus called for studying socialist theory and learning from nationalist role models, including the Mao-era hero Lei Feng.[25] Books that criticized the search for "Western solutions to China's problems" became popular reading on the same university campuses where the 1989 protests had begun. Chinese television stations were authorized to broadcast scenes of the chaos in Eastern Europe, as visual evidence of what would happen when the central control of a Communist Party eroded.[26] In case the implication was unclear, Li Xiannian said proudly in mid-July that if the leadership had not cracked down in 1989, "Wouldn't we be the same as Eastern Europe today?"[27]

Directives also emphasized the need to build up China's international image as a stable socialist country that would survive for decades to come. Citing the "rapid increase" in the number of foreign journalists working in China, one State Council directive called on the propaganda apparatus to "actively guide them to correctly understand China and promote China" while "limiting their negative effects."[28] The Chinese leadership also reestablished the Central Small Group on External Propaganda, which focused on developing messages for foreign audiences.[29]

Gradually, China's relations with the wider world warmed. Brent Scowcroft returned to Beijing for a public visit in December 1989, and George H. W. Bush renewed China's most-favored-nation status in May 1990, despite maintaining sanctions. As Wang Zhen had predicted in June 1989, "Foreign capitalists want to make money. . . . If they see your country is stable and can make money, they'll come."[30] Although it recovered from global condemnation, the CCP was determined to continue to increase its ability to shape international perceptions of China going forward.

Yet some members of the Chinese elite were concerned that the leadership of Li Peng and Jiang Zemin was drawing the wrong lessons from the "turmoil" of 1989 and the upheavals in the socialist world. They argued that "peaceful evolution" was a threat, but it did not require doubling down on economic policies that slowed growth.

Deng Xiaoping himself kicked off this debate. Although he remained officially retired, he wanted to make clear that the framework of "reform and opening," which was still in place, should focus on generating faster economic development. On March 3, 1990, freshly returned to Beijing from a visit to Shanghai, Deng met with Jiang, Li, and Yang Shangkun. On the international situation, he predicted a drift toward a "multipolar world" in which "China too will be a pole." However, he said forcefully that he was "worried" about "the drop in the economic growth rate." The people support the CCP, he said, "because over the last ten years our economy has been developing and developing visibly." Deng demanded rapid growth that would at least double gross national product in the decade ahead. He argued that slower growth rates were as likely as "peaceful evolution" to shake the CCP's authority and hoped that the official leadership would agree.[31]

At this point, Deng did not directly tie his objective of "rapid growth" to intensified marketization. Some officials were much more explicit. Xue Muqiao argued in 1990 in a letter to the Standing Committee that "peaceful evolution" was "not sufficient to explain . . . the dramatic changes in Eastern Europe." Although in late 1989 he had supported the retrenchment, Xue felt that "the main reason for the setbacks in Eastern Europe is that there was no thorough reform," and China must return to an agenda of rapid growth and intensive market reforms.[32]

Others, however, saw the entire paradigm of "reform and opening" as raising intolerable risks for China. One influential voice was He Xin, a researcher at the Chinese Academy of Social Sciences (CASS) and close adviser of Li Peng, who was reportedly living in the leadership compound of Zhongnanhai as of November 1989.[33] In 1990, He Xin wrote several reports arguing that China needed to put up economic defenses against the global capitalist system led by the United States. Criticizing market reform, foreign investment, and interdependence, he wrote, "The U.S. exploits other countries and inhibits their growth to satisfy its own interests." China needed to face facts: "The failure of the Soviet Union and Eastern Europe is due to their inability to compete economically with the developed countries." The stakes were existential, and "China cannot be another example of a failing socialist state." As China rose to greater power, He Xin argued, "developed countries feel threatened by the increasing competition. Hence, economic globalization has turned into economic protectionism."[34] If socialist China continued to open itself to the US-led international capitalist system, it would need to be prepared to "compete economically" with the same "protectionist" attitude that he ascribed to the United States. And if China remained open, he suggested that it would always be haunted by the risk that it would follow the Soviet Union and "fail."

These debates in 1990 raised anew questions that had preoccupied economic officials throughout the 1980s—the meaning of the market, the benefits and risks of fast growth, and the vulnerabilities of international interdependence—and many economists began to join in. They saw problems in the economy ranging from rising unemployment and temporary layoffs to factories that had all but stopped production. The profitability of the largest state firms plummeted by 57 percent in 1990, and rural enterprises were under severe pressure. Household purchases declined significantly, with household savings constituting nearly a quarter of income in 1989–1990.[35] Throughout the summer, CASS and the State Planning Commission held seminars on economic theory, and in July the Politburo Standing Committee invited economists to Zhongnanhai to discuss the economic situation. However, the political environment was still overwhelmingly critical of the hopes for market reform that attendees such as Xue Muqiao harbored. At one Zhongnanhai meeting, economist Wu Jinglian argued for a "commodity economy with market allocation as the basic operational mechanism" that could avoid "the pain and sacrifice of 'shock therapy'" and, in time, "market forces can create stability and a prosperous economy"; several other attendees dismissed these suggestions and blamed "market-oriented reforms" for causing the severe inflation of 1988 and even the "political turmoil" of 1989.[36] The leadership continued to assail bourgeois liberalization, tighten controls on intellectual life, and portray an existential global battle between socialism and capitalism.[37]

In this context, the new leadership team did not immediately respond to Deng's push for faster growth, taking the seemingly safer route of continuing to centralize control and bolster the planned economy. Only a few signs of pushback were visible. For example, at an Economic Work Conference in September, the central government attempted to bring the provinces under stricter fiscal control, but Ye Xuanping of Guangdong, Zhu Rongji of Shanghai, and Zhao Zhihao of Shandong successfully resisted these measures.[38] This provincial pushback aligned neatly with the increasing activity of some officials in the central government. In late September, the new head of the System Reform Commission, Chen Jinhua, read a report by economist Jiang Chunze that argued that planning and markets should not be seen as fundamental characteristics of either socialism or capitalism. Chen praised this "clear, reasonable, and targeted" argument and submitted it to Jiang Zemin and Li Peng, who circulated it more widely. In the subsequent months, the System Reform Commission held several seminars on planning and the market, including a joint conference with the World Bank and the United Nations Development Programme.[39] However, the leadership maintained the retrenchment policies.

Reflecting the continuing, if limited, tolerance for markets, the long-planned establishment of the Shanghai Stock Exchange was announced on November 26, 1990. A brief notice in *People's Daily* characterized its mission in ambiguous terms as "safeguarding the legitimate rights and interests of the state, enterprises, and the public, and promoting the healthy development of the securities market." The rising star Zhu Rongji presided over its opening with great fanfare, although prices and trading were still partially controlled.[40] Despite the fall in production, in major cities workers in state enterprises did not face significant job losses or wage cuts; however, Ezra Vogel notes that in less-developed parts of the country, approximately 20 million workers were laid off in 1989–1990 as factories scaled back on production.[41] Nevertheless, these large-scale layoffs due to slowed growth did not cause Jiang and Li to significantly shift their orientation, given the powerful sense of domestic and international threats everywhere they looked.

The ascendant critics of market reform and fast growth continued to push their arguments. In late December, Gao Di, chief editor of *People's Daily,* cast "the assistance of the United States and the Western world" as a strategic plot to overthrow the CCP through promoting "respect for human rights," "multiparty politics," and "a market-oriented economy." The same month, an essay by Chen Yun's son, Chen Yuan, who was an official at the Bank of China, demanded even greater centralization and assertion of economic control.[42]

As these voices grew louder, Deng Xiaoping traveled to Shanghai in early 1991 to stir up the energies of this internationalized city and encourage the limited steps that Zhu Rongji had taken during the period of retrenchment. Following his visit, the newspaper *Liberation Daily* published a series of commentaries under the pen name of Huangfu Ping—coordinated secretly by Deng's daughter and Zhu Rongji—that pushed Deng's successors to shift their economic policy agenda toward promoting faster growth and marketization. "Don't think that a planned economy is definitely socialism and a market economy is definitely capitalism," Deng said. "Both are means [to an end], and the market can also serve socialism." The commentaries emphasized that people should judge economic policies by whether they produced good results.[43]

Provincial leaders in Guangdong, Tianjin, Jiangxi, and Hebei followed the Huangfu Ping commentaries with essays calling for "emancipating the mind" and not seeing all markets as "capitalist." Others were furious at what they saw as subversion; according to Yang Jisheng, Gao Di of *People's Daily* even conducted an informal investigation to try to ferret out the "black hands" behind the Huangfu Ping series.[44] As the Baltic republics formally declared independence from the Soviet Union, Li Xiannian wrote to Jiang Zemin and Li Peng, exhorting them not to give up in the fight against "peaceful evolution" and "bourgeois liberalization."[45]

A series of personnel changes indicated that the prospects for market reform remained alive. Zhu Rongji was promoted in spring of 1991 to vice premier, and soon thereafter, three senior officials who had been removed from power in 1989—Hu Qili, Rui Xingwen, and Yan Mingfu—were rehabilitated.[46] Without a change in the top-level direction, these officials who had previously demonstrated their enthusiasm for market reform were focused on executing the retrenchment policies. The economic retrenchment proved even more effective at slowing growth than its designers had intended: In 1990, gross domestic product (GDP) grew by only 3.9 percent, and the size of total losses at state industrial firms surpassed 2 percent of GDP.[47]

Facing this situation, Deng decided to pursue an alternative avenue for advancing the modernization agenda: a restrengthened technology policy. Even officials who were committed to the retrenchment, such as Li Xiannian, encouraged further reforms to the science and technology (S&T) system that would raise working conditions for S&T personnel (although Li emphasized that it was essential to "adhere to the principle of self-reliance" and reject the temptation simply to "purchase foreign technologies and products").[48] Deng saw an opportunity. On April 23, 1991, Deng offered a personal inscription to the 863 Program and the Torch Program: "Develop high technology, achieve industrialization."[49] A week later, *People's Daily* published an essay that Deng's office had drafted on the "New S&T Revolution." Although the article did not mention Zhao, it closely followed his speeches on the global New Technological Revolution and used developments in fields such as information technology, biotechnology, and materials engineering to argue that China needed to act quickly because "competition about comprehensive national strength is essentially competition about S&T." Although this article's focus was primarily economic, the rapid victory of the United States in Operation Desert Storm in early 1991 also hammered home for many Chinese leaders that new technologies, such as precision-guided munitions, satellite communications, and the Global Positioning System (GPS), had enabled a "revolution in military affairs" that China could not miss.[50]

Deng's continued pushing seemed only to be generating ambiguous results. One way of interpreting Jiang Zemin's position at this moment is that he had not yet found a way to reconcile the new official narrative that emerged from the rectification—which emphasized the pervasive risk of bourgeois liberalization and antagonism between China and the capitalist world—with Deng's calls for faster growth and technological advancement. In a speech written by Hu Qiaomu on the seventieth anniversary of the CCP's founding, Jiang reflected on this medley of unresolved views. He indicated that planning and markets did not "differentiate socialism and capitalism," while also warning of "serious class struggle" and "peaceful evolution": "It is necessary to draw a clear line between two views of reform and opening—that is, the reform and opening that adheres to the Four Cardinal Principles, and the 'reform and opening' promoted by bourgeois liberalization that is actually capitalist," Jiang said.[51] The contradictions in his position were clear, but it was much less apparent how to resolve those tensions.

◇

On August 19, 1991, a group of Soviet generals launched a coup d'état, imprisoning Gorbachev at his dacha in Crimea and promising to roll back political liberalization. Many Chinese leaders were pleased with the news. The Politburo convened on the evening of August 19, and the dominant tone was that the situation could be beneficial to China. The Chinese ambassador called to congratulate the coup leaders, but Deng Xiaoping reached out to the top Chinese leadership to insist that they "carefully observe and study the situation" before taking action.[52]

The next day, Deng met with Jiang Zemin, Yang Shangkun, and Li Peng and offered his interpretation of the events. Praising China's stability, Deng stressed that China must now pursue "reform and opening" with greater vigor. "Many nations in this world have fallen, and the root cause has always been poor economic performance," he said, adding that a growth rate above 5 percent would be necessary to preserve CCP rule—and reaching that goal would require giving greater play to the market. The Soviet coup soon fell apart; while the Soviet Union would not officially collapse until December 26, 1991, after Gorbachev resigned and handed over power to Boris Yeltsin, the likelihood of its demise was already clear to China's leaders.[53]

Deng Xiaoping, facing the reality that his prior calls for renewing rapid economic growth had not produced a change of course from Jiang and Li, capitalized on this tumult in August 1991. After the sharp slowdown of 1989–1990, growth had begun to rebound—for example, Guangdong's industrial output rose by 27.2 percent in 1991—but nationwide, numbers were much lower, and Deng was dissatisfied. In a speech on the eightieth anniversary of the 1911 Revolution that had toppled the Qing dynasty, Yang Shangkun declared that "all other work must be subordinate to" economic construction. Deng repeatedly declared that the leadership should be less concerned about peaceful evolution and more concerned about promoting growth.[54]

Still, many members of the leadership were not persuaded that ending the retrenchment and moving to promote rapid market-oriented growth was worth the risk, and they were not sure how to promote growth again without permitting bourgeois liberalization. Other voices began to argue that a shift to promoting growth would be premature; if the CCP were to remain a socialist survivor over the long term, the leadership first needed to build a new argument for its rule.

The challenge raised by these voices was how to position the market-driven growth agenda *within* the paradigm of CCP dominance and the survival of Chinese socialism. Against the backdrop of the Soviet Union's collapse, thinkers such as Chen Yuan, Wang Huning, and Wang Xiaodong, many of whom had been active in advocating neo-authoritarianism in the late 1980s, proposed a set of distinctive, nationalistic ideas that came to be called "neoconservatism." This view was crystallized in an essay titled "Realistic Responses and Strategic Options for China after the Soviet Upheaval," which circulated widely in manuscript form before being published in *China Youth Daily*. Predicting significant new challenges for China as a result of the Soviet upheaval, this essay called for a firm rejection of "utopian capitalism," "radical reformism," and "shock therapy" in favor of gradual market reforms. It also proposed the dramatic idea of CCP control of all financial assets even as it increased the autonomy of enterprises. Most significantly, the essay argued forcefully that the CCP should elevate the concept of China's "national conditions" because they "dictate that only socialism can save China and only socialism can develop China." This influential essay argued that deploying the concept of "national conditions" could provide a compelling rationale for the CCP's rule and underscored that the CCP could hold to a mixed economic system that would promote faster growth without undermining the Four Cardinal Principles.[55] Deng Xiaoping was receptive to the concept of "national conditions," which built on ideas that he had previously endorsed, such as "socialism with Chinese characteristics," to argue that China's history, society, and level of development necessitated unorthodox policies.

In October, while meeting with a delegation from North Korea, Deng criticized the Soviet Union's decisions not to pursue rapid economic reform in the 1980s and the Soviet leadership's willingness to allow the

CPSU to fall from power.[56] Deng was maneuvering to use the Soviet collapse to strengthen his push for faster market-driven growth.

This renewed debate centered on what economic policies would best preserve China's status as a socialist survivor—faster or slower growth, more or less marketization, stronger or weaker state control. As the tensions among these views mounted, Jiang Zemin sought to understand his options better. To prepare for the 14th Party Congress scheduled for the fall of 1992, Jiang convened a large group of prominent Chinese economists at Zhongnanhai for a series of eleven economics seminars between October and December 1991.

These seminars focused on three clearly defined topics: (1) "Why had the capitalist system showed renewed vitality instead of collapsing?" (2) "What were the reasons for the dissolution of the system in the Soviet Union and Eastern Europe?" (3) "Given the foregoing, how should we proceed with our economic reforms going forward?" The group of economists who gathered to brief Jiang included Liu Guoguang, Wu Jinglian, Jiang Yiwei, Wang Huijiong, Zhou Xiaochuan, Justin Yifu Lin, and Guo Shuqing. Jiang also devoted himself to studying Western economic texts beginning with Adam Smith, seeking to "understand how the market works." Given the stringent constraints on open discussion, Zhou Xiaochuan recalled that the economists each prepared extremely cautious written statements, but Jiang's probing questions pushed them to speak more openly and make bolder proposals. Wu Jinglian argued that Western countries had actually achieved the much-discussed goal of "stability" by embracing the market and not by relying on planning. Guo Shuqing, meanwhile, directly attacked the Soviet-bloc countries, which, he argued, had too long continued "meddling in economic affairs" under reforms and had "dogmatic views of public ownership." Jiang Zemin responded to these presentations by setting out an important goal: "The Fourteenth Party Congress should articulate very clearly the contents of a 'planned commodity economy.'" Jiang was evidently pleased by what he had learned at these eleven internal meetings, and transcripts of the discussions were circulated among party cadres nationwide.[57]

What this meant in practice is that Jiang was coming to accept market-driven growth. "The failure of the Soviet Union and Eastern Europe is not the failure of socialism," he stated in his concluding remarks at the seminar. Jiang later recalled, "After spending a long time studying Western economics in 1991, I concluded that in a country with an underdeveloped economy . . . to push the economy forward, we must make use of the market economy."[58] This shift did not mark a refutation of the narrative of China's modernization that had emerged via the rectification. Rather, this gave an elevated role to market-driven growth as part of a model of state-led economic development with strict political control.

◇

After nearly eighteen months of trying to pressure his successor, Deng Xiaoping was starkly aware that Jiang still had not publicly embraced faster market-driven growth. In mid-January 1992, a month after Jiang's last economics seminar concluded, Deng set out on a trip to Wuchang, Shenzhen, Zhuhai, and Shanghai—what would come to be known as his Southern Tour. Planning for the trip had begun in late 1991, with officials in Shenzhen conducting preparatory work with Deng's aides. These aides claimed that Deng was only coming to "relax" and "look around," and they ordered that there were to be no public reports, speeches, pictures, banquets, or reporters other than those explicitly approved by Deng's office.[59]

When Deng arrived in Shenzhen and these other coastal cities, he personally told local officials and business leaders to move ahead with pursuing rapid growth: "Why was it that our country could remain stable after the June 4th Incident? It was precisely because we had carried out reform and opening, which have promoted economic growth and raised living standards." He dismissed excessive concern about whether a particular policy was "capitalist" or "socialist," calling instead for market reforms to produce economic results "as fast as possible." "Whoever is opposed to reform must leave office," Deng threatened.[60]

On this Southern Tour, Deng also continued to warn that "peaceful evolution" remained a risk in the ideological sphere. He emphasized the Four Cardinal Principles and even praised Singapore as a model of political control and public order, "thanks to a strict administration," and he said, "We should learn from its experience and surpass it in this respect."[61]

While Deng was on his Southern Tour, Li Peng was in Davos, Switzerland. On January 30, 1992, the man whom American politicians had denounced as the "butcher of Beijing" was, according to *People's Daily*'s front-page report, "warmly welcomed by Chairman [Klaus] Schwab" at the World Economic Forum's annual gathering. "We must further accelerate the pace of reform and opening," Li told the audience of government and business leaders. "We will further improve China's investment environment and welcome everyone to invest in China."[62] Although Li did not explicitly touch on questions of "capitalism" and "markets," his statements were remarkably in line with Deng's message in the south.

Even so, back in Beijing, it was not immediately clear whether Deng's gambit had worked. The retired Deng was no longer the official voice of the party, and the new "core" leader, Jiang, had not openly approved of Deng's statements. Deng's team prepared a condensed summary of his remarks and sought to release them via official media; news had also begun to leak out in the Hong Kong press about Deng's trip. However, any official acknowledgment on the mainland was delayed. Deng's trip was clearly an extremely important gesture from the octogenarian leader, but its relationship to the official line was uncertain.

The propaganda apparatus reacted with caution. On February 22, *People's Daily* published a front-page editorial on "taking economic construction as the center" and "making the economy develop faster in the year ahead," repeatedly invoking the need for a "faster speed" of growth but making no mention of Deng's Southern Tour.[63] Although the leadership circulated a summary of Deng's remarks on February 28, some officials who opposed a shift to faster market-driven growth clearly sought to bury Deng's message. The *People's Daily* editor, Gao Di, said dismissively, "We have already published two or three comments, and that is enough for the moment."[64] However, Jiang Zemin decided that it was to his advantage to endorse Deng's direction. At a Politburo meeting on March 9–10, Jiang delighted Deng by admitting that he had been too tepid in his support for reform and, with the unanimous backing of his colleagues, committed that accelerating reform and opening would be the central line of the 14th Party Congress.[65]

Soon thereafter, the propaganda organs finally announced to the Chinese public this shift toward faster market-driven growth. On March 12, 1992, *People's Daily* reprinted an article by a commentator in the *Zhejiang Daily* that described the retrenchment as "basically completed" and called for "speeding up the pace of reform and opening."[66] However, news of Deng's talks in the south had still not appeared in the party's mouthpiece.[67]

That changed on March 31 when *People's Daily* released a major front-page story on Deng's trip to Shenzhen. Photographs showed Deng speaking vigorously with his finger pointed commandingly in the air, as well as planting a tree and greeting troops accompanied by Yang Shangkun. Lavish prose celebrated the arrival of Deng as a heroic figure, "the chief architect of reform and opening" and a "great man who led a generation with genius." It also noted Deng's comparisons to Singapore and his call to "surpass" it in socialist spiritual civilization. Most importantly, it summarized, "Comrade Xiaoping's hope for Shenzhen is that it will seize the opportunity to pursue faster economic construction."[68]

The announcement marked the public unveiling of this historic event, but it also underscored what the meaning of the Southern Tour really was. The Southern Tour is often treated as a mythic turning point when liberalization was put "back on track."[69] In truth, Deng's focus was entirely on resuming rapid economic growth and marketization; he showed no interest in shifting away from the new official narrative of China's modernization that bifurcated economic and political change. The epistemic break of 1989 had been decisive and remained in place. Deng's Southern Tour accelerated market reforms but did not fundamentally change either the new historical narrative or the principles that had been developed to guide China's modernization.

Following this official announcement, the leadership moved intently to implement this economic agenda, embracing markets and trade to produce fast growth, while maintaining political control. New policies rolled out to open more cities on China's borders and along the Yangtze River to international trade, as well as to spread the status of the special economic zones (SEZs) to all provincial capital cities. A propaganda directive on May 25, 1992, called on all propaganda and ideological workers to "strengthen the spread of reform and opening."

Throughout 1992, denunciations of bourgeois liberalization continued to appear in official propaganda, which also frequently invoked the Soviet collapse; the intellectual atmosphere surrounding economic affairs was loosening, provided that political changes such as separating the party and the government were not discussed.[70]

On June 9, in a speech at the Central Party School, Jiang Zemin announced that China would build a "socialist market economy," a formulation that had been refined over the spring through discussions on the "goal model of the reform." Deng Xiaoping strongly approved, encouraging Jiang to circulate the speech internally first and then publicize the "socialist market economy" formulation "if the reaction is good."[71] However, Deng was no doubt aware that Li Peng was firmly in line, and Li Xiannian and Chen Yun were both extremely ill—with Li Xiannian passing away at the age of 83 on June 21, though Chen would live until 1995—so there would be no meaningful opposition within the leadership.[72]

Jiang's embrace of the "socialist market economy" concept provided the centerpiece of the upcoming 14th Party Congress. This formulation bears dwelling on. Although Deng had succeeded in returning market reform and faster growth rates to the top of the agenda, scholars such as Barry Naughton and Yasheng Huang have shown that the new "socialist market economy" gave much greater priority to promoting the government's interests and maintaining centralized management of the marketizing economy than the development strategy of the 1980s—underscoring that "socialist markets" were intended to be meaningfully different from capitalist markets.[73] A much faster growth target soon followed. After a discussion of the agenda for the 14th Party Congress between Deng and Jiang on July 13, the government's spokesperson signaled on July 17 that the five-year plan would be updated to increase the annual growth rate from 6 percent to 9 or 10 percent.[74]

China's shift back to high-growth market-oriented policies was reported ecstatically around the world. "Reality is overtaking ideology in China," celebrated the *Wall Street Journal*.[75] The publicity given to Deng's Southern Tour was not simply about doubling down on the nature of China's system after 1989 but also about explaining and even selling this bifurcation to international audiences. The *New York Times* reported on a clear decision "to show full support for economic liberalization and to put economic development back at the top of the national agenda."[76] However, political repression was now accepted as a long-lasting feature of the Chinese system—"Mr. Deng has given no indication that he intends to let up politically. The reality is the opposite," wrote a *Wall Street Journal* editorial—though many still held out for eventual change.[77]

As market reform and international trade resumed, the positive reviews of China's shift accumulated, treating market-oriented economic development paired with political repression as a natural model for China to follow. Even price liberalization moved ahead without the upheaval that had marked the 1988 attempt, with the government eliminating controls on the prices of nearly all major categories of production materials, agricultural products, and light industrial products over the course of 1992.[78] By August, the *New York Times* was announcing, "China sees Singapore as a model for progress": Combining "bustling markets with brutal repression . . . may be what China's leaders hope to adopt for themselves."[79]

In late 1992, the 14th Party Congress endorsed the "socialist market economy" as the means for achieving "socialism with Chinese characteristics." It heralded Deng as the "chief architect of our socialist reform, opening, and the modernization program." Jiang's work report endorsed the coastal development strategy of an "export-oriented economy" and gave significant attention to S&T development, among other clear continuities with the 1980s. However, there was no further talk of separating the party and the government. Even though the congress approved some administrative reforms to the government and the party, the Four Cardinal Principles received much more prominent billing than any political reform. "It would be absolutely wrong and harmful for anyone to doubt, weaken, or negate the party's position in power and its leading role," the work report stated. This represented a significantly different vision of China's modernization from what had been endorsed at the 13th Party Congress just five years earlier.[80]

Zhao, erased from history, remained under house arrest in Beijing. Soon thereafter, Li Peng rolled out a new civil service system for China, but it was as if Zhao's proposal from 1987 had been inverted. "The Chinese civil service will emphasize the principle of party control of the cadres," the drafting team determined. This policy stressed that "national conditions" required CCP dominance of the system.[81] Deng's status continued to rise, and a new official compilation in the fall of 1992 even placed him on an equal footing with Mao for his understanding of China's "national conditions."[82] On December 29, 1992, the *Financial Times* named Deng Xiaoping its person of the year, hailing "a nationwide renewal of enthusiasm for free-market reforms" but cautioning, "it cannot yet be concluded that free-market reforms mean the Communist system is on the way out."[83]

◇

Deng's Southern Tour and the economic policy shift in 1992 entrenched the new narrative about China's system that had been consolidated during the rectification of 1989, but it restored more specific market reforms and pursuit of very high growth rates to the concept of "reform and opening." This narrative has endured as the dominant official story of China's rise, carefully promoted by the CCP, which has flooded the public sphere with its narrative while assiduously censoring any writings that contradict this official story.[84] It is frequently repeated beyond China's shores; as China's GDP began once again to grow at an annual rate of more than 10 percent, its success seemed so staggering that its model—rapid economic growth with CCP-dominated authoritarian politics—seemed natural and inevitable to many in the commentariat. Images ran rife of China as a model "better than democracy" and "a rich, super-large Singapore," the fruits of a system that Nicholas Kristof acerbically termed "market Leninism."[85] (Of course, continued criticisms of the perils of fast growth would not disappear within China, though, as Joseph Fewsmith has noted, the resistance of figures such as Chen Yun and Li Xiannian to the fast-growth market-oriented economic model would be airbrushed out of their laudatory official obituaries.[86]) When China became the world's second-largest economy by GDP in 2010, a barrage of books and articles predicted the global ascendency of China's "market authoritarianism," which was poised to "dominate the twenty-first century."[87]

All the while, China's rulers remained haunted by the events of 1989–1991, seeing economic development and the CCP's continued dominance of society, the military, and the historical narrative as the keys to survival. China continued to pursue a policy of state-guided economic development and a CCP-dominated political system. To be sure, the CCP remained adaptive in its strategies of governance. In the 1990s and 2000s, it made attempts at collective leadership and gave leeway to some meaningful grassroots and legal reforms. There were also periods of vibrancy in journalism, culture, and civil society during these decades, including some I experienced personally when working in China at independent news magazine *Caijing* and non-governmental organizations in the 2000s. However, hopes for renewed political system reform have been repeatedly disappointed.[88]

Yet this was not the only path to modernization that China's rulers considered and experimented with in the 1980s. The CCP ensured that these alternative paths in ideology, the economy, technology, and especially political reform were erased or marginalized, while presenting a new official narrative that was forged in the crucible of the domestic and international crises of 1989–1991.

As the new millennium dawned, China's rulers—with Jiang Zemin still serving as the "core"—celebrated their successful achievement of the goals that Deng Xiaoping had set out for China's modernization before his death in 1997. China had surpassed the objective of quadrupling agricultural and industrial output by 2000, and the CCP remained dominant, with no significant political constraints on its power, let alone checks and balances. China was becoming a wealthy, powerful country under the firm leadership of the CCP.

In fact, more than surviving, the CCP was positively thriving in a capitalist world, and China was on the verge of joining the World Trade Organization (WTO) with the strong backing of US president Bill Clinton. Speaking at the Johns Hopkins University in March 2000, Clinton made his case for congressional approval of his deal. "The WTO agreement will move China in the right direction," he said, "and of course it will advance our own economic interests." Those economic and business interests were the primary motivation for US support, but Clinton used the first point to great political effect: "Membership in the WTO, of course, will not create a free society in China overnight or guarantee that China will play by global rules. But over time, I believe it will move China faster and further in the right direction. . . . So if you believe in a future of greater openness and freedom for the people of China, you ought to be for this agreement."[89] This rhetorical image of China was one in which faster market reforms, more trade, and deeper integration into the world economy would gradually produce "greater openness and freedom for the people of China." It was, in other words, a vision of China's modernization in which economic and political liberalization were deeply interlinked, even mutually reinforcing. This idea clearly resonated with the American public, or at least its elected representatives on Capitol Hill who voted in favor of the deal. However, this vision of how China would continue to modernize was at odds with the decisions that the Chinese leadership had made in the period chronicled in these pages. After the tumult of the 1980s and the crises of 1989–1991, the CCP was committed to keeping economic change bifurcated from political change.

A few months after Clinton's speech in Washington, DC, and less than a month before China's formal accession to the WTO, the top Chinese leadership gathered in Shenzhen. Jiang Zemin presided over a celebration of the twentieth anniversary of the SEZ's founding in 1980. The festivities took place atop Lianhua Mountain, overlooking the city that had boomed under "reform and opening." There, in front of a large group of dignitaries, Jiang pulled back a red silk cloth to unveil a twenty-foot-tall bronze statue of Deng Xiaoping, striding forward with a dignified, optimistic expression.[90] Surrounded by cypress and evergreen trees, the "Internationale" played. Deng's legacy, and the narrative he had constructed about China's modernization, were intact. As the bronze statue towered over them, the assembled crowd hailed Deng, once again, as "the chief architect of reform and opening."[91]

Conclusion

A New Era

On December 18, 2018, at the Great Hall of the People, Chinese president Xi Jinping led thousands of dignitaries in celebrating what they called "the fortieth anniversary of reform and opening." It was forty years to the day since the Third Plenum of 1978, but Xi did not want his audience to think too much about the past. He focused his speech on the strength of China's present-day position, issuing a triumphant and optimistic message despite the intensifying strategic competition with the United States and concerns about slowing growth. Where his speech did touch on the history of the preceding forty years, Xi offered up a simple story, saying that the party's decisions have been "absolutely correct." The fierce contestation and tumult of the 1980s—as well as, unsurprisingly, the central role of the purged Zhao Ziyang—went unmentioned. Xi also doubled down on the bifurcation of economic development and political system reform: "We will resolutely reform what should and can be reformed, and make no change where there should not and cannot be any reform," he said. "What should and can be reformed" included aspects of the economic, technological, and social welfare systems, but the CCP's dominance of the political system and refusal to tolerate dissent were principal domains in which "there should not and cannot be any reform."[1]

A few days before Xi's speech, I visited the National Museum of China, just across Tiananmen Square from the Great Hall of the People. The marquee exhibition was a celebration of the anniversary titled "Great Transformation." As I walked the halls, I realized something astonishing: the star of the show was Xi Jinping. His image appeared on nearly every wall of the museum, even though he had led China for only the last few years of the four decades being celebrated. Although the anniversary glanced back over history to glorify the CCP, its primary purpose was actually to celebrate Xi and what he calls a "new era" under his leadership.[2] Xi had recently proclaimed his official guiding ideology, the verbosely named Xi Jinping Thought on Socialism with Chinese Characteristics for a New Era. So, for the anniversary, directives to universities and workplaces across the country emphasized the importance of studying Xi Jinping's "guiding" words and thoughts.[3]

Then I noticed something else. Not only were there no signs of the purged Zhao Ziyang, or even Hu Yaobang, despite his formal rehabilitation. More startlingly, there were few images of Deng Xiaoping. Deng seemed to be a newly marginalized figure in a historical narrative with room for only one protagonist. The more I looked online, in newspapers, and on television, the more I realized that the celebrations were downplaying Deng. His image and name had been everywhere ten years earlier, for the thirtieth anniversary, but now those hagiographical portraits were fewer and farther between. The "chief architect of reform and opening" was no longer the most important figure in China's post-Mao history. That mantle had passed to Xi Jinping.

Xi was willing to celebrate Deng and his legacy only when it proved useful for his own purposes. In December 2012, just after becoming CCP general secretary, Xi traveled to Shenzhen to lay a wreath at the statue of Deng that overlooks the city. This bow to Deng was designed to make the new leader seem open minded and market oriented. Observers applauded, calling Xi's trip "a strong signal of support for greater market-oriented economic policies," with Xi sending the message that he was "the heir to Deng" and "not a conservative."[4]

Xi basked in the goodwill, then went ahead with his true plans: strengthening the role of the party across the economy, claiming for himself the mantle of the leadership "core" while removing term limits on his position, and clamping down on the media, civil society, and religious and ethnic minorities.[5] Soon, Xi declared, "Government, military, society, and schools—north, south, east, and west—the party is the leader of all."[6] That 2012 trip indicated nothing so much as Xi's skill at manipulating historical symbols to advance his ends.

In seeking to establish a distinctive political and ideological system with himself at the center, Xi Jinping clearly finds Deng Xiaoping's legacy less useful. More generally, although he invokes and celebrates the CCP's history and calls its decisions "absolutely correct," he is highly selective in the history he invokes, presenting it only to the extent that it is a "usable past."[7] This approach to history defined a new resolution on party history that Xi introduced for the CCP's hundredth anniversary in 2021. The 2021 resolution was a strikingly different kind of document than its predecessors, which it stated "remain valid to this day." It contained scant historical detail; less than an eighth of the document focused on the entire period between Mao's death in 1976 and Xi's rise in 2012. (As one metric, Xi's name appears over twenty times; Zhao goes unmentioned, of course, but even Deng's name appears only six times.)[8] Rather than evaluating the successes and failures of the past, the purpose of this resolution was to offer a forceful, far-reaching argument for the continued supremacy of the CCP, the transformational role of Xi personally, and the global importance of China's power—a "usable past" in action.

Yet history cannot be so easily written, rewritten, and then rewritten again at will. For example, Deng's symbolic power, built up by decades of propaganda, is a more durable and usable history for some than Xi may have realized. Critics of the regime have deployed Deng's sayings to criticize Xi's authoritarian, personalistic style of rule. After Xi amended the constitution to remove term limits, China's ubiquitous social media outlet WeChat buzzed with messages quoting Deng's August 1980 speech on political reform, with its denunciations of "over-concentration of power in the hands of individuals," "tenure for life in leading posts," and "practicing the cult of personality." These voices were using the party's own history and language to critique Xi's direction, transforming Deng from a font of legitimacy for the party into a source of pressure on the current leadership.[9] If the party was always "absolutely correct," as Xi has said, then how could Deng's criticisms of these practices be reconciled with Xi's embrace of them? One answer came in a new edition of an authoritative "short history" of the CCP published in 2021, which simply omitted these offending quotations from Deng that had appeared in prior versions.[10]

More broadly, in Xi's China, it is profoundly challenging to be a historian or even an ordinary person whose memories do not align with the CCP's "absolutely correct" version of history. Xi has called history "a mirror for people to draw wisdom."[11] However, he is adamant that this mirror should only reflect the single, correct interpretation of history the party creates. He warned in 2013, "Hostile forces at home and abroad often make trouble about the history of the Chinese revolution and New China, and do everything possible to attack, demonize, and sully this history."[12] He has imposed new penalties for the crime of "historical nihilism" and sought to control more strictly everything from the primary sources that inform scholarship to the historical movies and video games that represent history at its most popularized. His administration has even set up a hotline for Chinese citizens to report incidents of "historical nihilism." With fewer alternative narratives, Xi believes that the CCP—and China—will be stronger. The Tiananmen Mothers, bereaved parents who have become critics of the regime, once again faced persecution in 2019, on the thirtieth anniversary of the massacre, after decades of resilience in the face of house arrest and imprisonment. Magazines such as *China Annals* and *Remembrance* initially provided space to preserve memories of the Cultural Revolution and scholarship about the People's Republic of China's (PRC's) tumultuous past but ran into serious trouble with the authorities because, as Ian Johnson writes, they "recover memories that the Communist Party would prefer remained lost."[13] Book publications are routinely canceled or "indefinitely delayed"—even in Hong Kong, which was once a refuge for daring works on PRC history and politics.[14] Instead, the CCP offers up its official story of "the great path we have pioneered"—as Xi said at a celebration of the CCP's centenary—which it hopes "will go down in the annals of the development of the Chinese nation and of human civilization."[15]

If the CCP is becoming more successful in eliminating alternative narratives of its past, that strengthens the roots of its power within China and around the world.[16] This success enables the CCP to even more fully set the terms on which China's development success is understood—with clear geopolitical benefits. Xi declared in 2017 that China's experiences "blazed a new trail for other developing countries to achieve modernization. It offers a new option for other countries and nations who want to speed up their development while preserving their independence; and it offers Chinese wisdom and a Chinese approach to solving the problems facing mankind."[17] In September 2019, Xi went a step further: "The new type of state system founded by the CCP has enabled China to create a miracle of rapid economic growth and long-term social stability, and offered a new option for developing countries to realize modernity." Xi was explicit that this "new type of state system"—combining a single political party's authoritarian dominance and the pursuit of economic and technological development—was precisely what he believed developing countries could emulate "to achieve modernization."[18] This is a core part of his argument for China's increased global reputation and influence.

Thus, the history in these pages—and the evidence of its systematic manipulation by the CCP to construct the "China model"—is of great relevance to understanding the future of Chinese power. At a time of severe crisis in many democracies, with deep concerns about economic inequality, climate crisis, and political division, Xi's model may indeed be appealing to some countries. However, his portrait of that model and how it evolved in China is at best incomplete. The story of contestation, ferment, and experimentation as China found its way forward—and the alternative paths it experimented with during the 1980s—should be a core part of how people around the world understand China's rise. At a time of less stringent repression, we can hope this history becomes widely recognized within China as well.

Revisiting that history should also serve as a reminder that China's future is uncertain, despite the aura of inevitability and certainty the CCP seeks to project. Xi Jinping is not the end point of decades of transformation. Xi's China is not China forever, and China is still changing. Fundamental questions remain unanswered about the long-term viability of all aspects of the Chinese system, from its high debt burdens to widespread ecological crisis to its suppression of domestic debates about China's best path forward. And, of course, even if Xi remains as leader for life, what comes after him is profoundly uncertain as of this writing.

What would happen if the Chinese people were allowed to know this history? Would it produce the terrible chaos so feared by the Communist Party? Of course, the party's greatest horror is its own demise, but it is possible to imagine a process of historical reckoning that would not destabilize the entire party or country.[19] It is possible to imagine a China, even one ruled by the CCP, that rehabilitates Zhao Ziyang, praises the debate and contestation of ideas that characterized the 1980s, and even apologizes publicly for the violence of June 1989. It is possible to imagine China once again experimenting with meaningful political reforms, increasing the independence of the judiciary and the media, and giving ordinary people a greater say over the country's direction. All of this is not so difficult to imagine—and that is why the direction of CCP rule has profoundly disappointed so many people inside and outside of China. Instead of tolerating discussion of multiple paths to the future, China's rulers today offer up a new fable about the end of history. But history continues, in China as elsewhere. Just as greater openness can be found in China's past, it might well be found again in China's future.

ABBREVIATIONS

NOTES

ACKNOWLEDGMENTS

INDEX

ABBREVIATIONS

ADB	Asian Development Bank
BWAF	Beijing Workers' Autonomous Federation
CAC	Central Advisory Commission
CAS	Chinese Academy of Sciences
CASS	Chinese Academy of Social Sciences
CCDI	Central Commission for Discipline Inspection
CCHRC	中国当代史研究中心 [China Contemporary History Research Center], East China Normal University, Shanghai
CCP	Chinese Communist Party
CFELSG	Central Finance and Economics Leading Small Group
CMC	Central Military Commission
CoCom	Coordinating Committee for Multilateral Export Controls
COSTIND	Commission for Science, Technology, and Industry for National Defense
CPSU	Communist Party of the Soviet Union
CROPSR	Central Research Office on Political System Reform
CSFS	Chinese Society for Futures Studies
CYNP	Zhu Jiamu 朱佳木, ed., 陈云年谱 [Chronology of Chen Yun], 3 vols. (Beijing: Zhongyang wenxian chubanshe, 2000)

DRC Record   国务院发展研究中心大事记 (1980–2011) 征求意见稿 [Record of the State Council Development Research Center (1980–2011), draft for comments], internal (Beijing: Editorial Committee of the Record of the State Council Development Research Center, September 3, 2013)

DXGWX   党的宣传工作文件选编 [Selected documents on party propaganda work], 4 vols. (Beijing: CCP Central Party School Publishing House, 1994)

DXPNP   Leng Rong 冷溶, ed., 邓小平年谱, 1975–1997 [A chronology of Deng Xiaoping, 1975–1997] (Beijing: Central Literature Publishing House, 2004)

FBI   Federal Bureau of Investigation

GATT   General Agreement on Tariffs and Trade

GDP   gross domestic product

GSJTL   Committee on Historical Manuscripts of the People's Republic of China 中国人民共和国史稿委员会, ed., 邓力群国史讲谈录 [A record of Deng Liqun's talks on national history], internal manuscript, 7 vols. (2000–2002)

HGYFS   Beijing Armed Police Corps 武警北京市总队, 回顾与反思: 1989·制止动乱平息暴乱主要经验汇编 [Review and reflection: 1989—compilation of major experiences in stopping the unrest and quelling the rebellion], December 20, 1989, marked internal

HQMSXJ   Hu Qiaomu, 胡乔木书信集 [Letters of Hu Qiaomu], rev. ed. (Beijing: Renmin chubanshe, 2014)

HYBSXNP   Sheng Ping 盛平 and Wang Zaixing 王再兴, 胡耀邦思想年谱, 1975–1989 [Chronicle of Hu Yaobang's thought, 1975–1989], 2 vols. (Hong Kong: Taide shidai chubanshe, 2007)

HYBWX   胡耀邦文选 [Selected works of Hu Yaobang] (Beijing: Renmin chubanshe, 2015)

HYBZ   Zhang Liqun 张黎群, 胡耀邦专 [Biography of Hu Yaobang] (Beijing: Renmin chubanshe, 2005)

JFJB   解放军报 [PLA daily]

JJYJ   经济研究 [Economic research]

KMT   Kuomintang

LPLSRJ   Li Peng 李鹏, 李鹏六四日记 [Li Peng's June Fourth diary]

LXNNP   李先念年谱 [Chronology of Li Xiannian], 6 vols. (Beijing: Zhongyang wenxian chubanshe, 2011)

NCXB	内参选编 [Internal reference selections]. New China News Agency
NPC	National People's Congress
OTA	Office of Technology Assessment
PLA	People's Liberation Army
POS	Zhao Ziyang, *Prisoner of the State: The Secret Journal of Zhao Ziyang* (New York: Simon & Schuster, 2009)
PRC	People's Republic of China
RMRB	人民日报 [People's daily]
S&T	science and technology
SEZ	special economic zone
SJJJDB	世界经济导报 [World economic herald]
SPC	State Planning Commission
SSTC	State Science and Technology Commission
SWDXP	*Selected Works of Deng Xiaoping, 1975–1982* (Beijing: Foreign Languages Press, 1984)
SWDXP-3	*Selected Works of Deng Xiaoping, Vol. III, 1982–1994* (Beijing: Foreign Languages Press, 1994)
Toffler Papers	Papers of Alvin and Heidi Toffler, Columbia University Rare Books & Manuscripts
TERC	Technological and Economic Research Center
TVEs	township and village enterprises
WBA	World Bank Archives
WTO	World Trade Organization
XCDT	宣传动态 [Propaganda trends]
XCGWX	新闻出版工作文件选编, 1988–1989 [Selected documents on news and publishing work, 1988–1989] (Beijing: Zhongguo ISBN zhongxin, 1990), marked internal
XCJB	宣传简报 [Propaganda bulletin] (Propaganda Office of the PLA General Political Department, 1989
YHCQ	炎黄春秋 [Chinese annals]
ZFLZQJ	Fang Weizhong 房维中, ed., 在风浪中前进: 中国发展与改革编年记事 [Forward in the storm: Chronology of China's development and reform,

1977–1989], unpublished internal manuscript (2004). Available in the Fairbank Collection, Harvard University

ZHDMM   最后的秘密: 中共十三届四中全会"六四"结论文 [The last secret: The final documents from the June Fourth crackdown] (Hong Kong: New Century Press, 2019)

ZWCBWFWZX 中文出版物服务中心 [Service Center for Chinese Publications]. Available in Yenching Library, Harvard University

ZZGZWJXB 组织工作文件选编, 1989 年 [Selected organization work documents, 1989] (Beijing: General Office of the Organization Department of the CCP Central Committee, 1990), marked internal

ZZYWJ   赵紫阳文集, 1980–1989 [Collected works of Zhao Ziyang, 1980–1989], 4 vols. (Hong Kong: Chinese University Press, 2016)

ZZYYZZGG Wu Guoguang 吳國光, 趙紫陽與政治改革 [Zhao Ziyang and political reform] (Taipei: Yuanjing Publishing, 1997)

NOTES

A full bibliography is available at www.juliangewirtz.com.

Introduction

1.   Xinhua News Service, "赵紫阳同志逝世" [Comrade Zhao Ziyang passes away], RMRB, January 18, 2005.

2.   The detail on tank treads comes from Jonathan Mirsky, "Tiananmen: How Wrong We Were," *New York Review of Books,* May 20, 2014.

3.   Deng Xiaoping, "The Present Situation and the Tasks before Us," January 16, 1980; Klaus Mühlhahn, *Making China Modern: From the Great Qing to Xi Jinping* (Cambridge, MA: Belknap Press of Harvard University Press, 2019). Concepts of "modernization" and "development" are of course problematic when applied mechanically or as "universal," but they were constantly used by Chinese officials (on definitions, see Arif Dirlik, *Culture and History in Postrevolutionary China* [Hong Kong: Chinese University Press, 2011], 10–11; and He Ping, *China's Search for Modernity: Cultural Discourse in the Late 20th Century* [New York: Palgrave Macmillan, 2002], 1).

4.   He Li, *Political Thought and China's Transformation: Ideas Shaping Reform in Post-Mao China* (Basingstoke, UK: Palgrave Macmillan, 2015), 22; Jing Wang, *High Culture Fever: Politics, Aesthetics, and Ideology in Deng's China* (Berkeley: University of California Press, 1996), 97.

5.   "不走回头路" [Never turn back] in *Deng Xiaoping Commemoration Web,* January 23, 2017, http://cpc.people.com.cn/n1/2017/0123/c410539-29043742.html.

6.   Odd Arne Westad, "The Great Transformation: China in the Long 1970s," in *The Shock of the Global: The 1970s in Perspective,* ed. Niall Ferguson, Charles S. Maier,

Erez Manela, and Daniel J. Sargent (Cambridge, MA: Belknap Press of Harvard University Press, 2010), 65–79.

7.   Tony Saich, "Political and Ideological Reform in the PRC: An Interview with Professor Su Shaozhi," *China Information* 1, no. 2 (1986): 19–25. See also Huaiyin Li, *Reinventing Modern China: Imagination and Authenticity in Chinese Historical Writing* (Honolulu: University of Hawai'i Press, 2013), 204–235.

8.   For two major biographies of Deng, see Ezra Vogel, *Deng Xiaoping and the Transformation of China* (Cambridge, MA: Belknap Press of Harvard University Press, 2011); and Alexander V. Pantsov and Steven I. Levine, *Deng Xiaoping: A Revolutionary Life* (Oxford: Oxford University Press, 2015).

9.   Wu Guoguang, "Hard Politics with Soft Institutions: China's Political Reform, 1986–1989" (PhD diss., Princeton University, 1995), 93; Chen Jian, "China's Path toward 1989," in *The Fall of the Berlin Wall: The Revolutionary Legacy of 1989*, ed. Jeffrey A. Engel (Oxford: Oxford University Press, 2009), 109. See also Liu Xiaobo, "悲情的胡耀邦和赵紫阳" [The pathos of Hu Yaobang and Zhao Ziyang], 民主中国 [Democracy in China], January 2005, http://www.liu-xiaobo.org/blog/archives/7043; and Yao Jianfu 姚监复, "胡绩伟谈'胡赵十年新政'" [Hu Jiwei discusses the Hu-Zhao decade's new policies], January 5, 2008, https://2newcenturynet.blogspot.com/2008/03/blog-post_3505.html.

10.   "Streamlining Organizations Constitutes a Revolution," January 13, 1982, SWDXP; Vogel, *Deng Xiaoping*, 380.

11.   POS, 113. Whenever possible, I cite POS alongside other sources to corroborate its assertions.

12.   "Cable from Ambassador Katori to the Foreign Minister, 'Prime Minister Visit to China (Conversation with Chairman Deng Xiaoping),'" March 25, 1984, 2002-113, Act on Access to Information Held by Administrative Organs, obtained for CWIHP by Yutaka Kanda, http://digitalarchive.wilsoncenter.org/document/118849.

13.   These dynamics are now more visible due to revelatory leaked internal materials, including ZFLZQJ, ZZYWJ, and GSJTL.

14.   Pathbreaking works on this period include Joseph Fewsmith, *Dilemmas of Reform in China* (Armonk, NY: M. E. Sharpe, 1994); Richard Baum, *Burying Mao: Chinese Politics in the Age of Deng Xiaoping* (Princeton, NJ: Princeton University Press, 1994); Barry Naughton, *Growing out of the Plan* (Cambridge: Cambridge University Press, 1995); Susan Shirk, *The Political Logic of Economic Reform in China* (Berkeley: University of California Press, 1993); Merle Goldman, *Sowing the Seeds of Democracy in China: Political Reform in the Deng Xiaoping Era* (Cambridge, MA: Harvard University Press, 1995); Minxin Pei, *From Reform to Revolution: The Demise of Communism in China and the Soviet Union* (Cambridge, MA: Harvard University Press, 1998); Yasheng Huang, *Capitalism with Chinese Characteristics* (Cambridge:

Cambridge University Press, 2008); and Chen Fong-Ching and Jin Guantao, *From Youthful Manuscripts to River Elegy* (Hong Kong: Chinese University of Hong Kong Press, 1997). These works did not have available the sort of reliable internal primary source material that has appeared in recent years, which has been used in key studies such as Frederick C. Teiwes and Warren Sun, *Paradoxes of Post-Mao Rural Reform: Initial Steps toward a New Chinese Countryside, 1976–1981* (New York: Routledge, 2016); Sergey Radchenko, *Unwanted Visionaries: The Soviet Failure in Asia at the End of the Cold War* (Oxford: Oxford University Press, 2014); Taomo Zhou, "Leveraging Liminality: The Border Town of Bao'an (Shenzhen) and the Origins of China's Reform and Opening," *Journal of Asian Studies,* forthcoming 2021; Xiao Donglian, 歷史的轉軌: 從撥亂反正到改革開放, 1979–1981 [The historic transition: From bringing order out of chaos to reform and opening, 1979–1981] (Hong Kong: Chinese University of Hong Kong Press, 2008); and Jeremy Brown, *June Fourth: The Tiananmen Protests and Beijing Massacre of 1989* (Cambridge: Cambridge University Press, 2021). This book addresses different questions than those earlier studies—about the 1980s modernization project and the CCP's rewriting of this history—seeking to develop what Elizabeth Perry has termed "the promise of PRC [People's Republic of China] history." See Elizabeth Perry, "The Promise of PRC History," *Journal of Modern Chinese History* 10, no. 1 (January 2016): 114, 116.

15. Victor Shih, *Factions and Finance in China* (Cambridge: Cambridge University Press, 2008); Sebastian Heilmann and Elizabeth J. Perry, eds., *Mao's Invisible Hand: The Political Foundations of Adaptive Governance in China* (Cambridge, MA: Harvard University Press, 2011); Rebecca Karl, *The Magic of Concepts: History and the Economic in Twentieth-Century China* (Chapel Hill, NC: Duke University Press, 2017); Yuen Yuen Ang, *How China Escaped the Poverty Trap* (Ithaca, NY: Cornell University Press, 2016).

16. Policy debates were substantive and not simply a veil for personal clashes or conflict between purported factions. These policy ideas came from analyzing historical and contemporary conditions, learning from abroad, personal experience, and other sources, and evolved alongside "the pervasiveness of informal politics" in the 1980s (see reviews of *Prisoner of the State*: Alfred L. Chan, "Power, Policy and Elite Politics under Zhao Ziyang," *China Quarterly* 203 [September 2010]: 708–718; Joseph Fewsmith, "What Zhao Ziyang Tells Us about Elite Politics in the 1980s," *China Leadership Monitor* 30 [Fall 2009]: 1–20).

17. Richard Baum, "Epilogue: Communism, Convergence, and China's Political Convulsion," in *Reform and Reaction in Post-Mao China: The Road to Tiananmen,* ed. Richard Baum (New York: Routledge, 1991), 186.

18. On the "politics of historiography," see Jonathan Unger, ed., *Using the Past to Serve the Present: Historiography and Politics in Contemporary China* (Armonk, NY: M. E. Sharpe, 1993); and Zheng Wang, *Never Forget National Humiliation: Historical Memory in Chinese Politics and Foreign Relations* (New York: Columbia University

Press, 2012). On the artificiality of the decade as a periodization, see Zha Jianying 查建英, 八十年代访谈录 [Interviews on the 1980s] (Beijing: Sanlian shudian, 2006).

19.   This argument develops what Andreas Glaeser calls political epistemics, ways in which the East German socialist state "produced and certified knowledge about itself," in *Political Epistemics: The Secret Police, the Opposition, and the End of East German Socialism* (Chicago: University of Chicago Press, 2010), xvi—which he posits as a causal variable to explain the end of socialism and Communist Party rule there. "Epistemic" factors were crucial in the *continuation* of socialism and Communist Party rule in China.

20.   George Orwell, *1984* (New York: Penguin Classics, 2021), 40.

21.   Cao Yaxin 曹雅欣, "习近平: 灭人之国 必先去其史" [Xi Jinping: Destroying a nation begins with going after its history], August 6, 2015, http://star.news.sohu.com /20150806/n418305529.shtml.

22.   中共中央关于党的百年奋斗重大成就和历史经验的决议 [Resolution of the CCP Central Committee on major achievements and historical experiences of the Party over the past century], November 16, 2021, http://politics.people.com.cn/n1/2021/1116 /c1001-32284163.html.

23.   Glenn D. Tiffert, "Peering down the Memory Hole: Censorship, Digitization, and the Fragility of Our Knowledge Base," *American Historical Review* 124, no. 2 (April 2019): 550–568; Masha Borak, "Brain King Becomes First WeChat Mini Program Banned by Regulators for 'Distorting History,'" *TechNode,* January 31, 2018.

24.   Yan Lianke, "On China's State-Sponsored Amnesia," *New York Times,* April 1, 2013. See also Fang Lizhi, "The Chinese Amnesia," trans. Perry Link, *New York Review of Books,* September 27, 1990; and Margaret Hillenbrand, *Negative Exposures: Knowing What Not to Know in Contemporary China* (Chapel Hill, NC: Duke University Press, 2020).

25.   Chris Buckley, "Xi Jinping the Hidden Star of a TV Series about Deng Xiaoping," *New York Times,* August 27, 2014.

26.   Geremie Barmé, "Homo Xinesis Ascendant," *China Heritage,* September 16, 2018; Elizabeth Perry, *Anyuan: Mining China's Revolutionary Tradition* (Berkeley: University of California Press, 2012), esp. 247–281; and Rana Mitter, *China's Good War: How World War II Is Shaping a New Nationalism* (Cambridge, MA: Harvard University Press, 2020).

27.   中共中央关于党的百年奋斗重大成就和历史经验的决议.

28.   For example, Margaret MacMillan, *Dangerous Games: The Uses and Abuses of History* (New York: Modern Library, 2009); and James Mark, *Unfinished Revolution:*

Making Sense of the Communist Past in Central-Eastern Europe (New Haven, CT: Yale University Press, 2011).

29.   The CCP carried this tradition forward. Long before Zhao Ziyang, leaders such as Wang Ming, Liu Shaoqi, and Lin Biao were erased from positions of centrality. See Susanne Weigelin-Schwiedrzik, "In Search of a Master Narrative for 20th-Century Chinese History," *China Quarterly* 188 (December 2006): 1070–1091. For example, CCP historiography carries forward "evaluating figures" (人物评价) and "praise-blame" (褒贬) history so common in dynastic histories.

30.   Louisa Lim, *The People's Republic of Amnesia: Tiananmen Revisited* (New York: Oxford University Press, 2014). Wu Wei 吳偉, 中國 80 年代政治改革的台前幕後 [On stage and backstage: China's political reform in the 1980s] (Hong Kong: Xinshiji chuban ji chuanmei youxian gongsi, 2013).

31.   Henry Steele Commager, "The Search for a Usable Past," *American Heritage* 16, no. 2 (February 1965).

32.   Michel-Rolph Trouillot, *Silencing the Past: Power and the Production of History* (Boston: Beacon, 1995), xxiii.

33.   Stefan Link and Noam Maggor, "The United States as a Developing Nation: Revisiting the Peculiarities of American History," *Past & Present* 246, no. 1 (February 2020): 269–306.

Chapter 1: Reassessing History, Recasting Modernization

1.   Deng Xiaoping, "The Present Situation and the Tasks before Us" (January 16, 1980), SWDXP-3, https://dengxiaopingworks.wordpress.com/2013/02/25/the-present-situation-and-the-tasks-before-us/.

2.   Ezra Vogel, *Deng Xiaoping and the Transformation of China* (Cambridge, MA: Belknap Press of Harvard University Press, 2011), 176–177; Fan Shuo 范硕, 叶剑英在关键时刻 [Ye Jianying at the crucial moment] (Shenyang: Liaoning renmin chubanshe, 2001), 363–370.

3.   Zhang Gensheng 张根生, "华国锋谈粉碎'四人帮'" [Hua Guofeng Talks about smashing the 'Gang of Four'], YHCQ 7 (2004): 1–5.

4.   Richard Baum, *Burying Mao: Chinese Politics in the Age of Deng Xiaoping* (Princeton, NJ: Princeton University Press, 1994), 28, 38, 42; Vogel, *Deng Xiaoping*, 180.

5.   Andrew G. Walder, *Agents of Disorder: Inside China's Cultural Revolution* (Cambridge, MA: Belknap Press of Harvard University Press, 2019).

6.　Alexander V. Pantsov, with Steven I. Levine, *Deng Xiaoping: A Revolutionary Life* (Oxford: Oxford University Press, 2015).

7.　Pantsov, *Deng Xiaoping,* 293–309; Vogel, *Deng Xiaoping,* 157–174.

8.　Han Gang 韩钢, "'两个凡是'的由来及其终结" [The origin and end of the "two whatevers"], 中共党史研究 [CCP history studies] 11 (2009): 54–63; Frederick C. Teiwes and Warren Sun, "Hua Guofeng, Deng Xiaoping, and Reversing the Verdict on the 1976 'Tiananmen Incident,'" *China Review* 19, no. 4 (November 2019): 85–124.

9.　"Preserving Chairman Mao," *The Guardian,* September 11, 2016.

10.　出版工作文件选编 [Selected documents on publishing work, October 1976–December 1980] (Beijing: State Publishing Administration, 1981), marked internal, ZWCBWFWZX, 28: 65, 40–59, 290–291.

11.　"愤怒声讨'四人帮'反党集团篡党夺权的滔天罪行" [Angrily denounce the monstrous crime of usurping the power of the party by the "Gang of Four" anti-party clique!] (Shanghai: Shanghai renmin chubanshe, 1976), http://chineseposters.net/posters/g2-34.php.

12.　"学好文件抓住纲" [Study the documents and grasp the key links], RMRB, February 7, 1977.

13.　Han Gang, "'两个凡是'的由来及其终结."

14.　David Lague, "1977 Exam Opened Escape Route into China's Elite," *New York Times,* January 6, 2008.

15.　David M. Bachman, *Chen Yun and the Chinese Political System* (Berkeley: Institute of East Asian Studies, University of California, 1985); Xu Yongyue, "晚年陈云与邓小平: 心心相通" [The later years of Chen Yun and Deng Xiaoping: Kindred spirits], 百年潮 [Hundred year tide] 3 (2006): 13–17.

16.　Roderick MacFarquhar, foreword to POS, xviii.

17.　Hua Guofeng, "Unite and Strive to Build a Modern, Powerful Socialist Country," *Beijing Review* 21, no. 10 (March 10, 1982): 7–40; Frederick C. Teiwes and Warren Sun, "China's New Economic Policy under Hua Guofeng," *China Journal,* no. 66 (July 2011): 10–11; Chris Bramall, *Chinese Economic Development* (London: Routledge, 2009), 167–168.

18.　Joshua Eisenman, *Red China's Green Revolution: Technological Innovation, Institutional Change, and Economic Development under the Commune* (New York: Columbia University Press, 2018); Sigrid Schmalzer, *Red Revolution, Green Revolution: Scientific Farming in Socialist China* (Chicago: University of Chicago Press,

2016). See also Chris Bramall, "A Late Maoist Industrial Revolution? Economic Growth in Jiangsu Province, 1966–1978," *China Quarterly* 240 (2019): 1039–1065.

19.   Barry Naughton, *Growing out of the Plan* (Cambridge: Cambridge University Press, 1995), 42–50.

20.   Catherine H. Keyser, *Professionalizing Research in Post-Mao China: The System Reform Institute and Policymaking* (Armonk, NY: M. E. Sharpe, 2002), 27.

21.   Xiao Donglian 萧冬连, "中国改革开放之缘起" [The origins of China's reform and opening up], 中共党史研究 [CCP history research], no. 12 (2017); ZFLZQJ 1977–1978: 121–122; CYNP, 2:256.

22.   Xiao Donglian, "中国改革开放之缘起"; ZFLZQJ 1977–1978, 48–49, 124. On May 17, 1978, the State Council established a leading group for the introduction of new technologies led by Yu Qiuli.

23.   DXPNP, 1:320.

24.   They were so closely associated as to have been subject to joint criticism in 1976. See "邓小平、胡耀邦是怎样反对马克思主义青年运动路线" [How Deng Xiaoping and Hu Yaobang opposed the methods of the Marxist youth movement], April 1976, marked internal, in ZWCBWFWZX, 2:33; Tian Jiyun 田纪云 et al., "我们心中的胡耀邦" [Hu Yaobang in my heart], YHCQ 11 (2005), www.yhcqw.com/11/1514.html.

25.   "实践是检验真理的唯一标准" [Practice is the sole criterion of truth], 光明日报 [Guangming daily], May 11, 1978. See also GSJTL 3:352; Michael Schoenhals, "The 1978 Truth Criterion Controversy," *China Quarterly*, no. 126 (June 1991): 245, 259–262; Vogel, *Deng Xiaoping,* 211.

26.   Hu Qiaomu 胡乔木, "按照经济规律办事" [Act in accordance with economic laws] (delivered on July 28, 1978), RMRB, October 6, 1978, trans. in FBIS-CHI-78-197, October 11, 1978, E1–E23; Vogel, *Deng Xiaoping,* 224–225.

27.   Vogel, *Deng Xiaoping,* 299.

28.   Teiwes and Sun, "Hua Guofeng," 87, 102. Deng was traveling to Singapore as the conference got under way.

29.   "Hua Guofeng's Second Speech at the CCP Central Work Conference," November 25, 1978, History and Public Policy Program Digital Archive, Hubei Provincial Archives, SZ1-4-791, translated by Caixia Lu, http://digitalarchive.wilsoncenter .org/document/121689. Peng Dehuai and Tao Zhu were posthumously rehabilitated.

30.   HYBZ, 3:950–959; Teiwes and Sun, "Hua Guofeng," 87, 115.

31.   Deng Xiaoping, "Emancipate the Mind, Seek Truth from Facts, and Unite as One in Looking to the Future" (December 13, 1978), in SWDXP, 156–163; DXPNP, 1:450–452.

32.   "Hua Guofeng's Speech at the Closing Session of the CCP Central Work Conference," December 13, 1978, History and Public Policy Program Digital Archive, Hubei Provincial Archives, SZ1-4-791, translated by Caixia Lu, http://digitalarchive .wilsoncenter.org/document/121690.

33.   "中国共产党第十一届中央委员会第三次全体会议公报" [Official bulletin of the 3rd Plenary Session of the 11th CCP Central Committee], December 22, 1978; CYNP, 3:230–232; DXPNP, 454–456.

34.   CYNP, 2:301–303; Teiwes and Sun, "China's New Economic Policy," 17; Yu Guangyuan 于光远, "我亲历的那次历史转折" [That historical turnaround I personally experienced] (Beijing: Zhongguo bianyi chubanshe, 1998), 71–72, 272.

35.   CCP Central Committee and CCP Supreme People's Court Party Group, "关于抓紧复查纠正冤、假、错案认真落实党的政策的请示报告" [Report on request for instructions on paying close attention to the review and correction of unjust, false, and mistaken cases and conscientiously implementing party policy"], *The Maoist Legacy,* https://www.maoistlegacy.de/db/items/show/73.

36.   Andrew Nathan, *Chinese Democracy* (New York: Knopf, 1985), 10–22, 26–30; Benton and Hunter, eds., *Wild Lily, Prairie Fire* (Princeton, NJ: Princeton University Press, 1995), 157–263. Numerous videos are available on YouTube, including Helmut Opletal, "China 1979: Xidan Democracy Wall," uploaded March 29, 2016, YouTube, https://www.youtube.com/watch?v=HNdt4xC6Q7k.

37.   Hu Jiwei 胡绩伟, "胡耀邦与西单民主墙" [Hu Yaobang and the Xidan Democracy Wall], 争鸣 [*Cheng Ming*], April 2004; Vogel, *Deng Xiaoping,* 256.

38.   Wei Jingsheng, "The Fifth Modernization," *Wei Jingsheng Foundation,* https://weijingsheng.org/doc/en/THE%20FIFTH%20MODERNIZATION.html; Yan Jiaqi, *Toward a Democratic China,* trans. David S. K. Hong and Denis C. Mair (Honolulu: University of Hawai'i Press, 1992), 45–49; Susanne Weigelin-Schwiedrzik, "In Search of a Master Narrative for 20th-Century Chinese History," *China Quarterly* 188 (December 2006): 1076.

39.   Border clashes would continue throughout the decade. See Xiaoming Zhang, *Deng Xiaoping's Long War: The Military Conflict between China and Vietnam* (Chapel Hill: University of North Carolina Press, 2015).

40.   Deng Xiaoping, "Uphold the Four Cardinal Principles" (March 30, 1979), SWDXP.

41.   Ding Xing 丁邢, "李洪林与胡耀邦" [Li Honglin, and Hu Yaobang], September 17, 2008, 胡耀邦史料信息网 [Online repository of historical materials on Hu Yaobang], www.hybsl.cn/beijingcankao/beijingfenxi/2019-05-31/69838.html; Hu Jiwei, "胡耀邦与西单民主墙"; James P. Sterba, "Peking Closes Democracy Wall," *New York Times,* December 7, 1979.

42.   CCP Beijing Municipal Party Committee School Reference Office 中共北京市委党校资料室, 学习叶剑英同志的国庆讲话 [Study Comrade Ye Jianying's National Day speech], November 1979, marked internal, 1–7. Hu Yaobang, Hu Qiaomu, and Deng Liqun prepared the 1979 speech, consulting with Deng Xiaoping. See Vogel, *Deng Xiaoping*, 355–357; DXPNP, 554–555, 558, 562–563; Geremie Barmé, "History for the Masses," in *Using the Past to Serve the Present: Historiography and Politics in Contemporary China*, ed. Jonathan Unger (Armonk, NY: M. E. Sharpe, 1993), 261.

43.   Wang Junwei 王均伟, "重温'关于若干历史问题的决议'坚定'两个维护'的自觉" [Reviewing the Resolution on certain questions in the history of our party to strengthen consciousness of the "two upholds"], 求是 [Seeking truth], January 1, 2019.

44.   Xiao Donglian 萧冬连, "邓小平与'关于建国以来党的若干历史问题的决议'的起草" [Deng Xiaoping and the drafting of the Resolution on certain questions in the history of our party since the founding of the PRC], 江淮文史 [Lower Yangtze history and literature] 2 (2016): 4–23.

45.   ZFLZQJ 1980, 15–16; HYBSXNP), 1:481; Vogel, *Deng Xiaoping*, 358–359.

46.   Frederick C. Teiwes and Warren Sun, *Paradoxes of Post-Mao Rural Reform: Initial Steps toward a New Chinese Countryside, 1976–1981* (New York: Routledge, 2016); Joshua Eisenman, *Red China's Green Revolution: Technological Innovation, Institutional Change, and Economic Development under the Commune* (New York: Columbia University Press, 2018); Cai Wenbin 蔡文彬, ed., 赵紫阳在四川 1975–1980 [Zhao Ziyang in Sichuan, 1975–1980] (Hong Kong: Xin shiji chubanji, 2011). See also David Shambaugh, *The Making of a Premier: Zhao Ziyang's Provincial Career* (Boulder, CO: Westview, 1984), 81, 105. For a recent detailed biography of Zhao, see Lu Yuegang 盧躍剛, 趙紫陽傳: 一位失敗改革家的一生 [Zhao Ziyang: The life of a failed reformer] (Xinbei: INK Press, 2019). As he rose, Zhao promised to adhere to the readjustment, though with the Sichuan leadership he also committed to "striving for more substantial growth in agriculture and industry" and critiqued one effect of the "national economic readjustment": numerous enterprises "had no tasks to perform" (ZZYWJ, 1:9–10, 16–17). This complicates Teiwes and Sun's claim that Zhao was a consistent supporter of the readjustment.

47.   Frederick Teiwes and Warren Sun, "China's New Economic Policy under Hua Guofeng," *China Journal* 66 (July 2011): 19–20.

48.   Tian Jiyun 田纪云, "赵紫阳在四川" [Zhao Ziyang in Sichuan], November 2012, www.reformdata.org/index.do?m=wap&a=show&catid=359&typeid=&id=1680.

49.   See, for example, Vogel, *Deng Xiaoping*, 366–373.

50.   DXPNP, 2:730; Xiao Donglian, 歷史的轉軌: 從撥亂反正到改革開放, 1979–1981 [The historic transition: From bringing order out of chaos to reform and opening,

1979–1981] (Hong Kong: Chinese University of Hong Kong Press, 2008), 267–284; Deng Xiaoping, "Remarks on Successive Drafts of the 'Resolution on Certain Questions in the History of Our Party since the Founding of the PRC'" (March 1980–June 1981), SWDXP-3.

51.　"Erasing Traces of the Past," *Chinese Law & Government* 24, no. 4 (Winter 1991–1992): 86–93; Xiao Donglian, 歷史的轉軌, 276.

52.　*Selected Documents on Publishing Work, October 1976–December 1980,* 204–206.

53.　HQMSXJ, 282; see also 281, 293–294.

54.　Deng, "Remarks on Successive Drafts."

55.　Deng Xiaoping, "Answers to the Italian Journalist Oriana Fallaci" (August 21 and 23, 1980), SWDXP. Xinhua deputy director Mu Qing announced in June that news reporting and "external propaganda" would shift focus to the Four Modernizations, "especially economic construction." See XCDT 27, marked internal (June 25, 1980): 182.

56.　Pantsov, *Deng Xiaoping,* 165–176.

57.　Xiao Donglian, "邓小平与'关于建国以来党的若干历史问题的决议'的起草."

58.　HQMXSJ, 291.

59.　Guo Daohui 郭道晖, "四千老干部对党史的一次民主评议" [The 4,000 veteran cadres' first democratic deliberation on party history], YHCQ 4 (2010), http://www.yhcqw.com/34/7222.html; Xiao Donglian, 歷史的轉軌, 284–289.

60.　Deng Xiaoping, "Remarks on Successive Drafts."

61.　HQMXSJ, 295–300.

62.　ZFLZQJ 1980, 155–156.

63.　Alexander Cook, *The Cultural Revolution on Trial: Mao and the Gang of Four* (New York: Columbia University Press), 125–126.

64.　Deng Xiaoping, "Remarks on Successive Drafts." On the Sixth Plenum agenda, see also HQMXSJ, 301–302.

65.　Han Gang, "'两个凡是'的由来及其终结." On June 24, Zhao Ziyang praised the resolution as "very good" in a meeting with his adviser Ma Hong and drew attention to the fact that "the resolution has been amended on the matter of the utility of market regulation to the planned economy" (ZZYWJ, 1:190).

66.　"Resolution on Certain Questions in the History of Our Party since the Founding of the PRC," *Beijing Review* 24, no. 27 (July 6, 1981): 10–39.

67.   Weigelin-Schwiedrzik, "In Search of a Master Narrative," 1070–1091. The resolution never completely succeeded at "unifying thinking" about the Cultural Revolution's traumatic history. See Susanne Weigelin-Schwiedrzik and Cui Jinke, "Whodunnit? Memory and Politics before the 50th Anniversary of the Cultural Revolution," *China Quarterly* 227 (September 2016): 734–751.

68.   XCDT 36 (July 20, 1981): 210–211.

69.   "A Brief Account of the National Work Conference on Collecting Party History Materials," *Chinese Law and Government* 19, no. 3 (Fall 1986): 112–120.

70.   XCDT 33 (July 6, 1981): 201–202.

71.   Xiao Ke, "Criticism and Self-Criticism of Party Historiography," *Chinese Law & Government* 19, no. 3 (1986): 91–100.

72.   Deng Liqun 邓力群, "'关于建国以来党的若干历史问题的决议'的介绍和解释" [Introduction and explanation of the "Resolution on certain questions in the history of our party since the founding of the PRC"], July 21–24, 1981, ZWCBWFWZX, special file 18, no. 3.

73.   XCDT 7 (February 10, 1982): 29–31; Tan Zongji, "The Third Plenum of the Eleventh Central Committee Is a Major Turning Point in the History of the Party since the Founding of the PRC," *Chinese Law and Government* 28, no. 3 (May–June 1995): 5–88.

Part I: Ideology and Propaganda

1.   "Ideology" is a protean concept with many overlapping definitions. In China studies, see Stuart Schram, *Ideology and Policy in China since the Third Plenum, 1978–84* (London: Contemporary China Institute, 1984), 2. See also Franz Schurmann, *Ideology and Organization in Communist China* (Berkeley: University of California Press, 1968), 8–9, 18. For foundational treatments, see Karl Mannheim, *Ideology and Utopia: An Introduction to the Sociology of Knowledge* (London: Routledge and Kegan Paul, 1936) and Clifford Geertz, "Ideology as a Cultural System," in *The Interpretation of Culture* (New York: Basic Books, 1973), 211–252.

2.   Roderick MacFarquhar, *The Politics of China: The Eras of Mao and Deng*, 2nd ed. (New York: Cambridge University Press, 1997), 3; Evan Feigenbaum, *China's Techno-Warriors: National Security and Strategic Competition from the Nuclear to the Information Age* (Stanford, CA: Stanford University Press, 2000), 73. For other critiques of the widespread idea that post-Mao China was "post-ideological," see Joseph Fewsmith, *Elite Politics in Contemporary China* (London: Routledge, 2001), xv; Arif Dirlik, "Postsocialism? Reflections on 'Socialism with Chinese Characteristics,'" *Bulletin of Concerned Asian Scholars* 21, no. 1 (1989): 33–44.

3.   "The Great Pragmatist: Deng Xiaoping," *The Guardian,* December 17, 2008.

4.   Deng Xiaoping, "Uphold the Four Cardinal Principles," March 30, 1979, SWDXP.

5.   In this usage of "ideologue," I follow Geremie Barmé, *In the Red: On Contemporary Chinese Culture* (New York: Columbia University Press, 1999), 32, and *Shades of Mao: The Posthumous Cult of the Great Leader* (London: Routledge, 1995), 13. These classified materials—variously designated "internal" and grades of "secret"—contained instructions from the center to propaganda and publishing organs nationwide as well as classified reports prepared for top leaders.

6.   Peter Kenez, *The Birth of the Propaganda State: Soviet Methods of Mass Mobilization, 1917–1929* (New York: Cambridge University Press, 2009).

7.   Gao Hua, *How the Red Sun Rose: The Origin and Development of the Yan'an Rectification Movement, 1930–1945,* trans. Stacy Mosher and Guo Jian (Hong Kong: Chinese University Press, 2019). Although new sources of information emerged in the post-Mao period, the Chinese propaganda apparatus remained immensely powerful throughout the 1980s. See Anne-Marie Brady, *Marketing Dictatorship: Propaganda and Thought Work in Contemporary China* (Lanham, MD: Rowman & Littlefield, 2008); and Daniel C. Lynch, *After the Propaganda State: Media, Politics, and "Thought Work" in Reformed China* (Stanford, CA: Stanford University Press, 1999), 3.

8.   For example, foreign obituaries mocked Hu Qiaomu as "what counted for a leading theoretician on the CCP's Neanderthal wing" (Simon Long, "Obituary: Hu Qiaomu," *The Independent,* September 29, 1992).

9.   POS, 9; David Shambaugh, "China's Propaganda System: Institutions, Processes, and Efficacy," *China Journal* 57 (January 2007): 25–58.

10.   Schoenhals, *Doing Things with Words,* 1. On political metaphors and linguistic rhythms, see Perry Link, *An Anatomy of Chinese: Rhythm, Metaphor, Politics* (Cambridge, MA: Harvard University Press, 2013). Television viewership was also on the rise in this period, but CCP propagandists remained focused on print media, which provided the basis for highly scripted radio and television propaganda (with important exceptions such as the televised trial of the Gang of Four). See Lynch, *After the Propaganda State,* 45, 142–143.

11.   Schram, *Ideology and Policy in China,* 1, 2, 79. See also David Apter and Tony Saich, *Revolutionary Discourse in Mao's Republic* (Cambridge, MA: Harvard University Press, 1994), 4, 5, 7.

12.   Su Shaozhi, *Democratization and Reform* (Nottingham, UK: Spokesman, 1988), 79.

13.   An extensive literature has analyzed the CCP's changing claims on individuals and society in the post-Mao era; for example, Arthur Kleinman, Yunxiang Yan, Jing

Jun, Sing Lee, Everett Zhang, Pan Tianshu, Wu Fei, and Jinhua Guo, *Deep China: The Moral Life of the Person* (Berkeley: University of California Press, 2011); Yunxiang Yan, *Private Life under Socialism: Love, Intimacy, and Family Change in a Chinese Village, 1949–1999* (Stanford, CA: Stanford University Press, 2003); Emily Honig and Gail Hershatter, *Personal Voices: Chinese Women in the 1980s* (Stanford, CA: Stanford University Press, 1988); and Anita Chan, Richard Madsen, and Jonathan Unger, *Chen Village: Revolution to Globalization*, 3rd ed. (Berkeley: University of California Press, 2009).

14. The CCP did not invent these aspirations; in many ways, they echoed Chiang Kai-shek's New Life Movement in the 1930s (Ren Yimin 任一民, "新生活运动" [New Life Movement], RMRB, March 11, 1983).

15. Margaret E. Roberts, *Censored: Distraction and Diversion inside China's Great Firewall* (Princeton, NJ: Princeton University Press, 2018); Yuyu Chen and David Y. Yang, "The Impact of Media Censorship: 1984 or Brave New World?" *American Economic Review* 109, no. 6 (June 2019): 2294–2332. For context beyond the Chinese case, see Sergei Guriev and Daniel Treisman, "How Modern Dictators Survive: An Informational Theory of the New Authoritarianism" (NBER Working Paper No. 21136, Cambridge, MA, April 2015), www.nber.org/papers/w21136.

Chapter 2: Spiritual Pollutions and Sugar-Coated Bullets

1. Deng Xiaoping, "The Present Situation and the Tasks before Us," SWDXP.

2. Document No. 6 (no title, instructions on studying Deng Xiaoping's speech "The Present Situation and Tasks"), March 8, 1980, from 中共上海市日用五金公司委员会文件 (80) [Shanghai Daily Hardware Company Party Committee Records (1980)], in Folder En-021-109-004, CCHRC.

3. Chen Fong-Ching and Jin Guantao, *From Youthful Manuscripts to River Elegy* (Hong Kong: Chinese University of Hong Kong Press, 1997), 93; Daniel C. Lynch, *After the Propaganda State: Media, Politics, and "Thought Work" in Reformed China* (Stanford, CA: Stanford University Press, 1999), 88–90; Zha Jianying, "Bei Dao," in 八十年代访谈录 [*Interviews on the 1980s*] (Beijing: Sanlian shudian, 2006), 66–81. The leadership was also making changes to the ideological status of literature, art, and culture. On July 26, 1980, *People's Daily* declared, "Art serves the people and socialism" (rather than the Maoist idea that "art serves politics"). At the 4th Congress of Writers in October 1979, Deng Xiaoping had said, "The basic standard for judging all our work is whether it helps or hinders our effort to modernize" ("Speech Greeting the Fourth Congress of Chinese Writers and Artists," October 30, 1979, SWDXP, http://cpcchina.chinadaily.com.cn/fastfacts/2010-10/18/content_11425385.htm).

4.   Deng Xiaoping, "Implement the Policy of Readjustment, Ensure Stability and Unity," December 25, 1980, SWDXP.

5.   PLA Daily Special Commentator 本报特约评论员, "四项基本原则不容违反" [The Four Cardinal Principles must not be violated], JFJB, April 20, 1981; Merle Goldman, *Sowing the Seeds of Democracy in China: Political Reform in the Deng Xiaoping Era* (Cambridge, MA: Harvard University Press, 1995), 88–95; Richard Baum, *Burying Mao: Chinese Politics in the Age of Deng Xiaoping* (Princeton, NJ: Princeton University Press, 1994), 126–130. See also XCDT 20 (May 6, 1981): 120–122.

6.   XCDT 3 (January 13, 1982): 12–17.

7.   Keith Forster, "The 1982 Campaign against Economic Crimes," *Australian Journal of Chinese Affairs* 14 (1985): 7.

8.   ZFLZQJ 1981, 252. For a history of smuggling in China, see Philip Thai, *China's War on Smuggling: Law, Economic Life, and the Making of the Modern State, 1842–1965* (New York: Columbia University Press, 2018).

9.   CYNP, 2:330.

10.   HYBZ, 3:750–751.

11.   ZZYWJ, 1:437–438. See also XCDT 14 (March 15, 1982): 64–68.

12.   ZFLZQJ 1982, 43–45. For Deng Liqun, this "two hands" thesis was a significant contribution; see GSJTL, 5:446.

13.   XCDT 19 (April 14, 1982): 91–93.

14.   Jiang Jianzhang 姜建章, "职工守则-扶植正气, 抵制歪风, 拒腐蚀, 永不沾" [Foster a correct spirit, resist the evil spirit, resist corruption, never get involved with it] (Renmin meishu chubanshe, 1983), https://chineseposters.net/gallery/e13-413.php.

15.   XCDT 27 (May 17, 1982).

16.   Emily Honig and Gail Hershatter, *Personal Voices: Chinese Women in the 1980s* (Stanford, CA: Stanford University Press, 1988), 60–62. An entire book titled *How to Identify Pornographic Songs* (怎样鉴别黄色歌曲) was published by the People's Music Publishing House in 1982.

17.   Shen Rong 谌容, 杨月月与萨特之研究 [Yang Yueyue and the study of Sartre] (Beijing: Zhongguo wenlian chubanshe, 1984); Liu Mingjiu 柳鸣九, "给萨特以历史地位" [Placing Sartre in history], 读书 [*Dushu*] 7 (February 1980): 106–115; Liu Datao 刘大涛, "'萨特热'与改革开放初期的思想启蒙" ['Sartre fever' and the intellectual enlightenment of the early period of reform and opening up], 学术探索 [Academic exploration] 4 (2012): 1–5. Many also noted with pleasure Sartre's admiration for the Chinese revolution.

When Sartre died in April 1980, Chinese newspapers ran laudatory obituaries, leading to a surge of interest in his work.

18.   Hu Weimin 胡伟民, "肮脏的手: 导演阐述" [*Dirty Hands:* Director's statement], 戏剧艺术 [Theatre arts] 2 (1981): 120–127.

19.   XCDT 25 (May 4, 1982): 113–120.

20.   Guo Hongan 郭宏安, "第一届全国法国文学讨论会在无锡举行" [The first national French literature symposium held in Wuxi], 外国文学研究 [Foreign literature studies] 3 (1982): 138.

21.   "Oral Account by Cheng Xuliang," quoted in Honig and Hershatter, *Personal Voices,* 78.

22.   XCDT 32 (June 5, 1982): 185–190.

23.   Qiang Zhai, "Mao Zedong and Dulles's 'Peaceful Evolution' Strategy: Revelations from Bo Yibo's Memoirs," http://www.chinaheritagequarterly.org/features.php ?searchterm=0181959preventingpeace.inc&issue=018.

24.   XCDT 32 (June 5, 1982): 185–190; XCDT 39 (July 12, 1982): 234–237.

25.   HYBZ, 3:941–945.

26.   GSJTL, 3:408, 7:272–273; ZZYWJ, 1:643. Later statistics put the numbers at 164,000 economic crime cases examined, with 30,000 people "sentenced according to law"; more than 220 million yuan in stolen money and goods were reportedly recovered (HYBZ, 3:752–754).

27.   HYBZ, 3:933–936. The leadership established a "Civility and Politeness Month" in March 1982 (ZZYWJ, 1:421–422).

28.   XCDT 6 (January 29, 1983): 41–47.

29.   XCDT 8 (February 12, 1983): 51–52; XCDT 9 (February 17, 1983): 58–61.

30.   XCDT 3 (January 7, 1983): 19–20.

31.   David Palmer, *Qigong Fever: Body, Science, and Utopia in China* (New York: Columbia University Press, 2007), 70–72, 154–157, 296–298. In the 1990s, qigong emerged in the center of the political arena with the rise and political mobilization of Falun Gong (219–277).

32.   Yiu-chung Wong, *From Deng Xiaoping to Jiang Zemin: Two Decades of Political Reform in the PRC* (Lanham, MD: University Press of America, 2005), 147; Jing Wang, *High Culture Fever: Politics, Aesthetics, and Ideology in Deng's China* (Berkeley: University of California Press, 1996), 10–11.

33. Wang Ruoshui 王若水, "'清除精神污染'前后" [Recounting the anti-spiritual pollution campaign], November 1999, www.wangruoshui.net/CHINESE/QINGWUQH.HTM.

34. Wong, *From Deng Xiaoping*, 148; Wang, *High Culture Fever*, 26.

35. Ding Shaoping 丁晓平, "1980年代的周扬与胡乔木" [Zhou Yang and Hu Qiaomu in the 1980s], September 12, 2013, http://m.aisixiang.com/data/67597.html.

36. Gu Yan 顾骧, 周扬与清除精神污染 [Zhou Yang and eliminating spiritual pollution], YHCQ 10 (2013), www.yhcqw.com/34/9287.html; Ruan Ming, *Deng Xiaoping: Chronicle of an Empire* (Boulder: Westview Press, 1994), 132; Interview with Qin Chuan, "1983年清除精神污染" [1983's anti-spiritual pollution campaign], www.chinesepen.org/blog/archives/23178.

37. Charles Kraus, "More than Just a Soft Drink: Coca-Cola and China's Early Reform and Opening," *Diplomatic History* 43, no. 1 (2019): 122.

38. Honig and Hershatter, *Personal Voices*, 43–46.

39. XCDT 4 (January 15, 1983): 31–34. See also Thomas B. Gold, "'Just in Time!': China Battles Spiritual Pollution on the Eve of 1984," *Asian Survey* 24, no. 9 (September 1984): 948.

40. GSJTL, 4:446.

41. See, for example, Cai Zixiang 蔡子湘 and Wei Bing 韦炳, "采取具体措施加强反腐蚀教育" [Adopt specific measures to strengthen anti-corruption education], JFJB, March 30, 1982; "战胜糖弹 清除污染" [Defeat the sugar-coated bullets, eliminate spiritual pollution], JFJB, April 4, 1982.

42. Qin Chuan, former editor of the *People's Daily,* provided this excerpt from Deng's internal speech in a 1999 interview. Xu Qingquan 徐庆全, "邓力群与清除精神污染的真实关系" [The reality of Deng Liqun's relationship to the anti-spiritual pollution campaign], Aboluowang, March 19, 2017, https://www.aboluowang.com/2017/0319/898904.html.

43. Xu Jilin 许纪霖, "The Fate of an Enlightenment: Twenty Years in the Intellectual Sphere (1978–98)," trans. Geremie R. Barmé and Gloria Davies, in *Chinese Intellectuals between State and Market,* ed. Edward Gu and Merle Goldman (London: RoutledgeCurzon, 2004), 186. See also Baum, *Burying Mao,* 427.

44. Geremie Barmé, "History for the Masses," in *Using the Past to Serve the Present: Historiography and Politics in Contemporary China,* ed. Jonathan Unger (Armonk, NY: M. E. Sharpe, 1993), 264. Denunciations of foreign influences were common throughout China's modern history; see, for example, Education Minister Chen Lifu's attacks on Hollywood films as "traps of decadence" in the 1930s (Paul A.

Cohen, "Ambiguities of a Watershed Date: The 1949 Divide in Chinese History," in *China Unbound: Evolving Perspectives on the Chinese Past* [London: Routledge-Curzon, 2003], 136).

45.   GSJTL, 7:372–373.

46.   XCDT 41 (August 9, 1983): 266–291. See also XCDT 53 (October 20, 1983): 373–375.

47.   Cui Min 崔敏, "反思八十年代'严打'" [Rethinking "strike hard" in the 1980s], YHCQ 5 (2012), http://www.yhcqw.com/36/8779.html; CYNP, 2:387.

48.   ZZYWJ, 2:149–150.

49.   Ding Shaoping, "1980年代的周扬与胡乔木."

50.   "努力清除各个思想领域的精神污染" [Work hard to remove spiritual pollution in all ideological fields], JFJB, September 25, 1983.

51.   DXPNP, 2:939–940. The two Dengs discussed ideological matters on September 30 (DXPNP, 2:937–938).

52.   SWDXP-3, 47–58. Zhao asserted that Deng "believed Hu Yaobang should be held responsible for it since this realm was under Hu Yaobang's management" (POS, 162), though Deng Liqun recalled later that Deng Xiaoping had not endorsed criticisms of Hu as far as he knew (GSJTL, 7:190).

53.   CYNP, 2:388–389; Li Xiannian 李先念, "在全国工会十大上的致词" [Speech at the 10th National Congress of the All-China Federation of Trade Unions], RMRB, October 19, 1983.

54.   GSJTL, 7:372–373. Wang Zhen also called for eliminating spiritual pollution while visiting Nanjing.

55.   Gu Yan, "周扬与清除精神污染."

56.   Geremie Barmé, "China Blames the West for 'Spiritual Pollution,'" *National Times,* January 1984, 12. Even so, Zhao cautioned the Ministry of Public Security to focus on reeducating minor offenders, rather than more severe punishments (ZZYWJ, 2:195).

57.   Ding Shaoping, "1980年代的周扬与胡乔木"; Yiu-chung Wong, *From Deng Xiaoping,* 150; Liu Binyan, *Two Kinds of Truth: Stories and Reportage from China,* ed. Perry Link (Bloomington: Indiana University Press, 2006), 11–12.

58.   Xinhua News Service, "向精神污染作斗争" [Struggle against spiritual pollution], JFJB, November 1, 1983.

59.   XCDT 54 (October 26, 1983): 384–389, 390–392.

60.   Christopher S. Wren, "Peking Finds a New Enemy: Spiritual Pollution," *New York Times,* November 4, 1983; Gu Yan, "周扬与清除精神污染."

61.   Hu Qiaomu Biography Writing Group, "1983年, 反对精神污染的经过" [The events of the anti-spiritual pollution campaign of 1983], 读书文摘 [*Dushu wenzhai*] 19 (2015): 11–15; "建设精神文明　反对精神污染" [Building spiritual civilization, opposing spiritual pollution], RMRB, November 16, 1983.

62.   ZZYWJ, 2:249; POS, 163.

63.   ZZYWJ, 2:249–250.

64.   ZZYWJ, 2:275.

65.   GSJTL, 7:375; XCDT 62 (December 8, 1983): 446–473; XCDT 63 (December 13, 1983): 474–484.

66.   HYBSXNP, 2:942–944; Wei Jiuming 魏久明, "胡耀邦谈'反对精神污染'" [Hu Yaobang discusses "opposing spiritual pollution"], YHCQ 6 (2008): 38–42.

67.   Deng Liqun edited these remarks before they were circulated. Signaling how empowered he still felt, he made these edits himself and notified only Hu Yaobang; the edited version was circulated in the internal propaganda guidance publication *Propaganda Trends.* See GSJTL, 7:377 and XCDT 64 (December 23, 1983): 485–489.

68.   Hu Qiaomu 胡乔木, 关于人道主义和异化问题 [On the question of humanism and alienation] (Beijing: People's Publishing House, 1984); HQMSXJ, 457; Ding Shaoping, "1980年代的周扬与胡乔木"; Yiu-chung Wong, *From Deng Xiaoping,* 150; HQMSXJ, 457.

69.   HQMSXJ, 459–460.

70.   POS, 163; ZFLZQJ, 1983, 143; DXPNP, 2:949–950; Joseph Fewsmith, *Dilemmas of Reform in China* (Armonk, NY: M. E. Sharpe, 1994), 127–129; Christopher Wren, "China's Prey, 'Spiritual Pollution,' Proves Elusive," *New York Times,* December 20, 1983.

71.   DXPNP, 2:954; HYBZ, 3:756.

72.   Christopher Wren, "China Is Said to End a Campaign to Stop 'Spiritual Pollution,'" *New York Times,* January 24, 1984.

73.   Of course, proposing a separation of this sort would have been unthinkable a decade before. Although Mao had sometimes made statements suggesting an independent economic sphere (for example, in his speech on "The Ten Major Relationships" in 1956), during the Cultural Revolution, Mao said, "Political work is the lifeline of all economic work." See "毛主席论反对经济主义" [Chairman Mao discusses anti-economism] (unsigned news report), 光明日报 [Guangming daily], January 18, 1967.

74.   ZZYWJ, 2:274–276.

75.   HYPSXNP, 2:974.

76.   POS, 164; GSJTL, 7:380–381, 7:383–386. See also Michael Schoenhals, *Doing Things with Words in Chinese Politics: Five Studies* (Berkeley, CA: Institute of East Asian Studies, 1992), 50–51.

77.   ZZYWJ, 2:382; LXNNP, 6:242; GSJTL, 7:385.

78.   "熊复同志在第二次'红旗'联络员会议上的发言" [Xiong Fu's speech at the second *Red Flag* liaison conference], September 21, 1984, in 红旗杂志社文件选编 [Selected documents of *Red Flag* magazine], September 1986, marked internal, ZWCBWFWZX, 28:60, 90–91.

79.   GSJTL, 7:98–100.

Chapter 3: The Scourge of Bourgeois Liberalization

1.   "Resolution Concerning Guiding Policies for the Construction of a Socialist Spiritual Civilization," September 28, 1986, https://chinacopyrightandmedia .wordpress.com/1986/09/28/central-committee-resolution-concerning-guiding -policies-for-the-construction-of-a-socialist-spiritual-civilization.

2.   GSJTL, 7:98–100; HYBZ, 3:945–949.

3.   POS, 164–165.

4.   ZZYWJ, 3:101–104.

5.   HYBWX; HYBZ, 3:945–949, 3:756–761.

6.   Sheng Ping 盛平, "朱厚泽生前谈话见证胡耀邦富民政策出台始末" [Zhu Houze's testimony to Hu Yaobang's policies of enriching the people], 文史参考 [Literature and history reference] 11 (August 2010), http://www.people.com.cn/GB/198221/198819 /198855/12344176.html; Wu Wei 吴伟, 中國 80 年代政治改革的台前幕後 [On stage and backstage: China's political reform in the 1980s] (Hong Kong: Xinshiji chuban ji chuanmei youxian gongsi, 2013); GSJTL, 3:470–471. In early 1986, the CCP launched an initiative to "Develop Marxism" (Yan Sun, *The Chinese Reassessment of Socialism, 1976–1992* [Princeton: Princeton University Press, 1995], 191–192). The propaganda apparatus also continued to critique excessive admiration for foreign things, issuing a directive in the summer of 1986 on coverage of the Nobel Prize (XCDT, no. 12 [June 12, 1986]; 84–85).

7.   XCDT, no. 31 (October 24, 1986): 269–277, 337.

8.   Emily Honig and Gail Hershatter, *Personal Voices: Chinese Women in the 1980s* (Stanford University Press, 1988), 245, 252–253, 322–323.

9.   Stanley Rosen, "The Rise (and Fall) of Public Opinion in Post-Mao China," in Richard Baum, *Reform and Reaction in Post-Mao China* (New York: Routledge, 1991), 67.

10.   Li Zehou 李泽厚, "漫说'西体中用'" [Random thoughts on 'Western learning for fundamental principles and Chinese learning for practical applications'], www .personpsy.org/uploadfiles/file/books/lizhehou/enlightenment/漫说_西体中用_李泽厚 .pdf; Gloria Davies, "Discursive Heat: Humanism in 1980s China," in *A New Literary History of Modern China,* ed. David Der-wei Wang (Cambridge, MA: Harvard University Press, 2017), 758–764; He Li, *Political Thought and China's Transformation* (London: Palgrave Macmillan, 2015), 82–83.

11.   "Some Materials regarding Certain Theoretical Issues," *Chinese Law and Government* 21, no. 1 (Spring 1988): 63–102.

12.   Fang Lizhi, 危机感下的责任 [Responsibility under Crisis] (Singapore: Shijie keji chubanshe, 1989), 231. Hu Qiaomu had followed Fang Lizhi's increasingly bold writings since at least 1985, even consulting with Qian Xuesen on Fang's work (HQMSXJ, 567–568).

13.   Julie Kwong, "The 1986 Student Demonstrations in China: A Democratic Movement?" *Asian Survey* 28, no. 9 (September 1988): 970–971.

14.   Jeffrey Wasserstrom, *Student Protests in Twentieth-Century China: The View from Shanghai* (Stanford, CA: Stanford University Press, 1991), 299; "Obituary: Fang Lizhi," *The Economist,* April 14, 2012.

15.   HYBSXNP, 2:1297.

16.   Wu Wei, 中國 80 年代政治改革的台前幕後, 104–108.

17.   Yen-lin Chung, "The Ousting of General Secretary Hu Yaobang: The Roles Played by Peng Zhen and Other Party Elders," *China Review* 19, no. 1 (February 2019): 110. This meeting is not included in DXPNP.

18.   DXPNP, 2:1160–1162; SWDXP-3, 194–197; GSJTL, 7:390. Deng also criticized Fang Lizhi by name.

19.   POS, 172. See also HYBSXNP, 2:1298–1299.

20.   HYBSXNP, 2:1302; DXPNP, 2:1163; Fang Lizhi, *The Most Wanted Man in China: My Journey from Scientist to Enemy of the State,* trans. Perry Link (New York: Henry Holt, 2016), 246, 264. Liu Binyan and Wang Ruowang were also expelled from the party in January and widely criticized (Liu Binyan, *A Higher Kind of Loyalty: A Memoir by China's Foremost Journalist,* trans. Zhu Hong [New York: Pantheon Books, 1990], 260–262). Su Shaozhi was removed from all his posts (*Decision-Making in Deng's China: Perspectives from Insiders,* ed. Carol Lee Hamrin and Suisheng Zhao [Armonk, NY: M. E. Sharpe, 1995], 116).

21.   HYBSXNP, 2:1302–1307; Deng Liqun, 十二个春秋: 邓力群自述 [Twelve springs and autumns: An autobiography of Deng Liqun] (Hong Kong: Bozhi chubanshe, 2006), 417–445. Deng Xiaoping discussed Hu Yaobang's errors with Yang Shangkun on January 14, 1987 (DXPNP, 2:1165).

22.   Yang Jisheng, "First Visit to Zhao Ziyang," *Chinese Law & Government* 38, no. 3 (2005): 17; HYBSXNP, 2:1307.

23.   ZFLZQJ 1987, 56; DXPNP, 2:1166; Richard Baum, *Burying Mao: Chinese Politics in the Age of Deng Xiaoping* (Princeton, NJ: Princeton University Press, 1994), 206–207; CYNP, 3:401–402; HYBSXNP, 2:1313–1314.

24.   Lu Keng 陆铿, "胡耀邦访问记" [Interview with Hu Yaobang], 百姓 [Ordinary people], June 1, 1985; HYBSXNP, 2:1303–1304.

25.   POS, 169–170, 176–179.

26.   Li Rui, "Conversations."

27.   A report from Shanghai described "a comrade on the street who complains that Hu Yaobang is removed from office but Deng Xiaoping is still in office. He plans to gather a group to Beijing hoping to remove Deng Xiaoping from office" (Note from March 9, 1987, Folder As-0358-062-001, CCHRC).

28.   See Wu Jiang 吴江, 十年的路—和胡耀邦相处的日子 [The ten-year road: My days with Hu Yaobang] (Hong Kong: Jingbao wenhua qiye youxian gongsi, 1995); Hu Jiwei 胡绩伟, with Yao Jianfu 姚监复, 论胡赵十年新政 [On Hu and Zhao's decade of new policies] (China: n.p., 2009), available in the Fairbank Collection, Harvard University; POS, 176–179. Zhao also claimed that he was better suited to the role of premier (POS, 201; Ruan Ming, *Deng Xiaoping: Chronicle of an Empire* [Boulder, CO: Westview, 1994], 191).

29.   Ruan Ming, *Deng Xiaoping*, 173; see also LXNNP, 6:372.

30.   XCDT 5 (January 19, 1987): 16–17; XCDT 3 (January 13, 1987): 5–11.

31.   ZZYWJ, 4:20–24.

32.   ZFLZQJ 1987, 76–77; DXPNP, 2:1168. Navigating Chen and Deng's relationship remained a challenge for Zhao. Reportedly, Chen requested to have a Politburo Standing Committee in 1987 when Deng opposed holding such a meeting, leaving Zhao to tell Chen that if he felt strongly, he should take up the matter directly with Deng; Zhao demurred that he was simply "a big secretary" (大秘书长一个) (Yang Jisheng, 楊繼繩, 中國改革年代的政治鬥爭 [Political struggles in China's reform era] [Hong Kong: Excellent Culture Press, 2004], 299). I am grateful to Joseph Torigian for this point.

33. XCDT 9 (February 18, 1987): 21–28. Li even encouraged the establishment of a system for students to have "regular democratic channels to express their suggestions and needs" on campus rather than taking to the streets.

34. XCDT 22 (April 3, 1987): 54–58, 59; XCDT 24 (April 11, 1987): 69–74.

35. Orville Schell, "Fang Lizhi: China's Andrei Sakharov," *The Atlantic,* May 1988.

36. PLA Air Force Political Propaganda Department 空军政治宣传部编印, "坚持四项基本原则 反对资产阶级自由化专题教育材料" [Educational materials for upholding the Four Cardinal Principles and opposing bourgeois liberalization], February 1987, marked secret.

37. PLA Air Force Political Propaganda Department, "坚持四项基本原则 反对资产阶级自由化专题教育材料," 19–20, 42, 50–51, 60, 63, 88.

38. "Talk between Erich Honecker and Zhao Ziyang," June 8, 1987, History and Public Policy Program Digital Archive, SAPMO-BA, DY 30, 2437, http://digitalarchive .wilsoncenter.Org/document/122023.

39. ZZYWJ, 4:28–30, 4:43–45.

40. Xiong Fu 熊复, "我们党反对资产阶级自由化斗争的历史回顾" [The history of our party's struggle against bourgeois liberalization], May 25, 1987, in *Selected Documents of Red Flag Magazine,* 32; XCDT 25 (April 13, 1987): 75–88.

41. Wu Wei, 中國 80 年代政治改革的台前幕後, 129; XCDT 32 (June 13, 1987): 89–97.

42. Jim Mann, "Chinese Official Expelled from Party for Adultery," *Los Angeles Times,* May 30, 1987.

43. Jim Mann, "Student Corrupted by Works of Sartre and Nietzsche, Paper Says," *Los Angeles Times,* May 28, 1987.

44. ZZYWJ, 4:20–21; Ruan Ming, *Deng Xiaoping,* 177.

45. POS, 207–208; Ruan Ming, *Deng Xiaoping,* 180.

46. ZZYWJ, 4:107–108 and frontispiece of Zhao's handwritten communication with Deng; DXPNP, 2:1183; Wu Wei, 中國 80 年代政治改革的台前幕後, 130–131; POS, 194.

47. ZZYWJ, 4:108–110.

48. ZZYWJ, frontispiece; Wu Wei, 中國 80 年代政治改革的台前幕後, 133.

49. ZZYWJ, 4:96–101.

50. POS, 199; Deng Liqun, *Twelve Springs and Autumns,* 467–468; DXPNP, 2:1200.

51. LXNNP, 6:404; POS, 9.

52.   Wu Wei, 中國 80 年代政治改革的台前幕後, 144–145. *Red Flag* published its last issue in the summer of 1988 and was replaced by *Seeking Truth* (求是).

53.   XCDT 37 (July 9, 1987): 101–113.

54.   GSJTL, 4:192–194, 4:201.

Part II: The Economy

1.   This is the compound annual real growth rate; all figures are sourced from World Development Indicator Database.

2.   Yasheng Huang, *Capitalism with Chinese Characteristics* (Cambridge: Cambridge University Press, 2008), 53; National Bureau of Statistics of China, http://data.stats.gov.cn/english/easyquery.htm?cn=C01.

3.   Dwight H. Perkins, "Reforming China's Economic System," *Journal of Economic Literature* 26, no. 2 (June 1988): 623. See also Michael Schoenhals, *Doing Things with Words in Chinese Politics: Five Studies* (Berkeley, CA: Institute of East Asian Studies, 1992), 47–48.

4.   Yang Jisheng 杨继绳, 价格改革: 经济改革中的一步险棋 [Price reform: A difficult move in economic reform], YHCQ, no. 3 (2009), www.yhcqw.com/33/4685.html.

5.   Joseph Fewsmith, "Institutions, Informal Politics, and Political Transition in China," *Asian Survey* 36, no. 3 (March 1996): 242.

6.   In addition to the works cited in the Introduction, see Xiao Donglian 萧冬连, "1978–1984 年中国经济体制改革思路的演进" [The evolution of China's economic system reform, 1978–1984], 当代中国史研究 [Research on contemporary Chinese history] 11, no. 5 (September 2004): 59–70; Frederick C. Teiwes and Warren Sun, *Paradoxes of Post-Mao Rural Reform: Initial Steps Toward a New Chinese Countryside, 1976–1981* (London: Routledge, 2016); Liu Hong 柳红, 八0年代: 中国经济学人的光荣与梦想 [The eighties: Chinese economists' glory and dreams] (Guilin, Guangxi Province: Guangxi shifan daxue chubanshe, 2010); Isabella Weber, *How China Escaped Shock Therapy* (London: Routledge, 2021); Dorothy Solinger, *From Lathes to Looms: China's Industrial Policy in Comparative Perspective, 1979–1982* (Stanford, CA: Stanford University Press, 1991); Fan Qimiao and Peter Nolan, eds., *China's Economic Reforms: The Costs and Benefits of Incrementalism* (Basingstoke, UK: Macmillan, 1994); Edward S. Steinfeld, *Forging Reform in China: The Fate of State-Owned Industry* (Cambridge: Cambridge University Press, 1998); Victor Nee and Sonja Opper, *Capitalism from Below: Markets and Institutional Change in China* (Cambridge, MA: Harvard University Press, 2012).

7.   Julian Gewirtz, *Unlikely Partners: Chinese Reformers, Western Economists, and the Making of Global China* (Cambridge, MA: Harvard University Press, 2017).

Chapter 4: Liberating the Productive Forces

1.   Frederick C. Teiwes and Warren Sun, "China's Economic Reorientation after the Third Plenum: Conflict Surrounding 'Chen Yun's' Readjustment Program, 1979–80," *China Journal* 70 (July 2013): 167; Xiao Donglian 肖东连, 歷史的轉軌：從撥亂反正到改革開放, 1979–1981 [The historic transition: From bringing order out of chaos to reform and opening, 1979–1981] (Hong Kong: Chinese University Press, 2008), 473–479; CYNP, 3:253.

2.   Deng Liqun 邓力群, 向陈云同志学习做经济工作 [Learn to do economic work from Comrade Chen Yun] (Beijing: Zhonggong zhongyang dangxiao chubanshe, 1981), marked internal, 1–2.

3.   POS, 113.

4.   *Selected Works of Chen Yun* (Beijing: Foreign Languages Press, 1999), 3:255; Frederick C. Teiwes and Warren Sun, *Paradoxes of Post-Mao Rural Reform: Initial Steps Toward a New Chinese Countryside, 1976–1981* (London: Routledge, 2016), 169.

5.   Barry Naughton, *Growing Out of the Plan* (Cambridge: Cambridge University Press, 1995), 70–77. See also Hou Li, *Building for Oil: Daqing and the Formation of the Chinese Socialist State* (Cambridge, MA: Harvard-Yenching Institute, 2018).

6.   They also acknowledged three other objectives in addition to readjustment, "reform, consolidation, and improvement," but as scholars such as Frederick Teiwes, Warren Sun, and Xiao Donglian have shown, these were clearly subordinated to readjustment. See Teiwes and Sun, "China's Economic Reorientation," 163–170; Xiao Donglian, 歷史的轉軌, 473–479.

7.   In late March 1980, the leadership convened a Long-Term Planning Conference at which Deng Xiaoping and Zhao generally deferred to Chen Yun and Yao Yilin, requesting only that the rate of industrial development aim for 8 percent growth per year, with 7 percent growth "also acceptable." 邓小平、赵紫阳、姚依林同志关于编制长期规划的讲话 [The speeches of Comrades Deng Xiaoping, Zhao Ziyang, and Yao Yilin on drawing up long-term plans], and 赵紫阳同志在长期计划座谈会上讲话 (记录稿) [Comrade Zhao Ziyang's comments at the Long-Term Planning Conference (transcript)], April 22, 1980, Hubei Provincial Archives, March 19–April 2, 1980, SZ 1-8-174. I am grateful to Chuck Kraus for bringing this and other Hubei documents to my attention.

8.   Teiwes and Sun, *Paradoxes*, 128, 203, 218–225, 254–255; ZFLZQJ 1980, 62–66; ZZYWJ, 1:44–47; GSJTL, 241–243; POS, 138–140.

9.   Naughton, *Growing out of the Plan*, 100; Susan Shirk, *The Political Logic of Economic Reform in China* (Berkeley: University of California Press, 1993), 200–204.

10.   ZZYWJ, 1:43.

11.   Xiao Donglian, 歷史的轉軌, 557–558.

12.   Ezra Vogel, *Deng Xiaoping and the Transformation of China* (Cambridge, MA: Belknap Press of Harvard University Press, 2011), 396–397. Hua Guofeng presided over the meeting at which the SEZs were approved, though Deng would later take credit (Teiwes and Sun, "China's New Economic Policy," 1, 23).

13.   DXPNP, 305; Gu Mu, *Pioneer of China's Reform and Opening Up: An Autobiography* (Beijing, Foreign Languages Press, 2016), 295–296; ZFLZQJ-1977–1978, 121–130; Julian Gewirtz, *Unlikely Partners: Chinese Reformers, Western Economists, and the Making of Global China* (Cambridge, MA: Harvard University Press, 2017), 35–37.

14.   "吴庆瑞" [Goh Keng Swee], *Caijing*, June 6, 2010; DXPNP, 1:427–429; Vogel, *Deng Xiaoping*, 287–291.

15.   Gu Mu, *Pioneer*, 405–406, 425–444; Peter E. Hamilton, *Made in Hong Kong: Transpacific Networks and a New History of Globalization* (New York: Columbia University Press, 2020).

16.   "Economic Brief: Development and Performance Issues" (March 1980), 12, in IBRD / IDA EXC-09-3965S, Records of President A. W. Clausen, Country Files: China—Correspondence (1), WBA; "Operations Strategy" (March 1980), 1, in IBRD / IDA EXC-09-3965S, Records of President A. W. Clausen, Country Files: China—Correspondence (1), WBA.

17.   Liqun Jin and Chi-kuo Wu, eds., 回顾与展望: 纪念中国与世界银行合作十五周年 [Past and future: Fifteen years of China–World Bank cooperation] (Beijing: Ministry of Finance and Xinhua News Agency, 1995), 4–5, 25.

18.   Louis Galambos, William Becker, Jochen Kraske, and David Milobsky, "S. Shahid Husain," World Bank Group Oral History Program (March–June 1994, Washington, DC), http://documents.worldbank.org/curated/en/128041468161098257/pdf/790330TRNoHusao200andoJune014001994.pdf.

19.   ZZYWJ 1:49–52; "China—Mission Report and Recommendation" (July 27, 1980), 9, in IBRD / IDA EXC-09-3965S, Records of President A. W. Clausen, Country Files: China—Correspondence (1), WBA.

20.   World Bank, *China: Socialist Economic Development*, 3 vols. (Washington, DC: World Bank, 1983); Gewirtz, *Unlikely Partners*.

21.   XCDT 36 (August 28, 1980): 250.

22.   ZFLZQJ 1980, 141; Teiwes and Sun, "China's Economic Reorientation," 182; Shih, *Factions and Finance*, 99.

23.   ZZYWJ, 1:129–136. He made these remarks at the Central Work Conference of December 16–25, 1980.

24.   A third contemporary, Sun Yefang, returned to public life in 1977 after great suffering during the Cultural Revolution but died in 1983.

25.   LXNNP, 6:49; ZFLZQJ 1979, 80–132; Joseph Fewsmith, *Dilemmas of Reform in China* (Armonk, NY: M.E. Sharpe, 1994), 70–74. See also Xue Muqiao 薛暮桥, 中国社会主义经济问题研究 [Research on questions about China's socialist economy] (Beijing: Renmin chubanshe, 1979).

26.   Qian Liqun 钱理群, "'农村发展组': 八十年代的改革互动" [Rural Development Group: Reform activities in the 1980s], YHCQ, http://www.yhcqw.com/36/8881.html.

27.   CCP Central Committee and State Council, "转发国家农委 '关于积极发展农村多种经营的报告' 的通知" [Relaying the National Agriculture Commission's 'Report on promoting diversification in rural development'], March 30, 1981, in Folder En-0351-067-038, CCHRC.

28.   Alexander V. Pantsov, with Steven I. Levine, *Deng Xiaoping: A Revolutionary Life* (Oxford: Oxford University Press, 2015), 370–372. Beginning in December 1984, Soviet experts including Ivan Arkhipov would travel to China to study its economic reforms (Sergey Radchenko, *Unwanted Visionaries: The Soviet Failure in Asia at the End of the Cold War* [Oxford: Oxford University Press, 2014], 46–47).

29.   Gewirtz, *Unlikely Partners*, 61–62. See also Péter Vámos, "A Hungarian Model for China? Sino-Hungarian Relations in the Era of Economic Reforms, 1979–89," *Cold War History* 18, no. 3 (2018): 361–378.

30.   Edwin Lim 林重庚, "中国改革开放过程中的对外思想开放" [The opening of thinking to the outside world in the process of China's reform and opening], in 中国经济: 50人看三十年 [China's economy: Fifty people on thirty years], ed. Wu Jinglian 吴敬琏 (Beijing: Zhongguo jingji chubanshe, 2008), 30; Xiao Donglian 肖冬连, "中国改革初期对国外经验的系统考察和借鉴" [Observations of and references to foreign economic systems during the early reform period in China], 中共党史研究 [CCP history research] 4 (2006): 32.

31.   Naughton, *Growing out of the Plan*, 81, 82, 86.

32.   ZZYWJ, 1:154–156.

33.   Gewirtz, *Unlikely Partners*, 89–95.

34.   Ota Šik, letter, November 13, 1983, "Korrespondenz Ausland 1980–1983," Schreibersites' Sozialarchiv, Zurich; Lu Nan and Li Mingzhe, "Use of Input-Output Techniques for Planning the Price Reform," in *Chinese Economic Planning and*

Input-Output Analysis, ed. Karen R. Polenske and Chen Xikang (New York: Oxford University Press, 1991), 83–85.

35. Chen Zhongxuan 陈仲旋, "秘书陈仲旋眼中的赵紫阳" [Zhao Ziyang in the eyes of Secretary Chen Zhongxuan], https://renwuwang.org/node/2374.

36. ZZYWJ, 1:158, 161–179.

37. ZZYWJ, 1:187, 191–194; Xiao Donglian, 歷史的轉軌, 576. These enterprise reforms also sought to increase central government revenue (Naughton, *Growing out of the Plan,* 112–116).

38. Yasheng Huang, *Capitalism with Chinese Characteristics* (Cambridge: Cambridge University Press, 2008), 59, 62–63, 74.

39. Teiwes and Sun, *Paradoxes,* 232–238, 246–247.

40. ZZYWJ, 1:315.

41. ZZYWJ, 1:307–310.

42. Fewsmith, *Dilemmas of Reform,* 111–114.

43. Foreign Economics Research Group, ed., 外国经济学讲座 [Lectures on foreign economics] (Beijing: Chinese Social Sciences Press, 1980–1981), 1:1–2.

44. Gewirtz, *Unlikely Partners,* 83–87.

45. XCDT 53 (September 24, 1981): 320.

46. XCDT 79 (December 26, 1981): 493–495. Zhao Ziyang and Hu Yaobang also acknowledged disruptions due to the household contracting (ZZYWJ, 1:376).

47. ZFLZQJ 1982, 28–31; Gewirtz, *Unlikely Partners,* 105–106; POS, 101–105.

48. ZZYWJ, 1:453–454. The Chinese name is 经济体制改革委员会.

49. Zhou Chenghua 卓成华, "安志文: 中国改革的思考者" [An Zhiwen: Mind of China's reform], 中国老年 [China's elderly] 3 (2010), reformdata.org/index.do?m=wap&a=show&catid=100&typeid=&id=15066.

50. Hu Deping 胡德平, "耀邦同志如何看消费" [Comrade Hu Yaobang's views on consumption], 胡耀邦史料信息网 [Online repository of historical materials on Hu Yaobang], February 25, 2009, http://www.hybsl.cn/ybsxyj/shengpingyusixiang/2009-02-27/12815.html.

51. ZFLZQJ 1982, 70–74; CYNP, 3:298.

52. ZZYWJ, 1:483.

53. Dorothy Solinger, *States' Gains, Labor's Losses: China, France, and Mexico Choose Global Liaisons, 1980–2000* (Ithaca, NY: Cornell University Press, 2009), 77–81.

54. ZZYWJ, 1:645, 653–654; Shirk, *Political Logic*, 251–260; HYBSXNP, 2:746–748.

55. Zhao Ziyang, "Report on the Work of the Government" (June 6, 1983), trans. in Foreign Broadcast Information Service, FBIS-CHI-83-109, June 1983, K8–K16.

56. Hu Yaobang, "Report to the Twelfth Party Congress," Xinhua News Agency, September 1, 1982, trans. in Foreign Broadcast Information Service, FBIS-CHI-82-170, September 1982, K4–K6; CYNP, 3:299–305.

57. 领导同志与外宾谈话摘编(一) [Selected excerpts from dialogues between party leaders and foreign dignitaries (I)], February 6, 1982, marked secret, Shanghai Municipal Archive, B1-9-798-1, 4. I am grateful to Chuck Kraus for bringing this document to my attention.

58. Vogel, *Deng Xiaoping*, 452.

59. CYNP, 3:312–313; "Chen Yun Supports Constitution, Zhao Report," Xinhua News Agency, December 2, 1982, trans. in Foreign Broadcast Information Service, FBIS-CHI-82-233, December 3, 1982, K4–K5.

60. Wu Jinglian, *Understanding and Interpreting Chinese Economic Reform* (Mason, OH: Thomson / South-Western, 2005), 362.

61. ZZYWJ, 2:20.

62. ZFLZQJ 1983, 42–43; HYBSXNP, 2:841; GSJTL, 7:247.

63. DXPNP, 2:895; CYNP, 3:322; HYBSXNP, 2:852; POS, 115–117.

64. Yen-lin Chung, "The Ousting of General Secretary Hu Yaobang: The Roles Played by Peng Zhen and Other Party Elders," *China Review* 19, no. 1 (February 2019): 89–122.

65. Li Rui 李锐, "耀邦去世前的谈话" [Conversations with Hu Yaobang before his death], *Modern China Studies* 4 (2001).

66. See, for example, ZZYWJ, 2:42–47, 2:84.

67. ZZYWJ, 2:86–111; DXPNP, 2:911.

68. XCDT 13 (March 12, 1983): 114–118; XCDT 29 (June 4, 1983).

69. Jean C. Oi, "Corruption in Rural China," in *Reform and Reaction in Post-Mao China: The Road to Tiananmen*, ed. Richard Baum (London: Routledge, 1991), 152–153.

70. XCDT 30 (June 9, 1983): 216–222.

71.   Chen Daisun 陈岱孙, "现代西方经济学的研究和我国社会主义经济现代化" [Research on modern Western economics and China's socialist economic modernization], RMRB, November 16, 1983; Gewirtz, *Unlikely Partners*, 118.

72.   ZFLZQJ 1984, 5.

73.   DXPNP, 2:954–959; ZFLZQJ 1984, 11–13. See also SWDXP-3, 61–62.

74.   ZZYWJ, 2:17.

75.   ZFLZQJ 1984, 37–52; "福建省五十五名厂长、经理给省委领导写信: 请给我们'松绑'" [Fifty-five Fujian factory directors and managers write to members of the Provincial Party Committee: Please "untie" us], RMRB, March 30, 1984.

76.   ZZYWJ, 2:373–379.

77.   Hua Sheng, Xuejun Zhang, and Xiaopeng Luo, *China: From Revolution to Reform* (Basingstoke, UK: Macmillan, 1993), 103; ZFLZQJ 1984, 108–112; Fewsmith, *Dilemmas of Reform*, 132. Fewsmith notes, however, that officials there would subsequently stall and undermine implementation.

78.   XCDT 26 (1984), translated in *Chinese Law & Government* 24, no. 4 (1991): 34.

Chapter 5: The Powers of the Market

1.   Barry Naughton, *Growing out of the Plan* (Cambridge: Cambridge University Press, 1995), 174–176.

2.   See Joseph Stalin, *Economic Problems of Socialism in the USSR* (Moscow: Foreign Languages Publishing House, 1952).

3.   Chen Yizi 陈一谘, 陈一谘回忆录 [Memoirs of Chen Yizi] (Hong Kong: New Century Press, 2013), 314.

4.   POS, 113, 119. With the Central Economic and Finance Leading Small Group on May 4, 1984, Zhao said, "That which happens outside of the plan belongs to the sphere of market coordination" (ZZYWJ, 2:377–378).

5.   CYNP, 3:355–356; LXNNP, 6:249, 258.

6.   Gao Shangquan 高尚全, 改革历程 [The course of reform] (Beijing: Jingji kexue chubanshe, 2008), 9.

7.   Ma Hong 马洪, "关于社会主义制度下我国商品经济的再探索" [Further exploration of China's commodity economy under a socialist system], in ZFLZQJ 1984, 136–137; David Barboza, "Interviews with Wu Jinglian, Shelley Wu, and Wu's Biographer," *New York Times*, September 26, 2009.

8.   ZZYWJ, 2:453–456.

9.   World Bank Country Study, *China: The Achievement and Challenge of Price Reform* (Washington, DC: World Bank, 1993), 6, 9.

10.   Naughton, *Growing out of the Plan*, 250–251.

11.   ZZYWJ, 2:456–457; Hua Sheng, Xuejun Zhang, and Xiaopeng Luo, *China: From Revolution to Reform* (Basingstoke, UK: Macmillan, 1993), 108.

12.   Chen Yizi 陈一谘, 中国: 十年改革与八九民运 [China: Ten years of reform and the 1989 pro-democracy movement] (Taipei: Lianjing chuban shiye gongsi, 1990), 75–77; Chen Yizi, *Memoirs of Chen Yizi*, 309; Liu Hong 柳红, 八0年代: 中国经济学人的光荣与梦想 [The eighties: Chinese economists' glory and dreams] (Guilin: Guangxi Normal University Publishing House, 2010), 204–205. The Chinese name is 中国经济体制改革研究所.

13.   The organizers were Zhu Jiaming, Huang Jiangnan, Zhang Gang, and Liu Bocheng. Wang Qishan, son-in-law of Yao Yilin and currently China's vice president, attended. See Ma Xiaogang 马小冈, "从莫干山会议到京丰宾馆会议" [From the Moganshan Conference to the Jingfeng Hotel Conference], YHCQ 9 (2012), http://www.yhcqw.com/34/8896.html; Liu Hong 柳红, 1984: 莫干山会议 [1984: The Moganshan Conference] (Beijing: Dongfang chubanshe, 2019); Liu, *The Eighties*, 433.

14.   The Moganshan Conference and the proposal of the dual-track price system have attracted fierce and ongoing debate among the participants about what happened there. See, for example, Hua Sheng 华生, "双轨制始末" [The whole story behind the dual-track system], 中国改革 [China reform] 1 (2005): 22–25; Chen Yizi, *Memoirs of Chen Yizi*, 310–311; Liu Bocheng 刘佑成, "莫干山会议始末" [The Moganshan Conference from start to finish], 胡耀邦史料信息网 [Online repository of historical materials on Hu Yaobang], www.hybsl.cn/beijingcankao/beijingfenxi/2018-07-25/68021.html; Hua et al., *China: From Revolution to Reform*, 124.

15.   System Reform Commission, ed., 中国经济体制改革十年 [Ten years of China's economic system reform] (Beijing: Jingji guanli chubanshe, 1988), 454; ZFLZQJ 1985, 36.

16.   ZFLZQJ 1984, 171–174.

17.   ZZYWJ, 2:484–488.

18.   ZFLZQJ 1984, 179–180; CYNP, 3:360–361; see also LXNNP, 6:267–268.

19.   DXPNP, 2:1006; LXNNP, 6:274.

20.   POS, 119; DXPNP, 2:1006–1009; SWDXP-3, 90–99.

21.   Ma Hong, *Chinese Economists on Economic Reform: Collected Works of Ma Hong*, ed. China Development Research Foundation (London: Routledge, 2014), 113.

22. Huang Zihong 黄子鸿 and Xie Youxue 谢友学, "有关经济特区法规的几个认识问题" [Some questions regarding special economic zone regulations], 河北法学 [Hebei law science] 2 (1987): 41.

23. Jackie Sheehan, *Chinese Workers: A New History* (London: Routledge, 1998), 205–206.

24. *People's Daily* database search for the term "改革开放" conducted on February 10, 2020.

25. Naughton, *Growing out of the Plan*, 205, 220; Hua et al., *China: From Revolution to Reform*, 112, 125.

26. ZZYWJ, 3:16–18.

27. ZZYWJ, 3:105–121.

28. POS, 127–128. See also ZZYWJ, 3:79–80.

29. Wu Jinglian 吴敬琏, "经济改革初战阶段的发展方针和宏观控制问题" [Development policy in the beginning stages of economic reform and problems in macro-control], RMRB, February 11, 1985.

30. Zhu Jiaming 朱嘉明, "论我国正经历的经济发展阶段" [On China's current stage of economic development], 中青年经济论坛 [Young economists' forum] 2 (April 1985): 20–22; Susan Shirk, *The Political Logic of Economic Reform in China* (Berkeley: University of California Press, 1993), 284.

31. Li Yining 厉以宁, "改革的基本思路" [The fundamental idea of the reform], 北京日报 [Beijing daily], May 19, 1986, 3; Joseph Fewsmith, *Dilemmas of Reform in China* (Armonk, NY: M.E. Sharpe, 1994), 186; Isabella Weber, *How China Escaped Shock Therapy* (London: Routledge, 2021), 206–220. For a critique of the "misleading" notion that proponents of "coordinated reform" sought to implement "shock therapy," see Marcin Piatkowski and Zhang Chunlin, "Why China Never Wanted Shock Therapy and Thus Needed No Escaping from It," *China: An International Journal* 20, no. 1 (February 2022): 159–168.

32. Hua Sheng 华生 et al., "微观经济基础的重新构造" [Restructuring the micro-economic base], JJYJ 3 (1986): 21–24.

33. Ma Ding, "Ten Major Changes in China's Study of Economics," *Beijing Review*, December 9, 1985.

34. Julian Gewirtz, *Unlikely Partners: Chinese Reformers, Western Economists, and the Making of Global China* (Cambridge, MA: Harvard University Press, 2017), 136–155.

35. János Kornai, *Economics of Shortage* (New York: North-Holland, 1980), 4, 60–61, 191, 193.

36. "Discussion of the Paper by Professor Kornai," in *The Economics of Relative Prices,* ed. Bela Cšikós-Nagy, Douglas Hague, and Graham Hall (London: Macmillan, 1984), 82–83, 85.

37. Gewirtz, *Unlikely Partners,* 136–155.

38. ZFLZQJ 1985, 227, 235–236.

39. Zhao Renwei, "1985年巴山轮会议的回顾与思考" [Remembering and reflecting on the 1985 Bashan Conference]," JJYJ 12 (2008): 17–28; János Kornai, *By Force of Thought: Irregular Memoirs of an Intellectual Journey* (Cambridge, MA: MIT Press, 2016), 325.

40. ZZYWJ, 3:158.

41. ZZYWJ, 3:158–161, 3:209–210; DXPNP, 2:1045–1046, 2:1099–1100.

42. Gu Mu, *Pioneer of China's Reform and Opening Up: An Autobiography* (Beijing: Foreign Languages Press, 2016), 512–515.

43. Fewsmith, *Dilemmas of Reform,* 150; Hua et al., *China: From Revolution to Reform,* 112.

44. See, for example, XCDT 18 (June 21, 1985): 230–235. Given the CCP's longstanding fears of inflation, critics of market reforms grew louder and more influential when inflation soared (Victor Shih, *Factions and Finance in China* [Cambridge: Cambridge University Press, 2008]).

45. Hu Yaobang, "形势、理想、纪律和作风" [Circumstances, ideals, discipline, and work style], July 15, 1985, HYBWX, 599–615.

46. ZZYWJ, 3:157.

47. ZZYWJ, 3:180–186; HYBSXNP, 2:1140–1142; CYNP, 3:383–385; Zhang Xianyang 張顯揚 and Shi Yijun 史義軍, eds., 趙紫陽中南海十年紀事 [A record of Zhao Ziyang's ten years at Zhongnanhai] (Hong Kong: Shijie kexue jiaoyu chubanshe, 2005), which contains much intriguing but unattributed information, and which I have used only when a detail could be corroborated elsewhere.

48. XCDT 3 (March 12, 1985): 181–183.

49. XCDT 37 (October 13, 1985): 318.

50. Yu Guangyuan 于光远, "我国社会主义体制改革和政治经济学社会主义部分" [China's socialist reform and the political economy of socialism], JJYJ 8 (1986): 3–8.

51. Yasheng Huang, *Capitalism with Chinese Characteristics* (Cambridge: Cambridge University Press, 2008), 74–85.

52. On industrial policy in Asia, see Joe Studwell, *How Asia Works: Success and Failure in the World's Most Dynamic Region* (New York: Grove, 2013); and Robert

Wade, *Governing the Market: Economic Theory and the Role of Government in East Asian Industrialization* (Princeton, NJ: Princeton University Press, 1990).

53.   See Ma Hong et al., eds., 2000年的中国 [China in 2000] (Beijing: CASS Press, 1989); Wang Huijiong and Li Boxi, *China toward the Year 2000* (Beijing: New World Press, 1989); Carol Lee Hamrin, *China and the Challenge of the Future: Changing Political Patterns* (Boulder, CO: Westview Press, 1990), 119–128.

54.   Wang Huijiong and Li Shantong, "Economic Development and the Environment in China," in *Economic Development and Cooperation in the Pacific Basin* (New York: Cambridge University Press, 1998), 415.

55.   Yang Zhi 杨治, 产业经济学导论 [Introduction to industrial economics] (Beijing: Zhongguo renmin daxue chubanshe, 1985), 1–5, 7–12. See also Sebastian Heilmann and Lea Shih, "The Rise of Industrial Policy in China, 1978–2012" (Harvard Yenching Institute Working Paper, Cambridge, MA, 2013), 6, 9.

56.   "中华人民共和国国民经济和社会发展第七个五年计划 (摘要) " [The seventh five-year plan for national economic and social development of the PRC (summary)], http://guoqing.china.com.cn/2016-03/06/content_37950927.htm.

57.   Ma Hong 马洪, "把经济发展战略和产业政策的研究结合起来" [Bringing together research on economic development strategy and industrial policy], 开发研究 [Research on development] 6 (1987): 4–8.

58.   Douglas Zhihua Zeng, ed., *Building Engines for Growth and Competitiveness in China: Experience with Special Economic Zones and Industrial Clusters* (Washington, DC: World Bank, 2010), 9–10; Kwan-Yu Wong, "China's Special Economic Zone Experiment: An Appraisal," *Geografiska Annaler. Series B, Human Geography* 69, no. 1 (1987): 32, 38.

59.   "Memorandum, 'Re: Information Related to China,'" September 30, 1986, History and Public Policy Program Digital Archive, Historical Archives of the Hungarian State Security (ÁBTL). Obtained by Peter Vamos and translated by Katalin Varga, http://digitalarchive.wilsoncenter.org/document/119998.

60.   Gu Mu, *Pioneer,* 484–489.

61.   Juan Du, *The Shenzhen Experiment: The Story of China's Instant City* (Cambridge, MA: Harvard University Press, 2020), 74.

62.   Douglas Zhihua Zeng, ed., *Building Engines for Growth and Competitiveness in China: Experience with Special Economic Zones and Industrial Clusters* (Washington, DC: World Bank, 2010), 19, 58.

63.   Wu Jinglian, *Understanding and Interpreting,* 294; Harold Jacobson and Michel Oksenberg, *China's Participation in the IMF, the World Bank, and GATT* (Ann Arbor: University of Michigan Press, 1990), 83–92; ZZYWJ, 3:254.

64.   "China Pledge to Investors," Reuters, August 9, 1986.

65.   ZFLZQJ 1986, 140–141.

66.   Tage Vosbein, "Bankruptcy: The Limit of Economic Reform in China?" *China Information* 1, no. 3 (1986): 1–8; Nicholas Lardy, *China's Unfinished Economic Revolution* (Washington, DC: Brookings Institution Press, 1998), 131–132.

67.   ZZYWJ, 3:510.

68.   ZFLZQJ 1987, 82–86.

69.   ZFLZQJ 1987, 91–111.

70.   Office Files of David Bell, Box 2, Folder 21, International Division, Ford Foundation Archives, Rockefeller Archive Center, Sleepy Hollow, New York. For more on organizations such as the Ford Foundation and the Committee on Scholarly Communication with the PRC, see Steve Cohn, *Competing Economic Paradigms in China: The Co-evolution of Economic Events, Economic Theory and Economics Education, 1976–2016* (London: Routledge, 2017).

71.   Peter Geithner, letter of May 15, 1986, and "Memorandum: Opening the Beijing Office," June 18, 1987, Developing Countries Program, Office Files of William Carmichael, Box 1, Folder 22, Ford Foundation Papers.

72.   Peter F. Drucker, "No Jobs for the Millions Is China's Nemesis," *Wall Street Journal,* November 19, 1987; Edwin Lim 林重庚, "中国改革开放过程中的对外思想开放" [The opening of thinking to the outside world in the process of China's reform and opening], in 中国经济: 50人看三十年 [China's economy: Fifty people on thirty years], ed. Wu Jinglian 吴敬琏 (Beijing: China Economy Publishing House, 2008), 40.

73.   Naughton, *Growing out of the Plan*, 223.

74.   ZFLZQJ 1987, 115–122, 210–222.

75.   ZFLZQJ 1987, 199–204.

76.   Fewsmith, *Dilemmas of Reform*, 210–214; Qimiao Fan, "State-Owned Enterprise Reform in China: Incentives and Environment," in *China's Economic Reforms: The Costs and Benefits of Incrementalism*, ed. Qimiao Fan and Peter Nolan (Basingstoke, UK: Macmillan, 1994), 149–150.

77.   ZFLZQJ 1987, 222–224.

78.   Memorandum of Conversation of Todor Zhivkov and Deng Xiaoping, May 7, 1987, Central State Archive, Sofia, Fond 1-B, Record 60, File 395. Translated by Kalina Bratanova, https://digitalarchive.wilsoncenter.org/document/112704.

Part III: Technology

1.   ZZYWJ, 2:198. This section draws on Julian Gewirtz, "The Futurists of Beijing: Alvin Toffler, Zhao Ziyang, and China's 'New Technological Revolution,' 1979–1991," *Journal of Asian Studies* 78, no. 1 (February 2019): 115–140.

2.   Zuoyue Wang, "The Cold War and the Reshaping of Transnational Science in China," in *Science and Technology in the Global Cold War,* ed. Naomi Oreskes and John Krige (Cambridge, MA: MIT Press, 2014), 343–369; Covell F. Meyskens, *Mao's Third Front: The Militarization of Cold War China* (Cambridge: Cambridge University Press, 2020).

3.   US Congress, Office of Technology Assessment, *Technology Transfer to China* (Washington, DC: US Government Printing Office, 1987), 3.

4.   Aftonbladet Interview with PRC Deputy Prime Minister Wang Renzhong, March, 20, 1979, D790131-0570, Central Foreign Policy Files, 1973–1979, General Records of the Department of State, Record Group 59, National Archives at College Park—Electronic Records, https://aad.archives.gov/aad/createpdf?rid=196739&dt=2776&dl=2169.

5.   Denis Fred Simon, "China's Drive to Close the Technological Gap: S&T Reform and the Imperative to Catch Up," *China Quarterly* 119 (September 1989): 598–630.

6.   Susan Greenhalgh, *Just One Child: Science and Policy in Deng's China* (Berkeley: University of California Press, 2008).

7.   For perspectives on "science" (科学), expertise, and the CCP, see Joseph Fewsmith, "Promoting the Scientific Development Concept," *China Leadership Monitor* 11 (2004); Joel Andreas, *Rise of the Red Engineers: The Cultural Revolution and the Origins of China's New Class* (Stanford, CA: Stanford University Press, 2009); and Sigrid Schmalzer, *Red Revolution, Green Revolution: Scientific Farming in Socialist China* (Chicago: University of Chicago Press, 2016).

8.   Carol Lee Hamrin, *China and the Challenge of the Future: Changing Political Patterns* (Boulder, CO: Westview Press, 1990), 75–80; Paola Iovene, *Tales of Futures Past: Literature and Anticipation in Contemporary China* (Stanford, CA: Stanford University Press, 2014).

9.   Reinhart Koselleck, *Futures Past: On the Semantics of Historical Time* (Cambridge, MA: MIT Press, 1985), for example, 273–274; Matthew Connelly, "Future Shock," in *The Shock of the Global: The 1970s in Perspective,* ed. Niall Ferguson, Charles S. Maier, Erez Manela, and Daniel J. Sargent (Cambridge, MA: Harvard University Press, 2010); Jenny Andersson, *The Future of the World: Futurology, Futurists, and the Struggle for the Post Cold War Imagination* (Oxford: Oxford University Press, 2018).

Chapter 6: Responding to the New Technological Revolution

1.   Deng Xiaoping, "Speech at the Opening Ceremony of the National Conference on Science," March 18, 1978, SWDXP-2, 101–116. Although Deng used "science" (科学), "technology" (技术), and "S&T" (科技) loosely, scholars could place China's technological drive in the 1970s–1980s in dialogue with Paul Forman's periodization of the prioritization of technology relative to science beginning around 1980. See Paul Forman, "The Primacy of Science in Modernity, of Technology in Postmodernity, and of Ideology in the History of Technology," *History and Technology* 23, no. 1–2 (2007): 1–152. I am grateful to Zuoyue Wang for this observation.

2.   Zuoyue Wang, "The Cold War and the Reshaping of Transnational Science in China," in *Science and Technology in the Global Cold War,* ed. Naomi Oreskes and John Krige (Cambridge, MA: MIT Press, 2014), 343–369. Chinese scientists also participated in the joint nuclear research center at Dubna.

3.   Deng, "Speech at the Opening Ceremony"; Julian Gewirtz, "China's Long March to Technological Supremacy," *Foreign Affairs* (August 27, 2019).

4.   Pete Millwood, "An 'Exceedingly Delicate Undertaking': Sino-American Science Diplomacy, 1966–78," *Journal of Contemporary History* 56, no. 1 (January 2021): 166–190.

5.   Jan Wong, "China's Leap to American Campuses," *New York Times,* November 15, 1981; Zhou Wenting, "The History of Chinese Studying Abroad," *China Daily,* April 21, 2017; Jay Mathews, "Chinese Are the No. 1 Group of Foreign Students Here," *Washington Post,* May 2, 1989; "Memorandum of Record, January 1980 U.S.-PRC Educational Exchange Counterpart Discussions," in US-China Joint Commission on Science and Technology, 1980, Series I.3, Box 111, A. Doak Barnett Papers, Columbia University Rare Books and Manuscripts Library.

6.   "Request for Instructions regarding People Applying to Study Abroad at Their Own Expense," *Chinese Law and Government* 19, no. 4 (Winter 1986–1987): 30–33.

7.   "Record of a Conversation between the Prime Minister and Premier Zhao Ziyang," September 23, 1982, PREM19/962 f120, https://www.margaretthatcher.org/document/128397.

8.   Wong, "China's Leap"; Qian Ning 钱宁, 留学美国 [Studying in America] (Nanjing: Jiangsu Literature and Art Publishing House, 1996).

9.   Gerald B. Nolan, "On the FBI's Guidelines for Chinese Students" (letter to the editor), *Washington Post,* June 19, 1981.

10.   "Summary of the Vice President's Meeting with PRC Vice Premier Deng Xiaoping" (Document 264), in *Foreign Relations of the United States, 1977–1980, vol.*

8, China, ed. David P. Nickles (Washington, DC: United States Government Printing Office, 2013), 925; "Minutes of a National Security Council Meeting" (Document 287), in *Foreign Relations of the United States, 1977–1980, vol. 8, China,* ed. David P. Nickles (Washington, DC: United States Government Printing Office, 2013), 1030; Sergey Radchenko, *Unwanted Visionaries: The Soviet Failure in Asia at the End of the Cold War* (Oxford: Oxford University Press, 2014), 28–29.

11.   Evan Feigenbaum, *China's Techno-Warriors: National Security and Strategic Competition from the Nuclear to the Information Age* (Stanford, CA: Stanford University Press, 2000), 100; Tai Min Cheung, *Fortifying China: The Struggle to Build a Modern Defense Economy* (Ithaca, NY: Cornell University Press, 2013), 55.

12.   Denis Fred Simon, "China's Drive to Close the Technological Gap: S&T Reform and the Imperative to Catch Up," *China Quarterly* 119 (September 1989): 614.

13.   Feigenbaum, *China's Techno-Warriors,* 76–77.

14.   Xiaoming Zhang, *Deng Xiaoping's Long War: The Military Conflict between China and Vietnam* (Chapel Hill: University of North Carolina Press, 2015); Feigenbaum, *China's Techno-Warriors,* 80, 83–84.

15.   H. Lyman Miller, "Xu Liangying and He Zuoxiu: Divergent Responses to Physics and Politics in the Post-Mao Period," *Historical Studies in the Physical and Biological Sciences* 30, no. 1 (1999): 92–93; Zuoyue Wang, "The Chinese Developmental State during the Cold War: The Making of the 1956 Twelve-Year Science and Technology Plan," *History and Technology* 31, no. 3 (2015): 180–205; Du Lei 杜磊, "改革开放初期新技术革命对策大讨论研究" [A study on the discussion of the countermeasures to the new technological revolution during the initial stage of reform and opening], 中共党史研究 [CCP history research] 6 (2018): 38–47. Some Chinese scientists today assert that the long-term neglect of basic research in China is an important reason for continued dependence on foreign technology.

16.   Miller, "Xu Liangying and He Zuoxiu," 91–92.

17.   Introduction to Alvin Toffler 阿尔温·托夫勒, 第三次浪潮 [The third wave], trans. Zhu Zhiyan 朱志焱 et al. (Beijing: Sanlian shudian, 1983), 1.

18.   Carol Lee Hamrin, *China and the Challenge of the Future: Changing Political Patterns* (Boulder, CO: Westview Press, 1990), 1–2, 31–38; Eleonora Masini, J. Dator, and S. Rodgers, eds., *Futures of Development: Selections from the Tenth World Conference of the WFSF* (Paris: Future-Oriented Studies Programme, 1991), 491.

19.   William A. Callahan, *China Dreams* (Oxford: Oxford University Press, 2013).

20.   Dong Leshan 董乐山, "托夫勒的'三次浪潮'论" [On Toffler's "Third wave"], 读书 [Reading] 11 (1981): 146.

21.   Alvin Toffler, *Future Shock* (New York: Random House, 1970); Donella H. Meadows, Dennis L. Meadows, Jørgen Randers, and William W. Behrens III, *The Limits to Growth: A Report for the Club of Rome's Project on the Predicament of Mankind* (New York: Universe Books, 1972); Daniel Bell, *The Coming of Post-industrial Society: A Venture in Social Forecasting* (New York: Basic Books, 1973). The predictions of the Club of Rome report were also influential on Chinese population planning; see Susan Greenhalgh, *Just One Child: Science and Policy in Deng's China* (Berkeley: University of California Press, 2008).

22.   Alvin Toffler, *The Third Wave* (New York: Bantam, 1981), 10, 64.

23.   Toffler, *Third Wave*, 13–14.

24.   Toffler, *Third Wave*, 10, 275, 336, 419.

25.   Farhad Manjoo, "The Future Toffler Saw Is Already upon Us," *New York Times*, July 7, 2016.

26.   Toffler, *Third Wave*, 2, 6. Non-Marxist stages of growth were not novel; W. W. Rostow's *Stages of Economic Growth: A Non-Communist Manifesto* (Cambridge: Cambridge University Press, 1960) was translated prior to the Cultural Revolution. See 罗斯托, 经济成长的级段: 非共产党宣言 (Beijing: Commercial Press, 1962).

27.   Dong Leshan, "托夫勒的'三次浪潮'论," 146. See Wang Yan 王焱, "阿尔文•托夫勒: 第一次浪潮" [Alvin Toffler: The first wave], 金融时报 (Financial times), December 30, 2008, www.ftchinese.com/story/001023927?full=y.

28.   "Letter to Leshan Dong," May 14, 1982, Box 20, May 1982 Folder; Letter to Du Dagung [Dagong], November 19, 1982, and "Letter to Du Dagung [Dagong]," December 10, 1982, Box 30, Correspondence–Foreign–1982–II, Toffler Papers.

29.   "Letter to Hu Zhengqing," June 22, 1982, Box 20, June 1982 Folder, Toffler Papers; "Alvin Toffler Visit to China, 1983 January 2–12," Box 36, Folder 346, Papers of the National Committee on US-China Relations, Rockefeller Archive Center, Sleepy Hollow, New York.

30.   "Letter to Lennart Oldenburg," December 28, 1982, Box 30, Correspondence–Foreign–1982–I, Toffler Papers; Richard Baum, *Burying Mao: Chinese Politics in the Age of Deng Xiaoping* (Princeton, NJ: Princeton University Press, 1994), 166; Hamrin, *China and the Challenge of the Future*, 77.

31.   Miao Qihao 缪其浩, "托夫勒助上海推'第三次浪潮'" [Toffler visits Shanghai to promote *The Third Wave*], November 29, 2016, http://www.china-sorsa.org/n195/n203/n214/n227/u1ai11098.html.

32.   Alvin Toffler and Heidi Toffler, *Creating a New Civilization: The Politics of the Third Wave* (Atlanta: Turner Publishing, 1995); Miao Qihao, "托夫勒助上海推'第三次浪潮.'"

33.   "Transcript of 'Creating Alternative Futures,'" television interview, Box 23, June 1984 Folder, Toffler Papers.

34.   Tong Tianxiang 童天湘, "控制论的广泛影响" [The wide influence of cybernetics], RMRB, January 30, 1984.

35.   "首都出版一批科技新书" [New science and technology books published in Beijing], RMRB, April 16, 1978. Cybernetics had been included in the 1956 twelve-year plan for S&T, due primarily to Soviet influences on the plan.

36.   "控制论和系统论丛书" [Cybernetics and systems theory series], 自然辩证法通讯 [Journal of the dialectics of nature] 4 (1985): 65.

37.   Liu Yongzhen 刘永振, "一门应用广泛的方法性学科: 控制论" [Cybernetics: A methodological discipline with broad-ranging applications], RMRB, February 10, 1984.

38.   Greenhalgh, *Just One Child*, 126, 150–152, 189, 246–247, 264, 273, 285, 298.

39.   DRC Record, 34–35. Indeed, this provides one important lineage for policies such as the "social credit system."

40.   DRC Record; Wang Yan, "阿尔文•托夫勒."

41.   Ma Hong 马洪, "为我国社会主义现代化建设献计献策" [Advice and suggestions for construction of China's socialist modernization], 经济问题 [Economic problems] 1 (1984): 5–6; ZZYWJ, 2:197.

42.   ZZYWJ, 2:197–200; Huan Xiang, 宦乡文集 [Collected writings of Huan Xiang], 2 vols. (Beijing: World Affairs Press, 1994), 2:1004–1005.

43.   ZZYWJ, 2:197–198.

44.   DRC Record, 14, 36.

45.   ZZYWJ, 2:197–198.

46.   ZZYWJ, 2:198.

47.   ZZYWJ, 2:199–201.

48.   Mao Zedong, "Sixty Points on Working Methods" (February 2, 1958), in *Selected Works of Mao Tse-Tung*, vol. 8, www.marxists.org/reference/archive/mao/selected-works /index.htm.

49.   ZZYWJ, 2:204.

50.   Ma Hong, "为我国社会主义现代化建设献计献策," 2, 4–5.

51.   Xiao Donglian 萧冬连, "1978–1984年中国经济体制改革思路的演进" [The evolution of China's economic system reform, 1978–1984], 当代中国史研究 [Research

on contemporary Chinese history] 11, no. 5 (September 2004): 69; CCP Central Organization Department 中共中央组织部 et al., eds., 迎接新的技术革命: 新技术革命知识讲座 [Welcoming the new technological revolution: Lectures on the new technological revolution] (Changsha: Hunan Science and Technology Press, 1984).

52.   Chen Zujia 陈祖甲, "'银河'巨型计算机系统通过鉴定" [The "Galaxy" supercomputer passes appraisal], RMRB, December 22, 1983.

53.   Yao Cong 姚琮, "大趋势: 改变我们生活的十个新方向" [Megatrends: Ten new directions transforming our lives], 读书 [Reading] 10 (1983): 97–110.

54.   John Naisbitt, *Megatrends: Ten New Directions Transforming Our Lives* (New York: Warner Books, 1982), 1–2, 15, 19.

55.   Yang Mu 杨沐, "一个值得注意的信息 读西方关于新产业革命的几部著作" [Information worthy of our attention: Reading several Western works on the New Industrial Revolution], 读书 [Reading] 2 (1984): 15–20.

56.   Du Lei, "改革开放初期新技术革命对策大讨论研究."

57.   Wang Zijin 王子瑾, "赵紫阳在上海参观微电子技术及其应用汇报展览" [Zhao Ziyang visits the exhibition of microelectronics technology and its applications in Shanghai], RMRB, January 28, 1984.

58.   Guo Lihua 郭礼华, "邓小平王震视察宝钢" [Deng Xiaoping, Wang Zhen inspect Baosteel], RMRB, February 17, 1984; DXPNP, 2:961.

59.   Gu Mainan 顾迈南 and He Huangbiao 何黄彪, "我国现代化建设的一个基本方针 经济建设必须依靠科学技术 科学技术必须面向经济建设" [A new basic principle in China's modernization: Economic development must draw on science and technology, and science and technology must orient toward economic development], RMRB, December 18, 1983.

60.   Wei Mingyi 魏鸣一, "神通广大的微电子技术" [The remarkable abilities of microelectronics technology], RMRB, October 10, 1983.

61.   Chen Fong-Ching and Jin Guantao, *From Youthful Manuscripts to River Elegy* (Hong Kong: Chinese University Press, 1997).

62.   SWDXP-3, 50; DXPNP, 2:939–940.

63.   Ma Hong, "为我国社会主义现代化建设献计献策," 4–5.

64.   XCDT 6 (February 14, 1984): 50–52, trans. in *Chinese Law & Government* 24, no. 4 (1991): 31–33.

65.   XCDT 6 (February 14, 1984): 50–52, trans. in *Chinese Law & Government* 24, no. 4 (1991): 31–33.

66. Yang Jisheng 杨继绳, 邓小平时代: 中国改革开放二十年纪实 [Deng Xiaoping's era: A record of China's twenty years of reform and opening up] (Beijing: Central Compilation & Translation Press, 1998), 1:238.

67. Ma Hong 马洪, "开创社会科学事业的新局面" [A new situation in the cause of developing the social sciences], 江苏社联通讯 [Jiangsu Social Association newsletter] 7 (1984): 14–16.

68. ZFLZQJ 1984, 25.

69. DRC Record, 36; Liu Hong 柳红, 八0年代: 中国经济学人的光荣与梦想 [The eighties: Chinese economists' glory and dreams] (Guilin: Guangxi Normal University Publishing House, 2010), 137.

70. Liu Hong, 八0年代, 137–140; Wang Yan, "阿尔文•托夫勒."

71. "Letter to Jan Berris," February 21, 1984, Box 22, February 1984 Folder, Toffler Papers.

72. Feigenbaum, *China's Techno-Warriors*, 100–101, 126–127.

73. ZZYWJ, 2:372.

74. ZZYWJ, 2:521.

75. ZFLZQJ 1984, 7:166.

76. "国务院成立电子振兴领导小组" [The State Council establishes a leading group on the electronics industry], Xinhua News Service, September 19, 1984.

77. "万里会见美国企业家" [Wan Li meets with American entrepreneurs], RMRB, February 25, 1984.

78. Simon, "China's Drive," 609, 612.

79. "Decision of the Central Committee of the CCP on Reform of the Economic Structure," Xinhua News Agency, October 20, 1984, trans. in FBIS-CHI-84-205, October 22, 1984, K1–K19.

80. ZZYWJ, 3:86; Miller, "Xu Liangying and He Zuoxiu," 91–92, 112–114.

81. Marshall I. Goldman, *Gorbachev's Challenge: Economic Reform in the Age of High Technology* (New York: Norton, 1987); Benjamin Peters, *How Not to Network a Nation: The Uneasy History of the Soviet Internet* (Cambridge, MA: MIT Press, 2016).

82. Chris Miller, *The Struggle to Save the Soviet Economy: Mikhail Gorbachev and the Collapse of the USSR* (Chapel Hill: University of North Carolina Press, 2016), 29, 61.

83. Scott Kennedy, "The Stone Group: State Client or Market Pathbreaker?" *China Quarterly* 152 (December 1997): 752–756.

84.   Tan Feng 谈锋, "在'第三次浪潮'冲击下" [The impact of *The Third Wave*], RMRB, June 24, 1984.

85.   Alexander Woodside, "The Asia-Pacific Idea as a Mobilization Myth," in *What Is in a Rim? Critical Perspectives on the Pacific Region Idea,* ed. Arif Dirlik (Lanham, MD: Rowman & Littlefield, 1998), 41.

Chapter 7: A Matter of the Life and Death of the Nation

1.   DXGWX, 3:1681–1683.

2.   DRC Record, 50–52, Document No. 81 of 1985.

3.   Christopher Buckley, "Science as Politics and Politics as Science: Fang Lizhi and Chinese Intellectuals' Uncertain Road to Dissent," *Australian Journal of Chinese Affairs* 25 (January 1991): 8, 11.

4.   H. Lyman Miller, "Xu Liangying and He Zuoxiu: Divergent Responses to Physics and Politics in the Post-Mao Period," *Historical Studies in the Physical and Biological Sciences* 30, no. 1 (1999): 89–114; Dennis Overbye, "Einstein's Man in Beijing," *New York Times,* August 22, 2006; Merle Goldman, *China's Intellectuals: Advise and Dissent* (Cambridge, MA: Harvard University Press, 1988). See also Xu Ping 许评, ed., 许良英纪念文集 [Xu Liangying memorial collection] (Beijing: Liangzhi yingjian shuwu, 2016).

5.   Miller, "Xu Liangying and He Zuoxiu," 94; Buckley, "Science as Politics," 12.

6.   Miller, "Xu Liangying and He Zuoxiu," 109.

7.   Su Shaozhi 苏绍智 and Ding Xueliang 丁学良, "马克思对信息时代的预见" [Marx's predictions of the information era], RMRB, August 24, 1984.

8.   "中共中央关于科学技术体制改革的决定" [Decision on reform of the S&T management system], March 13, 1985, http://www.waizi.org.cn/law/5046.html.

9.   Tony Saich, "Political and Ideological Reform in the PRC: An Interview with Professor Su Shaozhi," *China Information* 1, no. 2 (1986): 20.

10.   Su Shaozhi, *Democratization and Reform* (Nottingham, UK: Spokesman, 1988), 89–97, 104.

11.   Pan Jianxiong 潘建雄, Zhao Zhiyi 赵志一, He Kuang 何况, and Zheng Xuping 郑绪平, "中国现代化过程中的文化冲突与社会发展" [Cultural conflict and social development in the process of China's modernization], 社会学研究 [Sociology research] 2 (1986): 64.

12.   Buckley, "Science as Politics," 12, 16–17.

13.   Gao Fang 高放, ed., 评'第三次浪潮' [Critiquing "the third wave"] (Beijing: Guangming Daily Publishing House, 1986).

14.   NCXB, no. 10 (March 5, 1986), in ZWCBWFWZX 21:9, 3–6.

15.   Han Zhongkun 韩钟昆, Zhai Huisheng 翟惠生, and Chen Hongyu 陈宏愚, "把科技'星火'引向燎原: 全国'星火计划'工作会议侧记" [From the technology "spark" to a prairie fire: Notes on the working meeting of the national "Spark Program"], 科技进步与对策 [Science & technology progress and policy] 4, no. 1 (1987): 10–13, 45; Denis Fred Simon, "China's Drive to Close the Technological Gap: S&T Reform and the Imperative to Catch Up," *China Quarterly*, no. 119 (September 1989): 620; ZZYWJ, 3:163.

16.   ZZYWJ, 3:223.

17.   Han, Zhai, and Chen, "把科技'星火'引向燎原." On the World Bank's support of the Spark Program, see "China: Country Strategy Paper Updating Memorandum," September 1993, WB IBRD / IDA DEC-03-42, Folder 1454402, Records of the Office of the Chief Economist. WBA: 14–15.

18.   Harry Harding, *China's Second Revolution: Reform after Mao* (Washington, DC: Brookings Institution Press, 1987), 134; Simon, "China's Drive to Close the Technological Gap," 617.

19.   Li Peng 李鹏, 李鹏经济日记: 市场与调控 (征求意见稿) [Li Peng's economic diary: Market and regulation (draft for comment)]. Held in the Fairbank Collection, Fung Library, Harvard University, 1:321; ZFLZQJ 1986, 11.

20.   Wan Runnan 万润南, "也谈'保护'" [On "Protection"], 万家述评 [Wan family review] (blog), *Wenxuecity*, published May 25, 2011, https://bbs.wenxuecity.com /origin/638413.html.

21.   Gregory Kulacki and Jeffrey G. Lewis, *A Place for One's Mat: China's Space Program* (Cambridge, MA: American Academy of Arts and Sciences, 2009), 22–25; Evan Feigenbaum, *China's Techno-Warriors: National Security and Strategic Competition from the Nuclear to the Information Age* (Stanford: Stanford University Press, 2000), 142.

22.   Julian Gewirtz, "The Futurists of Beijing: Alvin Toffler, Zhao Ziyang, and China's 'New Technological Revolution,' 1979–1991," *Journal of Asian Studies* 78, no. 1 (February 2019): 115–140.

23.   Mentioning international efforts on both sides of the Iron Curtain, including the Strategic Defense Initiative in the United States, they urged the creation of a unified technology strategy for China based on the principle of "civilian and military integration, placing civilian interests first" (Yang Lizhong 杨立忠 et al., 高技术战略: 跨世纪的挑战与机遇 [High-technology strategy: Challenges and opportunities in the new century] [Beijing: Military Science Press, 1991], 226–228).

24.　DXPNP, 2:1107–1108; Lu Jia 卢佳, "邓小平和中国高科技发展" [Deng Xiaoping and China's high-tech development], 中国共产党历史网 [CCP history web], December 23, 2014, www.zgdsw.org.cn/n/2014/1223/c244522-26259979.html.

25.　For example, Feigenbaum, *China's Techno-Warriors*, 141–188. This oversight is due to widespread use of a source released by an official People's Liberation Army publisher in 1991. See Yang Lizhong 杨立忠 et al., 高技术战略: 跨世纪的挑战与机遇 [High-technology strategy: Challenges and opportunities in the new century] (Beijing: Military Science Press, 1991).

26.　ZZYWJ, 3:300–301, 324.

27.　ZZYWJ, 3:323–326.

28.　ZZYWJ, 3:360–368. Compared to the 1956 Twelve-Year Plan, CAS played a much less central role in the 863 Program, reflecting that much of its defense-related capacity had been transferred to COSTIND as well as what historian Zuoyue Wang calls Zhao's dissatisfaction with CAS's focus on basic research.

29.　Tai Min Cheung, *Fortifying China: The Struggle to Build a Modern Defense Economy* (Ithaca, NY: Cornell University Press, 2013), 82; Feigenbaum, *China's Techno-Warriors*, 136; Sun Zhenhuan, 孙振环, "关于建立军民结合工业体制的探讨" [Inquiry into building an industrial system of military and civilian integration], JJYJ, no. 5 (1985): 68–73.

30.　Cheung, *Fortifying China*, 76.

31.　Cheung, *Fortifying China*, 73, 82–83.

32.　Feigenbaum, *China's Techno-Warriors*, 134. The focus on economic results, according to Cheung, negatively impacted the military's technological level (Cheung, *Fortifying China*, 53).

33.　ZZYWJ, 3:455–456; DRC Record, 62.

34.　Lu Jia 卢佳, "邓小平和中国高科技发展" [Deng Xiaoping and China's high-tech development], 中国共产党历史网 [CCP history web], December 23, 2014, www.zgdsw.org.cn/ n/2014/1223/c244522-26259979.html; Kulacki and Lewis, *A Place for One's Mat*, 24.

35.　SWDXP-3, 184; DXPNP, 2:1145–1146.

36.　Feigenbaum, *China's Techno-Warriors*, 167.

37.　Tian Sen 田森, "评'第三次浪潮'" [Critiquing *The third wave*], 红旗 [Red flag], no. 12 (1987): 30–34.

38.　U.S. Congress, Office of Technology Assessment (OTA), *Technology Transfer to China* (Washington, DC: U.S. Government Printing Office, 1987). OTA saw strengthening China's defense technological capacity as an effective source of pressure on the Soviet Union (11).

39.   OTA's China advisory board did note in passing the risk that "technology transfer will help China become a formidable competitor in the international economy." "Re: Progress Report," Letter to Technology Transfer to China Advisory Panel, May 22, 1986, OTA, 1985–1986, Series II.4, Box 140, A. Doak Barnett Papers, Columbia University Rare Books and Manuscripts.

40.   SWDXP-3, 222.

41.   ZZYWJ, 4:128.

42.   DXGWX, 3:1681–1683.

Part IV: Political Modernization

1.   "Ye Jianying's Speech at the Closing Session of the CCP Central Work Conference," December 13, 1978, History and Public Policy Program Digital Archive, Hubei Provincial Archives, SZ1-4-791, translated by Caixia Lu, http://digitalarchive.wilsoncenter .org/document/121691; Deng Xiaoping, "Emancipate the Mind, Seek Truth from Facts, and Unite as One in Looking to the Future," December 13, 1978, in SWDXP-2, 156–163.

2.   Wei Jingsheng, "The Fifth Modernization," Wei Jingsheng Foundation, https://weijingsheng.org/doc/en/THE%20FIFTH%20MODERNIZATION.html.

3.   Su Shaozhi, *Democratization and Reform* (Nottingham, UK: Spokesman, 1988), 16. Su noted, "Acton was a bourgeois and also a lord, but regardless of his status, what he said was quite reasonable."

4.   Ruan Ming, *Deng Xiaoping: Chronicle of an Empire* (Boulder, CO: Westview, 1994), 179.

5.   Andrew J. Nathan, *Chinese Democracy* (New York: Knopf, 1985), 228; Nina P. Halpern, "Economic Reform, Social Mobilization, and Democratization in Post-Mao China," in *Reform and Reaction in Post-Mao China: The Road to Tiananmen*, ed. Richard Baum (London: Routledge, 1991), 39.

6.   HYBZ, 3:950–959; Hongying Wang, "Zhao Ziyang's Visions: Victims of Political Turmoil or Seeds of a Democratic Future?" in *Zhao Ziyang and China's Political Future*, ed. Wu Guoguang and Helen Lansdowne (London: Routledge, 2012), 17–28; ZZYYZZGG, 448–485. On the Leninist state, see Barrett L. McCormick, *Political Reform in Post-Mao China: Democracy and Bureaucracy in a Leninist State* (Berkeley: University of California Press, 1990), 5–6.

7.　Elizabeth Perry, "The Populist Dream of Chinese Democracy," *Journal of Asian Studies* 74, no. 4 (November 2015): 903–915; Lei Guang, "Elusive Democracy: Conceptual Change and the Chinese Democracy Movement, 1978–79 to 1989," *Modern China* 22, no. 4 (October 1996): 420.

8.　Wu Guoguang, "Hard Politics with Soft Institutions: China's Political Reform, 1986–1989" (PhD diss., Princeton University, 1995), 264.

9.　They contrasted this "democracy" with feudal "despotism" and "patriarchy" (家长制). Other forms of socialist democracy, such as worker self-management in enterprises, were clearly undercut as a new market order took hold. See also Andrew J. Nathan, "Zhao Ziyang's Vision of Chinese Democracy," *China Perspectives* 3 (2008).

10.　These included limited local elections and legal reforms providing a measure of accountability. See, for example, Joseph Fewsmith, *The Logic and Limits of Political Reform in China* (Cambridge: Cambridge University Press, 2012).

11.　Merle Goldman, *Sowing the Seeds of Democracy in China: Political Reform in the Deng Xiaoping Era* (Cambridge, MA: Harvard University Press, 1995); Yiu-chung Wong, *From Deng Xiaoping to Jiang Zemin: Two Decades of Political Reform in the PRC* (Lanham, MD: University Press of America, 2005); Wu Guoguang and Helen Lansdowne, *Zhao Ziyang and China's Political Future* (London: Routledge, 2012).

12.　Wu, "Hard Politics," 315.

13.　Bao Tong, introduction to Wu Wei 吳偉, 中國 80 年代政治改革的台前幕後 [On stage and backstage: China's political reform in the 1980s] (Hong Kong: Xinshiji chuban ji chuanmei youxian gongsi, 2013), 1–4.

Chapter 8: Masters of the Country

1.　Deng Xiaoping, "On the Reform of the System of Party and State Leadership," August 18, 1980, SWDXP-2, 302–325.

2.　Deng Liqun, 十二个春秋: 邓力群自述 [Twelve springs and autumns: An autobiography of Deng Liqun] (Hong Kong: Bozhi Publishing House, 2006), 183; DXPNP, 1:641; GSJTL, 7:299. To a lesser extent, comments about "feudalism" were also warning shots to local bosses in the CCP and People's Liberation Army who had built powerful patronage networks.

3.　Ding Xueliang 丁学良, "丁学良口述: 为邓小平8·18讲话写奉命文章" [Ding Xueliang oral history: The writing of Deng Xiaoping's August 18 speech], August 19, 2017, https://2newcenturynet.blogspot.com/2017/08/818.html.

4.　Deng, "On the Reform."

5.   Deng, "On the Reform."

6.   XCDT, no. 42 (October 9, 1980): 256–258.

7.   Merle Goldman, *Sowing the Seeds of Democracy in China: Political Reform in the Deng Xiaoping Era* (Cambridge, MA: Harvard University Press, 1995), 67–68; Yiu-chung Wong, *From Deng Xiaoping to Jiang Zemin: Two Decades of Political Reform in the PRC* (Lanham, MD: University Press of America, 2005), 137–138. "*Gengshen*" refers to the designation for the year 1980 in the traditional sixty-year cyclical calendar.

8.   Michael Dobbs, "Poles Sign Strike Accord," *Washington Post*, September 1, 1980.

9.   "波兰工人讨论筹建全波独立自治工会" [Polish workers discuss preparations for establishing an independent and autonomous national union], RMRB, September 19, 1980; Goldman, *Sowing the Seeds*, 68–69.

10.   "The Death Knell of the Rule of the Privileged Class of Bureaucrats," in *Wild Lily, Prairie Fire: China's Road to Democracy, Yan'an to Tian'anmen, 1942–1989*, ed. Gregor Benton and Alan Hunter (Princeton, NJ: Princeton University Press, 1995), 259–262.

11.   HQMSXJ, 242–244; Ruan Ming, *Deng Xiaoping: Chronicle of an Empire* (Boulder, CO: Westview, 1994), 91–94.

12.   Wu Jiang 吴江, "对于我所提供的两条史料的补充说明" [Additional explanations of the two historical sources that I provided], 胡耀邦史料信息网 [Online repository of historical materials on Hu Yaobang], August 6, 2010, www.hybsl.cn /ybsxyj/shengpingyusixiang/2010-08-12/21786.html; Yang Jisheng 楊繼繩, 中國改革年代的政治鬥爭 (Hong Kong: Excellent Culture Press, 2004), 204.

13.   CYNP, 2:299; GSJTL, 7:267.

14.   GSJTL, 4:246.

15.   新闻出版工作文件选编 [Selected documents on news and publishing work] (edited and printed by Jiangsu Province News Publishing Bureau, 1990), 21–28; Wu Wei 吳偉, 中國 80 年代政治改革的台前幕後 [On stage and backstage: China's political reform in the 1980s] (Hong Kong: Xinshiji chuban ji chuanmei youxian gongsi, 2013), 23.

16.   XCDT, no. 13 (March 25, 1981): 77–78.

17.   Li Honglin 李洪林, "民主的权威: 关于权威的札记" [The authority of democracy: Notes on authority], RMRB, March 1, 1982.

18.   XCDT, no. 33 (July 6, 1981): 201.

19.   Wong, *From Deng Xiaoping*, 81; 领导同志与外宾谈话摘编 (十二) [Selected excerpts from dialogues between party leaders and foreign dignitaries (12)], December 10, 1982,

Shanghai Municipal Archives, B1-9-798-49, 11. I am grateful to Chuck Kraus for bringing this document to my attention.

20.　DXPNP, 2:797–799.

21.　Wong, *From Deng Xiaoping,* 90.

22.　ZZYWJ, 1:423–431; Zhiyong Lan, "Understanding China's Administrative Reform in Context," *Public Administration Quarterly* 24, no. 4 (Winter 2001): 442–443; Wu Wei, 中國 80 年代政治改革的台前幕後, 37.

23.　Wu Wei, 中國 80 年代政治改革的台前幕後, 38, 40.

24.　Richard Baum, *Burying Mao: Chinese Politics in the Age of Deng Xiaoping* (Princeton, NJ: Princeton University Press, 1994), 149–150; Gao Fang 高放, "中国政治体制改革的回顾与展望" [Recollection and outlook for China's political system reform], January 2010, at 胡耀邦史料信息网 [Online repository of historical materials on Hu Yaobang], http://www.hybsl.cn/beijingcankao/beijingfenxi/2018-06 -05/67727.html.

25.　XCDT, no. 31 (June 18, 1983): 223–225.

26.　Ding Xueliang, "丁学良口述"; Ding Xueliang, "切实改革 肃清封建主义残余影响" [Practical reform: Eliminating the residual influence of feudalism], RMRB, August 24, 1983.

27.　Liu Binyan, *Two Kinds of Truth: Stories and Reportage from China,* ed. Perry Link (Bloomington: Indiana University Press, 2006), 149–207; Liu Binyan, *A Higher Kind of Loyalty: A Memoir by China's Foremost Journalist,* trans. Zhu Hong (New York: Pantheon Books, 1990), 193–199; Goldman, *Sowing the Seeds,* 147–150.

28.　See, for example, ZZYWJ, 2:149.

29.　Timothy Cheek, *The Intellectual in Modern Chinese History* (Cambridge: Cambridge University Press, 2016), 203–205; Anita Chan, Stanley Rosen, and Jonathan Unger, eds., *On Socialist Democracy and the Chinese Legal System: The Li Yizhe Debates* (Armonk, NY: M. E. Sharpe, 1985), 1–28.

30.　ZZYWJ, 2:406–407; POS, 177. This internal letter has long been the subject of speculation because some commentators suspect it contained criticisms of Hu Yaobang.

31.　Wong, *From Deng Xiaoping,* 156; Goldman, *Sowing the Seeds,* 151.

32.　Li Rui 李锐, "耀邦去世前的谈话" [Conversations with Hu Yaobang before his death], *Modern China Studies,* no. 4 (2001), https://www.modernchinastudies.org/us /issues/past-issues/75-mcs-2001-issue-4/589-2012-01-03-12-11- 52.html.

33.   "Conference Puts Future into Younger Hands," *Beijing Review* 28, no. 39 (September 30, 1985): 6; Carol Lee Hamrin, *China and the Challenge of the Future: Changing Political Patterns* (Boulder, CO: Westview Press, 1990), 118.

34.   Baum, *Burying Mao*, 176; Daniel Southerland, "China Discloses Profiteering Scandal on Hainan," *Washington Post*, August 2, 1985.

35.   ZZYWJ, 3:252–253. See also Yan Sun, *Corruption and the Market in Contemporary China* (Ithaca, NY: Cornell University Press, 2004).

36.   SWDXP-3, 154.

37.   Du Guang 杜光, "回忆20年前的中国政治体制改革研究会" [Recalling the Political System Reform Research Society 20 years ago], December 14, 2008, *Boxun*, www.boxun.com/news/gb/z_special/2008/12/200812142206.shtml.

38.   John Gittings, "Su Shaozhi Obituary," *The Guardian*, September 3, 2019.

39.   NCXB, no. 9 (52) (February 26, 1986): 26–29.

40.   NCXB, no. 11 (54) (March 12, 1986): 24–28.

41.   J. Bruce Jacobs, *Democratizing Taiwan* (Leiden, the Netherlands: Brill, 2012), 62–66.

42.   Wu Guoguang, "Hard Politics with Soft Institutions: China's Political Reform, 1986–1989" (PhD diss., Princeton University, 1995), 223.

43.   NCXB, no. 12 (55) (March 19, 1986): 26–32.

Chapter 9: Explore without Fear

1.   Su Shaozhi, *Democratization and Reform* (Nottingham, UK: Spokesman, 1988), 116–119.

2.   Wu Guoguang, "Hard Politics with Soft Institutions: China's Political Reform, 1986–1989" (PhD diss., Princeton University, 1995), 27–28.

3.   Yiu-chung Wong, *From Deng Xiaoping to Jiang Zemin: Two Decades of Political Reform in the PRC* (Lanham, MD: University Press of America, 2005), 162; Merle Goldman, *Sowing the Seeds of Democracy in China: Political Reform in the Deng Xiaoping Era* (Cambridge, MA: Harvard University Press, 1995), 180.

4.   Carol Lee Hamrin and Timothy Cheek, *China's Establishment Intellectuals* (Armonk, NY: M. E. Sharpe, 1986).

5.   Qing Ming 青鸣, "政治体制改革的思考与探索" [Thinking on and exploring political system reform], 政治学研究 [Political science research] 5 (1986): 15, 58–60.

6.   Hu Qili 胡启立, "当代中国工人阶级的历史使命: 在纪念'五一'一百周年大会上的讲话" [The historical mission of the contemporary Chinese proletariat: Speech at the commemoration of the centennial of International Workers' Day], RMRB, May 1, 1986.

7.   "没有社会主义民主就没有社会主义现代化" [Without socialist democracy there is no socialist modernization], RMRB, May 8, 1986.

8.   Wu, "Hard Politics," 28; "Another Hundred Flowers," *New York Times*, September 26, 1986; Alexander V. Pantsov, with Steven I. Levine, *Deng Xiaoping: A Revolutionary Life* (Oxford: Oxford University Press, 2015), 329.

9.   ZFLZQJ 1986, 71–72; DXPNP, 2:1120–1121. The translation in SWDXP-3, 163, is significantly edited. See also Ezra Vogel, *Deng Xiaoping and the Transformation of China* (Cambridge, MA: Belknap Press of Harvard University Press, 2011), 571–572.

10.   DXPNP, 2:1125–1126; SWDXP-3, 166–167.

11.   Wu Wei 吳偉, 中國 80 年代政治改革的台前幕後 [On stage and backstage: China's political reform in the 1980s] (Hong Kong: Xinshiji chuban ji chuanmei youxian gongsi, 2013), 55–56.

12.   "赵紫阳谈我国经济政治体制改革" [Zhao Ziyang discusses China's economic and political system reforms], RMRB, July 11, 1986.

13.   "朱厚泽在政治体制改革理论研讨会上提出 思想要活跃学风要严谨" [At the Political System Reform Symposium, Zhu Houze says to think actively and study diligently], RMRB, July 15, 1986; Goldman, *Sowing the Seeds,* 181.

14.   Zou Aiguo 邹爱国, "王兆国在中央党校毕业典礼上讲话时强调 要有计划有步骤地进行政治体制改革" [At the Central Party School graduation ceremony, Wang Zhaoguo emphasizes that political system reform must be carried out in well-planned steps], RMRB, July 17, 1986.

15.   Wan Li 万里, "决策民主化和科学化是政治体制改革的一个重要课题: 在全国软科学研究工作座谈会上的讲话" [Democratization and scientization of policymaking are important for political system reform: Speech at the National Conference on Soft Science Research Work], RMRB, August 15, 1986, translated in "Democracy Essential to Policy Making," *Beijing Review* 29, no. 32 (August 11, 1986): 5.

16.   Wan Li, "决策民主化和科学化是政治体制改革的一个重要课题."

17.   Zhu Huaxin 祝华新, "万里: 实行决策的民主化科学化" [Wan Li: Implementing the democratization and scientization of policymaking], 中国共产党新闻网 [CCP news online], May 21, 2013, http://dangshi.people.com.cn/n/2013/0521/c364217 -21561993.html.

18.   Liu Binyan, *Two Kinds of Truth: Stories and Reportage from China*, ed. Perry Link (Bloomington: Indiana University Press, 2006), 217–220. Wan Li had a more

confrontational debate with Fang Lizhi in Hefei in November; see Fang Lizhi, *The Most Wanted Man in China: My Journey from Scientist to Enemy of the State,* trans. Perry Link (New York: Henry Holt, 2016), 255–256.

19.   "政治问题可以讨论" [Political questions can be discussed], RMRB, August 30, 1986.

20.   ZFLZQJ 1986, 65.

21.   NCXB 37 (September 10, 1986): 9–11.

22.   Zhang Mingshu 张明澍, "政治体制改革与经济体制改革学术讨论会纪要" [Summary of the academic seminar on political system reform and economic system reform], RMRB, November 3, 1986.

23.   "重读邓小平'党和国家领导制度改革'" [Rereading Deng Xiaoping's "On the reform of the system of party and state leadership"], SJJJDB, July 14, 1986. English translation in *Chinese Law & Government* 20, no. 1 (1987): 15–20.

24.   Tony Saich, "Political and Ideological Reform in the PRC: An Interview with Professor Su Shaozhi," *China Information* 1, no. 2 (1986): 25.

25.   Saich, "Political and Ideological Reform," 24.

26.   Su, *Democratization and Reform,* 165.

27.   Wei Haibo 魏海波, "政治体制改革与政治民主化" [On the reform of the political system and political democratization], 法学 [Legal studies], no. 10 (1986): 6–8, translated as "Reform of the Political System and Political Democratization," in *Chinese Law and Government* 20, no. 1 (Spring 1987): 74–77.

28.   Wang Huning 王沪宁, "当代西方政治多元主义思潮评析" [Analysis of contemporary Western political pluralism], 社会科学 [Social science] 4 (1986): 52–54.

29.   SWDXP-3, 178–179.

30.   DXPNP, 2:1136–1138; SWDXP-3, 179; Wu Wei, 中國 80 年代政治改革的台前幕後, 75.

31.   ZZYWJ, 3:453–454.

32.   Chen Yizi, "The Decision Process behind the 1986–1989 Political Reforms," in *Decision-Making in Deng's China: Perspectives from Insiders,* ed. Carol Lee Hamrin and Suisheng Zhao (Armonk, NY: M. E. Sharpe, 1995), 142; Wu Wei, 中國 80 年代政治改革的台前幕後, 77; Du Guang 杜光, "回忆20年前的中国政治体制改革研究会" [Recalling the Political System Reform Research Society 20 years ago], December 14, 2008, *Boxun,* www.boxun.com/news/gb/z_special/2008/12/200812142206.shtml.

33.   Wu Wei, 中國 80 年代政治改革的台前幕後, 89–90.

34.   Wu Wei, 中國 80 年代政治改革的台前幕後, 78–79.

35.   Zhu Xiaoqun, "Political Reform in Beijing City," in Hamrin and Zhao, *Decision-Making in Deng's China*, 177–178.

36.   ZZYWJ, 3:468–470, 3:490–492; Wu Wei, 中國 80 年代政治改革的台前幕後, 91–97; Chen Yizi 陈一谘, 陈一谘回忆录 [Memoirs of Chen Yizi] (Hong Kong: New Century Press, 2013), 403–410.

37.   ZZYWJ, 3:490–493; Wu Wei, 中國 80 年代政治改革的台前幕後, 98, 217; "政治体制改革要经过充分调查研究" [Reform of the political system must be fully investigated and studied], RMRB, December 8, 1986.

38.   Wu, "Hard Politics," 48–49.

39.   Wu Wei, 中國 80 年代政治改革的台前幕後, 113–114.

40.   Wu Wei, 中國 80 年代政治改革的台前幕後, 127; Chen Yizi, "The Decision Process," 145.

41.   ZZYWJ, 3:468; Wu, "Hard Politics," 56; Vogel, *Deng Xiaoping*, 575.

42.   I am grateful to Sergey Radchenko for suggesting this formulation.

43.   POS, 257.

44.   Wu Wei, 中國 80 年代政治改革的台前幕後, 232–234. See also DXPNP, 2:1172–1173, 2:1187–1188.

45.   Wu Wei, 中國 80 年代政治改革的台前幕後, 117; Chen Yizi, "The Decision Process," 146. Zhao recalled, "Frankly speaking, if there was anything new in the area of political reform in the Political Report for the 13th Party Congress, it certainly was not because of Deng" (POS, 208).

46.   Rana Mitter, *A Bitter Revolution: China's Struggle with the Modern World* (Oxford: Oxford University Press, 2004).

47.   Hsiao Pen, "Separating the Party from the Government," in Hamrin and Zhao, *Decision-making in Deng's China*, 153–163; see also, for example, ZFLZQJ 1986, 166.

48.   ZZYWJ, 3:473–474.

49.   ZZYWJ, 3:475; Yan Huai, "Establishing a Public Service System" in Hamrin and Zhao, *Decision-making in Deng's China*, 169–175; Yan Jiaqi, *Toward a Democratic China*, trans. David S. K. Hong and Denis C. Mair (Honolulu: University of Hawai'i Press, 1992), 79–85.

50.   ZZYWJ, 4:22, 3:470–472; Wu, "Hard Politics," 57–58.

51.   ZZYWJ, 3:471–472.

52. ZZYWJ, 3:470–471; POS, 262; Vogel, *Deng Xiaoping,* 575; Wu, "Hard Politics," 235–237.

53. Xinhua News Service, "十三大将提出政治体制改革方案" [Plans for political system reform to be announced at 13th Party Congress], JFJB, April 7, 1987.

54. ZZYWJ, 4:96–101; Vogel, *Deng Xiaoping,* 575; DXPNP, 2:1183.

55. Wu Wei, 中國 80 年代政治改革的台前幕後, 205–206, 223–225; Chen Yizi, "The Decision Process," 149–150.

56. ZZYWJ, 3:476–477, 237; Wu, "Hard Politics," 267–268. Zhao praised the bean elections during the civil war that allowed voters to select candidates by dropping beans into a bowl as an example of democracy in CCP history.

57. ZZYWJ, 3:476–477, 237; Wu Wei, 中國 80 年代政治改革的台前幕後, 226–229.

58. Leonard Silk, "Economic Scene; China's Debate on Reforms," *New York Times,* July 31, 1987.

59. "把政治体制改革提到日程上来 (社论)" [Putting political system reform on the agenda (editorial)], RMRB, July 1, 1987; Wu Wei, 中國 80 年代政治改革的台前幕後, 243. This version of the speech restored the section on the factory manager responsibility system that had been deleted at the time of first publication.

60. SWDXP-3, 247–248; DXPNP, 2:1191.

Chapter 10: Two Rounds of Applause

1. These paragraphs draw on Adi Ignatius, introduction to POS, ix–x; Jaime A. FlorCruz, "What Would China Look Like Today Had Zhao Ziyang Survived?" *ChinaFile,* August 18, 2016, www.chinafile.com/conversation/what-would-china-look -today-had-zhao-ziyang-survived; "General Secretary Zhao Meets the Press," *Beijing Review* 30, no. 45 (November 9–15, 1987): 12–15.

2. Wu Wei 吳偉, 中國 80 年代政治改革的台前幕後 [On stage and backstage: China's political reform in the 1980s] (Hong Kong: Xinshiji chuban ji chuanmei youxian gongsi, 2013), 249–252, 262–280; HYBSXNP, 2:1279.

3. Other important areas, such as foreign affairs, received scanty or no mention in Zhao's work report (Michel Oksenberg, "China's 13th Party Congress," *Problems of Communism* 36, no. 6 [November–December 1987]: 14).

4. DXPNP, 2:1213; LXNNP, 6:416; Richard Baum, *Burying Mao: Chinese Politics in the Age of Deng Xiaoping* (Princeton, NJ: Princeton University Press, 1994), 215–216. Oksenberg, "China's 13th Party Congress," 2, 5–7. After Hu Yaobang's purge, the

Politburo Standing Committee had ceased to function. Instead, Deng appointed a five-man committee of Bo Yibo, Hu Qili, Wan Li, Yang Shangkun, and Zhao Ziyang.

5.   POS, 199; Ruan Ming, *Deng Xiaoping: Chronicle of an Empire* (Boulder, CO: Westview, 1994), 185–186.

6.   Mao Zedong 毛泽东, 第一次郑州会议 [The first Zhengzhou conference], http://dangshi.people.com.cn/GB/151935/176588/176596/10556159.html; GSJTL, 7:306. This idea has clear parallels to the Stalinist two-stage theory.

7.   Su Shaozhi 苏绍智, "'社会主义初级阶段论'评析" [An analysis of the "initial stage of socialism theory"], *Modern China Studies* 4 (1998), http://www.modernchinastudies .org/cn/issues/past-issues/63-mcs-1998-issue-4/464-2011-12-29-18-13-29.html; Xue Muqiao, *China's Socialist Economy* (Beijing: Foreign Languages Press, 1981); Merle Goldman, *Sowing the Seeds of Democracy in China: Political Reform in the Deng Xiaoping Era* (Cambridge, MA: Harvard University Press, 1995), 245.

8.   GSJTL, 7:305; Joseph Fewsmith, *Dilemmas of Reform in China* (Armonk, NY: M. E. Sharpe, 1994), 69–70.

9.   Wu Wei, 中國 80 年代政治改革的台前幕後, 74–80; Chen Yizi 陈一谘, 陈一谘回忆录 [Memoirs of Chen Yizi] (Hong Kong: New Century Press, 2013), 383–386; ZZYYZZGG, 23–25, 32–33.

10.   ZZYWJ, 3:493; Wu Wei, 中國 80 年代政治改革的台前幕後, 98–99.

11.   POS, 205; ZZYWJ, 4:36. It was remarkably long term, designed to last 100 years (ZFLZQJ 1987, 288). This time frame has continued to be applied; see Richard Spencer, "China Promises Socialism for 100 Years," *Daily Telegraph*, February 28, 2007.

12.   Bao Tong 鲍彤, "社会主义的幼驹和资本主义的老马及其他" [The young horse of socialism, the old horse of capitalism, and other matters], RMRB, January 5, 1987; ZZYWJ, 4:14, 28–30; ZZYYZZGG, 312; Ezra Vogel, *Deng Xiaoping and the Transformation of China* (Cambridge, MA: Belknap Press of Harvard University Press, 2011), 586; Wu Wei, 中國 80 年代政治改革的台前幕後, 118–125.

13.   ZZYWJ, 4:47–48; DXPNP, 2:1173–1174; ZFLZQJ 1987, 112–114.

14.   Zhao Ziyang 赵紫阳, 沿着有中国特色的社会主义道路前进 [Advance along the road of socialism with Chinese characteristics] (Beijing: People's Publishing House, 1987), 27. The report defined the "main contradiction" in Chinese society as between "the backwardness of production" and "the people's growing material and cultural needs."

15.   Zhao Ziyang, 沿着有中国特色的社会主义道路前进, 7–14.

16.   Zhao Ziyang, 沿着有中国特色的社会主义道路前进, 2–6, 18, 22, 27–33; Oksenberg, "China's 13th Party Congress," 12–14; ZFLQZJ 1987, 335–342.

17.   Zhao Ziyang, 沿着有中国特色的社会主义道路前进, 16–18. When asked why he had not devoted more attention to foreign affairs, Zhao said, "If there were more about foreign affairs, I would have had to add 5,000 more Chinese characters. If I did that, it wouldn't have been possible for me to finish delivering the report in one morning" (*Beijing Review* 30, no. 45 [November 9–15, 1987]: 12).

18.   Wu Wei, "中共十三大报告起草过程述实" [Account of the drafting of the Thirteenth Party Congress work report], YHCQ 4 (2014): 47–48, 54–55; ZZYWJ, 4:202–216.

19.   Zhao Ziyang, 沿着有中国特色的社会主义道路前进, 34–48; Wu Wei, 中國 80 年代政治改革的台前幕後, 273–278.

20.   Oksenberg, "China's 13th Party Congress," 12.

21.   Zhao Ziyang, 沿着有中国特色的社会主义道路前进, 34–48.

22.   XCDT 57 (December 4, 1987): 130–141.

23.   XCDT 53 (November 6, 1987): 122–129; DXGWX, 3:1690–1696.

24.   ZZYWJ, 4:255–256. The existence of this secret protocol has long been known; Zhao confirmed it publicly in May 1989. However, prior to publication of the *Collected Works of Zhao Ziyang*, its precise text had not been available. On its appearance, see Julian Gewirtz, "Could Xi Jinping Stay in Power after He Retires? Here's How Deng Xiaoping Did It," *ChinaFile*, October 19, 2017.

25.   ZZYWJ, 4:256.

26.   Zhao Ziyang 趙紫陽, 改革歷程 [The course of reform] (Hong Kong: New Century Press, 2009), 231–232. Zhao's remarks were drafted in advance by Bao Tong.

27.   *Beijing Review* 30, no. 45 (November 9–15, 1987): 15.

28.   Even today, official summaries of the 13th Party Congress contain no negative language, whereas other congresses that endorsed ideas or promoted individuals subsequently removed—such as the 5th Congress of 1927 and the 10th Congress of 1973—contain critical language about their "errors" and "failures."

29.   Han Qingxiang, "New Thought for the New Era," *China Daily*, October 19, 2017.

Chapter 11: A Great Flood

1.   Wu Wei 吳偉, 中國 80 年代政治改革的台前幕後 [On stage and backstage: China's political reform in the 1980s] (Hong Kong: Xinshiji chuban ji chuanmei youxian gongsi, 2013), 287–288.

2.   Wu Guoguang, "Hard Politics with Soft Institutions: China's Political Reform, 1986–1989" (PhD diss., Princeton University, 1995), 221–222.

3.   ZFLZQJ 1987, 349–351.

4.   Wu Jinglian, "Economics and China's Economic Rise," in *The Chinese Economy: A New Transition,* ed. Masahiko Aoki and Jinglian Wu (New York: Palgrave Macmillan, 2012), 14.

5.   Wang Jian 王建, "走国际大循环经济发展战略的可能性及其要求" [Possibility and requirements of the great international cycle economic development strategy], in ZZYWJ, 3:294–299. See also Joseph Fewsmith, *Dilemmas of Reform in China* (Armonk, NY: M. E. Sharpe, 1994), 214–217.

6.   Gao Bowen 高伯文, "20世纪80年代沿海地区经济发展战略的选择及其效应" [The choice and effects of the 1980s' coastal development strategy], 当代中国史研究 [Research on contemporary Chinese history] 4 (2009): 92–100; Min Ye, *Diasporas and Foreign Direct Investment in China and India* (Cambridge: Cambridge University Press, 2014), 65–66.

7.   As discussed in Chapters 4 and 5, these countries used export-led growth to industrialize rapidly in the decades after World War II. See POS, 145–146; Fuh-Wen Tzeng, "The Political Economy of China's Coastal Development Strategy: A Preliminary Analysis," *Asian Survey* 31, no. 3 (March 1991): 273.

8.   ZFLZQJ 1987, 334–335.

9.   ZZYWJ, 4:305–306, 4:329–331; POS, 145–146.

10.   ZZYWJ, 4:342–343.

11.   ZZYWJ, 4:344–355, 4:363–365.

12.   DXPNP, 2:1223; ZZYWJ, 4:342.

13.   ZZYWJ, 4:366–368. The CCP's interactions with the World Economic Forum and its head, Klaus Schwab, dated to 1979, when Chinese Academy of Social Sciences Institute of World Economics director, Qian Junrui, led a Chinese delegation to the annual conference. Schwab visited China repeatedly and led delegations focused on modernizing enterprise management. He was honored for "outstanding contributions to forty years of China's reform and opening" in 2018.

14.   ZFLZQJ 1988, 86–88.

15.   "一件富有历史意义的大事: 论沿海地区经济发展战略" [A historic event: On the coastal development strategy], RMRB, May 19, 1988.

16.   XCDT 20 (June 10, 1988): 224–226.

17.   "成立中共中央政治体制改革研究室" [The establishment of the Central Research Office on Political System Reform], JFJB, February 28, 1988.

18.   Yan Xiu 严秀, "言论与兴衰" [Freedom of speech, prosperity and decline], RMRB, February 2, 1988.

19.   Yiu-chung Wong, *From Deng Xiaoping to Jiang Zemin: Two Decades of Political Reform in the PRC* (Lanham, MD: University Press of America, 2005), 102–103.

20.   Wang Huning 王沪宁, "转变中的中国政治文化结构" [Chinese political culture in transition], 复旦大学 (社会科学版) [Fudan University social science newsletter] 3 (March 1988): 55–64.

21.   Wu Wei, 中國 80 年代政治改革的台前幕後, 301–304; Xiao Guan'gen 萧关根, "江泽民在上海市人代会上说 党政机关及干部不得谋私和经商" [At the Shanghai Municipal People's Congress, Jiang Zemin prohibits party and government organs and cadres from engaging in business], RMRB, May 2, 1988. These proposals would be called the "two opennesses and one supervision."

22.   CYNP, 3:407–410.

23.   GSJTL, 1:410.

24.   ZFLZQJ 1988, 23–32, 47.

25.   ZFLZQJ 1988, 48; Tian Yuan 田源, "价格改革与产权制度转换" [Price reform and the changeover in the property rights system], JJYJ 2 (1988): 11–18.

26.   ZFLZQJ 1988, 90; POS, 146.

27.   ZFLZQJ 1988, 119.

28.   Chen Yizi 陈一谘, 陈一谘回忆录 [Memoirs of Chen Yizi] (Hong Kong: New Century Press, 2013), 505–509; Zhu Jiaming 朱嘉明 et al., "中国改革的道路" [The path of China's reform], November 3, 2012, http://www.21ccom.net/articles/zgyj/ggcx /article_2012110370279_2.html.

29.   Chen Yizi, 陈一谘回忆录, 509–512.

30.   Zhu Jiaming 朱嘉明, "智慧: 在于避免偏见" [Wisdom lies in refraining from bias], 读书 [Reading] 6 (1988): 120.

31.   Guo Shuqing 郭树清, "经济改革中的政策配合问题" [What policies suit reforms best], 管理世界 [Management world] 1 (1989): 75–76.

32.   Suisheng Zhao, *A Nation-State by Construction: Dynamics of Modern Chinese Nationalism* (Stanford, CA: Stanford University Press, 2004), 114; Rana Mitter, *Forgotten Ally: China's World War II, 1937–1945* (Boston: Houghton Mifflin Harcourt, 2013), 272–273.

33.   Dong Jianmin 董建民 and Liu Ren 刘仁, "近年来我国通货膨胀问题讨论综述" [Summary of the discussion on the recent problem of inflation in our country], 财经科学 [Finance and economics] 2 (1989): 63, 66.

34.   Cheng Xiaonong, "Decision and Miscarriage: Radical Price Reform in the Summer of 1988," in Carol Lee Hamrin and Suisheng Zhao, eds., *Decision-Making in Deng's China: Perspectives from Insiders* (Armonk, NY: M. E. Sharpe, 1995), 190. Li Peng was still consulting with Chen Yun with some regularity; they met on May 28, 1988 (CYNP, 3:413).

35.   Ezra Vogel, *Deng Xiaoping and the Transformation of China* (Cambridge, MA: Belknap Press of Harvard University Press, 2011), 600.

36.   ZFLZQJ 1988, 138–141.

37.   ZFLZQJ 1988, 164–165.

38.   ZZYWJ, 4:445–447.

39.   Mi Ling Tsui, ed., *China: Presenting River Elegy,* Deep Dish TV, https://archive.org/details/ddtv_40_china_presenting_river_elegy/.

40.   Tsui, *China.*

41.   Rana Mitter, *A Bitter Revolution: China's Struggle with the Modern World* (Oxford: Oxford University Press, 2004), 264; Jing Wang, *High Culture Fever: Politics, Aesthetics, and Ideology in Deng's China* (Berkeley: University of California Press, 1996), 118–136.

42.   The film also underscored intellectuals' frustrations with their status and compensation (Wu, "Hard Politics," 295).

43.   Su Xiaokang and Wang Luxiang, *Deathsong of the River: A Reader's Guide to the Chinese TV Series Heshang,* trans. Richard W. Bodman and Pin P. Wan (Ithaca, NY: East Asia Program, Cornell University, 1991), 182.

44.   Su and Wang, *Deathsong,* 172–173, 240.

45.   Su and Wang, *Deathsong,* 172–173, 176, 266, 268.

46.   GSJTL, 4:333; ZHDMM, 307–308; Yin Ming 尹明, "朱重的'河殇'" [Zhu Zhong's "River Elegy"], JFJB, August 14, 1988.

47.   Wu Wei, 中國 80 年代政治改革的台前幕後, 305–310.

48.   XCDT 12 (April 5, 1988): 202–206; XCDT 18 (June 1, 1988): 214–217.

49.   XCDT 20 (June 10, 1988): 218–223.

50.   ZFLZQJ 1988, 122–128.

51.   Torch Program, "Promoting Innovation and High-Tech Industrialization," 2014, www.chinatorch.gov.cn/english/xhtml/Program.html; Denis Fred Simon, "China's Drive to Close the Technological Gap: S&T Reform and the Imperative to Catch Up," *China Quarterly*, no. 119 (September 1989): 622, 624; ZZYWJ, 4:400.

52.   Wu Wei, 中國 80 年代政治改革的台前幕後, 316, 321, 331–336.

53.   Wu Wei, 中國 80 年代政治改革的台前幕後, 339–342; Wang Guixiu and Zhu Manliang, "A Research and Investigative Report on the Pioneering Implementation of a Civil Service System in the Shenzhen Special Economic Zone," *Chinese Law and Government* 23, no. 4 (Winter 1990–1991): 85–97; Hongying Wang, "Zhao Ziyang's Visions: Victims of Political Turmoil or Seeds of a Democratic Future?" in *Zhao Ziyang and China's Political Future*, ed. Wu Guoguang and Helen Lansdowne (London: Routledge, 2012), 17–21.

54.   Zhiyong Lan, "Understanding China's Administrative Reform in Context," *Public Administration Quarterly* 24, no. 4 (Winter 2001); Wu Wei, 中國 80 年代政治改革的台前幕後, 323–331, 353–360.

55.   Wu Wei, 中國 80 年代政治改革的台前幕後, 306, 312–314, 413–414.

56.   Wu, "Hard Politics," 70; Wu Wei, 中國 80 年代政治改革的台前幕後, 318–319.

57.   Du Guang 杜光, "回忆20年前的中国政治体制改革研究会" [Recalling the Political System Reform Research Society 20 years ago], December 14, 2008, *Boxun*, www.boxun.com/news/gb/z_special/2008/12/200812142206.shtml; Gao Fang 高放, "中国政治体制改革的回顾与展望" [Recollection and outlook for China's political system reform], January 2010, 胡耀邦史料信息网 [Online Repository of Historical Materials on Hu Yaobang], at http://www.hybsl.cn/beijingcankao/beijingfenxi/2018-06-05/67727.html.

58.   Wu Wei, 中國 80 年代政治改革的台前幕後, 366; DXPNP, 2:1229. Decades later, the participants in these events were still debating how Deng became so focused on price reforms; he does not appear to have been influenced by any particular proposal or report. "Perhaps Deng also felt at that time that his remaining time alive was limited," speculated one participant at a 2011 seminar. See Qiao Fu 樵夫, "赵紫阳同志谈价格改革" [Comrade Zhao Ziyang on price reform], 赵紫阳生平和思想研究 [Research on Zhao Ziyang's life and thought] 13 (April 1, 2009): 1–11, held in the Fairbank Collection, Fung Library, Harvard University.

59.   ZZYWJ, 4:435, 4:438–441; ZFLZQJ 1988, 143.

60.   SWDXP-3, 257–258; DXPNP, 2:1232–1233.

61.   ZZYWJ, 4:445–447; ZFLZQJ 1988, 154–155.

62.   DXPNP, 2:1240. See also Vogel, *Deng Xiaoping*, 469; ZZYYZZGG, 526–528.

63.   ZFLZQJ 1988, 167.

64.   Cheng Xiaonong, "Decision and Miscarriage: Radical Price Reform in the Summer of 1988," in *Decision-Making in Deng's China: Perspectives from Insiders,* ed. Carol Lee Hamrin and Suisheng Zhao (Armonk, NY: M. E. Sharpe, 1995), 193–194; Wu Jinglian and Bruce Reynolds, "Choosing a Strategy for China's Economic Reform," *American Economic Review* 78, no. 2 (1988): 461–466; Isabella Weber, *How China Escaped Shock Therapy* (London: Routledge, 2021), 247–252; Fewsmith, *Dilemmas of Reform,* 224.

65.   Cheng Xiaonong, "Decision and Miscarriage," 194. See also Wu Wei, 中國 80 年代政治改革的台前幕後, 371–373; POS, 231, 236.

66.   ZZYWJ, 4:483; Li Peng 李鹏, 李鹏经济日记: 市场与调控 (征求意见稿) [Li Peng's economic diary: Market and regulation (draft for comment)], held in the Fairbank Collection, Fung Library, Harvard University, 612.

67.   ZFLZQJ 1988, 191–193; 李鹏经济日记, 613–616.

68.   ZFLZQJ 1988, 198–221; CYNP, 3:414.

69.   ZZYYZZGG, 526, 530; DXPNP, 1243; 李鹏经济日记, 617–619.

70.   ZFLZQJ 1988, 221; Wu Wei, 中國 80 年代政治改革的台前幕後, 377–378.

71.   ZFLZQJ 1988, 221–224; ZZYYZZGG, 529.

72.   Wu Wei, 中國 80 年代政治改革的台前幕後, 378; "Panic Buying Clears Shelves in Chinese City," *Los Angeles Times,* August 16, 1988, http://articles.latimes.com/1988 -08-16/news/mn-711_1_bank-run.

73.   Xiao Huanhuan 肖欢欢 and Ni Ming 倪明, "1988年9月初武汉市民抢购金饰" [Wuhan residents rush to purchase gold jewelry in early September 1988], 广州日报 [Guangzhou daily], June 7, 2008.

74.   Zeng Jie 曾捷, dir., 激荡三十年·1978–2008 [The vibrant thirty years: 1978–2008], episode 11, www.youtube.com/watch?v=XaFuWneg3ok&feature=youtu.be&t=5m35s.

75.   Liu Binyan, *China's Crisis, China's Hope* (Cambridge, MA: Harvard University Press, 1990), 5; "China Presses Curbs on Spending," Reuters, June 15, 1988.

76.   "贯彻三中全会精神增强改革信心" [Acting in the spirit of the Third Plenary Session of the 13th Central Committee and strengthening confidence in the reform], 中国经济体制改革 [China's economic system reform] 36, no. 12 (December 23, 1988): 6–9.

77.   ZFLZQJ 1988, 227–230; CYNP, 3:414–415; Wu Wei, 中國 80 年代政治改革的台前 幕後, 381; 李鹏经济日记, 621–626.

78.   Vogel, *Deng Xiaoping,* 470.

79.   ZZYWJ, 4:484–485.

80.   POS, 227; 李鹏经济日记, 627; DXPNP, 2:1244.

81.   ZFLZQJ 1988, 231–234; 李鹏经济日记, 632.

82.   Wu Wei, 中國 80 年代政治改革的台前幕後, 388–389.

83.   ZFLZQJ 1988, 236–242; DXPNP, 1247–1248; Wu Wei, 中國 80 年代政治改革的台前幕後, 380–383.

84.   DXPNP, 2:1249–1250.

85.   ZFLZQJ 1988, 243, 246; ZZYWJ, 4:528–538; 李鹏经济日记, 638–642.

86.   王震传 [Biography of Wang Zhen] (Beijing: Contemporary China Press, 2001), 2:272–273; ZHDMM, 307–308.

87.   ZFLZQJ 1988, 255; Wu Wei, 中國 80 年代政治改革的台前幕後, 316–321.

88.   POS, 222, 233–236.

89.   Chen Yizi, 陈一谘回忆录, 515.

90.   "China: Position of Zhao Ziyang," UK National Archives, PREM19 / 2597 f187.

91.   Julian Gewirtz, "The Futurists of Beijing: Alvin Toffler, Zhao Ziyang, and China's 'New Technological Revolution,' 1979–1991," *Journal of Asian Studies* 78, no. 1 (February 2019): 132–133.

92.   On Friedman in China, see Julian Gewirtz, *Unlikely Partners: Chinese Reformers, Western Economists, and the Making of Global China* (Cambridge, MA: Harvard University Press, 2017), 209–214.

93.   ZZYWJ, 4:510–518; Zhang Liang 张亮, "赵紫阳会见弗里德曼时说 中国已大体具备推行股份制条件" [When meeting with Friedman, Zhao Ziyang states that China has largely implemented the conditions for a joint-stock system], RMRB, September 20, 1988.

94.   Zhang Liang, "赵紫阳会见弗里德曼时说 中国已大体具备推行股份制条件"; GSJTL, 4:206–207, 221; Steven N. Cheung, "Deng Xiaoping's Great Transformation," *Contemporary Economic Policy* 16, no. 2 (April 1998): 125–135.

95.   Fewsmith, *Dilemmas of Reform*, 231.

96.   CYNP, 3:471–472; ZFLZQJ 1988, 278–281; DXPNP, 2:1254.

97.   Xue Muqiao 薛暮桥, 薛暮桥回忆录 [Memoirs of Xue Muqiao] (Tianjin: Tianjin People's Press, 2006), 326.

98.   ZFLZQJ 1988, 286–296; ZZYWJ, 4:561–568.

99.   On December 3, Zhao called for "taking a step forward to implement the coastal development strategy during the period of economic retrenchment" (ZZYWJ, 4:569–571).

Chapter 12: We Came Too Late

1. Chris Buckley, "Q&A: Wu Wei Reflects on Reform, Now and in the 1980s," *New York Times*, January 12, 2014.

2. "Inflation Hits Peak in China," Reuters, November 29, 1988.

3. Suzanne Ogden, Kathleen Hartford, Nancy Sullivan, and David Zweig, eds., *China's Search for Democracy: The Student and Mass Movement of 1989* (Armonk, NY: M. E. Sharpe, 1992), 55–58.

4. Ren Yongfa 任永发, "一个银行副行长挪用公款七百二十六万元犯罪始末" [The case of a bank vice president who embezzled 7.26 million yuan in public funds], 党建 [Party building] 6 (1989): 18.

5. XCJB 16, May 15, 1989, in ZWCBWFWZX 27:43–45, 324–333.

6. Jane Macartney, "China Cracks Down on Corruption," United Press International, October 3, 1988; Richard Baum, *Burying Mao: Chinese Politics in the Age of Deng Xiaoping* (Princeton, NJ: Princeton University Press, 1994), 261.

7. ZZYWJ, 4:544–545, 4:608–609; Wu Guoguang, "Hard Politics with Soft Institutions: China's Political Reform, 1986–1989" (PhD diss., Princeton University, 1995), 74.

8. Ogden et al., *China's Search*, 54–55.

9. Xu Jian 徐建, "1988年深圳特区的政改方案" [The 1988 political reform plan of the Shenzhen SEZ], YHCQ 6 (2013), http://www.yhcqw.com/34/9170.html.

10. Ogden et al., *China's Search*, 31–32; Scott Kennedy, "The Stone Group: State Client or Market Pathbreaker?" *China Quarterly* 152 (December 1997): 761–762.

11. Michael J. Sullivan, "The 1988–89 Nanjing Anti-African Protests: Racial Nationalism or National Racism?" *China Quarterly* 138 (June 1994): 438, 450.

12. Jeremy Brown, *June Fourth: The Tiananmen Protests and Beijing Massacre of 1989* (Cambridge: Cambridge University Press, 2021), 156–158.

13. XCDT 31 (September 1, 1988): 271–276; XCDT 41 (December 15, 1988): 328–346.

14. DXPSW-3 273; DXPNP, 2:1256.

15. Zuoyue Wang, "Controlled Exchanges: Public-Private Hybridity, Transnational Networking, and Knowledge Circulation in U.S.-China Scientific Discourse on Nuclear Arms Control," in *How Knowledge Moves: Writing the Transnational History of Science and Technology,* ed. John Krige (Chicago: University of Chicago Press, 2019), 368–409; Eleonora Masini, J. Dator, and S. Rodgers, eds., *Futures of Development: Selections from the Tenth World Conference of the WFSF* (Paris: Future-oriented Studies Programme, 1991).

16. Su Shaozhi, *Marxism and Reform in China* (Nottingham, UK: Spokesman, 1993), 20–23.

17. Fang Lizhi, "China's Despair and China's Hope," trans. Perry Link, *New York Review of Books,* February 2, 1989.

18. Yiu-chung Wong, *From Deng Xiaoping to Jiang Zemin: Two Decades of Political Reform in the PRC* (Lanham, MD: University Press of America, 2005), 175; H. Lyman Miller, "Xu Liangying and He Zuoxiu: Divergent Responses to Physics and Politics in the Post-Mao Period," *Historical Studies in the Physical and Biological Sciences* 30, no. 1 (1999): 102.

19. Han Minzhu and Sheng Hua, eds., *Cries for Democracy: Writings and Speeches from the Chinese Democracy Movement* (Princeton, NJ: Princeton University Press, 1990), 17.

20. *China/Avant-Garde Exhibition* (Nanning: Guangxi People's Publishing House, 1989), https://aaa.org.hk/en/collection/search/archive/lu-peng-archive-1989-china-avantgarde-exhibition/object/chinaavant-garde-exhibition-catalogue; Xiao Lu, *Dialogue* (1989), Museum of Modern Art, https://www.moma.org/collection/works/114901.

21. DXPNP, 2:1262; Wu Wei 吳偉, 中國 80 年代政治改革的台前幕後 [On stage and backstage: China's political reform in the 1980s] (Hong Kong: Xinshiji chuban ji chuanmei youxian gongsi, 2013), 414, 417–419. Wu argues that these discussions had made some progress by April 1989, but after the crackdown, the leadership's view of "multiparty cooperation" shifted dramatically.

22. Wen Yuan 文远 and Xiao Chang 晓畅, "工会改革纲领要符合职 工群众的要求: 访中央政治体制改革研究室研究员陈小鲁" [The union reform program must adhere to workers' requirements: Interview with Central Research Office for Political System Reform member Chen Xiaolu], 中国劳动关系学院学报 [Journal of China University of Labor Relations] 1 (1989): 23–24.

23. Susan Finder, "Like Throwing an Egg against a Stone? Administrative Litigation in the People's Republic of China," *Journal of Chinese Law* 3, no. 1 (1989): 1–28.

24. "Letter to Paul Schroeder," April 9, 1989, Field Offices-China-General, 1979–1989, Office Files of William Carmichael, Box 3, Folder 24, Ford Foundation Papers; Hu Jiwei, 胡绩伟自述 [Hu Jiwei in his own words], 4 vols. (Hong Kong: Excellent Culture Press, 2006), 4:331–332.

25. ZZYWJ, 4:626, 634–636, 641; Joseph Fewsmith, *Dilemmas of Reform in China* (Armonk, NY: M. E. Sharpe, 1994), 230–231.

26. Ruan Ming, *Deng Xiaoping: Chronicle of an Empire* (Boulder, CO: Westview, 1994), 204–205; Chen Yizi 陈一谘, 陈一谘回忆录 [Memoirs of Chen Yizi] (Hong Kong: New

Century Press, 2013), 533–537; Liu Jun 刘军 and Li Lin 李林, eds., 新权威主义: 对改革理论纲领的论争 [Neo-authoritarianism: Debating the reform theory program] (Beijing: Beijing School of Economics Press, 1989).

27.   Wu Jiaxiang 吴稼祥, "新权威主义述评" [A review of neo-authoritarianism], SJJJDB, January 16, 1989; X. L. Ding, *The Decline of Communism in China: Legitimacy Crisis, 1977–1989* (Cambridge: Cambridge University Press, 2006), 175; Ma Shu Yun, "The Rise and Fall of Neo-authoritarianism in China," *China Information* 5, no. 3 (1990): 1. See also Wu Jiaxiang, 中南海日記 [Zhongnanhai diary] (Carle Place, NY: Mirror Publishing House, 2002), which ends in August 1987; Steven N. S. Cheung 張五常, "假若趙紫陽是個獨裁者" [If Zhao Ziyang were a dictator], 香港經濟日報 [Hong Kong economic daily], November 2, 1988; Samuel P. Huntington, 变化社会中的政治秩序 [Political order in changing societies], trans. Wang Guanghua 王冠华 et al. (Beijing: Sanlian shudian, 1988).

28.   Jie Li, "Gorbachev's *Glasnost* and the Debate on Chinese Socialism among Chinese Sovietologists, 1985–1999," *Journal of the British Association for Chinese Studies* 6 (November 2016): 36.

29.   Barry Sautman, "Sirens of the Strongman: Neo-authoritarianism in Recent Chinese Political Theory," *China Quarterly* 129 (March 1992): 72–102. See also Ryan Mitchell, "The Decision for Order: Chinese Receptions of Carl Schmitt since 1929," *Journal of Law and International Affairs* 8, no. 1 (2020): 183–263.

30.   Yang Jisheng, "Second Visit to Zhao Ziyang," *Chinese Law & Government* 38, no. 3 (May / June 2005): 29–30; Ruan Ming, *Chronicle of an Empire*, 194; DXPNP, 2:1268. Yang and Ruan use slightly different language. The dating is somewhat more complex. Zhao erroneously states that the conversation took place in late 1988, whereas Ruan Ming gives a date of March 6. However, Deng and Zhao discussed political stability on March 4, a date so close to Ruan's that it is the most plausible date for this conversation. However, this is further complicated by the fact that Wu Wei insists that DXPNP is incorrect and the meeting occurred on March 3 (Wu Wei, 中國 80 年代政治改革的台前幕後, 429–431).

31.   "Memorandum of Conversation between George H. W. Bush and Zhao Ziyang," February 26, 1989, History and Public Policy Program Digital Archive, Memcons and Telcons, George Bush Presidential Library and Museum, http://digitalarchive.wilsoncenter.org/document/133956.

32.   Wu Wei, 中國 80 年代政治改革的台前幕後, 431.

33.   CYNP, 3:420.

34.   Sautman, "Sirens"; Ma Shu Yun, "Rise and Fall of Neo-authoritarianism," 9; Qin Xiaoying, "Escaping from a Historical Vicious Cycle," *Chinese Sociology and Anthropology* 23, no. 4 (Summer 1991): 7–30.

35.   Pei Minxin 裴敏欣, "權威主義說的始作俑者亨廷頓談權威主義: 與哈佛大學政治系博士研究生裴敏欣的對話" [Huntington on his theory of authoritarianism: A dialogue with Pei Minxin, PhD student in political science at Harvard], SJJJDB, March 27, 1989. See also "China, Criticism," Samuel Huntington Papers, Harvard University Archives, HUM 178-26-30; and Lucian Pye, "Political Science and the Crisis of Authoritarianism," *American Political Science Review* 84, no. 1 (March 1990): 17.

36.   NCXB 204 (February 15, 1989): 28–30.

37.   Deng Xiaoping, "China Will Tolerate No Disturbances," March 4, 1989, in SWDXP-3, 279–280.

38.   Wu Wei, 中國 80 年代政治改革的台前幕後, 431–435.

39.   "Note about the Meeting between Hu Qili and Herbert Naumann," April 6, 1989, History and Public Policy Program Digital Archive, SAPMO-BA, DY 30, 2437, http://digitalarchive.wilsoncenter.org/document/122030.

40.   Zhang Lifan 章立凡, "胡耀邦治喪手记" [Notes on Hu Yaobang's funeral], YHCQ 6 (2012), http://www.yhcqw.com/34/8805.html.

41.   LPLSRJ, April 15, April 17. Given the many different editions of this document, I cite by date rather than page number. I quote from the edition available online at https://chinadigitaltimes.net/chinese/538060.html.

42.   Zhang Lifan, "胡耀邦治喪手记."

43.   Ezra Vogel, *Deng Xiaoping and the Transformation of China* (Cambridge, MA: Belknap Press of Harvard University Press, 2011), 595–639.

44.   "Document of 1989: Seven-Point Petition," Standoff at Tiananmen, April 18, 2009, www.standoffattiananmen.com/2009/04/document-of-1989-seven-point-petition.html?m=1.

45.   ZZYWJ, 4:652; GSJTL, 1:120; Wu Wei, 中國 80 年代政治改革的台前幕後, 442. On Deng's hair, see Zhang Lifan, "胡耀邦治喪手记."

46.   Philip J. Cunningham, *Tiananmen Moon: Inside the Chinese Student Uprising of 1989* (Lanham, MD: Rowman & Littlefield, 2009); Andrew J. Nathan, *China's Crisis: Dilemmas of Reform and Prospects for Democracy* (New York: Columbia University Press, 1990); ZFLZQJ 1989, 31–40, 50–52; Ian Johnson, "Ghosts of Tiananmen Square," *New York Review of Books,* June 5, 2014; Andrew Walder and Xiaoxia Gong, "Workers in the Tiananmen Protests: The Politics of BWAF," *Australian Journal of Chinese Affairs* 29 (January 1993): 1–29; Denise Chong, *Egg on Mao: The Story of an Ordinary Man Who Defaced an Icon and Unmasked a Dictatorship* (Berkeley, CA: Counterpoint, 2009).

47.   Yasheng Huang, "The Origins of China's Pro-Democracy Movement and the Government's Response: A Tale of Two Reforms," *Fletcher Forum* 14, no. 1 (Winter 1990): 32.

48.   DXPNP, 2:1271. There is evidence that leaders of the student movement were directly inspired by what they saw in Eastern Europe. See Wang Dan, "The Star of Hope Rises in Eastern Europe," in Ogden et al., *China's Search*, 46–47.

49.   M. E. Sarotte, "China's Fear of Contagion: Tiananmen Square and the Power of the European Example," *International Security* 37, no. 2 (Fall 2012): 161, 171.

50.   POS, 4–9. This meeting is not recorded in DXPNP.

51.   ZZYWJ, 4:644–646; POS, 6; Wu Wei, 中國 80 年代政治改革的台前幕後, 447–448. For insightful comments on why Zhao traveled to North Korea, see Brown, *June Fourth*, 91–93.

52.   This comment is quoted in LPLSRJ, April 25; DXPNP, 2:1273. Chen Xitong claims that he did not exaggerate the situation in Beijing and that Deng would not have been easily manipulated by such reports even if he had (Yao Jianfu 姚監復, ed., 陳希同親述: 眾口鑠金難鑠真 [Conversations with Chen Xitong] [Hong Kong: New Century Press, 2012], interview no. 1, 30–31). See also Zhang Liang, comp., *The Tiananmen Papers*, ed. Andrew J. Nathan and Perry Link (New York: Public Affairs, 2001), 71–74. I use *Tiananmen Papers* sparingly to confirm or elaborate on facts recorded elsewhere. Although they are well edited, vivid, and useful, this decision reflects what Vogel calls "questions [that] have been raised about the authenticity" of some of their contents (Vogel, *Deng Xiaoping*, 831). See Alfred L. Chan, with a rejoinder by Andrew J. Nathan, "The Tiananmen Papers Revisited," *China Quarterly* 177 (March 2004): 190–214.

53.   "必须旗帜鲜明地反对动乱" [It is necessary to take a clear-cut stand against the disturbances], RMRB, April 26, 1989; LPLSRJ, April 25; DXPNP, 2:1272–1274.

54.   Nicholas D. Kristof, "150,000 March in Defiance of Beijing," *New York Times*, April 28, 1989.

55.   "十支队司令部, 制乱平暴期间人民日报社的安全警卫" [10th Detachment Command, security of RMRB amid the riots], in HGYFS, in ZWCBWFWZX 27:26, 152.

56.   Ogden et al., *China's Search*, 119.

57.   Cheng Li and Lynn T. White III, "China's Technocratic Movement and the World Economic Herald," *Modern China* 17, no. 3 (July 1991): 352, 379; *Tiananmen Papers*, 91–95; see also LPLSRJ, April 26; Chen Yizi, 陈一谘回忆录, 574–577. Jiang subsequently briefed the Politburo on his handling of this matter (LPLSRJ, May 10).

58.   POS, 16–18; Wu Wei, 中國 80 年代政治改革的台前幕後, 457, 459–460, 464–465.

59.   ZZYWJ, 4:657–662; POS, 16.

60.   Xinhua News Service, "现在最需要的是冷静、理智、克制、秩序, 在民主和法制的轨道上解决问题" [What is needed most now is calm, reason, restraint, order, and solving problems on the path of democracy and rule of law], JFJB, May 5, 1989; Dingxin Zhao, *The Power of Tiananmen: State-Society Relations and the 1989 Beijing Student Movement* (Chicago: University of Chicago Press, 2001), 225–226; Wu Wei, 中國 80 年代政治改革的台前幕後, 469.

61.   CYNP, 3:423; Chen Yizi, 陈一谘回忆录, 582; Vogel, *Deng Xiaoping*, 608–609.

62.   LPLSRJ, May 4; Minzhu Han and Sheng Hua, eds., *Cries for Democracy: Writings and Speeches from the Chinese Democracy Movement* (Princeton, NJ: Princeton University Press, 1990), 134–135.

63.   Jackie Sheehan, *Chinese Workers: A New History* (London: Routledge, 1998), 211.

64.   LPLSRJ, May 4.

65.   LPLSRJ, May 8, May 11; Wu Wei, 中國 80 年代政治改革的台前幕後, 482–485; *Tiananmen Papers*, 126–138.

66.   ZHDMM, 283; Yao Jianfu, 陳希同親述.

67.   LPLSRJ, May 11.

68.   Buckley, "Q&A."

69.   Ogden et al., *China's Search*, 202; Lei Guang, "Elusive Democracy: Conceptual Change and the Chinese Democracy Movement, 1978–79 to 1989," *Modern China* 22, no. 4 (October 1996): 435.

70.   POS, 21; DXPNP, 2:1275; LPLSRJ, May 13. Li Peng was told the details about Deng's complaints by Yang Shangkun. See also *Tiananmen Papers*, 147–151.

71.   Wu Wei, 中國 80 年代政治改革的台前幕後, 494–498, 621–623; "Memorandum of Conversation: President Bush's Meeting with Premier Li Peng," February 26, 1989, George H. W. Bush Presidential Library, 19–20.

72.   LPLSRJ, May 15.

73.   DXPNP, 2:1275–1276.

74.   "Excerpts from Conversation between Mikhail Gorbachev and Zhao Ziyang," May 16, 1989, in Mikhail Gorbachev, *Zhizn' i Reformy* (Moscow: Novosti, 1995), 2:441–445, History and Public Policy Program Digital Archive, http://digitalarchive.wilsoncenter.org/document/119290.

75.   "Excerpts from the Conversation between Mikhail Gorbachev and Rajiv Gandhi," July 15, 1989, trans. and comp. Sergey Radchenko, History and Public Policy Program Digital Archive, Archive of the Gorbachev Foundation, http://digitalarchive.wilsoncenter

.org/document/119291. Gorbachev's relative youth, political reform credentials, and especially the partly free March 1989 Soviet elections for the Congress of People's Deputies inspired the students, some of whom even petitioned to meet Gorbachev while he was in Beijing (Sergey Radchenko, "'I Do Not Want Red Square to Look Like Tiananmen Square,'" *Foreign Policy,* June 4, 2014).

76.   Wu Wei, 中國 80 年代政治改革的台前幕後, 499, 505–506.

77.   Ogden et al., *China's Search,* 225; Yan Jiaqi, *Toward a Democratic China,* trans. David S. K. Hong and Denis C. Mair (Honolulu: University of Hawai'i Press, 1992), 154–155.

78.   Nicholas D. Kristof, "Crowds in Street Ask Deng's Ouster," *New York Times,* May 18, 1989.

79.   POS, 11; Yang Jisheng, "First Visit to Zhao Ziyang," *Chinese Law & Government* 38, no. 3 (2005): 9–10; *Tiananmen Papers,* 184–190; DXPNP, 2:1276–1277. Zhao and Bao Tong drafted a resignation letter after this meeting (Wu Wei, 中國 80 年代政治改革的台前幕後, 514). *The Tiananmen Papers* report a subsequent Politburo Standing Committee meeting that day that voted on the martial law decision, though other accounts dispute this (*Tiananmen Papers,* 191–193). That evening, Bao Tong held an emergency CROPSR meeting, where he allegedly revealed the decision to impose martial law.

80.   LPLSRJ, May 18.

81.   "就治理整顿深化改革发展生产和当前形势等问题 李鹏同首钢职工座谈" [Rectifying administration, deepening reform, developing production, the present situation and other issues: Discussion with Li Peng and Capital Iron and Steel workers], RMRB, May 15, 1989; Walder and Gong, "Workers in the Tiananmen Protests," 16–17; Ogden et al., *China's Search,* 255–256.

82.   "25 Years Ago: Zhao Ziyang: 'We Came Too Late,'" *China Digital Times,* May 19, 2014. Zhao's speech is available online at https://www.youtube.com/watch?v=JRshth1Nyb4.

83.   "赵紫阳李鹏昨晨到天安门广场看望绝食请愿的部分高校学生 赵总书记恳切希望同学们健康地活着看到中国实现四化" [At Tiananmen Square yesterday morning, Zhao Ziyang and Li Peng visited students on hunger strike; General Secretary Zhao sincerely hopes students will stay healthy and live to see China realize the Four Modernizations], RMRB, May 20, 1989.

84.   Michel Oksenberg, Lawrence R. Sullivan, and Marc Lambert, eds., *Beijing Spring 1989: Confrontation and Conflict, The Basic Documents* (Armonk, NY: M. E. Sharpe, 1990), 287–288.

85.   Ruan Ming, *Chronicle of an Empire,* 254; Chen Yizi, 陈一谘回忆录, 601–604; Yao Jianfu, 陳希同親述.

86.   Andrew Jacobs and Chris Buckley, "Tales of Army Discord Show Tiananmen Square in a New Light," *New York Times*, June 2, 2014; Joseph Torigian, "Prestige, Manipulation, and Coercion: Elite Power Struggles and the Fate of Three Revolutions" (PhD diss., MIT, 2016), 533–544.

87.   "Li Peng Delivers Important Speech on Behalf of Party Central Committee and State Council," Beijing Television Service, May 19–20, 1989, FBIS-CHI, May 22, 1989, 9–13; Wang Fang 王芳, 王芳回忆录 [Memoirs of Wang Fang] (Hangzhou: Zhejiang People's Publishing House, 2006), 369.

88.   DXPNP, 2:1277; LPLSRJ, May 21; Yang, "Second Visit," 32; see also *Tiananmen Papers*, 257–264.

89.   Wu Wei, 中國 80 年代政治改革的台前幕後, 535.

90.   Ogden et al., *China's Search*, 261, 272–273.

Chapter 13: Political Crackdown and Narrative Crisis

1.   Andreas Glaeser, *Political Epistemics: The Secret Police, The Opposition, and the End of East German Socialism* (Chicago: University of Chicago Press, 2010), xvi.

2.   Gao Hua, *How the Red Sun Rose: The Origin and Development of the Yan'an Rectification Movement, 1930–1945*, trans. Stacy Mosher and Guo Jian (Hong Kong: Chinese University Press, 2019); Frederick C. Teiwes, *Politics and Purges in China: Rectification and the Decline of Party Norms, 1950–1965* (White Plains, NY: M. E. Sharpe, 1979); Jeremy Brown, *June Fourth: The Tiananmen Protests and Beijing Massacre of 1989* (Cambridge: Cambridge University Press, 2021), 218–242.

3.   Li Peng 李鹏, 关于赵紫阳同志在反党反社会主义的动乱中所犯错误的报告 [Report on Comrade Zhao Ziyang's mistakes in the anti-party, anti-socialist turmoil], June 24, 1989, http://www.tiananmenduizhi.com/2015/06/blog-post_23.html.

4.   Song Keda 宋克达, "深入学习理解军委邓主席在接见首都戒严部队军以上干部时的讲话" [Deepen the study and understanding of CMC Chairman Deng's speech delivered to martial law unit cadres in the capital] (June 21, 1989), in XCJB, 334–339.

5.   As Jeffrey Wasserstrom argues, there is "no simple way to separate myth from history when dealing with the protests and repression of 1989." Jeffrey Wasserstrom, "History, Myths, and Tales of Tiananmen," in *Popular Protest and Political Culture in Modern China*, ed. Jeffrey Wasserstrom and Elizabeth J. Perry (Boulder, CO: Westview, 1994), 275. See also Louisa Lim, *The People's Republic of Amnesia: Tiananmen Revisited* (Oxford: Oxford University Press, 2014), 6. Important works on 1989 include Timothy Brook, *Quelling the People: The Military Suppression of the Beijing Democracy Movement* (Stanford, CA: Stanford University Press, 1999); Philip J. Cunningham, *Tiananmen*

Moon: Inside the Chinese Student Uprising of 1989 (New York: Rowman & Littlefield, 2009); Andrew J. Nathan, *China's Crisis: Dilemmas of Reform and Prospects for Democracy* (New York: Columbia University Press, 1990); Craig Calhoun, *Neither Gods nor Emperors: Students and the Struggle for Democracy in China* (Berkeley: University of California Press, 1997); and Wu Renhua's three important books, most recently 六四事件全程實錄 [The full record of the June Fourth incident] (Taipei: Zhenxiang Press, 2014).

6.　　　Robin Munro, "Who Died in Beijing, and Why," *The Nation* 250, no. 23 (June 11, 1990): 811–822; Andrew Walder and Xiaoxia Gong, "Workers in the Tiananmen Protests: The Politics of BWAF," *Australian Journal of Chinese Affairs,* no. 29 (January 1993): 9–10; Anita Chan, "China's Long Winter," *Monthly Review* 41, no. 8 (January 1990): 1–14.

7.　　　LPLSRJ, May 24, 1989.

8.　　　LXNNP, 6:481; Lu Zhichao 卢之超, 海边忆往: 围绕中南海的回忆与思考 [Seaside recollections: Memories and reflections around Zhongnanhai] (China: n.p., 2008), 173. Held in the Fairbank Collection, Fung Library, Harvard University.

9.　　　POS, 37–38; Wu Wei 吳偉, 中國 80 年代政治改革的台前幕後 [On stage and backstage: China's political reform in the 1980s] (Hong Kong: Xinshiji chuban ji chuanmei youxian gongsi, 2013), 541–544; see also *Tiananmen Papers,* 307–308.

10.　　 LPLSRJ, May 22.

11.　　 "李鹏会见三国新任驻华大使 介绍中国当前形势并重申我对外政策 强调改革开放总设计师是邓小平同志" [In meetings with three countries' new ambassadors to China, Li Peng explains China's current situation, reiterates our foreign policy stance, and emphasizes that Comrade Deng Xiaoping is the chief architect of reform and opening], RMRB, May 26, 1989; LPLSRJ, May 25.

12.　　 LPLSRJ, May 22; Michel Oksenberg, Lawrence R. Sullivan, and Marc Lambert, eds., *Beijing Spring 1989: Confrontation and Conflict, The Basic Documents* (Armonk, NY: M. E. Sharpe, 1990), 331–333. In CYNP, 3:480–481, only "the first part" of his remarks is included.

13.　　 ZFLZQJ 1989, 69–73; DXPNP, 2:1277–1278. This meeting is incorrectly dated in *Tiananmen Papers,* 324–328.

14.　　 Joseph Torigian, "Prestige, Manipulation, and Coercion: Elite Power Struggles and the Fate of Three Revolutions" (PhD diss., MIT, 2016), 534–535.

15.　　 "坚持正面引导, 把干部战上的思想统一到中央精神上来" [Continue positive guidance, unify comrades' military thinking with the Central Party's spirit], in XCJB, 805–810. The *Tiananmen Papers* include an alleged transcript of a meeting that

Deng Xiaoping hosted on June 2, 1989, but no other source (including Li Peng's diary) gives any indication of this meeting.

16.   "Telegram from Romanian Embassy in Beijing to Ministry of Foreign Affairs, 03:00 a.m.," June 4, 1989, trans. Mircea Munteanu, History and Public Policy Program Digital Archive, AMAE, Telegrame, Folder Beijing / 1989, vol. 3, 110–111, http:// digitalarchive.wilsoncenter.org/document/113156.

17.   POS, 33.

18.   "保卫广播电影电视部" [Defending the Ministry of Radio, Film, and Television], in HGYFS, 309–311.

19.   "被围困情况下的部队思想政治工作" [Ideological and political work of the troops under siege], in HGYFS, 239.

20.   Ezra Vogel, *Deng Xiaoping and the Transformation of China* (Cambridge, MA: Belknap Press of Harvard University Press, 2011), 619, 629–631.

21.   Brown, *June Fourth,* 177–187; Lim, *People's Republic,* 182; Anne Gunn, "The Student Movement in Shenyang," in *The Pro-Democracy Protests in China: Reports from the Provinces,* ed. Jonathan Unger and Geremie Barmé (Armonk, NY: M. E. Sharpe, 1991), 78.

22.   Li Rui 李銳, "事已做絕, 何以對天下" [Now that things have come to this, how can we face the world?], June 4, 1989, republished in *Ming Pao,* May 27, 2019, https://news.mingpao.com/pns/要聞/article/20190527/s00001/1558894891137/記六四鎮壓-十里長街槍聲近-李銳日記-事已做絕-何以對天下.

23.   Jim Mann and David Holley, "Protests for Democracy in Tiananmen Square; Troops Fire on Beijing Crowds," *Los Angeles Times,* June 4, 1989.

24.   "Cable from Department of State to U.S. Embassy Beijing Concerning Secretary of State James Baker's meeting with Chinese Ambassador Han Xu," June 7, 1989, George H. W. Bush Presidential Library, www.chinafile.com/library/reports/us -china-diplomacy-after-tiananmen-documents-george-hw-bush-presidential-library.

25.   "Secret Instructions by State Security (MfS) Chief Erich Mielke to Heads of all State Security Units," June 10, 1989, trans. Christian F. Ostermann, History and Public Policy Program Digital Archive, State Security Archives, reprinted in German in Armin Mitter / Stefan Wolle, *Ich liebe Euch doch alle! Orders and Situation Reports of the MfS, January to November 1989* (Berlin: BasisDruck, 1990), 78, https:// digitalarchive.wilsoncenter.org/document/117222.

26.   Oksenberg et al., *Beijing Spring,* 363–376; Charles Stuart Kennedy, "Interview with Ambassador James Lilley," May 21, 1998, Foreign Affairs Oral History Collection, Association for Diplomatic Studies and Training (2001), 138, http://www.adst .org › Lilley, James R.toc.pdf.

27.　CYNP, 3:482. This statement is not included in the 2000 edition of CYNP and appears only in the 2015 edition.

28.　Clyde Haberman, "Economic Penalties Are Placed on China by Belgium and Italy," *New York Times*, June 25, 1989; Paul Gecelovsky and T. A. Keenleyside, "Canada's International Human Rights Policy in Practice: Tiananmen Square," *International Journal* 50, no. 3 (1995): 577.

29.　NCXB 220 (June 7, 1989): 4–5.

30.　DXPNP, 2:1279–1280; ZFLZQJ 1989, 73–76; LXNNP, 6:482. When Deng's remarks were made public in July, "market economy" had been demoted to "market-regulated economy" (市场调节经济).

31.　ZFLZQJ 1989, 73–76, translated at www.tsquare.tv/chronology/Deng.html.

32.　XCGWX, 269.

33.　Song Keda, "深入学习理解军委邓主席在接见首都戒严部队军以上干部时的讲话."

34.　ZFLZQJ 1989, 76–82; DXPNP, 2:1281–1282.

35.　Prior to ZHDMM, documentation on these meetings was available in limited form in, for example, DXPNP, 2:1282; LXNNP, 6:483; LPLSRJ, June 20–22; POS, 39–41.

36.　ZHDMM, 149–151, 162–163.

37.　LPLSRJ, June 22; ZHDMM, 231.

38.　LPLSRJ, June 20; "Zhao Ziyang's Speech in His Own Defense," *Chinese Law & Government* 38, no. 3 (May / June 2005): 51–68; *Tiananmen Papers*, 441–446.

39.　LPLSRJ, June 19, June 20; POS, 40.

40.　ZHDMM, 165, 173. It is unclear whether Zhao remained present for Chen Xitong's comments. ZHDMM shows that he remained, responding to a follow-up question from Song Renqiong (ZHDMM, 175), but Zhao gives a somewhat different account in POS.

41.　XCDT 21 (June 20, 1989): 125–127; David Shambaugh, *China's Communist Party: Atrophy and Adaptation* (Washington, DC: Woodrow Wilson Center Press, 2008), 43–45. This speech is not included in ZHDMM.

42.　ZHDMM, 187, 242–249, 226; CYNP, 3:483.

43.　ZHDMM, 190, 194. Li also attacked Zhao's meeting with Milton Friedman in September 1988.

44.　ZHDMM, 263–264, 272, 313.

45. ZHDMM, 177–186; Xin Can 辛灿, ed., 西方政界要人谈和平演变 [Western political figures talk about peaceful evolution] (Beijing: New China Press, 1989). See also LPLSRJ, May 27, 1989.

46. ZHDMM, 251–255.

47. ZHDMM, 312.

48. ZHDMM, 275–280, 288, 309.

49. ZHDMM, 311.

50. Wang also compared Zhao's "brain trust" to Lin Biao's "small fleet" of conspirators against Mao.

51. ZHDMM, 313.

52. Yang Jisheng, "Second Visit to Zhao Ziyang," *Chinese Law & Government* 38, no. 3 (2005): 35.

53. See, for example, GSJTL, 4:191–196, 206–207.

54. Lim, *People's Republic,* 162–163.

55. "Call on Lee Kuan Yew: Hong Kong / China," UK National Archives, PREM19 / 2597 f9.

56. "中国共产党第十三届中央委员会第四次全体会议公报" [Communiqué of the Fourth Plenary Session of the 13th Central Committee of the CCP], June 23, 1989, http://cpc.people.com.cn/GB/64162/64168/64566/65386/4441846.html. This kind of partial official acknowledgment and brief praise of Zhao's role would not continue after the documents passing judgment on him.

57. LPLSRJ, June 24.

58. Liu Chengdong 刘成栋, Zhang Zhiyi 张志义, and Han Bingcheng 韩秉成, "要坚信党的基本路线、方针政策的正确性" [We must firmly believe in the correctness of the party's fundamental line and principles], in XCJB, 339–344.

59. Song Keda, "深入学习理解军委邓主席在接见首都戒严部队军以上干部时的讲话."

60. "这场风波是不以人的意志为转移的" [This storm will not be moved by human will], June 28, 1989, in XCJB, 353–363. There was also a renewed focus on "class struggle" going forward.

61. NCXB 22 (June 1989): 11–16.

62. Richard Baum, *Burying Mao: Chinese Politics in the Age of Deng Xiaoping* (Princeton, NJ: Princeton University Press, 1994), 298; Scott Kennedy, "The Stone Group: State Client or Market Pathbreaker?" *China Quarterly* 152 (December 1997):

746, 764; James L. Tyson, "High-Tech Star Falls from Grace," *Christian Science Monitor,* September 18, 1989.

63. Dongfeng Han, "Chinese Labor Struggles," *New Left Review* 34 (July / August 2005), https://newleftreview.org/issues/II34/articles/dongfang-han-chinese -labour-struggles; Merle Goldman, "Vengeance in China," *New York Review of Books* 36, no. 17 (November 1989): 5–9.

64. "中央组织部关于在当前斗争中如何处理党员退党问题的答复意见" [Organization Department suggestions on tackling the issue of party members withdrawing from the party in the current struggle], June 22, 1989, in ZZGZWJXB, in ZWCBW-FWZX, 26:113, 232–233.

65. "国务院办公厅转发国家教委关于当前高等学校毕业生分配几个问题请示的通知" [The General Office of the State Council Office relays the State Education Commission notice on issues concerning employment of graduating university students], ZZGZWJXB, in ZWCBWFWZX, 26:113, 365–367.

66. XCGWX, 88, 271.

67. XCGWX, 272–273.

68. Yao Jianfu 姚監復, ed., 陳希同親述: 眾口鑠金難鑠真 [Conversations with Chen Xitong] (Hong Kong: New Century Press, 2012), 163. "I did not participate in writing the report," Chen recounted. "I did not change even a punctuation mark" before delivering it (Lu Zhichao, 海边忆往, 189–190). On Central Document No. 3, see Brown, *June Fourth,* 218–219.

69. Chen Xitong 陈希同, 关于制止动乱和平息反革命暴乱的情况报告 [Report on the suppression of the unrest and quelling the counterrevolutionary rebellion] (Beijing: People's Publishing House, 1989), www.chinadaily.com.cn/epaper/html/cd /1989/198907/19890707/19890707004_1.html.

Chapter 14: Recasting Reform and Opening

1. "在中组部召开的座谈会上, 老前辈语重心长话党建" [At the Central Organization Department's symposium, old veterans focus on long-term party building], RMRB, July 28, 1989.

2. See Julian Gewirtz, "'Loving Capitalism Disease': AIDS and Ideology in the People's Republic of China, 1984–2000," *Past & Present* 241 (November 2020): 251–294.

3. Zhou Zhiliang 周之良, "要重新学习两类矛盾的学说" [Relearning the doctrine of the two types of contradictions], 光明日报 [Guangming daily], August 31, 1989.

This article draws on Mao's February 1957 speech "On the Correct Handling of Contradictions among the People."

4.　Ding Suoming 丁锁明, "'思想病'种种" [Types of "thought diseases"], RMRB, October 8, 1989.

5.　"在中组部召开的座谈会上, 老前辈语重心长话党建."

6.　On July 3, the NPC Standing Committee discussed a draft law on "assemblies, processions, and demonstrations," which outlawed any such activities that opposed the CCP's leadership or would harm unity and stability, which was passed as the Law of 1989 on Assemblies, Processions, and Demonstrations on October 31, 1989, https://www.refworld.org/docid/3ae6b592e.html.

7.　"Memorandum of Conversation: LTG Brent Scowcroft, Deng Xiaoping, et al.," July 2, 1989, George H. W. Bush Presidential Library, https://www.chinafile.com /library/reports/us-china-diplomacy-after-tiananmen-documents-george-hw-bush -presidential-library; Charles Stuart Kennedy, "Interview with Ambassador James Lilley," May 21, 1998, Foreign Affairs Oral History Collection, Association for Diplomatic Studies and Training (2001), 146–148.

8.　Wang Fang 王芳, 王芳回忆录 [Memoirs of Wang Fang] (Hangzhou: Zhejiang People's Publishing House, 2006), 374–377; Marianne Yen, "Fund's Representatives Arrested in China," *Washington Post,* August 8, 1989; Yang Jisheng, "Second Visit to Zhao Ziyang," *Chinese Law & Government* 38, no. 3 (2005): 32–33.

9.　"宋平同志在全国省、自治区、直辖市党委组织部长会议上的讲话" [Comrade Song Ping's speech at the national meeting of leaders of party committees of provinces, autonomous regions, and municipalities], August 18, 1989, in ZZGZ-WJXB, in ZWCBWFWZX, 26:113, 25.

10.　"Letter to Cde. Erich Honecker from Cde. Schabowski on a Meeting with Jiang Zemin," July 14, 1989, History and Public Policy Program Digital Archive, SAPMO-BA, DY 30, 2437, http://digitalarchive.wilsoncenter.org/document/122031.

11.　"Excerpts from the Conversation between Mikhail Gorbachev and Rajiv Gandhi," July 15, 1989, trans. Sergey Radchenko, History and Public Policy Program Digital Archive, http://digitalarchive.wilsoncenter.org/document/119291.

12.　XCGWX, 274–279.

13.　Elizabeth J. Perry, "Cultural Governance in Contemporary China: 'Re-orienting' Party Propaganda," in *To Govern China: Evolving Practices of Power,* ed. Vivienne Shue and Patricia Thornton (New York: Cambridge University Press, 2017), 36. See also Geremie Barmé and Linda Jaivin, eds., *New Ghosts, Old Dreams: Chinese Rebel Voices* (New York: Times Books, 1992), 363–368.

14. Ezra Vogel, *Deng Xiaoping and the Transformation of China* (Cambridge, MA: Belknap Press of Harvard University Press, 2011), 661.

15. XCDT 26 (July 25, 1989): 163–172.

16. XCGWX, 337–338.

17. Yu Jianwen 于建文, "邓小平同志是中国改革开放的总设计师" [Deng Xiaoping is the chief architect of reform and opening], July 10, 1989, in XCJB, 392–397.

18. "全军各大单位认真学习深刻领会党的十三届四中全会精神" [All major military units attentively study and thoroughly understand the spirit of the Fourth Plenary Session of the 13th Central Committee of the CCP], July 20, 1989, in XCJB, 410–414.

19. NCXB 234 (September 13, 1989): 4.

20. LXNNP, 6:487–488.

21. Du Guang 杜光, "回忆20年前的中国政治体制改革研究会" [Recalling the Political System Reform Research Society 20 years ago], December 14, 2008, *Boxun*, www.boxun.com/news/gb/z_special/2008/12/200812142206.shtml.

22. NCXB 227 (July 26, 1989): 11–13.

23. "China Replaces Head of Beijing University," *New York Times*, August 24, 1989.

24. CYNP, 2:486–487.

25. ZFLZQJ 1989, 83–86; CYNP, 2:484–486.

26. ZFLZQJ 1989, 106–115, 161–179; Vogel, *Deng Xiaoping*, 660.

27. DXPNP, 2:1286–1288; SWDXP-3, 307–308.

28. Yuan Mu 袁木, "中国第三代领导集体的政治宣言" [The political statement of China's third generation of leadership], RMRB, October 10, 1989.

29. POS, 49, 54–55; "Bao Tong and the End of Glasnost," *Chinese Law & Government* 31, no. 3 (1998): 38–48. The full text of the unpublished draft investigative report on Zhao's actions is included in POS, 63–70.

30. XCDT 25 (July 10, 1989): 150–162; 平暴英雄谱 [Guidebook to the heroes of quelling the rebellion] (Beijing: Guangming Daily Publishing House, 1989). Official media repeatedly announced that no deaths had occurred in Tiananmen Square.

31. The phrase "peaceful evolution" had last appeared in the title of an RMRB article in 1967, but starting in July 1989, it appeared with great regularity. After 1992, the term would again fall out of view.

32. Zhou Borong 周伯荣, "国际大气候与反革命暴乱" [The international political climate and counterrevolutionary unrest], July 10, 1989, in XCJB, 397–401.

33. "正确看待国际舆论对我国平息 反革命暴乱的反应" [Correctly interpreting international public opinion on China's quashing of the counterrevolutionary unrest], July 10, 1989, in XCJB, 402–404.

34. XCDT 27 (August 1, 1989): 176–180, translated as "Forum Held by Central Foreign Propaganda Units on Studying How to Strengthen the Current Struggle of World Public Opinion," *Chinese Law and Government* 25, no. 1 (Spring 1992): 83–86.

35. Henry A. Kissinger, "Caricature of Deng as Tyrant Is Unfair," *Washington Post*, August 1, 1989; Jeffrey Wasserstrom, "History, Myths, and Tales of Tiananmen," in *Popular Protest and Political Culture in Modern China*, ed. Jeffrey Wasserstrom and Elizabeth J. Perry (Boulder, CO: Westview Press, 1994), 292.

36. Zhou Xiangguang 周象光, "邓小平会见基辛格时说'中国现在很稳定，我也放心'" [When meeting Kissinger, Deng Xiaoping said, "China is now stable and my mind is at ease"], RMRB, November 11, 1989.

37. Richard Baum, *Burying Mao: Chinese Politics in the Age of Deng Xiaoping* (Princeton, NJ: Princeton University Press, 1994), 316–317.

38. "人事部关于少数博士后研究人员出国逾期不归问题的通知" [Ministry of Personnel Notice on the number of postdoctoral researchers who have overstayed their time abroad], December 27, 1989, in ZZGZWJXB, in ZWCBWFWZX, 26:113, 408–409.

39. "中央纪委关于印发共产党员和党的组织参加动乱反革命暴乱活动党纪处分的若干规定的通知" [Notice from the CCDI on distributing certain decisions on disciplinary actions against Communist Party members and party organizations for participating in unrest and counterrevolutionary activities], July 20, 1989, in ZZGZWJXB, in ZWCBWFWZX, 26:113, 258, and the following documents from July 21, 31, and September 7, 1989.

40. "国家行政机关工作人员贪污贿赂行政处分暂行规定实施细则" [Detailed rules for implementing provisional injunctions against corruption and bribery among workers in state administrative organs], September 8, 1989, in ZZGZWJXB, in ZWCBWFWZX, 26:113, 386. Some of the highest-ranking targeted officials, such as Hainan governor Liang Xiang, were linked to Zhao Ziyang, but many of the mid- and lower-level targets were not.

41. David Shambaugh, "The Soldier and the State in China: The Political Work System in the People's Liberation Army," *China Quarterly* 127 (September 1991): 551, 554.

42. See Margaret E. Roberts, *Censored: Distraction and Diversion inside China's Great Firewall* (Princeton, NJ: Princeton University Press, 2018); Yuyu Chen and David Y. Yang, "The Impact of Media Censorship: 1984 or Brave New World?" *American Economic Review* 109, no. 6 (June 2019): 2294–2332; Sergei Guriev and Daniel Treisman, "How Modern Dictators Survive: An Informational Theory of the

New Authoritarianism" (Working Paper No. 21136, National Bureau of Economic Research, Cambridge, MA, April 2015), www.nber.org/papers/w21136.

43. LXNNP, 6:491.

44. DXPNP, 2:1286–1288.

45. LXNNP, 6:491–492.

46. Uli Schmetzer, "Security Heavy for China's 40th," *Chicago Tribune*, October 2, 1989; Jeff Sommer, "Army Ensures a Smooth China Anniversary Fest," *Newsday*, October 2, 1989.

47. "在庆祝中华人民共和国成立四十周年大会上江泽民总书记的讲话" [General Secretary Jiang Zemin's speech at the celebration of 40th anniversary of the PRC's founding], RMRB, September 30, 1989; GSJTL, 1:111. Li Xiannian, Yang Shangkun, and other elders advised on the drafting of Jiang Zemin's speech (LXNNP, 6:495).

48. Zheng Wang, *Never Forget National Humiliation: Historical Memory in Chinese Politics and Foreign Relations* (New York: Columbia University Press, 2012).

49. Wang Jin 王瑾文世芳 and Wen Shifang 文世芳, "1949~1989年《人民日报》对历史虚无主义的解析" [Analysis of historical nihilism in RMRB, 1949–1989], 当代中国史研究 [Studies in contemporary Chinese history] 24, no. 2 (2017), http://www.dswxyjy.org.cn/n1/2017/0907/c398751-29521602.html.

50. Xiao Donglian 萧冬连, "中国改革是如何越过市场化临界点的" [How China's reforms crossed the threshold of marketization], December 10, 2018, https://mp.weixin.qq.com/s/aM1XhDzHBXgYPQ9dEB4lZg.

51. XCDT 34 (October 15, 1989): 244–250.

52. Beijing Municipal Propaganda Bureau 中共北京市委宣传部, 资产阶级自由化言论辑录 [Record of speeches on bourgeois liberalization] (Beijing: China Youth Publishing House, 1989), 1–6.

53. Qian Xuesen 钱学森, "基础科学研究应该接受 马克思主义哲学的指导" [Basic scientific research should be guided by Marxist philosophy], 哲学研究 [Philosophy research] 10 (1989): 3–8.

54. XCDT 1 (January 1, 1990): 1–13.

Chapter 15: The Socialist Survivor in a Capitalist World

1. Li Peng 李鹏, 和平、发展、合作: 李鹏外事日记 [Peace, development, cooperation: Li Peng's foreign affairs diary], 2 vols. (Beijing: New China Press, 2008).

2.   "建国40年来的民主德国" [The GDR's past 40 years], RMRB, October 17, 1989; "姚依林将出访民德" [Yao Yilin to visit the GDR], RMRB, September 22, 1989. See also Quinn Slobodian, "China Is Not Far! Alternative Internationalism and the Tiananmen Square Massacre in East Germany's 1989," in *Alternative Globalizations: Eastern Europe and the Postcolonial World*, ed. James Mark, Artemy Kalinovsky, and Steffi Marung (Bloomington: Indiana University Press, 2020).

3.   Li Peng, 和平、发展、合作, 1:212, 235. See also NCXB 245 (November 29, 1989).

4.   "李鹏总理谈东欧局势" [Li Peng discusses the situation in Eastern Europe], NCXB 247 (December 13, 1989): 5–7. Li also called Gorbachev "powerless."

5.   DXPNP, 2:1302–1303.

6.   Li Peng, 和平、发展、合作, 1:236. See also Kristina Spohr, *Post Wall, Post Square: How Bush, Gorbachev, Kohl, and Deng Shaped the World after 1989* (New Haven, CT: Yale University Press, 2020).

7.   Xiao Donglian 萧冬连, "中国改革是如何越过市场化临界点的" [How China's reforms crossed the threshold of marketization], December 10, 2018, https://mp .weixin.qq.com/s/aM1XhDzHBXgYPQ9dEB4lZg.

8.   LXNNP, 6:498–499.

9.   ZFLZQJ 1989, 76; Barry Naughton, *Growing out of the Plan* (Cambridge: Cambridge University Press, 1995), 274–276; Joseph Fewsmith, *China since Tiananmen: The Politics of Transition* (New York: Cambridge University Press, 2001), 36–38.

10.   Wei Xinghua, "China Cannot Go in Fully for a Market Economy," in *Chinese Economic Studies* 25, no. 2 (Winter 1991–1992): 83–89.

11.   LXNNP, 6:499–500.

12.   Xue Muqiao, "牢记历史经验 坚决执行治理整顿的方针" [Remember the lessons of history as we resolutely implement rectification policies], RMRB, December 18, 1989.

13.   XCDT 37 (November 10, 1989): 268–273. See also LXNNP, 6:489.

14.   Xu Kehong 徐克洪 and Jiang Shaogao 江绍高, "十年改革开放坚持了社会主义方向" [Ten years of reform and opening up have upheld the direction of socialism], RMRB, January 11, 1990.

15.   "国务院发布命令 北京市部分地区解除戒严" [State Council releases order to lift martial law in parts of Beijing], RMRB, January 11, 1990.

16.   XCDT 42 (December 25, 1990): 547–552.

17.   David Remnick, "Lithuanians Assail Gorbachev Plan," *Washington Post*, January 13, 1990.

18. "Excerpts of Gorbachev Speech to Central Committee," Associated Press, February 5, 1990, https://apnews.com/5011f29fba9f7d9c4ae812ca4b5a53ec. Li Peng traveled to the Soviet Union in April 1990.

19. "维护国家的长治久安是中共和各民主党派的神圣责任" [Protecting China's lasting political stability is the sacred responsibility of the CCP and every democratic party], RMRB, February 8, 1990. This editorial briefly mentioned "reforming the political system" but saying only vaguely it would entail "gradually establishing and improving various specific democratic systems."

20. Ezra Vogel, *Deng Xiaoping and the Transformation of China* (Cambridge, MA: Belknap Press of Harvard University Press, 2011), 657.

21. Lei Jieqiong 雷洁琼, "我国推进社会主义民主建设和深化政治体制改革的一件大事" [A big event in China's pushing for the establishment of socialist democracy and deepening of political system reform], RMRB, February 10, 1990. One important exception would be enterprises, where separating party and government functions was eventually permitted to continue, though within the broader centralizing framework noted above.

22. Jiang Zemin 江泽民, 江泽民文选 [Selected works of Jiang Zemin], 3 vols. (Beijing: People's Publishing House, 2006), 1:112, cited in Jie Li, "Sovietology in Post-Mao China, 1980–1999" (PhD diss., University of Edinburgh, 2017), 144.

23. Wang Renzhi 王忍之, "关于反对资产阶级自由化" [On opposing bourgeois liberalization], RMRB, February 22, 1990.

24. Geremie Barmé, "China: The Party Has Its Way with History," *Index on Censorship* 20, no. 7 (July 1991): 14. Hu's statements about party history were heightened by the public sensation of Zhang Zhenglong 张正隆, 雪白血红 [White snow, red blood] (Beijing: PLA Publishing House, 1989), which included revelations such as the smuggling of opium by PLA officers during the Chinese Civil War that caused it to be banned.

25. XCDT 24 (July 10, 1990): 294–309.

26. Geremie Barmé, "To Screw Foreigners Is Patriotic: China's Avant-Garde Nationalists," *China Journal* 34 (July 1995): 209–234; Xu Guangqiu, "Anti-Western Nationalism in China, 1989–99," *World Affairs* 163, no. 4 (Spring 2001): 153, 156.

27. LXNNP, 6:519–520.

28. "国务院关于加强外国记者管理问题的通知" [Notice from the State Council on strengthening management of foreign journalists], January 20, 1990, in DXGWX, 4:1941–1945.

29. "中共中央关于恢复中央对外宣传小组的通知" [Notice from the CCP Central Committee on reestablishing the Central Small Group on External Propaganda], March 19, 1990, in DXGWX, 4:1904.

30.   ZHDMM, 312.

31.   SWDXP-3, 341–343; DXPNP, 2:1309–1311. See also Vogel, *Deng Xiaoping,* 667.

32.   薛暮桥年谱 (A chronology of Xue Muqiao). Unpublished, no pagination, entry for September 17, 1990.

33.   Geremie Barmé, translator's introduction in He Xin, "A Word of Advice to the Politburo," *Australian Journal of Chinese Affairs* 23 (January 1990): 62.

34.   何新政治经济论文集 [Collected works of He Xin on political economy] (Ha'erbin: Heilongjiang Education Press, 1993) and 何新对美国对华政策的看法 [He Xin's views on America's China policy] (manuscript). Both held in the Fairbank Collection, Fung Library, Harvard University.

35.   Naughton, *Growing out of the Plan,* 280–285.

36.   Xiao Donglian, "中国改革是如何越过市场化临界点的." See also Barry Naughton, ed., *Wu Jinglian: Voice of Reform in China* (Cambridge, MA: MIT Press, 2013), 224–229.

37.   In June 1990, Fang Lizhi and his wife, Li Shuxian, finally received permission to leave China (Jim Abrams, "Dissident Fang Lizhi and Wife Allowed to Leave China," Associated Press, June 25, 1990).

38.   Fewsmith, *China since Tiananmen,* 40–41.

39.   Xiao Donglian, "中国改革是如何越过市场化临界点的."

40.   Liu Shi'an 刘士安, "建国以来大陆第一家 上海证券交易所成立" [The first in the mainland since the founding: Shanghai Stock Exchange established], RMRB, November 27, 1990.

41.   DXPNP, 2:1322–1324; Vogel, *Deng Xiaoping,* 660.

42.   Gao Di 高狄, "社会主义必定代替资本主义" [Socialism must replace capitalism], RMRB, December 17, 1990; Fewsmith, *China since Tiananmen,* 49.

43.   DXPNP, 2:1325–1328.

44.   Fewsmith, *China since Tiananmen,* 45–46; Yang Jisheng 楊繼繩, 中國改革年代的政治鬥爭 (Hong Kong: Excellent Culture Press, 2004), 479.

45.   LXNNP, 6:548–549.

46.   Fewsmith, *China since Tiananmen,* 47; Richard Baum, *Burying Mao: Chinese Politics in the Age of Deng Xiaoping* (Princeton, NJ: Princeton University Press, 1994), 315.

47.   Naughton, *Growing out of the Plan,* 285–287.

48.   LXNNP, 6:521–522.

49.   DXPNP, 2:1329.

50.   Ren Guojun 任国钧, "向新科技革命进军" [Advance toward the New Techno-logical Revolution], RMRB, May 2, 1991; Fewsmith, *China since Tiananmen,* 47; Jacqueline Newmyer, "The Revolution in Military Affairs with Chinese Characteris-tics," *Journal of Strategic Studies* 33, no. 4 (2010): 483–504.

51.   Vogel, *Deng Xiaoping,* 660.

52.   Fewsmith, *China since Tiananmen,* 52; DXPNP, 2:1330.

53.   DXPNP, 2:1330–1331; Hu Shuli 胡舒立, Huo Kan 霍侃, and Yang Zheyu 杨哲宇, "改革是怎样重启的: 社会主义市场经济体制的由来" [How reform was restarted: Origins of the socialist market economic system], 中国改革 [China reform] 12 (2012), http://magazine.caixin.com/2012-11-29/100466603.html. The collapse of the Soviet Union also heightened concerns among the Chinese leadership about the succes-sionist potential of ethnic minorities (such as Uighurs and Tibetans in particular), among many other consequences.

54.   Vogel, *Deng Xiaoping,* 665–669; Fewsmith, *China since Tiananmen,* 54.

55.   "Realistic Responses and Strategic Options for China after the Soviet Up-heaval," *Chinese Law and Government* 29, no. 2 (March–April 1996): 13–31; Fewsmith, *China since Tiananmen,* 98–100.

56.   Vogel, *Deng Xiaoping,* 658; DXPNP, 2:1332.

57.   Julian Gewirtz, *Unlikely Partners: Chinese Reformers, Western Economists, and the Making of Global China* (Cambridge, MA: Harvard University Press, 2017), 243–245.

58.   Xiao Donglian, "中国改革是如何越过市场化临界点的."

59.   Li Luoli 李罗力, "亲历邓小平南巡" [Experiencing Deng Xiaoping's Southern Tour], YHCQ 2 (2011), http://www.yhcqw.com/34/8236.html; Tian Jiyun 田纪云, "怀念小平同志" [Remembering Comrade Xiaoping], YHCQ 8 (2004), www.yhcqw.com/11/1200.html.

60.   Deng Xiaoping, "Excerpts from Talks Given in Wuchang, Shenzhen, Zhuhai, and Shanghai," January 18–February 21, 1992, SWDXP-3, 358–370; DXPNP, 2:1334–1341. Yang Shangkun accompanied Deng on several stops.

61.   Deng Xiaoping, "Excerpts from Talks." Diplomatic ties with Singapore had been reestablished in 1990.

62.   Ma Shichen 马世琨, "李鹏总理出席世界经济论坛年会 施瓦布主席热烈欢迎李鹏总理" [Premier Li Peng attends annual meeting of the World Economic Forum, is warmly welcomed by Chairman Schwab], RMRB, January 31, 1992.

63.   "更好地坚持以经济建设为中心" [Maintain better focus on economic construction as the center], RMRB, February 22, 1992.

64.   DXPNP, 2:1341–1345; Vogel, *Deng Xiaoping*, 680; Fewsmith, *China since Tiananmen*, 59.

65.   DXPNP, 2:1345–1346; CYNP, 2:501.

66.   "加快改革开放的步伐" [Hasten the pace of reform and opening up], RMRB, March 12, 1992.

67.   For a bold essay from April 1992 that was critical of the efforts to squelch Deng's calls for market reform, see Hu Jiwei 胡绩伟, "论防'左'为主" [On prioritizing guarding against "left" deviation], April 4, 1992, in 历史的潮流—学习邓小平南巡重要讲话辅导材料 [The trend of history: Materials to study Deng Xiaoping's important Southern Tour talks] (Beijing: Renmin University of China Press, 1992), 143–157.

68.   Chen Xitian 陈锡添, "东方风来满眼春: 邓小平同志在深圳纪实" [East winds herald the spring: Record of Comrade Deng Xiaoping in Shenzhen], RMRB, March 31, 1992. This article originally appeared in the *Shenzhen SEZ News* on March 26; it was also broadcast on Chinese Central Television on March 31.

69.   See, for example, Keith Bradsher and Li Yuan, "China's Economy Became No. 2 by Defying No. 1," *New York Times*, November 25, 2018.

70.   Vogel, *Deng Xiaoping*, 681; DXGWX,1988–1992, 2195–2205.

71.   DXPNP, 2:1347–1348.

72.   DXPNP, 2:1348; CYNP 2:504.

73.   Barry Naughton, "China: Economic Transformation before and after 1989," prepared for the conference "1989: Twenty Years After," University of California, Irvine, November 6–7, 2009, 2. Township and village enterprises suffered particularly seriously from Zhao's "inappropriate exaggeration" of their contributions (Yasheng Huang, *Capitalism with Chinese Characteristics* [Cambridge: Cambridge University Press, 2008], 125).

74.   DXPNP, 2:1349; Sheryl WuDunn, "China Talks of Raising Economic Growth Target," *New York Times*, July 17, 1992.

75.   James McGregor, "Reality Is Overtaking Ideology in China: Data Show Explosion in Private-Sector Growth," *Wall Street Journal*, March 2, 1992.

76.   Sheryl WuDunn, "Some Chinese See Return to Reform," *New York Times*, February 12, 1992.

77.   "China's Desperate Capitalist," *Wall Street Journal*, February 28, 1992.

78.　Yang Jisheng 杨继绳, "价格改革: 经济改革中的一步险棋" [Price reform: A difficult move in economic reform], YHCQ, no. 3 (2009), www.yhcqw.com/33/4685.html.

79.　Nicholas Kristof, "China Sees Singapore as a Model for Progress," *New York Times,* August 9, 1992.

80.　Jiang Zemin, "Accelerating the Reform, the Opening to the Outside World, and the Drive for Modernization," October 12, 1992, www.bjreview.com.cn/document/txt /2011-03/29/content_363504.htm; DXPNP, 2:1352–1355.

81.　Hon S. Chan, "The Making of Chinese Civil Service Law: Ideals, Technicalities, and Realities," *American Review of Public Administration* 46, no. 4 (2016): 388; Xu Songtao 徐颂陶, ed., 国家公务员制度教程 [National civil service course] (Beijing: China Personnel Press, 1992), 5–6.

82.　毛泽东邓小平论中国国情 [Mao Zedong and Deng Xiaoping on China's national conditions] (Beijing: CCP Central Party School Publishing House, 1992).

83.　DXPNP, 2:1357; "Long March to the Market," *Financial Times,* December 29, 1992.

84.　This includes the publication of a third volume of the *Selected Works of Deng Xiaoping* (DXPNP, 2:1365–1366) and enshrining "Deng Xiaoping Theory" in the constitution in 1997. For official histories, see, for example, 中华人民共和国编年史 [Record of the PRC] (Beijing: People's Publishing House, 2010); 当代中国编年史 [Record of contemporary China] (Beijing: People's Publishing House, 2007); and Li Lanqing, *Breaking Through: The Birth of China's Opening-Up Policy* (Oxford: Oxford University Press, 2009).

85.　Joshua Cooper Ramo, *The Beijing Consensus* (London: Foreign Policy Centre, 2004), 2; Nicholas D. Kristof, "China Sees 'Market Leninism' as Way to Future," *New York Times,* September 6, 1993.

86.　Fewsmith, *China since Tiananmen,* 69.

87.　Stefan Halper, *The Beijing Consensus: How China's Authoritarian Model Will Dominate the Twenty-First Century* (New York: Basic Books, 2010); Eric X. Li, "A Tale of Two Political Systems," TED.com, June 2013, www.ted.com/talks/eric_x_li_a_tale _of_two_political_systems.

88.　David Shambaugh, *China's Communist Party: Atrophy and Adaptation* (Washington, DC: Wilson Center Press, 2008), 2–3; Elizabeth Perry and Merle Goldman, eds., *Grassroots Political Reform in Contemporary China* (Cambridge, MA: Harvard University Asia Center, 2007); Joseph Fewsmith, *The Logic and Limits of Political Reform in China* (Cambridge: Cambridge University Press, 2012); Paul Gewirtz, "The U.S.-China Rule of Law Initiative," *William & Mary Bill of Rights Journal* 11 (2003): 603–621.

89.   "Full Text of Clinton's Speech on China Trade Bill," March 9, 2000, www
.nytimes.com/library/world/asia/030900clinton-china-text.html. See also Alastair
Iain Johnston, "The Failures of the 'Failure of Engagement' with China," *Washington
Quarterly* 42, no. 2 (2019): 99–114.

90.   Carolyn Cartier, "Transnational Urbanism in the Reform-Era Chinese City:
Landscapes from Shenzhen," *Urban Studies* 39, no. 9 (2002): 1513–1514.

91.   Jiang Zemin, "在深圳经济特区建立二十周年庆祝大会上的讲话" [Speech at the
20th anniversary celebration of the Shenzhen SEZ], RMRB, November 15, 2000.

Conclusion

1.   "Highlights of President Xi Jinping's Remarks on China's Reform and Opening-
Up," Xinhua, December 20, 2018, http://www.xinhuanet.com/english/2018-12/20/c
_137687815.htm; Chris Buckley and Steven Lee Myers, "China's Leader Says Party
Must Control 'All Tasks,' and Asian Markets Slump," *New York Times,* December 18,
2018, www.nytimes.com/2018/12/18/world/asia/xi-jinping-speech-china.html.

2.   "40 Years & Onward: Into the New Era," Xinhua News Service, m.china.com
.cn/plug/v2/zt.htm?ztId=784669. On museums and CCP historiography, see Rana
Mitter, "Behind the Scenes at the Museum: Nationalism, History and Memory in the
Beijing War of Resistance Museum, 1987–1997," *China Quarterly* 161 (March 2000):
279–293.

3.   山东师大党办字 [Shandong Normal University Party Office Note], no. 5 (2018).
Copy in the author's possession.

4.   Edward Wong, "Signals of a More Open Economy in China," *New York Times,*
December 9, 2012; Leslie Hook and Simon Rabinovitch, "Xi Stokes Economic Reform
Hopes in China," *Financial Times,* December 12, 2012.

5.   Richard McGregor, "Party Man: Xi Jinping's Quest to Dominate China,"
Foreign Affairs (September / October 2019), www.foreignaffairs.com/articles/china
/2019-08-14/party-man.

6.   Chris Buckley, "Xi Jinping Opens China's Party Congress, His Hold Tighter
than Ever," *New York Times,* October 17, 2017.

7.   Commager, "The Search for a Usable Past."

8.   中共中央关于党的百年奋斗重大成就和历史经验的决议 [Resolution of the CCP
Central Committee on major achievements and historical experiences of the Party
over the past century], November 16, 2021, http://politics.people.com.cn/n1/2021/1116
/c1001-32284163.html.

9.   See, for example, Sheng Hong, "Sino-U.S. Relation Is Critical for China's Reform and Opening-Up," Unirule Institute of Economics, October 25, 2018, http://english.unirule.cloud/highlights/2018-10-25/1124.html.

10.   Chun Han Wong and Keith Zhai, "China Repackages Its History in Support of Xi's National Vision," *Wall Street Journal*, June 15, 2021.

11.   "Xi Congratulates on CASS Chinese History Institute's Establishment," Xinhua News Service, January 3, 2019, http://www.xinhuanet.com/english/2019-01/03/c_137717406.htm.

12.   Zhu Jiamu 朱佳木, 掌握同历史虚无主义思潮斗争的思想武器 [Take up ideological weapons to struggle against the trend of historical nihilism], October 2018, https://mp.weixin.qq.com/s/ea2sP1fhBfFFeZ97OdVgZQ. This includes underscoring the fundamental unity of Chinese history both before and after 1978.

13.   "举报网上历史虚无主义错误言论请到 12377" [Go to "12377" to report erroneous remarks about historical nihilism on the internet], Central Cyberspace Affairs Office, April 9, 2021, www.12377.cn/wxxx/2021/fc6eb910_web.html; Ian Johnson, "China's Brave Underground Journal," *New York Review of Books*, December 4, 2014, www.nybooks.com/articles/2014/12/04/chinas-brave-underground-journal. See also Sebastian Veg, *Minjian: The Rise of China's Grassroots Intellectuals* (New York: Columbia University Press, 2019), 84–122.

14.   Ilaria Maria Sala, "In Hong Kong's Book Industry, 'Everybody Is Scared,'" *The Guardian*, December 28, 2016.

15.   "Speech by Xi Jinping at a Ceremony Marking the Centenary of the CPC," Xinhua News Service, July 1, 2021, http://www.xinhuanet.com/english/special/2021-07/01/c_1310038244.htm. See also 中共中央关于党的百年奋斗重大成就和历史经验的决议.

16.   Qu Qingshan, "把握历史大势 掌握历史主动" [Seize the historical trend, grasp the historical initiative], 求是 [Seeking truth] 11 (2021), http://www.qstheory.cn/dukan/qs/2021-06/01/c_1127509092.htm.

17.   "Xi Jinping's Report at the 19th CCP Congress," October 18, 2017, www.xinhuanet.com/english/special/2017-11/03/c_136725942.htm.

18.   "Xi Stresses Modernizing China's Governance System, Capacity," Xinhua News Service, September 25, 2019, www.xinhuanet.com/english/2019-09/25/c_138419199.htm.

19.   Figures such as Li Rui have called for such a reckoning; Li Rui 李锐, "耀邦去世前的谈话" [Conversations with Yaobang before his death], *Modern China Studies*, no. 4 (2001), https://www.modernchinastudies.org/us/issues/past-issues/75-mcs-2001-issue-4/589-2012-01-03-12-11- 52.html.

ACKNOWLEDGMENTS

I owe a great debt of gratitude to the mentors and teachers who helped make this book possible. There could be no better doctoral supervisor than Rana Mitter, who was profoundly generous with guidance, wisdom, and encouragement over many years. I also thank Micah Muscolino and Henrietta Harrison in Oxford's History Faculty; Charles Conn and Mary Eaton at Rhodes House; and Stephen (S.A.) Smith and Sebastian Heilmann, who gave detailed and incisive feedback as dissertation examiners. I returned to Harvard in 2017 to work with Arne Westad, whose mentorship and sage judgment have contributed immeasurably to my growth as a thinker and writer. I am grateful to the other scholars who welcomed me back to Harvard: Erez Manela, Elizabeth Perry, Fredrik Logevall, Graham Allison, Michael Szonyi, Mark Wu, Arunabh Ghosh, Meg Rithmire, Victor Seow, and two much-missed giants of the field, Roderick MacFarquhar and Ezra Vogel. I will always be thankful to Ezra for serving as commentator at my presentation of this project to the Harvard Academy, with the energy and kindness that continued through our last exchanges in the weeks before his passing. Another great benefit of Harvard was the Fung Library, built into a national and international treasure by Nancy Hearst, who offered precious sources and warm support in equal measure. I also am deeply grateful to Minxin Pei for his invaluable encouragement.

Two workshops significantly strengthened this book. First, the Harvard Academy convened virtually a group of leading scholars just as the COVID-19 pandemic began, a feat that would have been impossible without Melani Cammett, Bruce Jackan, and Kathleen Hoover. For probing and generous comments, I thank workshop chair Elizabeth Perry and commenters Sergey Radchenko, Zuoyue Wang, Stephen Platt, and Lei Guang. Second, Tarun Chhabra, with the intelligence and care he brings to so many endeavors, organized a lively workshop with Mark Wu, Shanthi Kalathil, John Culver, Andrew Batson, Gerard DiPippo, Seth Center, D. L. McNeal, and Susan Jakes; I am grateful to them all for their feedback.

I benefited from several other opportunities to present this project. David Shambaugh chaired a panel on Zhao Ziyang at the Association of Asian Studies, with important perspectives offered by Wu Guoguang, Robert Suettinger, and Winston Lord. A conference at the British Academy on "Global Neoliberalisms," organized by James Mark and his colleagues at the University of Exeter, broadened my ambitions. Participants in a conference at Yale on the thirtieth anniversary of 1989, organized by Fritz Bartel and the late Nuno Montiero, helped hone my arguments, as did audiences at presentations at SciencesPo, the Weatherhead Forum at Harvard University, the Center for Security and Emerging Technology, Harvard Business School, Harvard Kennedy School, the University of Vienna, and the Council on Foreign Relations. I am also grateful to Harvard University Press's anonymous reviewers for their thoughtful feedback that improved the book. A portion of Part III was first published in "The Futurists of Beijing: Alvin Toffler, Zhao Ziyang, and China's 'New Technological Revolution,' 1979–1991," *Journal of Asian Studies* 78, no. 1 (February 2019): 115–140.

I completed this book while working as Senior Fellow for China Studies at the Council on Foreign Relations and Lecturer in History at Columbia University. The Council gave me a vibrant professional home and numerous opportunities: I extend my thanks to Richard Haass; in the Studies Program, James Lindsay and his excellent team; and to colleagues including Elizabeth Economy, Adam Segal, Mira Rapp-Hooper, Philip Gordon, and Dan Kurtz-Phelan. Kirk Lancaster and Katherine Enright both provided excellent research assistance. At Columbia,

Thomas Christensen welcomed me into the China and the World Fellowship community, and I have benefited greatly from his kindness and counsel. I am also grateful to Daniel Suchenski at CWP and to Kim Brandt in the History Department.

I am delighted to return to Harvard University Press and once again benefit from Kathleen McDermott's judicious guidance and steady hand. I also thank Katrina Vassallo and Stephanie Vyce, as well as Kimberly Giambattisto and Brian Ostrander of Westchester Publishing Services.

In addition to those named above, I gained important perspectives on this project from conversations and exchanges with Andrew Walder, Barry Naughton, Brinton Ahlin, Chan Koon-chung, Charles Kraus, Chris Buckley, Chris Miller, David Adler, David Shimer, Edward Steinfeld, Eric Schmidt, Evan Osnos, Fan Shitao, Frank Gavin, Ganesh Sitaraman, Geremie Barmé, Hal Brands, Han Gang, Hon S. Chan, Isaac Stanley-Becker, James McAuley, Jamie Martin, Jared Cohen, Jason Kelly, Jason Matheny, Jeffrey Ding, Jeffrey Prescott, Jeffrey Wasserstrom, Jessica Chen Weiss, Joanna Waley-Cohen, John Krige, Jonathan Chatwin, Joseph Torigian, Karl Gerth, Kristina Spohr, Matan Chorev, Matt Wills, Matthew Shutzer, Max Harris, Moira Weigel, Molly Dektar, Noah Feldman, Orville Schell, Pete Millwood, Philip Zelikow, Quinn Slobodian, Rebecca Lissner, Richard McGregor, Rowena Xiaoqing He, Rush Doshi, Sahana Ghosh, Sheena Chestnut Greitens, Stephen Wertheim, Steven Lee Myers, Sulmaan Khan, Taylor Fravel, Thomas Gold, Tobias Rupprecht, Wendy Leutert, William Kirby, Wu Guoguang, Xiaolu Guo, Yafeng Xia, Yakov Feygin, Yang Zheyu, Yangyang Cheng, Yen-lin Chung, Yuan Yang, Zha Jianying, Zhang Jing, and Zoë Hitzig. I am especially thankful for all those in China who spoke with me about their firsthand experiences of the 1980s; at a time when so many voices are being silenced there, I have not named them.

Finally, I dedicate this book to my parents, to my brother Alec, and to Fareed. This book, and this life, would not be the same without your support and love.

INDEX

Leap Forward, 123; human suffering caused by, 14–15; Jiang on,
28; legacy of, 14; New Democracy
concept, 146; "peaceful evolution"
and, 250; purges by, 251; *Quotations
of Chairman Mao* (*Little Red Book*),
26, 46; rectification movement,
237; Resolution on Party History
and, 24, 26–27, 28; in *River Elegy*,
202; *Selected Works*, 16; status of,
293; successor of, 14 (*see also* Hua
Guofeng)
Mao Zedong Thought, 23, 31, 34, 133,
146, 158. *See also* Four Cardinal
Principles
market, 67–68, 104, 105, 185, 281,
282, 283, 288. *See also* economic
modernization
market, international, 195
market authoritarianism, 293
marketization, 54, 219, 276, 280.
See also economic modernization
market Leninism, 293
market reform, 38, 81, 85–86, 95–97,
212, 231, 263–264, 291–292; criticism
of, 280–281, 282–283; disagreement over, 80, 86, 93–95. *See also*
economic development; economic
modernization
markets, 67–68
market socialism, 78, 291
martial law, 230, 233, 237, 239, 241,
277. *See also* Tiananmen protests
(1989)
Marx, Karl, 43, 81, 94, 133–134, 201
Marxism, 34, 43, 54, 87–88, 117,
118, 120, 127, 135, 245. *See also*
ideology
Marxism-Leninism, 4, 23. *See also*
ideology

Marxism–Leninism–Mao Zedong
Thought, 31–32, 34, 133, 146, 158.
See also Four Cardinal Principles
May Fourth Movement (1919), 133,
217, 227
media, 154, 161, 214–215, 246, 255,
272. *See also* press; press freedom
media, foreign / Western, 210, 260
military, 108, 115–116, 128, 132, 139–140,
269, 284. *See also* defense sector;
People's Liberation Army (PLA)
modernization, 21, 29–30, 66; agenda
for, 58, 61; announcement of, 21;
assessment of Mao and, 27; bourgeois liberalization and, 59;
changing assessments of, 201;
China's path to, 3, 222; consolidation of new vision for, 239; Deng
and, 3, 13, 18, 19, 262–263, 294;
disagreement over meaning of,
222; economic development and, 3;
expanding definition of, 161; experimentation with, 294; Four
Cardinal Principles and, 22–23
(*see also* Four Cardinal Principles);
historical revision and, 7; history
and, 13, 21, 23, 26; Hua and, 17, 19;
ideological and political work and,
33; ideology and, 3, 51, 60–61; initial
stage of socialism concept and,
184; Marxist humanism and, 43;
new narrative of, 273–278 (*see also*
narrative, official); official history
of, 294 (*see also* narrative, official);
overseas study and, 114; political
democracy and, 197; rectification
and, 257; retrenchment and, 277;
S&T and, 110, 111 [*see also* science
and technology (S&T)]; socialist,
26, 32, 39, 42, 61, 63; Su on, 217–218;